MEETING
Jesus
in the
SACRAMENTS

MEETING Jesus *in the* SACRAMENTS

Ave Maria Press AVE Notre Dame, Indiana

The Subcommittee on the Catechism, United States Conference of Catholic Bishops, has found that this catechetical high school text, copyright 2018, is in conformity with the *Catechism of the Catholic Church* and that it fulfills the requirements of Core Course V of the *Doctrinal Elements of a Curriculum Framework for the Development of Catechetical Materials for Young People of High School Age.*

Nihil Obstat: Reverend Monsignor Michael Heintz, PhD
                Censor Librorum

Imprimatur: Most Reverend Kevin C. Rhoades
                Bishop of Fort Wayne–South Bend
                Given at: Fort Wayne, Indiana, on 17 May, 2017

The *Nihil Obstat* and *Imprimatur* are official declarations that a book or pamphlet is free of doctrinal or moral error. No implication is contained therein that those who have granted the *Nihil Obstat* or *Imprimatur* agree with its contents, opinions, or statements expressed.

Scripture texts in this work are taken from the *New American Bible, revised edition* © 2010, 1991, 1986, 1970 Confraternity of Christian Doctrine, Washington, DC, and are used by permission of the copyright owner. All Rights Reserved. No part of the *New American Bible* may be reproduced in any form without permission in writing from the copyright owner.

English translation of the *Catechism of the Catholic Church* for the United States of America copyright © 1994, United States Catholic Conference, Inc.—Libreria Editrice Vaticana. Used with permission.

Catechetical Writing Team
Janie Gustafson, PhD
Michael Amodei
Gloria Shahin

Theological Consultant
John Sehorn, PhD
Assistant Professor of Theology
Augustine Institute

Pedagogical Consultant
Michael J. Boyle, PhD
Director, Andrew M. Greeley Center for Catholic Education
Loyola University Chicago

Theology of the Body Consultant
Sr. Helena Burns, F.S.P.

© 2010, 2018 by Ave Maria Press, Inc.

www.avemariapress.com

Founded in 1865, Ave Maria Press is a ministry of the United States Province of Holy Cross.

Paperback: ISBN-13 978-1-59471-733-8

E-book: ISBN-13 978-1-59471-734-5

Cover and text design by Andy Wagoner.

Printed and bound in the United States of America.

ENGAGING MINDS, HEARTS, AND HANDS for FAITH

An education that is complete is the one in which hands and heart are engaged as much as the mind. We want to let our students try their learning in the world and so make prayers of their education.

Bl. Basil Moreau
Founder of the Congregation of Holy Cross

In this text you will:

 gain an understanding of the sacraments from their foundations in Jewish religious practices to their institution by Christ to their establishment and practice in the Church.

 grow in appreciation of the celebratory nature of the sacraments, remaining mindful of how they make present Christ and his Paschal Mystery.

 recognize more deeply the graces of the sacraments and how these graces are able to transform your life.

CONTENTS

THE CHURCH AND THE
SACRAMENTAL
ECONOMY
OF SALVATION

ON THE ROAD TO GOD

When Lam Minh Hua came with his family to the United States as a young boy, he carried with him one childhood memory of Vietnam: walking with his family to Mass every Sunday. Lam Minh Hua says today, "I remember clearly; it was far, but we walked together every Sunday, no matter what."

The family settled in Tacoma, Washington, where Hua lived a normal American life. While in high school, Hua began helping out with the youth program in his parish. As high school was coming to a close, he happened to read a book about the Jesuit missionary Pierre-Jean de Smet. Hua began to feel a call toward mission work. His pastor gave him a copy of *Maryknoll* magazine, and thus began his journey to the priesthood as a Maryknoll missioner.

As a seminarian, Hua was sent to Tanzania in Africa, where he noticed that the villagers had to walk more than an hour to get to church, just as he and his family had done in Vietnam. Hua encouraged them to build their own village church so that the priest could come to them. They gathered wood and tarp and set up poles to raise the roof.

Hua comments, "The beauty of this experience is that because I said, 'OK, let's do it,' they were able to build that little outpost church. If I hadn't gone out there, they would have had no one to say yes. That's all they were waiting for. They were all ready."

Fr. Lam Minh Hua was ordained a Maryknoll priest on May 31, 2014. Through a convergence of his experience with three cultures—American, Vietnamese, and Tanzanian—he was able to help others to open themselves to God's sacramental gifts. You will find him "on the road again," bringing Jesus to all he meets.

(Based on Gabriela Romeri, "The Road to God," *Maryknoll*, May/June 2014.)

1

FOCUS QUESTION

How does the Church
• **REVEAL AND COMMUNICATE**
Christ's saving work through
the sacraments?

Chapter Overview

Introduction — Jesus Christ and the Sacramental Life of the Church

Section 1 — The Church, the Universal Sacrament of Salvation

Section 2 — The Sacraments Transform the Church and the World

Section 3 — Breaking Open a Definition of the Sacraments

INTRODUCTION
Jesus Christ and the Sacramental Life of the Church

MAIN IDEA

Jesus himself is the way to God the Father. He is the mystery of salvation and the living, ever-present sacrament of God.

You have, by now, probably learned about at least some of the Seven Sacraments of the Church. Your learning may have begun as far back as second grade, when you were preparing to celebrate First Penance and First Eucharist. In this course, your learning will go deeper into the meaning of the sacraments, collectively and individually. In this chapter and the next, you will learn a definition of *sacrament* and examine how Jesus Christ is himself the living, ever-present sacrament of God. In fact, only in understanding the sacramentality of Christ can you come to an understanding of the meaning, signs, and effects of each of the Seven Sacraments.

Jesus Christ, the Sacrament of God

St. Augustine of Hippo described the sacraments as "visible signs of invisible grace." To understand the sacraments, you must think about making the invisible

> **sacraments** Efficacious and visible signs of God's grace, instituted by Christ and entrusted to the Church, by which divine life is dispensed to us. The Seven Sacraments are Baptism, Confirmation, Eucharist, Penance, Anointing of the Sick, Holy Orders, and Matrimony.

NOTE TAKING

Identifying Main Ideas. Create a two-column chart like the one here to help you organize the content in this section. Fill in the second column with further details.

MAIN IDEA	SUMMARY
The Son of God was incarnate.	
Christ is the living, ever-present sacrament of God.	
The mysteries of Christ's life are efficacious signs.	

St. Anne, the mother of Mary, offers a blessing to the infant Jesus.

And the Word became flesh
and made his dwelling among us,
and we saw his glory,
the glory as of the Father's only Son,
full of grace and truth. (Jn 1:14)

Jesus Christ "assumed a human nature in order to accomplish our salvation in it" (*CCC*, 461). When Christ assumed a human nature, he did so without losing his divine nature. This union of Christ's human nature and divine nature did not end with Christ's Death or Resurrection; in fact, this union cannot be broken. Christ, now ascended to the Father, has ascended with the union of both natures in his Divine Person.

The desire of the Son of God to be with you remains strong today. Jesus longs to share your life, both the tragedies and joys. The sacraments and **liturgy**—known together as the **sacramental economy**—are the means Christ uses to make himself and his saving graces present on earth. The sacramental economy is the way the fruits of Christ's redemption are given to you in the Church's liturgy through the work of the Blessed Trinity.

Jesus Christ, the Mystery of Salvation

Sacraments are mysteries that are so rich, so deep, and so profound that they cannot be easily captured or expressed in limited human language. Christ is a mystery in this sense, too; human language and speech

visible. This understanding can be facilitated by first reflecting on the mystery of the **Incarnation**.

For example, consider the story of a young child awoken by the sound of thunder who runs into her mother's room and stands near the edge of her sleepy mom's bed. "Honey, you can go back to your room. You aren't alone. God is with you," the mother gently tells her.

"Mommy, I know God is with me," the little girl says in return. "But I want someone with skin."

The message of this story is that everyone wants to be near to the ones who know us, protect us, and most of all, love us. That is why the Son of God, the Second Person of the Blessed Trinity, took on flesh and became a man. At a time in history chosen by God, the Son of the Father became incarnate:

Incarnation The act by which the Father sent his Son into the world, and by the power of the Holy Spirit, the Son came to exist as a man within the womb of Mary. The Son of God assumed human nature and became man in order to accomplish salvation for humanity in that same nature. Jesus Christ, the Son of God, the Second Person of the Trinity, is both true God and true man, not part God and part man.

liturgy The official public worship of the Church. The sacraments and the Divine Office constitute the Church's liturgy. Mass is the most important liturgical celebration.

sacramental economy The communication or dispensation of the fruits of Christ's Paschal Mystery through the celebration of the sacramental liturgy.

are incapable of expressing completely the mystery of the Son of God, God's Word made flesh. Jesus is truly human, like you in all ways, "yet without sin" (Heb 4:15). Jesus is also truly divine, the Second Divine Person of the Blessed Trinity—without beginning or end.

It is impossible to know *how* Jesus can be fully man yet fully divine at the same time. This mystery is known as the **hypostatic union**. This doctrine of faith, first expressed by St. Cyril of Alexandria (d. 444), teaches that in Jesus there are two divine natures—one human and the other divine—in one Divine Person. These natures are united in such a way that Jesus was human like every human, except for the presence of sin. He was born as a baby, grew as a child, experienced adolescence, and finally became an adult. He needed to eat, sleep, drink, breathe, bathe, and learn—just as any person does. He laughed, cried, and felt real pain. And because he had a real human body, he was subject to death.

It is important to always remember that Jesus never ceased to be God when he became man. Being both God and man, Jesus has a human intellect and human will that is always perfectly in tune with his divine

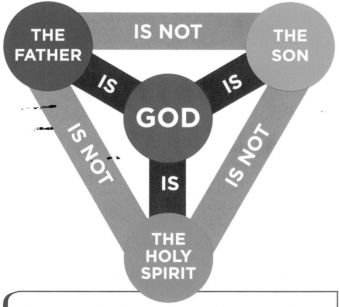

hypostatic union The doctrine of faith that recognizes two natures (one human and one divine) in the one Divine Person of Jesus Christ.

intellect and divine will. His human will "does not resist or oppose but rather submits to his divine and almighty will" (*CCC*, 475). For example, because of the union of his human and divine natures, in his human nature Jesus is able both to make present his "intimate and immediate knowledge" of God the Father and to know the secret thoughts of humans. Christ "showed the divine penetration he had into the secret thoughts of human hearts" (*CCC*, 473).

Jesus is the living, ever-present sacrament of God because he is the only Son of the Father, the eternal Word made flesh. As the Son of God, Jesus is one of the Three Divine Persons of the Blessed Trinity. He told his disciples the night before his Death, "Whoever has seen me has seen the Father. . . . I am in the Father and the Father is in me" (Jn 14:9–10). God the Father's eternal being and love are manifested in the missions of Christ and the Holy Spirit.

Throughout the Gospels, Jesus not only tells people about God's love, but he also personally manifests and makes that love present in his very Person. In fact,

> his humanity appeared as a "sacrament," that is, the sign and instrument of his divinity and of the salvation he brings: what was visible in his earthly life leads to the invisible mystery of his divine sonship and redemptive mission. (*CCC*, 515)

For example, Jesus doesn't just talk about water or use it as a sign of God's love; rather, he himself is the source of the living water of eternal life: "Whoever drinks the water I shall give will never thirst; the water I shall give will become in him a spring of water welling up to eternal life" (Jn 4:14).

Jesus doesn't just multiply bread as visible proof of God's love. He himself is the living bread come down from heaven: "I am the living bread that came down from heaven; whoever eats this bread will live forever; and the bread that I will give is my flesh for the life of the world" (Jn 6:51).

Likewise, Jesus doesn't merely talk about light in his parables as a way to explain the absence of darkness (see Luke 11:33–36). He himself is God's light to a world darkened by sin; "I am the light of the world. Whoever follows me will not walk in darkness, but will have the light of life" (Jn 8:12).

The *Catechism of the Catholic Church* teaches that Christ himself is the mystery of salvation: "For there is no other mystery of God, except Christ" (St. Augustine, quoted in *CCC*, 774). To put it more simply, Jesus himself is the only way to God the Father; he says, "I am the way and the truth and the life. No one comes to the Father except through me" (Jn 14:6).

Your Participation in Christ's Mission

These examples of words and actions from Jesus' ministry on earth do not simply "point to" or "reveal" God's love to the world. Jesus' teaching and actions *are* this love and saving grace in the world, personally present. "God is love" (1 Jn 4:8). In fact, Christ's whole life—beginning with the mystery of the Incarnation and culminating in the saving events of the Paschal Mystery—manifests God's love to the world. These mysteries of Christ's life are efficacious signs of God's love. The word *efficacious* means "capable of producing a desired effect." Sacraments, too, are efficacious but only due to Christ himself acting in and through them.

Christ established the Church on the foundation of the Apostles (through the gift of the Holy Spirit) and instituted the Seven Sacraments so that his Church could administer them and he could be present to her always. "God himself is an eternal exchange of love, Father, Son, and Holy Spirit, and he has destined us to share in that exchange" (*CCC*, 221).

Your participation in Christ's mission is intended to bring you into communion with the Father, Son, and Holy Spirit. Through the Seven Sacraments, the Church continues Christ's work of perfectly worshipping the Father and of making redeeming grace available.

New Life in Christ

Jesus came into the world to bring full, abundant life for all (see John 10:10). St. Irenaeus, a second-century bishop who was killed for his faith, said it brilliantly: "The glory of God is the human person fully alive." Think about it: God rejoices when you live a full, abundant life. God's will is that you should live with him forever. The saving effect of the Paschal Mystery of Christ is a vibrant new life in the Blessed Trinity. You participate in this new life through the sacraments. The sacraments, in turn, empower you to share this new life with others.

ASSIGNMENT

Read the following Scripture passages. Summarize each as it pertains to the new life you receive in the sacraments and how you can share this new life with others.

- similes of salt and light (Matthew 5:13–16)
- parable of the mustard seed (Matthew 13:31–33)
- parable of the weeds among the wheat (Matthew 13:24–30)

SECTION ASSESSMENT

NOTE TAKING

Use the chart you created to help you answer the following questions.

1. Why did the Son of God assume a human nature?

2. What does it mean to say that Christ is the "living, ever-present sacrament of God"?

3. What does it mean to say that the mysteries of Christ's life—beginning with the mystery of the Incarnation—are efficacious?

COMPREHENSION

4. Share an example from the Gospels of how Jesus witnessed that "God is love."

VOCABULARY

5. Define *hypostatic union*.

CRITICAL THINKING

6. How do the sacraments enable the Church to continue Christ's work of perfectly worshipping the Father and of making redeeming grace available to humanity?

SECTION 1

The Church, the Universal Sacrament of Salvation

MAIN IDEA
The Church is the universal sacrament of salvation. She makes the saving action of Jesus present to you and completes his mission.

The Church's sacraments have meaning only in and through Jesus. All of the events of Jesus' entire life and saving work become the sacrament of salvation, "revealed and active in the Church's sacraments" (*CCC*, 774). Each sacrament is primarily and fundamentally a personal act of Christ himself acting through his Mystical Body, the Church. Each sacrament is the saving action of Christ in visible form; it is the act of Christ the High Priest who "entered once for all into the sanctuary, not with the blood of goats and calves but with his own blood, thus obtaining eternal redemption" (Heb 9:12). In the words of the *Catechism of the Catholic Church*, "it really is Christ who acts in the sacraments through the Holy Spirit for the Church" (*CCC*, 1120). Jesus continues to live and work in the Church, especially in the Seven Sacraments. He acts through the sacraments he instituted to communicate his grace to all. And, as the *Catechism* teaches, the sacraments "are *efficacious* because in them Christ himself is at work; it is he who baptizes, he who acts in his sacraments in order to communicate the grace that each sacrament signifies" (*CCC*, 1127). Understanding this can help you recognize that the Church is the "universal sacrament of salvation" because Christ works through her. Thus she is the visible channel of grace to the whole human race. The late Cardinal Joseph Bernardin of Chicago once explained, "As Christ is the sacrament of God—the visible and incarnate, efficacious and gratuitous bestowal of divine grace and life, so the Church is the sacrament of Christ in human history." The Church makes Christ present in today's world.

An analogy can be drawn here to the relationship between the moon and the sun. Just as the moon has no light of its own but shines in the night sky because it reflects the light of the sun, the Church is a light to the world because she reflects the light of Christ.

NOTE TAKING

Summarizing the Section. Create an outline like the one below in your notebook. As you read the section, use the outline to help you summarize the material.

I. The Church meets the definition of *sacrament*
    A. As mystery:
    B. As visible sign:
    C. As efficacious sign:

II. The Church completes the mission of Christ
    A. The Church as the Body of Christ
    B. Implications of this understanding
        1. Communion with Christ:
        2. Communion with the Church:
        3. Communion with people throughout the world:

She makes this light—the grace of salvation and new life—available to all people.

To consider further how the Church is the sacrament of Christ, think about how the Church herself meets the definition of sacrament. First, a sacrament is a *mystery*. Second, it is a *visible sign* of the unseen (invisible) divine reality. Third, a sacrament is an *efficacious sign*—something that makes real what it signifies. The Church also has these same three dimensions, explained in the following chart.

THE CHURCH AS **MYSTERY**

St. Paul spoke of the Church as a great mystery—something that cannot be fully explained or understood (see Ephesians 5:32). For this reason, he and the other writers of the New Testament described the Church in symbolic language. They used images that would help people understand the Church as mystery. Some of the images for the Church found in the New Testament include a flock of sheep (see John 21:15–19), a cultivated field or vineyard (see John 15:1–10), the Bride of Christ (see Ephesians 5:25–27), and the New Jerusalem (see Revelation 21:9–27).

THE CHURCH AS **VISIBLE SIGN**

The Church is the visible sign of Jesus Christ, whom we can no longer see in human form and who is the perfect sign of the Father's saving love. In more detail:

> The church is both human and divine, visible but endowed with invisible realities, zealous in action and dedicated to contemplation, present in the world, yet a migrant, so constituted that in it the human is directed toward and subordinated to the divine, the visible to the invisible, action to contemplation, and this present world to that city yet to come, the object of our quest (see Hebrews 13:14). (*Sacrosanctum Concilium*, 2)

THE CHURCH AS **EFFICACIOUS SIGN**

The power of the Church to effect what she signifies was given by Christ to Peter and the Apostles when he told them, "I will give you the keys to the kingdom of heaven" (Mt 16:19) and "Whatever you bind on earth shall be bound in heaven; and whatever you loose on earth shall be loosed in heaven" (Mt 18:18). He further promised them, "And behold, I am with you always, until the end of the age" (Mt 28:20) and

> "Amen, amen, I say to you, whoever believes in me will do the works that I do, and will do greater ones than these, because I am going to the Father. And whatever you ask in my name, I will do, so that the Father may be glorified in the Son. If you ask anything of me in my name, I will do it." (Jn 14:12–14)

Because of the power Jesus gave her, "The Church, then, both contains and communicates the invisible grace she signifies" (*CCC*, 774). As *Lumen Gentium* (*Dogmatic Constitution on the Church*) explains, "The Church is in Christ like a sacrament or as a sign and instrument both of a very closely knit union with God and of the unity of the whole human race." This was the reason the Fathers of the Second Vatican Council called the Church "the universal sacrament of salvation" (*Lumen Gentium*, 48).

As part of Christ's Body, you need to spend time with other members to worship God and grow together in your faith.

The Church Completes the Mission of Christ

The Church, the universal sacrament of salvation, completes the mission of Christ. This mission is to bring Catholics into communion with the Three Divine Persons of the Blessed Trinity—Father, Son, and Holy Spirit. It is Christ who pours out his Spirit among the members of his Church. "Through the Church's sacraments, Christ communicates his Holy and sanctifying Spirit to the members of his Body" (*CCC*, 739).

When you respond in faith to God's Word and become a member of Christ's Body, you become intimately united with him. You are also united to other members of the Body of Christ and to people throughout the world. Through all the sacraments, you are "united in a hidden and real way to Christ in his Passion and glorification" (*CCC*, 790). In Baptism, in particular, you are united to Christ's Death and Resurrection. In the Eucharist, you share in the Body and Blood of the Lord, strengthening the bond of charity between you and Christ while reinforcing the unity of the Church as the Mystical Body of Christ. Your participation in the sacraments helps you to live morally.

When you are united to Christ, you are first and foremost united to other members of the Body of Christ, the Church. This communion encompasses all members of the Church, both living and dead—the **Communion of Saints**. In addition, because you are united to Christ, you are also in communion with all other people throughout the world.

> **Communion of Saints** The unity in Christ of all those he has redeemed: the Church on earth, in heaven, and in Purgatory.

Your Communion with Christ

Through your participation in the Church—and particularly due to the graces of the sacraments—you are in communion with Christ. The *Catechism of the Catholic Church* describes the intimacy of this communion:

> The comparison of the Church with the body casts light on the intimate bond between Christ and his Church. Not only is she gathered *around him*; she is united in *him*, in his body. (*CCC*, 789)

> [The Church] draws her life from the word and the Body of Christ and so herself becomes Christ's Body. (*CCC*, 752)

> The Church . . . is the visible sign of the communion in Christ between God and men. (*CCC*, 1071).

In his encyclical *Redemptor Hominis* (*Redeemer of Man*), Pope John Paul II (canonized by Pope Francis in 2014) wrote that communion with Christ is the Church's main purpose for existing—so that "each person may be able to find Christ, in order that Christ may walk with each person the path of life" (*Redemptor Hominis*, 13). That is why the Church is "the sacrament of unity" (*CCC*, 1140).

You also encounter Christ and delve more deeply into a relationship with the Blessed Trinity *whenever* you come together as Church. This means that when you celebrate the liturgy and when you do the things Christ did and in his name—minister to the sick, care for the needy, and show compassion to the stranger—you grow even more deeply in communion with Christ.

Your Communion with the Church

The Communion of Saints is defined as the "unity of all the redeemed, those on earth and those who have died" (*CCC*, Glossary). The *Catechism of the Catholic Church* also teaches that "the Communion of Saints is

the Church" (*CCC*, 946). This statement has two meanings that help to explain how your membership in the Church brings you into union with all who belong to the Body of Christ.

First, everyone in the Church shares a communion in spiritual goods. Among these goods are the following:

COMMUNION IN THE FAITH.
The faith you share with other Catholics today is the same faith inherited from the Apostles.

COMMUNION OF THE SACRAMENTS.
The sacraments of the Church unite you to the Communion of Saints because they unite you to God in Christ. The term *communion* is applicable to all of the sacraments, but it "is better suited to the Eucharist than to any other, because it is primarily the Eucharist that brings this communion about" (*CCC*, 950).

COMMUNION OF CHARISMS.
A *charism* is a special gift, talent, or ability given to each Church member by the Holy Spirit. Charisms are intended to help build up the Church; they are for the good of all. The Church collectively shares the charisms her members have received individually.

COMMUNION OF GOODS.
The early Christians held everything in common. So, too, "all Christians should be ready and eager to come to the help of the needy" (*CCC*, 952).

COMMUNION IN CHARITY.
Every act of charity performed by Catholics benefits the entire Body of Christ. Every sin harms this communion.

Second, there is a communion of all holy people—in the Church in heaven, the Church in Purgatory, and the Church on earth. The saints in heaven intercede for those who are living and for the dead who are still being purified. The living can receive strength and aid from the saints in heaven, and living members of the Church can pray for those who have died. "Our prayer for them is capable not only of helping them, but also of making their intercession for us effective" (*CCC*, 958).

Your membership and participation in the Church highlights the diversity of gifts and talents given for the welfare of the Church, with love as the foremost gift. The unity of the Mystical Body of Christ is able to succeed over any human divisions.

Your Communion with People throughout the World

The Church is the universal sacrament of salvation. The Church has a missionary mandate to proclaim the Gospel to all peoples and to baptize in Christ's name. "The ultimate purpose of mission is none other than to make men share in the communion between the Father and the Son in their Spirit of love" (*CCC*, 850). Such unity can be understood by understanding *catholicity*, a mark of the Church. This mark has several implications for a Catholic's participation in the world and communion with others that apply to the relationship of Catholics with other members of the Church, with others who believe in Christ, and finally with all of humankind who are called by God's grace to salvation.

The Church is joined, albeit imperfectly, to those who are baptized Christians but do not profess the Catholic faith in its entirety or have not remained united under the pope. With Orthodox churches, the communion is profound and, in the words of Pope Paul VI, "lacks little to attain the fullness that would permit a common celebration of the Lord's Eucharist" (quoted in *CCC*, 838).

Non-Christians, too, are related to the Church in different ways. Jewish people hold a special place of honor because Jews first received God's covenant. Because of a shared belief in one God, Muslims also are related to the Church.

The task to make all people disciples of Christ and sharers in the communion of love of the Blessed Trinity is a missionary mandate directed by the Holy Spirit. God wills the salvation of all people through the knowledge of the truth. The task requires that missionaries and all who witness the Gospel live lives of penance, accept the Cross, and abide in a deep respect for those who do not yet accept the Gospel.

Catholics must see all people as interconnected and part of the human family. Because God is the Father of all people, we must care about everyone as we care about the members of our own families. If people in another part of the world are suffering from famine, a natural disaster, or oppression, you and your community suffer with them and try to help them. This type of concern for others is called *human solidarity*.

BUILDING the Body of Christ

Read what St. Paul wrote about the Church as a body with many parts (1 Cor 12:14–26) and the Church as a community (Rom 12:9–18). Then research information from Catholic Relief Services for ideas on how you can practically be a witness to the faith by serving others both in and out of the Catholic Church. Write a proposal for your plan of service in this area. Incorporate a reference to some of St. Paul's words into your plan. Make sure your plan can be started and well on the way to completion during the course of this semester. Put the plan into action.

Remembering the Communion of Saints

Make a prayer card as a reminder of the Communion of Saints. Cut an equilateral triangle out of construction paper or card stock. On the front at one corner, list one or more names of living people who are pilgrims with you in the journey of faith. In the second corner, list one or more names of people of faith who have died but are not canonized saints. In the third corner, list one or more names of saints in heaven to whom you have a particular attachment. Finally, put your own name in the center of the triangle. On the back, write your own prayer of communion with these people. Pray for their spiritual well-being, and also ask them to help you be a better Catholic.

SECTION ASSESSMENT

NOTE TAKING

Use the outline you created to help you answer the following questions.

1. How does the Church meet the definition of mystery as the term is applied to the sacraments?
2. In what ways is the Church a visible sign of the Father's love?
3. How does the Church complete the mission of Christ?

COMPREHENSION

4. Explain how the Church shares a communion in charity.

VOCABULARY

5. Define *Communion of Saints*.

APPLICATION

6. Reflect on a special gift, or charism, the Holy Spirit has given you. Explain how you can use this charism in a way that benefits others and builds up the Church.

SECTION 2

The Sacraments Transform the Church and the World

MAIN IDEA
The Church is the instrument of God's grace. Members of the Church are called to participate in Christ's mission as priest, prophet, and king.

As sacrament, the Church is the instrument Christ uses for the salvation of all people. As the universal sacrament of salvation, the Church makes the mystery of God's love present to all.

The Church "is the visible plan of God's love for humanity" because God desires "that the whole human race may become one People of God, form one Body of Christ, and be built up into one temple of the Holy Spirit." (*CCC*, 776, quoting Pope Paul VI)

The Church, as the sacrament of Christ, has the power to transform the world. While the transformation has already begun, the Church is also a sign and an instrument of the unity that has yet to be realized.

How does Christ use the Church as his instrument of salvation for all? At Baptism, you are incorporated into the Church and become a member of the Body of Christ. "The baptized have become 'living stones' to be 'built into a spiritual house, to be a holy priesthood'" (*CCC*, 1268, quoting 1 Pt 2:5). By becoming a member of the Church through Baptism, you receive the rights of a Christian, including the right to receive the other

NOTE TAKING

Using a Concept Diagram. Create a diagram like the one to the right describing how Catholics are transformed through the grace of each of the sacraments. Then summarize how the Seven Sacraments shape a Catholic's mission to be priest, prophet, and king.

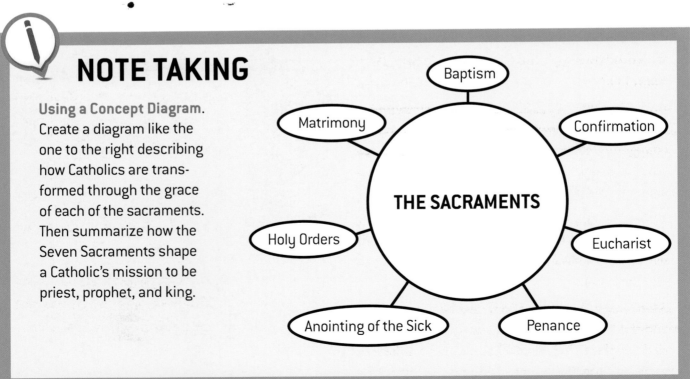

sacraments. You also are charged with the responsibility to profess the faith and share it with others as part of the Church's missionary mandate.

The Second Vatican Council summarized how Catholics deepen their participation in the Church through their participation in the sacraments. Here is an overview of the Council's statements on the sacraments and how they impact you:

- *Baptism.* Your faith and participation in this sacrament make you a member of the Church and the People of God. You are "reborn" as a son or daughter of God (*Lumen Gentium*, 11).

- *Confirmation.* Your identity as a Catholic is strengthened. "The Holy Spirit endows you with special strength" so that you may act as a true witnesses of Christ, spreading and defending the faith (*Lumen Gentium*, 11).

- *Eucharist.* "Strengthened in Holy Communion by the body of Christ, [you] manifest in a concrete way that unity of the people of God which is suitably signified and wondrously brought about" by this sacrament (*Lumen Gentium*, 11).

- *Penance and Reconciliation.* Every sin is not only an offense against God; it is also an offense against the Church. Sin separates you from the Church. This sacrament forgives sin and restores your unity with God and with the Church (cf. *Lumen Gentium*, 11).

- *Anointing of the Sick.* This sacrament strengthens the sick and suffering members of the Church to "contribute to the welfare of the whole people of God by associating themselves freely with the passion and death of Christ" (*Lumen Gentium,* 11).

- *Holy Orders.* This sacrament enables bishops, priests, and deacons to "feed the Church in Christ's name with the word and the grace of God" (*Lumen Gentium*, 11).

- *Matrimony.* As a sign of oneness between Christ and the Church, this sacrament strengthens married couples to help one another attain holiness in their lives together and to build up the Church by "the rearing and education of their children" in the faith (*Lumen Gentium*, 11).

As a member of the Church, you join in carrying out the mission of Christ in today's world. Just as Jesus had a threefold mission as priest, prophet, and king, so "the whole People of God participates in these three offices of Christ and bears the responsibilities for mission and service that flow from them" (*CCC*, 783).

Now consider how participating in the Church helps you to participate in Christ's mission as priest, prophet, and king.

PRIEST

- All the baptized share in the priesthood of Christ.

- You participate in Christ's priestly mission when you provide spiritual support, such as through your prayers, to another person.

PROPHET

- A prophet witnesses to the Catholic faith and proclaims God's truth.

- Being a prophet sometimes means you have to go against the tide of public opinion.

KING

- Jesus fulfilled his kingly mission by dying for the sins of all.

- You can participate in Christ's kingly mission when you put the needs of others before your own needs.

Your Mission as Priest

On the basis of your Baptism, you are to act as Christ. You are to offer yourself to God in worship, become holy, and help others grow in holiness. Baptism makes you a member of a holy priesthood. This *common priesthood* differs from the hierarchical or *ministerial priesthood* of bishops and priests (see page 46). Duties of the common priesthood include:

- *Spiritual sacrifices to God.* You have a responsibility and duty to worship God at all times and in all places by your holy actions. "All [the laity's] works, prayers, and apostolic undertakings, family and married life, daily work, relaxation of mind and body, if they are accomplished in the Spirit—indeed, even the hardships of life if patiently born—all these become spiritual sacrifices acceptable to God through Jesus Christ" (*CCC*, 901).

- *Personal holiness.* Through the Church, God sanctifies your life, transforming you with his presence and grace through the Holy Spirit. Grace is not a particular thing or a quantifiable amount. Rather, grace is a sharing in the actual life and love of the Trinity. You become holy because you are united with God in grace. Each sacrament enables you to share God's life in a particular way. In other words, each sacrament gives a special grace. For example, the Sacrament of the Anointing of the Sick brings you the healing dimension of God's life and love. The Sacrament of Penance and Reconciliation offers you the forgiving dimension of God's life and love. All sacraments also dispense *sanctifying grace* (a grace that heals your human nature, wounded by sin, and gives you a share in the divine life) and *actual grace* (divine help to perform some good action you would not ordinarily be able to do on your own, such as forgiving an enemy, avoiding a habitual sin, or remaining faithful to Jesus through torture or death). Grace is never something you "earn." Your holiness is God's wonderful and generous gift to you.

- *Helping others grow in holiness.* In making you holy, the sacraments help to infuse the three **theological virtues** into your life. They also help you form a community of faith, hope, and charity with others.

Your Mission as Prophet

While prophets can foretell and have foretold the future, a prophet does more than just that. A prophet speaks God's Word to others, witnesses to the truth about Jesus Christ, and reminds people to persevere in the true faith. As part of his threefold office of priest, prophet, and king, Jesus called people to repent of their sins and turn back to God's covenant of love. As a member of the Church, you share in the prophetic mission of Christ whenever you give witness to him through your words, actions, or example. You also act as prophet whenever you encourage others in the Church to persevere in faith despite times of discouragement, disillusionment, and confusion.

Among the graces of the Church's sacraments are those that inspire Catholics to greater discipleship, including enabling some to become *evangelists*—people who spread the message of Christ throughout the world. In effect, you become "God's co-worker," "God's field," and "God's building" (1 Cor 3:9). You help proclaim the faith to others *in* the Church through discussions, religious education classes, Bible study groups, and the use of social media. Furthermore, you help proclaim the Good News of Jesus Christ to those outside the Church by your every word and action.

> **theological virtues** Three important virtues, first infused at Baptism, that enable Catholics to know God and lead them to union with him; they are faith (belief in, and personal knowledge of, God), hope (trust in God's salvation and his bestowal of graces needed to attain it), and charity (love of God and love of neighbor). Catholics can also receive an increase in the theological virtues through reception of the other sacraments and through the application of the theological virtues in their lives.

As a member of the universal church (see page 323), you are able to join with people from around the world in prayer and worship.

While ordained bishops and priests work as prophets mainly within the Church, the **laity** carry out their prophetic mission primarily *outside* the Church, in the secular world—in neighborhoods, workplaces, shopping malls, schools, hospitals, and so forth. The Second Vatican Council clarified that laypeople have "the special vocation" to help build God's Kingdom "by engaging in temporal affairs and by ordering them according to the plan of God. . . . They are called by God to work for the sanctification of the world from within as a leaven" (*Lumen Gentium*, 31).

Think about it: Everywhere you go, you can bring Christ's presence and love to others. In everything you

> **laity** All the unordained members of the Church who have been initiated into the Church through Baptism.

do—whether it is working in a grocery store, expressing yourself on a social networking site, counseling a friend, competing in sports against a rival school, or talking with your parents—you can be Christ to others. As St. Augustine once said, "Let us rejoice then and give thanks that we have become not only Christians, but Christ himself."

Your Royal Mission

Many people equate royalty with worldly power and riches. However, the true role of those in power is to serve the people they are charged to protect and provide for. True royalty—as Jesus represented by his life—does not seek to be served but rather seeks to serve others, especially the poor and the suffering. Just as Jesus came "to bring glad tidings to the poor" (Lk 4:18) and "to seek and to save what was lost" (Lk

19:10), so you participate in his royal mission whenever you work for justice and peace and serve others in charity.

You can participate in Christ's mission as king by serving others individually, such as by showing care and compassion for a classmate or neighbor in need, or as part of a Church ministry, such as the St. Vincent de Paul Society, a food pantry, or a ministry that serves the elderly in your community. When you serve others and seek to treat them as Christ would—with love, patience, understanding, and genuine caring—you are living your royal mission.

As sacrament, the Church brings the healing, forgiving, and comforting love of God to all those in need. When you involve yourself in the Church's priestly, prophetic, and royal mission, you become—as the Church—a sign and an instrument of Christ's presence in every part of today's world.

SECTION ASSESSMENT

NOTE TAKING

Use the diagram you created to help you answer the following questions.

1. How is a person transformed through the graces of the Sacrament of Baptism?
2. How is a Catholic transformed through the Sacrament of Penance?
3. How can the sacraments help you live your mission as prophet?

COMPREHENSION

4. Why is the mission to serve others known as a royal mission?
5. Describe the prophetic mission.

REFLECTION

6. Choose either the prophetic mission or the royal mission, and write a paragraph explaining how you can more fully commit to living out that mission. Make your answer practical and specific.

Breaking Open a Definition of the Sacraments

MAIN IDEA
In the sacraments, God freely dispenses his grace to you and makes you a sharer in the divine life.

In the remaining chapters of this text, you will explore the meaning, signs, and effects of each of the Seven Sacraments.

This primary definition of *sacraments* is taken from the *Catechism of the Catholic Church*:

> The sacraments are efficacious signs of grace, instituted by Christ and entrusted to the Church, by which divine life is dispensed to us. The visible rites by which the sacraments are celebrated signify and make present the graces proper to each sacrament. They bear fruit in those who receive them with the required dispositions. (*CCC*, 1131)

This definition contains some complex and important ideas. The next sections break open the ideas.

Sacraments Are Efficacious Signs of Grace

St. Thomas Aquinas wrote that sacraments "have efficacy from the incarnate Word himself." Recall that *efficacious* is a term that means "capable of producing a desired effect." The sacraments themselves are efficacious signs, meaning they effect, or bring about,

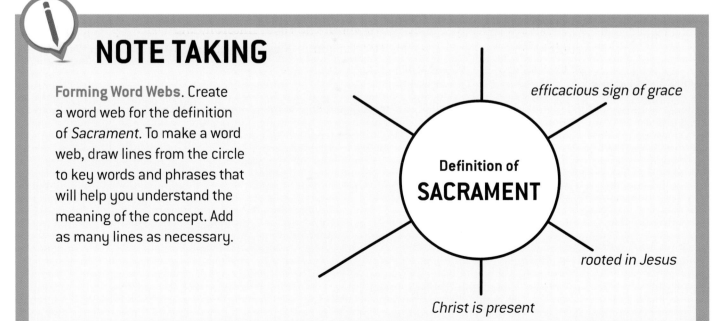

NOTE TAKING

Forming Word Webs. Create a word web for the definition of *Sacrament*. To make a word web, draw lines from the circle to key words and phrases that will help you understand the meaning of the concept. Add as many lines as necessary.

efficacious sign of grace

Definition of SACRAMENT

rooted in Jesus

Christ is present

what they signify and signify what they effect. As an "efficacious sign of grace," each sacrament confers a grace that is proper to it and that comes from Christ.

The *Catechism of the Catholic Church* defines grace as "free and undeserved help that God gives us" so that we can respond to his call (*CCC*, 1996). Grace is "a participation in the life of God" (*CCC*, 1997).

It is important to understand that grace is not some *thing* that is outside of the relationship you have with God. Rather, grace is the gift by which you participate in the life of the Blessed Trinity. Grace is, first and foremost, the gift of God's very own life, but grace also includes the ability God gives you to participate in, and collaborate with, his work. As the *Catechism of the Catholic Church* teaches, "the fruits of the sacraments also depend on the disposition of the one who receives them" (*CCC*, 1128).

God gives you his grace in many ways and through many opportunities in your life. When they are celebrated "worthily in faith," the Seven Sacraments "confer the grace that they signify," providing opportunities for encountering God the Father and God the Son, through the grace of the Holy Spirit (see *CCC*, 1127). Sacraments strengthen and deepen your relationship with Jesus, with the Church, and with all people throughout the world. They draw you into the wonder and completeness of the divine life.

Sacraments Are Instituted by Christ

The sacraments are rooted in Jesus and traceable to him. "Christ instituted the sacraments of the new law" (*CCC*, 1210). His ongoing presence in the Church through the gift of the Holy Spirit has helped the Church know and understand the Seven Sacraments as times when Christ is present with the Church in a special way. The same Jesus who in the efficacious signs of his earthly ministry healed the sick, forgave the sinner, celebrated marriage with his friends, and fed thousands with bread and fish and with his words is present today in the Seven Sacraments. As St. Leo the Great put it, "What was visible in our Savior has passed over to his sacraments."

Sacraments Are Commemorations of the Paschal Mystery

The sacraments celebrate the Paschal Mystery—the Passion, Death, Resurrection, and Ascension of Christ—that brought about the salvation of humankind. In each sacrament, the saving actions of Christ are made present. The way Christ dispenses the fruits of the Paschal Mystery until he comes again is the sacramental economy. The term *economy* originates from a Greek word that means "management of the household." The *sacramental economy* refers to the way Christ cares for his household, the Church.

St. Leo the Great

Of course, the actual historical events of the Paschal Mystery occurred only once, but by the power of the Holy Spirit the liturgy makes the events truly present today. The Paschal Mystery brings a person into communion with the Blessed Trinity and with Christ's Body, the Church. Chapter 2 explores more about how the Blessed Trinity works in the liturgy.

Sacraments Are the Masterworks of God

In the sacraments, God really becomes present. No created object, spoken word, or ritualized action can ever "force" God to be present. Nothing anyone says or does can control what God himself says or does. Pouring water over someone's head or saying certain words doesn't produce God "on demand." Instead, God comes to you in the sacraments because he has chosen these rituals and times, places, and ways to be present. As the *Catechism of the Catholic Church* simply and beautifully puts it, the sacraments are "the masterworks of God" (*CCC*, 1116).

A sacrament always involves a relationship between God and humanity. When you participate in a sacrament, God acts first, and then you act in response. God takes the initiative of being present, of offering you a share in his own life and love. You, in turn, open your heart to the divine, giving to God through your worship and by accepting God's Word as the truth on which to base your life. In other words, every sacrament is an encounter with Christ, a dialogue, and a two-way street.

This means that a sacrament is a visible sign that confers the grace that the liturgical rite of the sacrament signifies. When a sacrament is properly administered and celebrated worthily in faith, grace is received. Grace is necessary for salvation. Through the sacraments, God invites you to enter into communion with him and with all those who are celebrating with you.

But even this definition falls short of what a sacrament truly is. You also need to realize that each sacrament fills you with grace and *transforms* you. Each sacrament works to make you completely whole and holy. You grow in God's likeness through your participation in the sacraments. Each sacrament empowers you to come alive in the Holy Spirit, so that your every thought and action can praise God and give witness to Christ's saving power.

In summary, every sacrament has four aspects, or dimensions:

1. *memorial*—a remembering that God is present now and has always acted for the benefit of all in the past;

2. *celebration*—a Church-approved ritual, involving objects, words, and actions, that gives worship and thanks to God for salvation in Christ;

3. *communion*—a real encounter of union with Christ, with members of the Church, and with people throughout the world; and

4. *transformation*—an empowerment to become more holy and to minister to others through the gift of God's grace.

It is important to realize that these four aspects are not like stages or steps. One does not necessarily happen before the other, nor is there any particular order. Rather, each sacrament—in its entirety—is a memorial, a celebration, a communion, and a transformation that must be understood through the sacramentality of Christ, particularly through the mysteries of the Incarnation and the hypostatic union.

WHY SEVEN SACRAMENTS?

Why are there exactly Seven Sacraments in the Catholic Church? The simple answer is that Jesus instituted exactly seven. Take some time to read the following Gospel passages to discover how the sacraments are connected to Jesus' ministry and how he met people in their time of need. Answer:

1. Which sacrament is each set of passages connected with?

2. What value(s) of Jesus appear in the passages?

GOSPEL PASSAGES

- Matthew 9:35–38 and Matthew 28:16–20
- Luke 22:14–20 and John 6:47–58
- John 2:1–11
- Luke 12:8–12 and John 16:5–16
- Luke 7:36–50 and John 20:19–23
- Mark 1:40–45 and Mark 8:22–26
- Matthew 3:13–17 and John 3:3–8

Why Seven Sacraments? In the thirteenth century, St. Thomas Aquinas expanded on the simple answer and taught that human development is likewise marked by a similar seven stages. He thought that while it was not mandatory for Christ to institute exactly Seven Sacraments, it was reasonable because of the way human lives unfold:

- You are born. (Baptism)
- You grow. (Confirmation)
- You are fed. (Eucharist)
- You are healed. (Penance)
- You recover. (Anointing of the Sick)
- You need, and form, family. (Matrimony)
- You need, and respond to, leaders. (Holy Orders)

What do you think of St. Thomas's reasoning?

SECTION ASSESSMENT

NOTE TAKING

Use the word web you created for this section to help you complete the following items.

1. Name and explain four aspects, or dimensions, of the sacraments.

2. What are some words that show that the sacraments are traceable to Christ?

COMPREHENSION

3. What does it mean to say that the Paschal Mystery is made present in the celebration of the sacraments?

4. The *Catechism of the Catholic Church* describes the sacraments as "the masterworks of God" (*CCC*, 1116). Briefly explain what is meant by this phrase.

REFLECTION

5. Recall your participation in one of the sacraments. Write a paragraph describing any way you have noticed God's grace transforming your life through a sacrament.

Section Summaries

Focus Question

How does the Church reveal and communicate Christ's saving work through the sacraments?

Complete one of the following:

 Create a collage that creatively expresses how the Church reveals Christ's saving work to the faithful and to the world.

→ Write a journal entry summarizing what you have learned about the Church and her role in carrying on Christ's work of salvation. Then write questions you have that you can seek answers to throughout this course.

→ Write a three-paragraph essay explaining how the Church reveals and communicates Christ's saving work. Imagine that your audience for the essay is unfamiliar with the Catholic faith.

INTRODUCTION (PAGES 3–7)

Jesus Christ and the Sacramental Life of the Church

Christ makes himself known in the sacraments and liturgy, known as the *sacramental economy*. Christ is the living sacrament of God by virtue of his Incarnation and hypostatic union. The mysteries of Christ's life—the Incarnation, his ministry, and the Paschal Mystery—are efficacious signs of God's love. Christ's entire holy and sanctifying humanity is an efficacious sign. The Son of God makes God's love present to the world. The sacraments, too, are efficacious signs, but only because of Christ acting in and through them.

 Write a two- to three-paragraph journal entry describing how you have experienced God's love through the work of Jesus Christ.

SECTION 1 (PAGES 8–13)

The Church, the Universal Sacrament of Salvation

In the Church, especially in her sacraments, Jesus continues to live and work among us. The Church is the "universal sacrament of salvation" and an efficacious sign because she makes the saving actions of the Risen Christ present to you through the work of the Holy Spirit. The Church completes the mission of Christ, which is to bring the Church into communion with the Blessed Trinity.

 Read paragraphs 1088 and 1089 of the *Catechism of the Catholic Church*. Write a two-paragraph summary that supports the statement that the Church "makes the saving actions of the Risen Christ present to us."

SECTION 2 (PAGES 14–18)

The Sacraments Transform the Church and the World

As sacrament, the Church is the instrument Christ uses to offer and facilitate the gift of salvation. Baptism incorporates you into the Church and makes you a member of the Body of Christ. This gives you the rights of a Christian, including the right to receive the other sacraments. You are also charged to profess your faith and share the faith with others.

Tell two concrete ways you can profess and share your faith in Christ with others.

SECTION 3 (PAGES 19–23)

Breaking Open a Definition of the Sacraments

The sacraments are efficacious signs, meaning they effect what they signify and signify what they effect. They are instituted by Christ and entrusted to the Church, and through them divine life is dispensed to us.

Write one or two paragraphs explaining your understanding of the meaning of the phrase "they effect what they signify" as it pertains to the sacraments.

Chapter Assignments

Choose and complete at least one of the following three assignments assessing your understanding of the material in this chapter.

1. Creating a Musical Collection

Using contemporary Christian music, liturgical hymns, or other music with suitable themes, create a music medley (e.g., the audio portion via YouTube) that connects to, or supports, the themes covered in this chapter. Your compilation should include at least seven songs. Suggested themes include the following:

- Jesus as the Way to the Father
- the Church as the instrument of salvation
- the Church as the Body of Christ
- your mission as priest, prophet, and king (or specifically one of these titles)
- one or more of the individual sacraments

For Catholic hymns, check the index of a parish or school hymnal for titles. After you have made your music selections, give your medley a title. Create suitable cover art or a cover slide, if possible.

2. Developing a Lesson Plan

Develop a lesson plan that can be used for teaching the main content of this chapter to a group in a parish youth ministry setting. The object of the lesson plan is to make sure teens who do not attend Catholic high school are able to answer the chapter's Focus Question—How does the Church reveal and communicate Christ's saving work through the sacraments?—by the end of a ninety-minute session. The plan should include the following elements:

- an icebreaker to begin the session that has a connection with the sacraments
- a succinct one-page script that summarizes the chapter and that could be read by a youth minister to the teens
- one suggestion for a small-group activity to help teens reflect on, respond to, or teach one another a key part of the material
- five test items (in several different formats) that can be used at the end of the session to assess the teens' understanding of the material

3. Understanding Primary Sources

→ Read chapter 1 of the Second Vatican Council document *Lumen Gentium*. You can find the document on the Vatican website. Write a two- or three-page essay summarizing the mystery of the Church as explained in this chapter of *Lumen Gentium*. Include at least five quotations from the document in your essay, and provide proper citations for the quotations. Conclude your essay by explaining how your reading of chapter 1 of *Lumen Gentium* strengthened your understanding of what you learned in this chapter of your text.

Faithful Disciple

St. John Paul II

Pope John Paul II gives Communion to people attending open-air Mass at the People's Stadium in Kinshasa, Zaire, on August 15, 1985.

In 1978, after the short reign of Pope John Paul I, when the College of Cardinals gathered again to elect a new pope, they surprised the world by electing the first Polish pope in history. His name was Karol Wojtyla, and he took the name John Paul II. His papal reign was the third longest in history: nearly twenty-seven years.

As a young man growing up in Poland, Karol Wojtyla followed a road to the priesthood that was neither easy nor simple. When World War II began, the Nazis closed the university where Karol had been a student. He was then forced to work in a quarry and later in a chemical plant. Deciding to be a priest, he studied in a secret "underground" seminary. He was ordained a priest in 1946, just after World War II ended. After ordination, Karol Wojtyla served as a parish priest and chaplain for university students in Poland. At only age thirty-eight he was named a bishop, and he later attended the Second Vatican Council.

Pope John Paul II frequently expressed his love of the sacraments. He explained how the mission of God the Father through the Son and the Holy Spirit is present in them:

> What else are the sacraments (all of them!), if not the action of Christ in the Holy Spirit?
> When the Church baptizes, it is Christ who baptizes; when the Church absolves, it is
> Christ who absolves; when the Church celebrates the Eucharist, it is Christ who celebrates

it: "This is my body." And so on. All the sacraments are an action of Christ, the action of God in Christ. (*Crossing the Threshold of Hope*)

Pope John Paul II died on April 2, 2005. At his funeral Mass, many in the vast crowd outside St. Peter's Basilica took up the chant "Magnus, Magnus, Magnus," meaning "Great, Great, Great." It was a public proclamation that Pope John Paul II should be given the title "Pope John Paul the Great" and should be remembered as a man who had great influence in the twentieth century while helping usher in the new millennium. This title is still used to describe him today. Even more significantly, Pope John Paul II was canonized by Pope Francis in April 2014.

Reading Comprehension

1. What was one surprising fact about the election of Karol Wojtyla?

2. Name two jobs that Karol Wojtyla held during World War II.

3. Who always acts in the sacraments?

Writing Task

- Choose one sentence from St. John Paul II's quotation on the sacraments, and write a paragraph expressing what it means for you.

Explaining the Faith

Why do we need sacraments at all? Aren't the sacraments just celebrations to mark significant times in a person's life? And why not just approach God without signs, set prayers, or the help of the Church and a priest?

You may associate the celebration of sacraments with the commemoration of certain age markers in life; for example, Baptism shortly after birth or Confirmation during adolescence. However, sacraments are much more than simply celebrations of significant life moments. In the sacraments, you can encounter God in a uniquely powerful, grace-giving way. Far from blocking your full individual experience of God, sacraments bring you closer to him. Sacraments give you a point of contact with God's grace through things you can feel, smell, see, taste, and touch: water, wine, bread, oil, and the laying on of hands. Hearing the words of sacramental rituals spoken aloud, and speaking them yourself, can transform you in profound ways.

Sacraments proclaim and celebrate the mysteries professed in the Apostles' Creed, especially the Paschal Mystery by which Christ redeemed the world. These words and signs don't replace or diminish your interior prayer; instead, they strengthen and nourish it. They affirm your identity and your unity with every child of God.

This is true not just because of the words and the signs themselves but because of their connection to the Church. "Christ lives and acts in and with his Church" (*CCC*, 1076). That means Christ is truly present in the sacraments when they are conferred by an ordained minister of the Church. Through them, Christ acts in the Church to fill with his grace each person who receives the sacraments. This is the sacramental economy, the way in which the Church brings Christ's living and real presence to all people and the way in which Christ continues his work to bring about the salvation of humanity. Because the Church "both contains and communicates the invisible grace she signifies" (*CCC*, 774)—that is, the grace of Christ—you are able to access his grace directly in the sacraments.

Of course, all people can always pray directly to God. The prayers we say in the silence of our hearts are of irreplaceable value. However, Christ gave us the Church to teach and enrich us with his grace. He gave us the sacraments for our salvation. The sacraments are irreplaceable in Christian life.

 # Further Research

- Read paragraphs 774 to 776 of the *Catechism of the Catholic Church*. Write a one-paragraph summary answering the following questions: How are the sacraments connected to Christ's saving work on earth? How do the sacraments figure into "the visible plan of God's love for humanity" (*CCC*, 776)?

Prayer
Jesus, Abide in Me

Lord, you said, "Remain in me, as I remain in you . . . because without me you can do nothing" (Jn 15:4–5).

> Lord Jesus, reveal yourself to me.
> Give me the strength to go out and
> profess that I am your disciple.
> Show me that you alone can fill my heart.
> Teach me to accept your freedom
> and embrace your truth.
> Make me a messenger of the
> certainty that I have truly been liberated
> through your Death and Resurrection.
> Let my experience of your love
> generate through me a more just
> society and a better world.
>
> —based on a prayer by St. John Paul II

WHAT HAPPENS IN THE SACRAMENTS

THE JOURNEY
BACK TO GOD

Mike Walterman remembers the day he turned his back on God. It was his eighteenth birthday, and his best friend had committed suicide. Mike explains, "I wanted no part of a God who would allow these types of things to happen. I couldn't understand. I basically gave up on God."

Thus began a spiral into both depression and arrogance. Thinking he was smart enough to get through college without studying, he failed his classes and then dropped out. His mother begged him to return to the Church. He said he would, but he didn't. Then, one Mother's Day when Mike was about thirty, his mother shared her personal struggle with the family: she had been diagnosed with kidney cancer. In addition, she began to show signs of early onset dementia. Not long after, her condition deteriorated enough that the family had to admit her into a nursing home.

Mike began to think that he should be going to Mass. He realized that he did believe in God and no longer blamed God for his own heartache and his mother's sufferings. Then, one Sunday morning, he heard in his deepest self what he believed to be God's voice saying, "Mike, it's time to go back to church." This time he went.

He prepared for Confirmation and received this sacrament at the Easter Vigil in 2013. Mike visited his mother in the nursing home and told her all about his newly recovered faith and his return to the sacraments. Mike slowly began to realize that perhaps God had called him back in order to give him the strength and faith he needed to deal with his mother's illness. She died of complications from Alzheimer's disease about a month after Easter.

Since then, Mike has put his life back on track. He has earned a degree in construction technology and is in an apprenticeship program for carpentry. Mike sums up his journey this way: "If you are depressed or lost or lonely or confused or hopeless, just remember that even if you have lost your faith in God, he still has faith in you. You are never too far gone for God to find you."

(Based on John Shaughnessy, "Young Adult Catholic Returns to the Church after Journey of Heartbreak and Separation," *The Criterion* [published by the Archdiocese of Indianapolis], February 28, 2014.)

FOCUS QUESTION

How can the sacraments **TRANSFORM** YOUR LIFE?

INTRODUCTION
Celebrating Redemption

When you come together with others to celebrate the Church's liturgy, you celebrate the Paschal Mystery—Christ's work of salvation through his Passion, Death, Resurrection, and Ascension. It is in the Paschal Mystery that Christ redeemed the world.

What is redemption? One definition of *redeem* is "to recover ownership by paying a sum." Another meaning is "to set free or ransom." For Christians, redemption is Jesus Christ's act of paying the price of his own Death on the Cross to save humans from sin and return them to new, eternal life in union with the Blessed Trinity.

In the liturgy—particularly in the celebration of the Eucharist—"it is principally his own Paschal mystery that Christ signifies and makes present" (*CCC*, 1085). When you participate in the sacraments, you don't only remember the events that accomplished your redemption, as if watching a rerun of a past event. Instead, by the power of the Holy Spirit, you actually *participate* in the events of the Paschal Mystery. You are present to those events.

Your participation in the liturgy transforms you so that your entire life takes up the pattern of Jesus' very life from the time of his Incarnation to the saving events of the Paschal Mystery.

Dom Columba Marmion (1858–1923) was an Irish diocesan priest in Dublin. At age thirty he changed the course of his vocation and entered a Benedictine monastery in Belgium. He became a prolific and influential spiritual writer. A central theme of his writings is *divine adoption*—that is, because God became man, you can become an adopted child of God. His understanding of the Paschal Mystery and how Catholics participate in the Paschal Mystery through the liturgy reflects this theme:

> It is above all by sacramental Communion that we now assimilate the fruits of this mystery. What indeed do we receive in the Eucharist? We receive Christ, the Body and Blood of Christ. . . .
>
> Still in our days, Christ, ever living, repeats to each soul the words that he said to his disciples when at the time of the Pasch [the Passover], he was about to institute his sacrament

NOTE TAKING

Recognizing Main Ideas. In this section, you will read how Bl. Columba Marmion speaks of *divine adoption*. In three or four bullet points, explain what this phrase means and how, according to Bl. Columba, God effects your divine adoption.

- *God wills your complete joy.*
-
-

of love: "With desire I have desired to eat this pasch with you" (Lk 22:15). Christ Jesus desires to effect in us the mystery of his Resurrection. He lives entirely for his Father above all that is earthly; he wills, for our joy, to draw us with him into this divine current. If, after having received him in Communion, we leave him full power to act, he will give to our life, by the inspirations of the Holy Spirit, that steadfast orientation towards the Father in which all holiness is summed up; so all our thoughts, all our aspirations, all our activity will refer to the glory of our Father in heaven. (*Spiritual Writings*)

The liturgy, particularly the Eucharist, is the way Christ communicates the fruits of the Paschal Mystery, the redemption of the world, until he comes again. It helps you move your life into the course of the "divine current." With this attitude, which you increase through faith and your participation in the sacraments, every facet of your life—from misery to joy—becomes intertwined with the life of Jesus as you grow in union with the Blessed Trinity. "The event of the Cross and Resurrection *abides* and draws everything toward life" (*CCC*, 1085). You will learn how this takes place in the sacramental economy—that is, what happens in the sacraments—in this chapter.

SECTION ASSESSMENT

NOTE TAKING

Use your notes to help you complete the following item.

1. Bl. Columba Marmion used the phrase *divine adoption*. Write one persuasive sentence to explain this concept to someone who does not understand it or is skeptical about such an idea.

COMPREHENSION

2. What do you think Bl. Columba meant by the term "divine current"?

3. To *redeem* is "to recover ownership by paying a sum" or "to set free or ransom." How do these definitions apply to Christ's work of redemption?

REFLECTION

4. How do you imagine the "divine current" is present in your life?

Christ Acts through the Sacraments

MAIN IDEA
The Three Divine Persons—Father, Son, and Holy Spirit—have distinct roles in the liturgy.

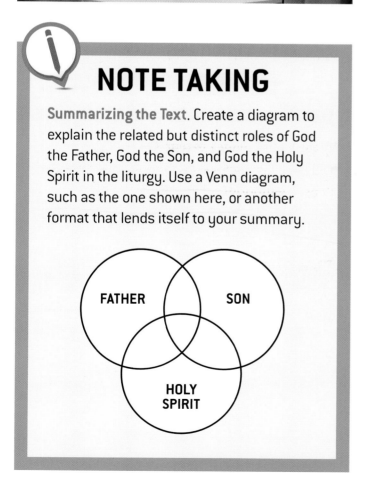

NOTE TAKING

Summarizing the Text. Create a diagram to explain the related but distinct roles of God the Father, God the Son, and God the Holy Spirit in the liturgy. Use a Venn diagram, such as the one shown here, or another format that lends itself to your summary.

FATHER   **SON**

HOLY SPIRIT

Have you ever experienced the departure of a close relative or friend, who was perhaps moving to a far-away place that would limit your ability to visit and spend time together? The occasion probably caused you sadness, or even anxiety. This was the situation the Apostles found themselves in at the time of Jesus' Ascension. Jesus had been the Apostles' teacher and leader. Now they would have to fulfill the mission he gave to them—to teach and baptize people of all nations (see Matthew 28:16–20)—without Jesus' being physically present to them. But, like a person dear to you who moves away but remains in close touch with you and an integral part of your life, Jesus did not abandon the Apostles. Instead, he sent the Holy Spirit to strengthen and empower them to fulfill their mission. On the Jewish Feast of **Pentecost**, the **Paraclete** that Jesus had promised descended on the Apostles:

> When the time for Pentecost was fulfilled, they were all in one place together. And suddenly there came from the sky a noise like a strong driving wind, and it filled the entire house in which they were. Then there appeared to them tongues as of fire, which parted and came to rest on each one of them. And they were all filled with the holy Spirit and began to speak in different tongues, as the Spirit enabled them to proclaim. (Acts 2:1–4)

It is not hard to imagine the dramatic effect this experience had on the Apostles. Before Pentecost, with Jesus physically departed from them, they gathered together in prayerful reflection and expectation; they may have been a bit afraid of meeting the same earthly

Pentecost From a Greek word meaning "fiftieth day," the day on which the Church celebrates the descent of the Holy Spirit upon Mary and the Apostles.

Paraclete Another name for the Holy Spirit, it means "advocate," "defender," or "consoler."

St. Peter and St. John are depicted exhorting the faithful.

would need to appoint others to carry on their work of teaching, baptizing, serving, and building up the Church. By the power of the Holy Spirit, they entrusted this power and authority to their successors (see *CCC*, 1087). Through an unbroken chain of this **apostolic succession**, today's Church can trace a continuous line of leadership back to the days of the first Christians, the Apostles, and to Christ himself, the founder of the Church.

From a historical perspective, the events of salvation—Jesus' Passion, Death, Resurrection, and Ascension—occurred only once. But by the power of the Holy Spirit, the events commemorated in the liturgy are present and real for Catholics today. Because Christ is present, you are in intimate communion with God and with one another when you participate in the liturgy. At the liturgy you are also able to participate in Christ's prayer to the Father, made in the Holy Spirit.

The distinct roles of the Three Divine Persons—Father, Son, and Holy Spirit—help you understand the work of the Blessed Trinity in the liturgy and how Christ acts through the sacraments.

fate as Christ. After the Holy Spirit came to them, they became enlivened, rejuvenated, and filled with courage. They understood that Jesus had fulfilled his promise not to abandon them. They no longer hid in fear; they spoke openly to the "Jews from every nation" (Acts 2:5) who had come to Jerusalem to celebrate Pentecost. Acts says this of St. Peter's preaching: "Those who accepted his message were baptized, and about three thousand persons were added that day" (2:41). The Church of Jesus, prepared for from the beginning of time, had been brought into the public.

The Holy Spirit continued to be present in the Apostles, just as Jesus had promised. The Apostles became "sacramental signs of Christ" (*CCC*, 1087), bringing the grace of Jesus to the members of the early Church. Before the Apostles died, they realized they

God the Father: Source and Goal of the Liturgy

In the same way that God the Father is the source of all creation, he is the source of the blessings you receive from the liturgy. From the beginning of the world to the end of time, all of God's work is a blessing. You return the blessings you receive to the Father when you respond to his grace.

> **apostolic succession** An unbroken chain of power and authority connecting the pope and bishops to St. Peter and the other Apostles through the Sacrament of Holy Orders.

Initially, your response involves recognizing the Father's blessings in the story of creation, in the covenants he established with the Chosen People of the Old Testament, and, finally, in the fullness of Divine Revelation in the coming of the Son of God, Jesus Christ.

Throughout human history, people have seen visible signs of God's blessings in creation. As St. Paul reminds the faithful, "Ever since the creation of the world, his invisible attributes of eternal power and divinity have been able to be understood and perceived in what he has made" (Rom 1:20). Many people have experienced God's majesty, power, and greatness in things like the roar of an ocean's waves, a hurricane or an earthquake, the beauty of a new day dawning, or the gurgling of a mountain stream. Many ancient peoples mistakenly confused their experiences of creation with God. They worshipped the sun, mountains, oceans, and various trees as gods in themselves. But, as God's Chosen People, the Israelites gradually learned that these visible signs of creation merely point to the divine; they aren't the same as the God who created them.

While creation can point to the sacred, creation is not a sacrament in itself. Unlike signs of God's greatness in creation, the sacraments make God's presence real. A sacrament not only points to God's existence; it also makes God truly present to you. "In the Church's liturgy the divine blessing is fully revealed and communicated" (*CCC*, 1082).

In a sacrament, God acts first, and then you act in response. As the source of the liturgy, God the Father takes the initiative of being present, of offering a share in his own life and love. In the liturgy, God the Father fully reveals and communicates his blessings to you and all the Church. The Father is the source and the end of all blessings. As the priest raises the Body and Blood of Christ at Mass, he prays on behalf of the Church:

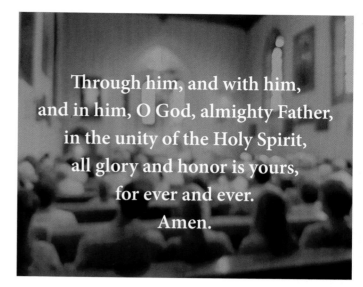

Through him, and with him, and in him, O God, almighty Father, in the unity of the Holy Spirit, all glory and honor is yours, for ever and ever. Amen.

You respond to God by giving him worship and accepting his Word as the truth on which to base your life.

The Work of Christ in the Liturgy

The sacraments are words and actions instituted by Christ through the Holy Spirit that are perceptible to you through your senses and accessible to your human nature. Now, seated at the right hand of the Father, the Son of God pours out his blessings on the Church and acts through the sacraments to bestow his grace upon you. In the liturgy he primarily makes present his own Paschal Mystery.

Jesus is God-in-the-flesh. His entire life reveals God the Father. The Paschal Mystery transcends time and place. Because Jesus brought about the redemption of the world through the saving actions of the Paschal Mystery, he remains present in the sacraments.

Christ is always present in the Church. After Jesus gave his Apostles a worldwide mission to share the Gospel, he added, "And behold, I am with you always, until the end of the age" (Mt 28:20). By giving the Holy Spirit to the Apostles and their successors, he gave them the power to make his work of salvation present in the sacraments, most especially in the Eucharist.

Christ's presence is clearly seen in the liturgy in the following ways:

Jesus is present in the minister of the sacrament. ✗

Through the Sacrament of Holy Orders, Christ is present in the ordained minister who offers the Sacrifice of the Mass. In point of fact, it is Christ himself who is the minister of the sacrament. By his ordination, the priest is given particular grace to act *in persona Christi capitis* (a Latin phrase meaning "in the person of Christ, Head [of the Body, the Church]")—that is, to serve the Body, the Church, in Jesus' name by the celebration of the sacraments, which is the distinctive work of Holy Orders. Take into account that Jesus is also present "when anybody baptizes" (*CCC,* 1088, quoting *Sacrosanctum Concilium,* 7). Note that "anybody" does not have to be an ordained minister.

Jesus is present in Scripture. ✗

It is Christ who speaks when the Scriptures are read at the liturgy. Jesus is the Word of God made flesh (see John 1:14). As God himself, Jesus alone has "the words of eternal life" (Jn 6:68).

Jesus is present when the Church prays and sings and is gathered in his name. ✗

Jesus told his disciples, "For where two or three are gathered together in my name, there am I in the midst of them" (Mt 18:20).

Jesus is especially present in the Eucharistic species, his own Body and Blood. ✗

This mystery is called the Real Presence of Christ (see pages 142–143) in the Eucharist because it is Jesus' presence in the fullest sense: "It is a *substantial* presence by which Christ, God and man, makes himself wholly and entirely present" (*CCC,* 1374).

Besides these ways that Christ is present in the earthly liturgy, he is also present in the heavenly liturgy that is celebrated with the angels and saints. You should hope to one day share in the heavenly liturgy and, in some way, Christ's glory.

The Work of the Holy Spirit in the Liturgy

The Holy Spirit is the teacher of faith, the one Christ promised. The Holy Spirit's role in dispensing the graces of the sacraments is to prepare the Church to encounter Jesus in the liturgy. The Holy Spirit desires that you might live the life of the Risen Christ. When you cooperate with the Holy Spirit in this desire, he brings about unity in the Church. This common work of the Holy Spirit and the Church takes place in the liturgy.

Christ is the center of the liturgy, and every dimension of it points to him. The *Catechism of the Catholic Church* teaches that "every liturgical action, especially the celebration of the Eucharist and the sacraments, is an encounter between Christ and the Church" (*CCC,* 1097). The Holy Spirit prepares the faithful for Christ in several ways. First, the Holy Spirit enables the Church to understand the Old Testament as the preparation for the New Testament. In the liturgy this is accomplished by:

- reading the Old Testament,

- praying the psalms, and
- recalling how the saving events and significant realities of the Old Covenant have been fulfilled in the mystery of Christ.

Rereading these events with the inspiration of the Holy Spirit and in light of the life of Christ reveals their new meaning. For example, salvation by Baptism was prefigured by Noah's ark during the flood and by the crossing of the Red Sea. Water from the rock in the Sinai desert prefigured the spiritual gifts of Christ, and the reception of manna in the desert prefigured the Eucharist, "the true bread from heaven" (Jn 6:32).

The Holy Spirit prepares you to be properly disposed to encounter Christ in the liturgy. For example, he offers you the grace of a prayerful, reflective heart to properly ready yourself for the sacraments. The Holy Spirit also uses the liturgy—especially the Eucharist—to strengthen the unity between Christ and the Church. The Holy Spirit helps you and other participants see Christ in one another and gather into one Body of Christ.

The Holy Spirit also serves as the "living memory" of the Church, helping you to understand the words of the liturgy, including the inspired Word of Scripture. The "remembering of" (e.g., the events detailed in the Old Testament) is known by a Greek word, *anamnesis*. Note what is meant by "living memory": anamnesis is more than a recollection of past events. "In the liturgical celebration of these events, they become in a certain way present and real" (*CCC*, 1363; cf. *CCC*, 1364). The Scripture readings in the **Liturgy of the Word** at Mass recall all that God has done for humankind. At

> **Liturgy of the Word** The part of the Mass that includes the "writings of the prophets" (the Old Testament reading and psalm), the "memoirs of the Apostles" (the New Testament epistles and the Gospel), the homily, the Profession of Faith, and the intercessions for the world.

Devotion to Jesus in the Eucharist

The Church uses two traditional prayers to honor the Real Presence of Christ during Eucharistic processions on the Solemnity of the Most Holy Body and Blood of Christ (Corpus Christi), on Holy Thursday, and during the Rite of Eucharistic Exposition and Benediction.

TANTUM ERGO

Come adore this wondrous presence
Bow to Christ the source of grace.
Here is kept the ancient promise
Of God's earthly dwelling place.
Sight is blind before God's glory,
Faith alone may see his face.

Glory be to God the Father,
Praise to his coequal Son,
Adoration to the Spirit,
Bond of love, in Godhead one.
Blest be God by all creation
Joyously while ages run.

PRAYER FOR BENEDICTION

Lord our God,
In this great sacrament
We come into the presence of Jesus Christ, your Son,
Born of the Virgin Mary
And crucified for our salvation.
May we who declare our faith in this fountain of love and mercy
Drink from it the water of everlasting life.
We ask this through Christ our Lord. Amen.

Read and meditate on both of these prayers. Then write your own prayer, poem, or song lyrics to express your own thoughts and feelings about the Real Presence of Jesus under the appearances of consecrated bread and wine.

Sunday Mass, the Scripture readings are typically taken from the Old Testament, a New Testament epistle, and the Gospel. The Holy Spirit awakens your memory of this story of the faith.

Anamnesis is also central to the Liturgy of the Eucharist. The Church fulfills the memorial of Christ ("Do this in memory of me") by recalling his Paschal Mystery in the Eucharistic Prayer. Once again, anamnesis involves more than just remembering the events of salvation. It also makes them present today. By the outpouring of the Holy Spirit, you are present in the here and now to the saving actions of Christ.

The Holy Spirit is called upon in the liturgy to come and sanctify the elements used in the liturgy, such as the bread and wine or the water and chrism used in Baptism. The *epiclesis* or "invocation prayer" is the intercessory prayer the priest makes at Mass in which he asks the Father to send the Spirit so that the gifts of bread and wine can become the Body and Blood of Christ. Then, when you receive them, you become a living offering to God.

The epiclesis is also the prayer for the full effect of the Church's communion with the mystery of Christ. The fruit you receive of the Spirit, described in Galatians 5:22–23, is love, joy, peace, patience, kindness, generosity, faithfulness, gentleness, and self-control.

SECTION ASSESSMENT

NOTE TAKING

Use your notes to help you answer the following questions.

1. What is the role of God the Father in the liturgy?
2. How is Jesus present in the liturgy?
3. How does the Holy Spirit work in the Liturgy of the Word at Mass?

VOCABULARY

4. What is the Holy Spirit's role in the *epiclesis* at liturgy?

COMPREHENSION

5. How does the Paschal Mystery transcend time and place in the sacraments?
6. When were the Apostles empowered to begin the mission of Jesus?
7. How do the faithful return God the Father's blessing to him in the liturgy?

CRITICAL THINKING

8. Read Mark 6:34–44. How does Jesus' miracle provide a foretaste of the heavenly liturgy you may one day experience?

Introducing the Seven Sacraments

MAIN IDEA
The liturgical life of the Church revolves around the celebration of the sacraments, instituted by Christ and entrusted to the Church.

The Church's entire liturgical life revolves around the sacrifice of the Eucharist and the other sacraments. The sacraments make the events of the Paschal Mystery present to you today. The Seven Sacraments are Baptism, Confirmation (or Chrismation), Eucharist, Penance and Reconciliation, Anointing of the Sick, Holy Orders, and Matrimony. The upcoming chapters explore each of these sacraments in detail. For now, consider some elements common to all the sacraments.

The Sacraments of Christ

The sacraments can be called Sacraments of Christ because Christ instituted each of them while he was on earth. This doesn't mean that Jesus, during his human life, literally celebrated all Seven Sacraments in precisely the form you know them today. However, it does mean that the Church's sacraments begin and end through Christ's words and actions, which

> announced and prepared what he was going to give the Church when all was accomplished. The mysteries of Christ's life are the foundations of what he would henceforth dispense in the sacraments, through the ministers of his Church, for "what was visible in our Savior has passed over in his mysteries." (*CCC*, 1115, quoting St. Leo the Great)

Christ is present and acting in all the sacraments. Each sacrament is rooted in and based on his Paschal Mystery. They are "powers that come forth" (cf. Luke 5:16, 6:19, 8:46) from the Body of Christ.

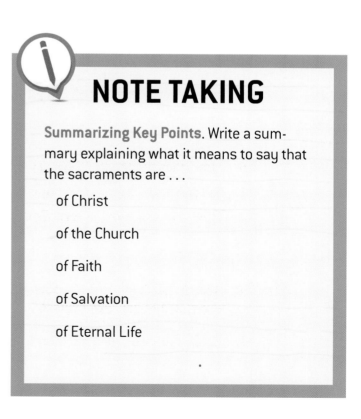

NOTE TAKING

Summarizing Key Points. Write a summary explaining what it means to say that the sacraments are . . .

of Christ

of the Church

of Faith

of Salvation

of Eternal Life

The Sacraments of the Church

Before his Ascension, Christ entrusted his Apostles, and hence his Church, with the power of the Holy Spirit. Christ gave his Church the power to make God's grace available through the sacraments. Specifically, the Church, by the guiding power of the Holy Spirit, has determined that there are Seven Sacraments instituted by Christ and that there is an "immutable part, a part that is divinely instituted and of which the Church is the guardian" (*CCC*, 1205, quoting Pope John Paul II). Christ gave the Church authority to occasionally change parts of the liturgy to adapt to the culture of people who have recently been evangelized. The sacraments are of the Church because they bring people into communion with God and form them into a holy people, the Body of Christ (see *CCC*, 1117–1121).

How does this work? Through Baptism and Confirmation, the faithful are enabled to celebrate the liturgy, while the Sacrament of Holy Orders appoints those who have been ordained "to nourish the Church with the word and grace of God in the name of Christ" (*Lumen Gentium*, 11). This teaching points out how the **ministerial priesthood** is at the service of the **common priesthood**. The ordained priesthood guarantees that it is really Christ who ministers in the sacraments through the Holy Spirit for the Church. This teaching also points out why Baptism, Confirmation, and Holy Orders confer an indelible **sacramental character** or "seal" by which Christians share in the priesthood of Christ according to different states and functions.

The Sacraments of Faith

Christ gave the Church the mission to **evangelize** others. It was always a sacramental mission—to "make disciples of all nations" and "to baptize" (see Matthew 28:19). Before a person can be baptized, he or she must assent, or say yes, to God's Word. This assent is the meaning of faith, but the faith of the Church comes before the faith of the believer. That is why the Church baptizes infants, who are not able to assent for themselves, for example. That is also why sacraments are celebrated communally. They are rooted not in the individuals who participate in them (the minister of the sacraments or the recipients, for example) but in the faith of the whole Church. In celebrating the sacraments, the Church confesses the faith she received from the Apostles. The sacraments are Sacraments of Faith because the faith of the Church has preserved them in the Church's history.

The particular words the Church prays in the sacramental rites express the faith. This statement is the origin of the ancient saying *lex orandi, lex credendi*, which means "the law of praying is the law of believing." It can also be expressed in reverse: *lex credendi, lex orandi*. In this order, it expresses the role liturgy and prayer have in shaping and nurturing the faith. The words of the liturgy, like the words of the creeds,

ministerial priesthood A unique sharing in the one priesthood of Christ received in the Sacrament of Holy Orders. By his ordination, a man is configured to Christ by a special gift of the Holy Spirit so that he can act as a representative of Christ, Head of the Church. As a representative of Christ, the ordained man is enabled to serve the common priesthood by building up and guiding the Church.

common priesthood The priesthood of the faithful. Christ has made the Church a "kingdom of priests" who share in his priesthood through the Sacraments of Baptism and Confirmation.

sacramental character An indelible spiritual mark that is the permanent effect of the Sacraments of Baptism, Confirmation, and Holy Orders. The mark is a permanent configuration to Jesus Christ and a specific standing in the Church. Because of their permanent effect, the reception of the Sacraments of Baptism, Confirmation, and Holy Orders is never repeated.

evangelize To bring the Good News of Jesus Christ to others.

The Sacrament of the Eucharist is a sacrament of communion that unites the faithful with one another and binds them to Jesus Christ.

are a foundational element of the Church's **Sacred Tradition**. For this reason, no sacramental rite may be modified by an ordained minister or by the will of the community.

The Sacraments of Salvation

The sacraments are called Sacraments of Salvation because they confer the grace they signify. They are efficacious *ex opere operato* ("by the very fact of the action's being performed"). Thus, the grace of a sacrament is not dependent on the worthiness of either the celebrant or the recipient. Instead, whenever a sacrament is celebrated in accordance with the intention of the Church, the power of Christ and the Holy Spirit act in and through it, independently of the holiness of the minister or the recipient. Yet recall that the "fruits of the sacraments also depend on the **disposition** of the one who receives them" (*CCC*, 1128).

In this life, the sacraments help people avoid sin and live as disciples of Jesus. They bring healing and forgiveness. As the *Catechism of the Catholic Church*

Sacred Tradition The living transmission of the Church's Gospel message found in the Church's teaching, life, and worship. It is faithfully preserved, handed on, and interpreted by the Church's Magisterium.

disposition The interior attitude of a person upon receiving the sacraments. "Celebrated worthily in faith, the sacraments confer the grace they signify" (*CCC*, 1127). Disposition includes the recipient's openness to the life of grace and willingness to avoid sin. Unrepented and unforgiven mortal sin affects a person's disposition to receive the sacraments.

explains, through the sacraments, "the Spirit heals and transforms those who receive him by conforming them to the Son of God" (*CCC*, 1129). This definition helps you understand why the sacraments, like faith, are necessary for salvation.

The Sacraments of Eternal Life

An ancient prayer of the Church was *Marana tha*, an Aramaic expression that means "O Lord, come!" This prayer expresses the ultimate meaning of the sacraments and of all Christian life: the prospect of welcoming the Lord at the end of time and spending eternal life with him in the Kingdom he has established.

Defining the sacraments as Sacraments of Eternal Life reminds us that the sacraments are celebrated until the Lord comes again, assuring the faithful the graces necessary to enter eternal life. The sacraments unite you with the Blessed Trinity in an experience of oneness, communion, and joy in the hope of everlasting life. This life, which you will experience fully only after death, begins to live in you now through the sacraments. Through them you are made holy; you become a "partaker of the divine nature" (*CCC*, 1721; see also *CCC*, 1130).

SECTION ASSESSMENT

NOTE TAKING

Use the summary statements you wrote to help you complete the following item.

1. Write a paragraph explaining the following five aspects of the sacraments: they are of Christ, of the Church, of Faith, of Salvation, and of Eternal Life.

CRITICAL THINKING

2. Explain the connection and interrelatedness of these five aspects of the sacraments.

COMPREHENSION

3. Explain the roles of the ministerial priesthood and common priesthood in celebrating the liturgy.

4. What is the meaning of the ancient saying *lex orandi, lex credendi* and its reverse *lex credendi, lex orandi*?

5. What does it mean to say that the "fruits of the sacraments also depend on the disposition of the one who receives them"?

APPLICATION

6. How do you say yes to God's Word by your own words? By your own actions?

7. What do you do to be properly disposed to receive sacraments?

Celebrating the Church's Liturgy

MAIN IDEA
All Catholics have a role in celebrating the liturgy; signs, proper matter, and form play a role in the celebration.

Why do Catholics say "we" celebrate the sacraments? It is proper to say "we" celebrate the sacraments because the sacraments are acts of divine worship and the faithful are involved in them through their participation in the liturgy. Sacraments are celebrations that are "woven from signs and symbols" (*CCC*, 1145). Signs and symbols, along with their proper matter and form, play a role in the celebration of the sacraments. In this section you will consider the particulars of how the sacraments are celebrated, specifically the *who*, *how*, *when*, and *where* of the celebration of the liturgy. Reflecting on these questions gives you a deeper understanding and appreciation of the sacraments.

Who Celebrates the Liturgy?

In the broadest sense, the liturgy is an action of the "whole Christ" (*Christus totus*)—Head and Body. As High Priest of the liturgy, Christ celebrates with the Church in heaven and on earth. The heavenly liturgy is celebrated by the hosts of angels and saints, including those of both the Old Testament and the New Testament, especially Mary, the Mother of God, the Apostles, the martyrs, and the saints.

NOTE TAKING

Summarizing the Material. Elements from the material world are used to celebrate the sacraments. Jesus, too, used earthly signs from creation in his ministry. Read each of the Scripture passages noted here. For each, tell what material element Jesus used and what effect it had on, or change it brought about in, those who experienced it. (The effect or change can be physical or spiritual.)

SCRIPTURE PASSAGE	ELEMENT FROM CREATION	CHANGE OR EFFECT IT BROUGHT ABOUT
John 2:1–12		
Matthew 14:13–21		
Luke 10:29–37		
John 13:1–15		
Luke 7:36–50		

The pilgrim Church on earth participates in the heavenly liturgy whenever we participate in the sacramental liturgy on earth, including keeping the memorials of the saints—first those of Mary, the Mother of God, and then the Apostles, martyrs, and other saints on fixed days in the **liturgical year**, or Church Year. Because it is the whole *community* united with Christ that celebrates the liturgy, liturgical services are best celebrated communally.

The celebration of the liturgy involves all members of the Body of Christ, each according to his or her calling. God calls bishops, priests, and deacons in and through the Church to special service in the liturgy. The Sacrament of Holy Orders enables these men to act in the liturgy in the Person of Christ the Head, for the service of all the Church. This is most evident in the Eucharist, where the bishop and the priests in communion with him offer the Sacrifice of the Mass.

When it is necessary and ministers are lacking, laypersons, even if they are not lectors or acolytes, may assist at liturgy in certain offices such as the ministry of the Word, presiding over liturgical prayers, conferring Baptism, and distributing Holy Communion. The bishop, in following liturgical traditions and pastoral needs, determines these ministries in accordance with Church law.

How Is the Liturgy Celebrated?

The sacraments are celebrated with signs and symbols. These include words, actions, and objects that express the meaning of each sacrament. Drawn from human

The essential signs of the Eucharistic sacrament are wheat bread and grape wine.

experience, they allow God to speak to us through visible creation.

Christ instituted the Seven Sacraments; he directly instituted the physical elements, gestures (actions), and words of some the sacraments. "In his preaching, the Lord Jesus often makes use of the signs of creation to make known the mysteries of the Kingdom of God" (*CCC*, 1151). In the sacraments, the Church uses elements from creation (such as water, bread, and wine) and human culture (such as washing or anointing) to make God's grace available to us. The traditional physical element(s) and/or gesture(s) used in each sacrament are called the *matter* of the sacrament.

The celebration of each sacrament also involves solemnity. The traditional words said for each sacrament are called the *form* of the sacrament. When you hear these words, you know that the sacrament is taking place. God is truly present, filling you and others with his love and grace.

> **liturgical year** Also known as the Church Year, it organizes the seasons of Advent, Christmas, Lent, the Easter Triduum, Easter, and Ordinary Time around the major events of Jesus' life.

The form and matter of each of the Seven Sacraments are as follows.

SACRAMENT	FORM	MATTER
BAPTISM	"I baptize you in the name of the Father, and of the Son, and of the Holy Spirit."	**Element:** water **Gestures:** triple pouring of water over candidate's head or immersion in water
CONFIRMATION (or Chrismation)	"Be sealed with the Gift of the Holy Spirit."	**Element:** oil (sacred chrism) **Gestures:** laying on of hands, anointing with oil
EUCHARIST	"This is my Body. This is my Blood."	**Elements:** wheat bread and grape wine **Gesture:** the institution narrative spoken by the priest
PENANCE AND RECONCILIATION	"Through the ministry of the Church may God give you pardon and peace, and I absolve you from your sins in the name of the Father, and of the Son, and of the Holy Spirit."	**Gestures:** three acts of the penitent: contrition, confession, and satisfaction
ANOINTING OF THE SICK	"Through this holy anointing may the Lord in his love and mercy help you with the grace of the Holy Spirit." **Response:** Amen. "May the Lord, who frees you from sin, save you and raise you up." **Response:** Amen.	**Element:** oil (oil of the sick) **Gesture:** anointing with oil
HOLY ORDERS	"Grant, we pray, Almighty Father, to this your servant the dignity of the priesthood; renew deep within him the Spirit of holiness; may he henceforth possess this office which comes from you, O God, and is next in rank to the office of Bishop; and by the example of his manner of life, may he instill right conduct." (Prayer of Ordination for Priests)	**Gestures:** laying of the bishop's hands on the head of the ordinand and the bishop's specific prayer of consecration
MATRIMONY	"I, N., take you, N., to be my wife/husband. I promise to be true to you in good times and in bad, in sickness and in health. I will love you and honor you all the days of my life."	**Gesture:** consent of the man and woman and the exchange of vows

The words spoken and the actions performed by the assembly are other signs at the liturgy. The fact that people say and do the same thing at the same time is a sign of unity, which the liturgy establishes and strengthens.

In particular, the liturgy makes use of the Word of God, given to the Church in Sacred Scripture. The Church has a three-year cycle of Sunday Scripture readings and a two-year cycle of weekday Scripture readings so that Catholics at Mass can hear a good selection from the Old Testament and virtually all of the books of the New Testament during that period. The Liturgy of the Word at Sunday Masses consists of two Scripture readings, the responsorial psalm, and the Gospel reading. The following signs accompany the Liturgy of the Word:

- Scripture is contained in a special book—the lectionary or Book of the Gospels.
- The Book of the Gospels is venerated with a procession, incense, and candles.
- Scripture is proclaimed from a special place—a lectern or an ambo.
- Scripture is read audibly and with dignity.
- Scripture's proclamation is extended by the ordained minister's **homily**.
- With acclamations, meditation psalms, litanies, and a profession of faith, the assembly responds to Scripture.

> **homily** A reflection given by a bishop, priest, or deacon based on the Scripture read at Mass or a sacramental celebration. The homily helps you hear God's Word and apply it to your life today.
>
> **Eastern Catholic Churches** The twenty-one Churches of the East that are in union with the Roman Catholic Church and the bishop of Rome, the pope. They have developed their own liturgical and administrative traditions.

Liturgical singing and music are an important part of celebrating the liturgy. Music allows the faithful to express what is in their hearts. The Second Vatican Council described music as "a necessary or integral part of solemn liturgy" (*Sacrosanctum Concilium*, 112). Songs chosen for the liturgy should conform to Catholic doctrine in their texts and should be drawn primarily from Scripture and liturgical sources. Songs and music at the liturgy should encourage all the faithful to sing.

Sacred images are also a significant part of celebrating the liturgy. Representations of Christ, the Blessed Virgin, and saints in sculptures, painting, or stained glass help those participating in the liturgy to understand more deeply the truths of faith and inspire them to a devotion to Christ, Mary, the angels, and the saints.

Although the essential elements of the liturgy remain unchanged, different liturgical traditions and customs can make up the celebration of the liturgy. In fact, the twenty-one **Eastern Catholic Churches** that are united with the Roman Catholic Church celebrate the liturgy according to one of the following rites:

- the Byzantine Rite, which developed out of the Church in Constantinople;
- the Alexandrian (Coptic or Ethiopian) Rite, which developed out of the Church in Alexandria (Egypt) or Ethiopia;
- the Antiochene or Syriac Rite, which developed out of the Church in Antioch (Syria);
- the Armenian Rite, which developed out of the Church in Armenia;
- the Maronite Rite, which has roots in Antioch and is named for St. Maron, a fifth-century monk; or
- the Chaldean Rite, which developed out of the Church in Iraq and eastern Syria.

Each of the twenty-one Eastern Catholic Churches adheres to its own liturgical traditions and customs, celebrates in its own language, and has its own bishop. These particular Churches are fully Catholic through their communion with the Church of Rome. The criterion that assures that there is unity amid the diversity of liturgical rites is that each is faithful to apostolic Tradition, is united under the bishop of Rome (the pope), and celebrates and passes on the sacraments received by the bishops, the successors of the Apostles. Since apostolic times, the Church's liturgy has been one with the Paschal Mystery, though it has been celebrated in a variety of forms.

God's Word in the Sacraments

Listed below are some of the Scripture readings often proclaimed for each sacrament. Choose one sacrament and read the Scripture passages for it. Write a short essay explaining (1) what the Bible passages recall and (2) what reality is made present to the Church in these readings (that is, how is God acting the same way in your life today?). Be prepared to summarize your ideas with the class.

SACRAMENT	SCRIPTURE READINGS
Baptism	Exodus 17:3–7; John 4:5–14
Confirmation (or Chrismation)	Isaiah 11:1–4a; Luke 4:16–22a
Eucharist	Exodus 16:2–4, 12–15; Luke 9:11b–17
Penance and Reconciliation	Isaiah 1:10–18; Matthew 3:1–12
Anointing of the Sick	Acts 3:1–10; Matthew 8:1–4
Holy Orders	Deuteronomy 1:9–14; Mark 1:14–20
Matrimony	Genesis 2:18–24; John 2:1–11

When Is the Liturgy Celebrated?

When God entered human history through the Incarnation, he made history and time sacred. The Church's celebration of the saving work of Jesus is therefore set in time, structured around daily, weekly, and yearly schedules that all revolve around Sunday, the first day of the week. This was the day Jesus rose from the dead, and it has become for Christians "the first of all days, the first of all feasts, the Lord's Day" (*CCC*, 2174).

Liturgical celebrations are celebrations of the whole Church. The *Catechism of the Catholic Church* teaches,

> Participation in the communal celebration of the Sunday Eucharist is a testimony of belonging and of being faithful to Christ and to his Church. The faithful give witness by this to their communion in faith and charity. Together they testify to God's holiness and their hope of salvation. They strengthen one another under the guidance of the Holy Spirit. (*CCC*, 2182)

When you celebrate the liturgy, you are brought into the presence of those saving moments in the life of Christ. You become present to these events as if they were happening today. This understanding is true not only for your commemoration of the Sunday feast but for all the holy seasons and days of the liturgical year. Through the feasts and seasons of the liturgical year, the Church makes present to you the life of Jesus, from his conception and birth to the events of the Paschal Mystery.

The Liturgical Year Begins: Advent

Although the mystery of Christ's Incarnation is celebrated throughout the year, the Incarnation is a

Jesus Is RISEN!

Read John 20:19–29, which tells of appearances of the Risen Jesus to his disciples. Then work with a group of classmates to act out the passage as a narrator reads it aloud. Perform the pantomime in several venues of your choosing; for example, in a classroom of younger children, at a retirement home, or at school for a parent/teacher meeting. Write a reflection on your experience along with at least one lesson you gleaned from the passage.

prominent focus of the seasons of Advent and Christmas. The word *advent* means "coming." This season begins the Church Year and starts with the first evening prayer of the Sunday that falls on or closest to November 30. During Advent, the Church prepares for the coming of the Messiah in two main ways. First, the Church celebrates the anticipation of the second coming of Christ at the end of time, when he will judge all people at the Final Judgment and bring about God's Kingdom in its fullness. Second, the Church remembers the centuries of people who waited with faith and hope that God's promise to send a Savior would one day be fulfilled. The Church especially recalls the ministry of St. John the Baptist, who prepared people to receive Jesus as the Messiah. Also remembered is the response of Mary to the announcement that she would be the Mother of God.

The Christmas Season

The Christmas season begins at the Christmas Eve vigil Mass and ends on the Feast of the Baptism of the Lord.

The Bible does not report the exact date of the birth of Jesus, but ever since the fourth century, the Church has celebrated his birth on December 25. Some historians note that this date was originally celebrated by the Romans to honor a sun god. If this Roman celebration did, in fact, predate the celebration of Christ's birth (it is not certain), by choosing this day as the birthday of Christ, the Church was perhaps counteracting pagan belief by offering Jesus as the true "sun god," the Son of God and Light of the World.

The Christmas season includes several other feasts of Christ. On the Sunday between Christmas and New Year's Day, the Church celebrates the Feast of the Holy Family—Jesus, Mary, and Joseph. On the Sunday after New Year's Day, the Church celebrates the Feast of the Epiphany—the revelation of Jesus' universal mission as the Messiah. On the following Sunday, the Church celebrates the Baptism of the Lord. These days are joyous

feasts for Christians as the Church thanks God for the gift of his own Son.

Lent

During the season of Lent, which begins on Ash Wednesday and ends on Holy Thursday evening, the Church especially recalls and celebrates the Paschal Mystery of Christ. In Latin, the word for *lent* (*Quadragesima*) means "fortieth." In English, *lent* means "springtime." The Church sees Lent not only as a time of new life but also as a time of "spring cleaning" and personal renewal. Originally, Lent was when catechumens began their immediate preparation to receive the Sacraments of Baptism, Confirmation, and First Eucharist at the Easter Vigil service. Over the centuries, Lent was extended to the forty days (excluding Sundays) before Easter as a period of penance, fasting, and prayer. This period recalls the forty years the Israelites spent wandering in the desert before God led them into the Promised Land. Lent also recalls the forty days Jesus spent in the desert immediately after his Baptism—praying, fasting, and facing temptation—in preparation for his public ministry.

Like Jesus, the New Adam who does not give in to temptation, you are called throughout Lent to conquer your own temptations and discipline yourself spiritually in preparation for the Resurrection. During this time, the Church proclaims the Gospel account of the Transfiguration of Jesus (see Matthew 17:1–9, Mark 9:2–10, Luke 9:28–36), Jesus' discourse about "living water" with the woman at the well (see John 4:5–42), Jesus' cure of a blind man (see John 9:1–41), and Jesus' raising of Lazarus from the dead (see John 11:1–45).

> **catechumens** Unbaptized persons who are preparing for full initiation into the Church through the Sacraments of Christian Initiation by engaging in formal study, prayer, and spiritual reflection.

The last Sunday of Lent, known as Passion Sunday or Palm Sunday, celebrates Jesus' triumphal entry into Jerusalem as king (see Luke 19:28–40). On this day, the entire Passion of Jesus (the account of his suffering, Death on the Cross, and burial) is read at Mass. The Church thanks God for the great gift of Jesus, who became "obedient to death, even death on a cross" (Phil 2:8). Palm Sunday marks the beginning of Holy Week.

The Easter Triduum

The Easter Triduum begins the most sacred days in the Church Year. Although it takes place over three days, the Triduum is considered one single liturgy. The Triduum begins with the Holy Thursday liturgy, which commemorates the Lord's Supper. This Mass celebrates Jesus' institution of the Eucharist at the Last Supper, as well as his washing of the Apostles' feet (see John 13:1–15). The liturgy focuses on Jesus as the Lamb of God, as the Suffering Servant who willingly went to death so that the sins of the world might be forgiven. The Triduum also includes Good Friday and Holy Saturday and concludes with an evening prayer on Easter Sunday.

On Good Friday, the Church has a solemn communion service recalling the Passion and Death of Jesus. This is the only day of the Church Year when Mass is not celebrated. The Passion account from the Gospel of John is read (see John 18:1–19:42). The Church remembers and reflects on the mercy of Christ's sacrifice and how his Death on the Cross reveals God's immense love. The faithful take time to appreciate the enormity of the gift Jesus gave us—the gift of salvation and eternal life. On Holy Saturday there are no Masses during the day. The Church observes a period of quiet, recalling the time Jesus spent in the tomb.

Then, on Holy Saturday evening after sundown, the Church celebrates the glorious Easter Vigil. The Paschal or Easter candle is lit from new fire. Scripture accounts following salvation history since the beginning of creation are read. The Church welcomes catechumens into the Church through the administration of the Sacraments of Baptism, Confirmation, and the Eucharist. And there is great rejoicing in the central proclamation of faith: Christ is indeed risen from the dead!

The Easter Vigil is the first celebration of Easter, the occasion when the Church celebrates the Resurrection of Jesus to new life. The word *easter* derives from the German *ostern* for "east" or, according to St. Bede the Venerable, from *Eastre*, a spring deity. Christians understand Easter's relationship with the Jewish Passover: just as God saved the Israelites by helping them pass safely through the Red Sea to freedom from the Egyptians, so Easter celebrates Christ's Passover. Jesus passed through death, once and for all, and entered into new life—a new life you are also promised as one of his faithful followers. As the *Catechism of the Catholic Church* states,

Jesus and his disciples were together at the Last Supper to celebrate the Feast of Passover.

Easter is not simply one feast among others, but the "Feast of feasts," the "Solemnity of solemnities," just as the Eucharist is the "Sacrament of sacraments" (the Great Sacrament). St. Athanasius calls Easter "the Great Sunday" and the Eastern Churches call Holy Week "the Great Week." The mystery of the Resurrection, in which Christ crushed death, permeates with its powerful energy our old time, until all is subjected to him. (*CCC,* 1169)

The date of Easter changes from year to year. This is because the feast, which was determined at the First Council of Nicaea in 325, follows the lunar calendar rather than the solar calendar. According to the bishops at Nicaea, Easter is to be celebrated on the Sunday following the first full moon after the spring equinox. Because the date of the full moon changes from year to year, the date of Easter changes as well. Even though the Church set the timing of the celebration of Easter in the fourth century, the Latin (Roman) and Eastern Churches celebrate Easter at different times, usually one or two weeks apart. This discrepancy occurs because since the sixteenth century the Latin Church has followed the Gregorian calendar, while the Eastern Churches continue to follow the older, Julian calendar. The First Council of Nicaea also rejected a method popular in Asia Minor for celebrating Easter on the same day as the Jewish Passover (14 Nisan), since this day always falls on a Sunday.

The Easter Season

The Easter season lasts for fifty days. In the liturgies of the Easter season, the accounts of the Resurrection appearances of Christ are proclaimed. This time is sometimes called the **mystagogia** because it is when the **neophytes** first immerse themselves in the divine mysteries (sacraments). (See page 82 for more information on mystagogia.) The neophytes participate in the entire Mass, instead of being dismissed at the end

of the Liturgy of the Word as they were prior to Easter. They are encouraged to participate fully in the life of the Church.

The Church celebrates Jesus' Ascension to heaven on a Thursday, the fortieth day after Easter. (The United States Conference of Catholic Bishops recently allowed the option of celebrating the Ascension on the Sunday closest to the fortieth day after Easter.) This day commemorates Jesus' bodily ascension into heaven, where he is seated at the right hand of the Father and from where he promised to send the Holy Spirit.

The Feast of Pentecost (see pages 39–40), the coming of the Holy Spirit to the Apostles and Mary (see Acts 2:1–42), occurs on a Sunday fifty days after Easter. Just as Jesus had promised, he sent the Holy Spirit, the Third Divine Person of the Blessed Trinity, to be with his disciples forever. Pentecost is a celebration of the gift of the Holy Spirit and a recognition that, like the Apostles, you are sent forth to proclaim Jesus' Gospel of salvation to all people.

Ordinary Time

Ordinary Time occurs twice in the liturgical year: between the Christmas season and Lent (a period of five to eight weeks) and between the Easter Season and Advent (twenty-three to twenty-eight weeks). Ordinary Time is the longest liturgical season. The season gets its name from the word *ordinal*, meaning "numbered," as all the Sundays of Ordinary Time are designated numerically. Although the season has always existed, it was not until the liturgical reforms

> **mystagogia** A Greek term that means "leading into the mystery"; the period following the Baptism of adults. During this time, the newly baptized are to open themselves more fully to the graces received in Baptism.
>
> **neophytes** Those newly received into the Church through the Sacraments of Christian Initiation at the Easter Vigil.

of the Second Vatican Council that it came to be called "Ordinary Time."

A purpose of Ordinary Time is to teach Christians how to follow Jesus in everyday, ordinary life. During Ordinary Time, the Scripture readings focus on how you should relate to family members, the poor, people you may not like (represented as tax collectors and sinners), and those for whom you work. You learn more about the teachings and miracles of Jesus and how you are to keep the two greatest commandments: "You shall love the Lord, your God, with all your heart, with all your soul, and with all your mind" and "You shall love your neighbor as yourself" (Mt 22:37, 39).

During Ordinary Time, as in other liturgical seasons, the Church celebrates solemnities, feasts, and memorials. Solemnities have the greatest importance. These include Sundays and other holy days of obligation. The Gloria and Creed are both recited on solemnities. There is also a vigil Mass on the evening before the solemnity. Feast days are second in importance. They do not have a vigil Mass unless the feast day occurs on a Sunday.

An example of a solemnity is the Solemnity of Christ the King (celebrated the last Sunday of Ordinary Time). The Solemnity of Christ the King recognizes and acknowledges Christ's kingship as "ruler of the kings of the earth" (Rv 1:5) and therefore directs people to order their lives according to his rule. The Church looks forward to the second coming of Christ, when he will rule as King and invite all the faithful to enter his Kingdom.

Two examples of feasts during Ordinary Time are the Feast of the Presentation of the Lord (February 2) and the Feast of the Transfiguration (August 6). The Feast of the Presentation of the Lord commemorates the date forty days after Jesus' birth when Mary came with her infant to the Temple to offer sacrifice and present herself to the priests for purification. The Feast of the Transfiguration marks not only Christ's Transfiguration on the mountain (see Matthew 17:1–8) but also our own future transfiguration in Christ when God the Father will say to each of us, "You are my beloved child" (cf. Mk 9:7).

Mary and the Sanctoral Cycle

Though the Church Year is basically structured around the Incarnation and Paschal Mystery of Jesus Christ, it also prominently includes the feasts of Mary, the Mother of God. The *Catechism of the Catholic Church* explains why this is so:

> In celebrating this annual cycle of the mysteries of Christ, Holy Church honors the Blessed Mary, Mother of God, with a special love. She is inseparably linked with the saving work of her Son. In her the Church admires and exalts the most excellent fruit of redemption and joyfully contemplates, as in a faultless image, that which she herself desires and hopes wholly to be. (*CCC,* 1172, quoting *Sacrosanctum Concilium,* 103)

Mary is the perfect model of Christian discipleship. "By her complete adherence to the Father's will, to his Son's redemptive work, and to every prompting of the Holy Spirit, the Virgin Mary is the Church's model of faith and charity" (*CCC,* 967). We honor her not only as a symbol of the Church but also as the Mother of the Church (see *CCC,* 967–968).

Throughout the year, the Church celebrates a number of feasts in Mary's honor. Three of these are holy days of obligation: the Solemnity of Mary, Mother of God (January 1), the Feast of the Assumption (August 15), and the Feast of the Immaculate Conception (December 8). Other feast days that honor Mary include Our Lady of Lourdes (February 11), the Visitation (May 31), the Queenship of Mary (August 22), the Birth of

> **holy days of obligation** The days in the Church Year when all Catholics are obliged to participate in Mass.

The Feast of the Immaculate Conception is celebrated with a light festival at Lyon Cathedral in Lyon, France.

Mary (September 8), Our Lady of the Rosary (October 7), and Our Lady of Guadalupe (December 12).

In addition to celebrating feasts of Jesus and feasts of Mary, the Church honors numerous saints throughout the year. Saints are role models of holiness and charity. The Church honors these deceased Church members because they "have suffered and have been glorified with Christ" (*CCC*, 1173, quoting *Sacrosanctum Concilium*, 104). In their lives, they courageously lived and proclaimed the Paschal Mystery of Christ. Among the honored saints are popes, bishops, martyrs, pastors, Apostles, Doctors of the Church, virgins, and holy members of the laity, including men, women, and children. The calendar of saints is called the **sanctoral cycle**. The Church honors all saints, known and unknown, on November 1. This Feast of All Saints is a holy day of obligation.

Where Is the Liturgy Celebrated?

Jesus said, "God is Spirit, and those who worship him must worship in Spirit and truth" (Jn 4:24). The *Catechism of the Catholic Church* teaches that "worship 'in Spirit and in truth' of the New Covenant is not tied to any one place. . . . What matters is that, when the faithful assemble in the same place, they are the 'living stones,' gathered to be 'built into a spiritual house'" (*CCC*, 1179). Incorporated by the Holy Spirit into Christ, they are made a "temple of the living God" (2 Cor 6:16).

That the worship is not tied to any one place does not diminish the importance of physical church buildings. When they are free to do so, Catholics construct buildings for divine worship. Such a building is called a church:

> A house of prayer in which the Eucharist is celebrated and reserved, where the faithful assemble, and where is worshipped the presence of the Son of God our Savior, offered for us on the sacrificial altar for the help and consolation of the faithful—this house ought to be in good taste and a worthy place for prayer and sacred ceremonial. (*CCC*, 1181)

The first church buildings constructed after the practice of worship in house churches ceased were based on the floor plan of Roman government assembly halls. Known as a *basilica*, this type of building was long and narrow. The altar was at one end, usually on an elevated platform. Because there were no pews or chairs, the people stood or knelt in the *nave*, or main body of the building, while the celebration was in progress.

In the late Middle Ages, church buildings became larger and more elaborate, culminating in the huge

> **sanctoral cycle** The feasts of saints found throughout the year on the Church's liturgical calendar.

Gothic cathedrals of Europe, dozens of which still stand today. These buildings are many stories high and often have a cruciform (cross-shaped) layout. Typical features of Gothic cathedrals include intricate sculptures, wood-carvings, pointed arches, and stained-glass windows.

Even though the architecture of modern-day church buildings has become simplified in several ways, the buildings themselves remain consecrated ground, holy places that "signify and make visible the Church living in this place, the dwelling of God with men reconciled and united in Christ" (*CCC*, 1180). When you walk into any Catholic church today, regardless of its architectural style, you will usually find the following furnishings:

1. **altar** (which serves for the Sacrifice of the Mass and the Eucharistic Communion)

2. **tabernacle** (sometimes located in a "chapel of reserve"), which contains the Blessed Sacrament, the consecrated species of bread from Mass

3. **chair** (*cathedra*) of the bishop or chair of the priest (the presider of the sacraments)

4. **lectern or ambo**, for proclaiming the Word of God

5. **ambry** (a niche or container for storing the sacred chrism used in sacramental anointings, the oil of catechumens, and the oil of the sick)

6. **baptismal font** (a basin for baptismal water in which a baptismal candidate is immersed or washed over)

The Church at PRAYER

The liturgy is a participation in Christ's prayer to the Father in the Holy Spirit. When you pray personally, you continue to share in the graces of your redemption and in the Father's great love for you that you receive in the liturgy.

St. John Damascene described prayer as "the raising of one's mind and heart to God or the requesting of good things from God." Prayer is a gift. Effective prayer is made in humility. Only in acknowledging that you are not able to pray as best you ought are you able to freely receive the gift of prayer.

The prayer of the Church was born at Pentecost when the Holy Spirit descended on the Apostles who were gathered in prayer. The Holy Spirit taught the Church what she should know about prayer and formed her in the life of prayer. The following forms of prayer—present in the Scriptures throughout all of salvation history—remain normative for the Church today:

- *Adoration* is the first attitude of a person in prayer. You acknowledge that you are but a creature before God, the Creator. This prayer is made in "respectful silence" in the presence of the "ever greater" God (see *CCC*, 2628).
- *Blessing* is the fundamental movement of prayer. You dialogue with God, blessing God for his goodness to you and asking for his graces. God blesses you by giving you what you ask for.
- *Petition* is an "asking" prayer or, more concretely, a "begging" prayer. The first object of petition is to plead for God's mercy. Christian petition is centered on "the desire and search for the Kingdom to come" (*CCC*, 2632).
- *Intercession* is a prayer of petition for the needs of others. You pray for both your fellow Christians and those who reject God and the Gospel. You pray for their salvation.
- *Thanksgiving*, characterized by the Eucharist, is a prayer expressing your gratitude to God for answering every need in your life.
- *Praise* "lauds God for his own sake and gives him glory" (*CCC*, 2639). Praise brings together all the other forms of prayer and raises them up to God in heaven.

Prayer is essential to your faith life and helps you form an ongoing relationship with God, just as conversation with a friend or loved one can help you enrich your relationship with that person. You can engage in conversation with God throughout the day, at any time of day. Here are some of the ways you can pray outside the liturgy:

- *Vocal prayer.* This way of praying is probably the most familiar to you. In vocal prayer, you pray with words, either your own extemporaneous address to God or the traditional prayers of the Church, such as the Hail Mary or the Lord's Prayer, which is also known as the Our Father (see page 326).
- *Meditation.* Meditation involves a search or a quest for God. You actively use your thoughts, emotions, imagination, and desires to think about God's presence in the world and in your life. To be fruitful, meditation must be done regularly. Common ways to engage in meditation are through **lectio divina** or by praying the Rosary.
- *Contemplation.* This form of prayer is similar to meditation. However, contemplation involves simply being in the presence of God. It is silent, wordless prayer that leads you to rest in the presence of God's all-encompassing love.

To engage in meditation or contemplation effectively, it's ideal to reserve a set time, place, and duration for prayer.

You can also pray the **Liturgy of the Hours**, the official public prayer of the Church. The Liturgy of the Hours, or Divine Office, extends the mystery of Christ, celebrated in the Eucharist, through the hours of each day. The Church recites this prayer, in its complete form, seven times each day in response to St. Paul's exhortation to "pray without ceasing" (1 Thes 5:17).

> **lectio divina** Literally, "divine reading"; a prayerful way to read, and meditate on, Sacred Scripture.
>
> **Liturgy of the Hours** The public prayer of the Church that makes holy the entire course of the day and night. It is also called the Divine Office.

Priests and consecrated religious pray the Liturgy of the Hours each day. Many Catholics today pray a shortened form of the Divine Office, which includes an Office of Readings, Morning and Evening Prayer, Daytime Prayer, and Night Prayer.

Perhaps you can make the Divine Office a part of your prayer life. Many resources are available that can help you pray the Liturgy of the Hours.

Popular Piety

Another way to enrich your prayer life and your participation in the sacraments is through various forms of popular piety. Popular piety refers to a great number of devotions and religious practices. Some of these are not strictly liturgical or sacramental yet are approved by the Church. Many devotions of popular piety do make use of *sacramentals.* See Explaining the Faith on page 70 for more information on sacramentals. Devotions and religious practices include the veneration of relics, making pilgrimages, participating in religious processions (such as for a patron saint's feast day), praying the Stations of the Cross (see page 330), praying the Rosary (see pages 328–330), and wearing religious medals.

eschatological Related to the "last things" (death, judgment, heaven, hell, Purgatory, the second coming of Christ, and the resurrection of the body).

Churches have an **eschatological** significance. The threshold you pass when you enter a Catholic church symbolizes the passage from this world to the everlasting Kingdom of God.

SECTION ASSESSMENT

NOTE TAKING

Use the chart you created to help you complete the following items.

1. Identify three material elements Jesus used in his ministry.

2. How do Jesus' actions provide the Church with a basis for the physical elements used in the sacraments?

3. Choose one of the passages you read, and describe parallels between the Scripture events and what takes place in one or more of the sacraments.

VOCABULARY

4. Write a sentence using the terms *ministerial priesthood* and *common priesthood*.

5. Explain the *sanctoral cycle*.

COMPREHENSION

6. Why is the liturgy best celebrated communally?

7. Explain what *form* and *matter* mean regarding the sacraments.

8. How does the liturgical year help you commemorate the Paschal Mystery?

9. What are the main seasons of the Church Year?

APPLICATION

10. Name and describe three ways you can pray, apart from the liturgy.

Section Summaries

Focus Question

How can the sacraments transform your life?

Complete one of the following:

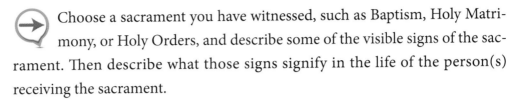

→ Choose a sacrament you have witnessed, such as Baptism, Holy Matrimony, or Holy Orders, and describe some of the visible signs of the sacrament. Then describe what those signs signify in the life of the person(s) receiving the sacrament.

→ Review paragraph 1131 of the *Catechism of the Catholic Church*. Choose one statement made in the paragraph, and write a reflection on what the statement means in your life.

→ Create artwork (print or digital) that represents the grace of the sacraments or of one particular sacrament.

INTRODUCTION (PAGES 37–38)
Celebrating Redemption

The liturgy celebrates the Paschal Mystery of Christ, through which you are redeemed. In the liturgy, particularly the Eucharist, you proclaim the mystery of your redemption. The liturgy transforms you so that your entire life is patterned after the life of Christ.

 What does it mean to say that through the liturgy, your entire life takes up the pattern of Christ's life?

SECTION 1 (PAGES 39–44)
Christ Acts through the Sacraments

By the power of the Holy Spirit, the events of Christ's life—especially the Paschal Mystery—are present and real for you today in the liturgy. The Holy Spirit transforms you to meet Christ in the liturgy, of which God the Father is the source and the goal.

 Describe how God the Father is the source and goal of the liturgy.

SECTION 2 (PAGES 45–48)

Introducing the Seven Sacraments

The Seven Sacraments have several doctrinal elements in common with one another and can be described as Sacraments of Christ, Sacraments of the Church, Sacraments of Faith, Sacraments of Salvation, and Sacraments of Eternal Life.

 Choose one of the titles for the sacraments, and write a short poem or meditation on what the title means for you.

SECTION 3 (PAGES 49–63)

Celebrating the Church's Liturgy

Christ instituted the Seven Sacraments, directly instituting the words, physical elements, and gestures of some of the sacraments. These are signs that play an important role in the celebration of the sacraments.

Answer these questions related to a liturgy you recently attended: (1) When was the liturgy? (2) Where was the liturgy? (3) Why did you attend? (4) What did you celebrate?

Chapter Assignments

Choose and complete at least one of the following three assignments assessing your understanding of the material in this chapter.

1. A Liturgical Calendar Presentation

The liturgical calendar is a way to recall and commemorate the major events of Jesus' life through the Church's liturgy. Create a presentation that further explains the liturgical year. Draw a cyclical calendar that highlights the seasons and some of the feast days of the Church Year. Use liturgical colors to differentiate the seasons. For each season, add symbols, words, and pictures to depict some important days in the Church Year that occur during that season. Then write a report addressing the following points:

- What do the colors of each season represent? How are those colors used in the liturgy?

- In addition to the three holy days of obligation dedicated to Mary, name at least three other Marian feast days not previously mentioned in the text, provide their dates, and tell what events they commemorate.

- Research the origins of your name and whether it has roots in the faith (such as the name of a saint or a connection to a feast day). If so, identify the Christian origins of your name and the feast day that is associated with it.

2. Reporting on the Eastern Churches

Although they share the same apostolic faith and the same Seven Sacraments, the Churches of the East and West have developed different liturgical practices and customs over the centuries. One example is the different dates for the celebration of Easter, noted on page 57. What other practices and customs differ between the Churches of the East and West? Complete your research in two parts, as follows:

- List five liturgical rites of the Eastern Catholic Churches, and write two or three sentences explaining the origins or roots of each.

- Identify several other practices, other than the date for celebrating Easter, that differ between the Eastern Catholic Churches and the Roman Catholic Church.

3. Participating in Parish Ministries

Read what St. Paul had to say about different ministries in the Church (see 1 Corinthians 3:5–9; 12:4–11, 27–31). Then follow these instructions for completing the assignment:

1. Make a list of the ministries in your parish that people your age can participate in (your list should include at least five ministries).

2. Meet with the coordinator of one of these ministries. Videotape an interview. Ask the person to tell (1) the essential tasks of the ministry, (2) the purpose of the ministry (how it serves the Church through the parish community), and (3) who is eligible to participate.

3. Attend one meeting or event sponsored by the ministry. Tape an interview with several participants who minister or are ministered to. Ask them why they feel this ministry is important.

4. Edit both tapes into one. Play the entire video for your teacher or class.

5. Write a three-paragraph essay explaining why you would or would not like to participate in this ministry.

Faithful Disciple

St. Juan Diego

St. Juan Diego

How did the beautiful Basilica of Our Lady of Guadalupe, which stands today in Mexico City, come to be? It came about through the simple faith of a poor peasant who, on his way to Mass, met and spoke with a wondrous lady. She asked for a shrine.

This lady was Mary, the Mother of God. She appeared as a young, pregnant native Mexican woman, and she spoke to Juan Diego in his own language. Mary told him to ask the local bishop to build the shrine. Juan Diego did so, but the bishop was skeptical and asked for a sign. On December 12, 1531, Mary told Juan Diego to climb a hill and pick the flowers there. He climbed up and, in the midst of winter, found roses blooming. Juan Diego gathered them in his *tilma,* or cloak, and took them to the bishop. The bishop was surprised by the roses. But he was even more surprised by the image of the beautiful lady imprinted on the inside of Juan Diego's cloak. The bishop ordered the shrine built. The image remains there and is honored to this day.

God's miracles are not only in the past. During Pope John Paul II's visit to Mexico in 1990 to beatify Juan Diego, another miracle occurred. A young man addicted to drugs stabbed himself and jumped off a third-story balcony. Inspired by the beatification, this man's mother prayed to Juan Diego that her son be saved from death. Doctors did not expect him to survive, and he received the final sacraments of the Church. (See Chapter 7 for more information on the Sacrament of the Anointing of the Sick.) Yet within a week, the man made a full recovery. Even more, he gave up his drug habit and changed his life. Doctors declared his recovery to be a miracle. As a result of this and other miracles associated with prayer to the blessed peasant, Pope John Paul II declared Juan Diego a saint in 2002.

Both a devout and simple peasant and a recovered drug addict in Mexico City witness, over a span of five centuries, to the power of the sacraments. In one sense, every sacrament is a miracle, because every sacrament brings an encounter with the Risen Christ and his power into your life.

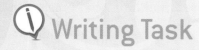

Reading Comprehension

1. What was the sign Mary gave Juan Diego?

2. What was the miracle attributed to St. Juan Diego in 1990?

3. In what sense is every sacrament a miracle?

Writing Task

- Research how Catholics in Mexico celebrate the Feast of Our Lady of Guadalupe. Why has December 12 become one of the most important dates on the Mexican calendar?

Explaining the Faith

How can objects and actions enrich our prayer life as Catholics?

What sacred objects have you seen used in prayer or have you used when you pray? Some common objects Catholics use in prayer, and which you yourself may have used, include holy water, candles, statues of saints, and holy pictures. These objects are called *sacramentals*. Another type of sacramental is actions or gestures. These include making the Sign of the Cross, blessing ourselves or another person, and participating in a religious procession.

Sacramentals are usually accompanied by a special prayer. The Church instituted sacramentals to enrich Catholics in receiving the fruits of the sacraments by making holy the various circumstances of our lives. Among sacramentals, blessings hold the most important place. Blessings praise God for the gifts he has given to his people. A common blessing you may pray frequently is Grace at Meals (see page 327). Blessings are usually addressed to the Trinity, through the Sign of the Cross.

Further Research

- Read about the Church's teaching on sacramentals (see *CCC*, 1667–1679). Name at least two sacramental objects and two sacramental actions not mentioned in the preceding text. Then explain the origins of sacramentals.

Prayer
A Prayer of Thanksgiving for the Sacraments

Thank you, God, for the Sacrament of Baptism, for making me your child, for giving me life in you.

Thank you, God, for the Sacrament of Holy Eucharist. As I journey through life, strengthen me always with the Living Bread, the Body and Blood of your Son.

Thank you, God, for the Sacrament of Confirmation, for the gift of the Holy Spirit in my life. May I listen to his voice and follow his ways!

Thank you, God, for forgiveness in the Sacrament of Penance and Reconciliation. May I always come to you with my burdens, knowing that, as I surrender them to you, I will find freedom.

Thank you, God, for the comfort you bring to the sick and the dying in the Sacrament of the Anointing of the Sick. Gather your suffering people into your arms, and give them peace.

Thank you, God, for the Sacrament of Holy Orders. Thank you for the bishops, priests, and deacons you give to your people. May they be true to this gift of ordained ministry, and may they lead us to you.

Thank you, God, for the Sacrament of Matrimony, for giving life and joy to men and women who are pledged to each other, and for the children they will bring into the world. You promise to be with them in all their joys and sorrows as they witness to your love.

Amen.

THE SACRAMENT OF
BAPTISM

A Phone Call *from*
ROME

A phone call received by a young Italian woman in September 2013 falls into the category of biggest surprises ever. About four months before the call, this young woman, Anna Romano, had found that she was pregnant. When Anna told her boyfriend the news, he revealed that he was already married and told Anna to get an abortion. Anna refused.

Anna felt betrayed. "The perfect man" for her had never had any intention of making a home with her. Anna decided to pour out her heart to Pope Francis in a letter. She no doubt felt that he would appreciate her decision to carry the child to term. She never really expected a reply.

While on vacation, Anna was surprised to get a phone call from Rome. She recognized the city's area code. Who could be calling from Rome? When she answered the phone, she recognized the voice immediately: it was the voice of Pope Francis!

During the call, the pope told Anna that she had been "brave and strong" for her unborn child. In turn, Anna told the pope that she was worried about baptizing this baby because she had been married before and then divorced and now she was a single mother. Pope Francis assured her that he would be her spiritual father and guide and offered to baptize the baby himself. The pope signaled that, no matter what the circumstances, every child is welcome in the household of the faith.

Anna says that this phone call changed her life. Anna hopes that her letter will "be an example for other women who feel they may be distant from the Church simply because they have chosen the wrong man, they are divorced, or they are with men who are not worthy of being fathers."

Anna added at the time, "I don't know the sex of the baby, but if the pope does baptize it and it's a boy I have no doubt of his name—Francis."

(Based on "Pope Calls Single Mother, Offers to Baptize Child," *Catholic News Agency*, September 9, 2013.)

FOCUS QUESTION

How does the Sacrament of Baptism make you **A CHILD OF GOD** and a **SHARER IN THE PASCHAL MYSTERY**?

Chapter Overview

Introduction	**Saying No to Sin**
Section 1	**Understanding the Sacrament of Baptism**
Section 2	**Celebrating the Sacrament of Baptism**
Section 3	**The Graces of the Sacrament of Baptism**

INTRODUCTION
Saying No to Sin

In the Sacrament of Baptism, a series of six questions is asked of the parents and godparents or, in the case of adults, the catechumens. Three of the questions involve things to reject (sin, evil, and Satan, the "father of sin and prince of darkness") and require "I do [reject]" for answers.

In a homily he once shared on the Feast of the Baptism of the Lord, Pope Benedict XVI explained that in the ancient Church, three responses of no rejected the *pompa diaboli* ("the devil's procession"), which referred to the morally permissive pagan culture of the day and its perversion of the true meaning of life. Today, the rejections of sin, evil, and Satan spoken at Baptism are also a rejection of cultural values that promote a pursuit of happiness through material possessions, egotism, sexual promiscuity, and moral relativism in so many spheres of life. Pope Benedict, in addressing those who had come for Baptism and to accompany those being baptized, said,

Let us say "no" to this promise of apparent happiness, to this "pompa" of what may seem to be life but is in fact merely an instrument of death, . . . in order to cultivate instead the culture of life.

In the Sacrament of Baptism, this no to the lure of sinful culture rings out loud and clear for all to hear. The parents and godparents, or catechumens, also affirm the culture of life in responding "I do" when asked if they believe in God: Father, Son, and Holy Spirit.

What do people hope for when they are baptized in the Church? Pope Benedict explained in simple words:

We hope for a good life, the true life . . . and also for happiness in a future that is still unknown. We are unable to guarantee this gift for the entire span of the unknown future, so we turn to the Lord to obtain this gift from him.

At his Wednesday audience on January 8, 2014, the Sunday before the Feast of the Baptism of the Lord,

NOTE TAKING

Summarizing Main Ideas. Create and complete a simple outline like the one below to help you summarize the main points of this section.

WHAT YOU REJECT IN BAPTISM

- In the three no responses of the rite:
- In the rejection of the *pompa diaboli* in the ancient Church:
- What this means today:

WHAT YOU AFFIRM IN BAPTISM

- In the three affirmative responses of the rite:
- In how you live as a Christian:

Pope Francis began a new series of catechesis on the sacraments, focusing first on the Sacrament of Baptism. Speaking to the thousands gathered at St. Peter's Square, he said,

> With Baptism we become immersed in that inexhaustible source of life that is the death of Jesus, the greatest act of love in all of history; and thanks to his love we can live a new life, no longer at the mercy of evil, of sin and death, but in communion with God and with our brothers and sisters.

In this chapter you will consider the new life offered in Baptism and how this Sacrament of Christian Initiation frees you from sin and configures you to Christ so that you are empowered to live as his disciple and as a member of his Church.

The Culture of Life

Baptism makes real the new life that Christ won for you. In Baptism, Catholics join with Christ in saying no to sin and yes to moral goodness. In other words, you say yes to the culture of life. In doing so, you obey each of the Ten Commandments.

Listed below are examples of saying yes to life in today's world. Think about each example. Then write one practical way you will try to carry out each example this week. Follow through on your plan.

- Say yes to a God who gives meaning to life (Commandments 1–3).
- Say yes to the family (Commandment 4).
- Say yes to life (Commandment 5).
- Say yes to responsible love (Commandment 6).
- Say yes to social responsibility and justice (Commandment 7).
- Say yes to the truth (Commandment 8).
- Say yes to respect for others and their belongings (Commandments 9 and 10).

SECTION ASSESSMENT

NOTE TAKING

Use the outline you created to respond to the following questions.

1. What three things do you reject in Baptism?
2. What three beliefs do you affirm in Baptism?

COMPREHENSION

3. What are some examples of the *pompa diaboli* in the world today?

REFLECTION

4. What are some sinful elements of popular culture that you have rejected?
5. By word or action, how do you affirm your baptismal promise of belief in God?

SECTION 1
Understanding the Sacrament of Baptism

MAIN IDEA

Baptism is prefigured in the Old Testament and clarified by its connection with the Paschal Mystery of Jesus Christ; it has always been the way to membership in the Church.

The word *baptism* comes from the Greek word *baptizein*, which means "to plunge or immerse." Thus the Sacrament of Baptism takes its name from the central rite by which it is carried out. The immersion of the catechumens into water represents their burial with Christ. Their rising up out of the water represents their resurrection with Christ as "new creatures." St. Paul wrote:

> Or are you unaware that we who were baptized into Christ Jesus were baptized into his death? We were indeed buried with him through baptism into death, so that, just as Christ was raised from the dead by the glory of the Father, we too might live in newness of life. (Rom 6:3–4)

Baptism is the first **Sacrament of Christian Initiation**. Its place in the sacramental economy is remembered in the Easter Vigil liturgy, in which several events of the Old Testament prefigure Baptism. Christ's own Baptism reveals more of the sacrament's meaning.

> **Sacrament of Christian Initiation** One of the three sacraments—Baptism, Confirmation, and Eucharist—through which a person enters into full membership in the Church.

NOTE TAKING

Outlining Main Ideas. Create a chart like the one below to outline the main ideas explained in this section.

MAIN IDEA	DETAILS
Other Names for Baptism	
Baptism Prefigured in the Old Testament	
The Rite of Christian Initiation in the Early Church and Today	

OTHER NAMES *for* BAParTISM

THE WASHING OF REGENERATION AND RENEWAL BY THE HOLY SPIRIT

This name refers to the regeneration or rebirth of a person by water and Spirit that the sacrament brings about. Jesus spoke of this rebirth: "Amen, amen, I say to you, no one can enter the kingdom of God without being born of water and Spirit" (Jn 3:5).

ENLIGHTENMENT

St. Justin Martyr called Baptism *enlightenment* "because those who receive this [catechetical] instruction are enlightened in their understanding." Jesus is the light of the world, who enlightens everyone.

THE SACRAMENT OF FAITH

St. Augustine described Baptism as the Sacrament of Faith because by receiving it, you profess your faith in all the Church teaches.

Finally, the history of Baptism in the Church teaches that through the sacrament a person is purified, justified, and sanctified by the Holy Spirit. The following sections explain more of the history of the sacrament.

Baptism Prefigured in the Old Testament

The Sacrament of Baptism is prefigured, or anticipated, in the Old Testament with the first creation account

in the Book of Genesis, the Great Flood, the crossing of the Red Sea, and the crossing of the Jordan into Canaan. These four events of salvation history are commemorated when the water is blessed for Baptism.

The Waters of Creation

The Old Testament roots of the Sacrament of Baptism begin in the creation account in the Book of Genesis when the Holy Spirit hovered over the waters

and brought new life from them: "In the beginning, when God created the heavens and the earth—and the earth was without form or shape, with darkness over the abyss and a mighty wind sweeping over the waters" (Gn 1:1–2). Thus, since the beginning of the world, water has been a source of life (see *CCC*, 1218). Through the waters of Baptism, you are brought to new life with the Blessed Trinity.

The Great Flood

Just as water can be life-giving, it can also bring great destruction. This is witnessed in the Book of Genesis, in the account of the Great Flood (see Genesis 6:5–8:22). In this event, God sent a deluge to wipe out all human life, which had been overwhelmed by sin, saving only Noah and his family. Through the waters of the flood, God created a new beginning. Humanity's sinfulness was buried, and, through the remnant people—Noah and his family—a new creation established.

The death and new life brought about by the flood foreshadow the death and new life you experience in Baptism. In Baptism, you are buried in water, symbolizing your death to sin, and rise to new life with Christ. The waters of Baptism signify and make real "an end of sin and a new beginning of goodness" (Easter Vigil 42, Blessing of Water, *Roman Missal*).

Crossing the Red Sea

In the waters of Baptism, the Church also recalls God's saving plan to rescue Moses and the Israelites from slavery in Egypt. With God's help, the Israelites crossed the Red Sea and reached the opposite side, free to continue on their journey to the Promised Land (see Exodus 14:10–31). God gave them new life as free people. He made a covenant with them and taught them to live

by the Ten Commandments as his own people. They were to choose life rather than death by "loving the Lord . . . heeding his voice, and holding fast to him" (Dt 30:19–20).

The waters of Baptism remind you of the promise God made to be with the Israelites always and to bring them safely to their home in Canaan. Furthermore, they free you from sin and allow you safe passage on your journey to the Promised Land of eternal life with God.

Crossing the Jordan

To reach the Promised Land, the Israelites still had to cross the waters of the Jordan River. God led Joshua and the Israelites safely across the Jordan into the land of Canaan (see Joshua 3:13–17). In the same way, the waters of Baptism enable you to enter the Church and live as a member of the New Covenant, one of God's own People.

The Baptism of Jesus

It was in the Jordan River that Jesus himself was baptized. In the time of Jesus, John the Baptist, sometimes referred to as the "last Old Testament prophet," preached repentance of sin and urged people to prepare for the coming of the long-awaited Messiah. Even though Jesus was without sin, he went to John to be baptized (see Matthew 3:13–17, Mark 1:9–11, Luke 3:21–22, John 1:31–34).

In all four Gospels, the Baptism of Jesus marks the beginning of his public ministry, his preaching of the coming of God's Kingdom *and* the necessity of his own Death and Resurrection for the forgiveness of sins. His Baptism with water prefigured his Baptism in blood at his Death on the Cross. This association is clear in the dialogue between Jesus and his Apostles in Mark's Gospel:

> [James and John said to Jesus], "Grant that in your glory we may sit one at your right and the other at your left." Jesus said to them, "You do not know what you are asking. Can you drink the cup that I drink or be baptized with the baptism with which I am baptized?" (Mk 10:37–38)

Jesus further clarified the connection between Baptism and the Paschal Mystery in Luke's Gospel: "There is a baptism with which I must be baptized, and how great is my anguish until it is accomplished!" (Lk 12:50). Further, in the Gospel of John's account of the Passion, it was reported that "one soldier thrust his lance into [Jesus'] side, and immediately blood and water flowed out" (Jn 19:34). The water from Christ's side alludes to Baptism. His Death is not the end but a new beginning. Jesus will conquer death just as he conquered sin. He will rise again to new life.

Finally, the Risen Jesus commissioned the Apostles to baptize: "Go, therefore, and make disciples of all nations, baptizing them in the name of the Father, and of the Son, and of the holy Spirit" (Mt 28:19). Note that examples from the beginning, the middle, and the end of Christ's ministry all teach the Church the primacy of Baptism.

The Sacrament of Baptism recalls the Baptism of Jesus as a revelation of his true character. You express your own faith that he is the Messiah, the Son of God, who has saved you from sin and brings you to new life. You also recall the Paschal Mystery—his suffering, dying, and rising from the dead. Your immersion in water signifies his Death. Your rising from the water signifies his Resurrection. As St. Paul explained to the Colossians, "You were buried with [Christ] in baptism, in which you were also raised with him through faith in the power of God, who raised him from the dead" (Col 2:12).

Christian Initiation in the Church

On the day of Pentecost, when the Holy Spirit descended upon Mary and the Apostles gathered in the Upper Room, before St. Peter said to the crowds gathered in the streets of Jerusalem, "Repent and be baptized, every one of you, in the name of Jesus Christ for the forgiveness of your sins; and you will receive the gift of the holy Spirit" (Acts 2:38), he shared with them the story of faith, recounting for them an account of salvation history. According to the Acts of the Apostles, three thousand were baptized that day (see Acts 2:41).

Likewise, when the Apostle Philip offered Baptism to the Ethiopian eunuch (see Acts 8:27–38), he first showed the man how the Old Testament prophecies connected with the mission of Jesus as Messiah (see also page 82).

From the time of the Apostles, reception of Baptism by adults was preceded by preparation in the faith. Christian initiation continues to be accomplished in several stages, requiring certain essential elements: proclamation of the Word, conversion, a profession of faith, Baptism, the outpouring of the Holy Spirit, and Eucharistic communion. In the first three centuries, the journey to Christian initiation consisted of these four steps:

Catechumens study Church teaching and learn about the Gospels from catechists, who can be priests, deacons, or laypeople.

1. *Precatechumenate.* This period consisted of evangelization and initial conversion. From the words and actions of practicing Christians, the person heard the Good News that Jesus is the Messiah and sought to learn more. People at this stage of initiation were called "inquirers." Inquirers were guided by sponsors, members of the Christian community who got to know them and supported them in their faith formation. (As infant Baptisms became more common, the role of sponsor was replaced by that of godparents. Infant Baptism is the subject of Section 2.) Inquirers were then admitted into the order of catechumens. From that moment on, these catechumens were considered part of the Church.

2. *Catechumenate.* During two or three years of study, known as the **catechumenate**, the catechumens met to receive instruction in the Gospels and Church teaching. They were taught by **catechists** (priests, deacons, and lay teachers). Through the example of their sponsors, the catechumens learned about the Christian life. They celebrated the Liturgy of the Word at Mass and attended the celebration of other liturgical rites of the Church. They participated in the local church's work of charity and service.

3. *Purification, Enlightenment, or Illumination.* This part of the initiation process usually coincided with Lent. On the first Sunday of Lent, the catechumens who were ready to proceed to the celebration of the sacraments took part in the Rite of Enrollment. The catechumens entered their names in the *Book of the Elect*. From then on, they were known as the *elect*

At the Easter Vigil, small candles are lit from the Paschal Candle.

or "chosen ones." During Lent, the elect intensified their prayer and preparation for the sacraments. They underwent three or more **scrutinies**—liturgical rites that aid the elect in self-examination and repentance, and support them through prayers of intercession and **exorcisms**. The prayer services also were intended to strengthen the resolve of the elect to choose good and live for Christ. The scrutinies usually took place on the third, fourth, and fifth Sundays of Lent. They reminded everyone—not just the catechumens—of the need for constant repentance and conversion. At the end of Lent, the catechumens celebrated Baptism, Confirmation, and Eucharist at the Easter Vigil service. At this great Feast of the Resurrection, the catechumens joined themselves to the Paschal Mystery of Jesus and began a new life as full members of the Church.

catechumenate From a Greek word that means "study or instruction." In the early Church, the catechumenate was a two- to three-year period of study about Jesus and the Christian faith. Celebration of the Sacraments of Christian Initiation did not occur until after the catechumenate.

catechists Ordained ministers and laypeople who instruct others in Christian doctrine and for entry into the Church.

scrutinies Rites within the Rite of Christian Initiation of Adults that aid the elect in self-examination and repentance and support them through prayers of intercession and exorcism.

exorcisms Prayerful rites in preparation for Baptism that invoke God's help in overcoming the power of Satan and the spirit of evil.

4. *Mystagogia.* Recall that this Greek term for the fourth step of Christian initiation means "leading into the mystery." This step lasted for the entire Easter season, and sometimes longer. The newly baptized, who were now called neophytes, immersed themselves in the mysteries of Christ, the Church, and the sacraments. They took an active part in the local church community—meditating on the Gospel, sharing in the entire Mass and receiving Holy Communion, and performing works of charity.

The Second Vatican Council restored the practice of the adult catechumenate, called the **Rite of Christian Initiation of Adults (RCIA).** As in the early Church, it includes several distinct steps. (See page 83.) A difference between the Eastern and Western Churches is that the Eastern Churches confer all three Sacraments of Christian Initiation in infancy: babies are baptized and receive Confirmation and First Eucharist at the same time. In the celebration of Eucharist, the priest puts a small spoonful of the Blood of Christ under the species of consecrated wine into their mouths. The babies become full members of the Church at this time. In the Western Church, after infant Baptism there are years of preparation preceding reception of the Sacrament of the Eucharist (and the Sacrament of Penance) and often a few more years of preparation prior to reception of the Sacrament of Confirmation. Infant Baptism by its nature requires a postbaptismal catechumenate of instruction in faith for the child as he or she grows and an opportunity for the "flowering of baptismal grace in personal growth" (*CCC,* 1231).

> **Rite of Christian Initiation of Adults (RCIA)** The process by which an unbaptized adult or an adult baptized in another ecclesial community prepares for full initiation into the Catholic Church.

📖 Easter Vigil
READINGS

The Apostle Philip did not just tell the Ethiopian eunuch about the life and message of Jesus. He explained to the man how even the ancient prophecies of Isaiah foretold Jesus' mission as Messiah (see Acts 8:27–38). Likewise today, when the Church baptizes new members at the Easter Vigil, it precedes these Baptisms with nine Scripture readings—seven from the Old Testament and two from the New Testament—that encompass all of salvation history. They recall for the Church how everything in the past either prefigured or prepared people for the coming of Jesus. These readings are listed below. Consider the sequence of readings, and write one or two paragraphs telling how you think the sequence relates to Baptism.

- God creates the world (Genesis 1:1–2:2).
- God makes a covenant with Abraham (Genesis 22:1–18).
- The Israelites cross the Red Sea (Exodus 14:15–15:1).
- God's love for his people brings blessing and protection (Isaiah 54:5–14).
- Come to God and you will have life (Isaiah 55:1–11).
- God's commandments bring life (Baruch 3:9–15, 32–4:4).
- God will give you a new heart (Ezekiel 36:16–28).
- We are baptized into Christ Jesus (Romans 6:3–11).
- Jesus has been raised from the dead (Matthew 28:1–10 *or* Mark 16:1–8 *or* Luke 24:1–12).

THE RITE OF **CHRISTIAN** **INITIATION** OF ADULTS

The RCIA includes four periods with three additional steps. Here is a brief description of each.

1 PERIOD OF INQUIRY

Known also as the period of evangelization and precatechumenate, this is the time when a person interested in being baptized in the Catholic Church learns about the Catholic faith and discerns a call to live a life of discipleship as a Catholic. The person seeks out a Catholic, usually an official of the Church like a priest, and inquires about how to belong. The priest will usually encourage the person to participate in the catechumenate.

First Step: Acceptance into the order of catechumens.

In the Rite of Acceptance, the catechumens publicly express their desire to follow Christ and are accepted into the order of catechumens.

PERIOD OF THE CATECHUMENATE **2**

This is a time of formation for the catechumens. They are instructed in the Catholic faith in the following four ways: catechesis, spiritual development, participation in the liturgy, and engaging in apostolic witness.

Second Step: The Rite of Election.

This rite, also called the Enrollment of Names, usually occurs on the first Sunday of Lent. The rite takes place after the homily, when the catechumens are asked to affirm their desire to receive the sacraments of the Church. The catechumens are then invited to sign their names in the *Book of the Elect* to show that they wish to receive the Sacraments of Christian Initiation at the Easter Vigil.

3 PERIOD OF PURIFICATION

The Rite of Election begins the period of purification and enlightenment. During this period the elect participate in three scrutinies and two optional presentations—the Apostles' Creed or Nicene Creed and the Lord's Prayer. The catechumens listen to these presentations, which represent the handing on of the faith.

Third Step: Celebration of the Sacraments of Christian Initiation.

At the Easter Vigil, the catechumens receive the Sacraments of Baptism (for those who have not been previously baptized), Confirmation, and Eucharist.

PERIOD OF MYSTAGOGY **4**

This is also known as the period of postbaptismal catechesis. As the name suggests, during this time the newly initiated Catholics (neophytes) continue to study together to "deepen their grasp of the paschal mystery" (*RCIA*, 244). The period usually lasts only until Pentecost, but it sometimes lasts until Advent.

SECTION ASSESSMENT

NOTE TAKING

Use your completed chart to help you answer the following questions.

1. What are two other names by which the Sacrament of Baptism is known?

2. Explain the meaning of one of the other names for the Sacrament of Baptism.

3. Name and briefly describe two Old Testament events that prefigure Baptism.

4. Name and briefly explain the four steps of the catechumenate process in the early Church.

COMPREHENSION

5. What does the plunging of the candidate at Baptism represent?

6. Explain the connection between Baptism and the Paschal Mystery of Jesus Christ.

7. How do the Roman, or Western, Church and the Eastern Catholic Churches confer the Sacraments of Christian Initiation differently?

REFLECTION

8. Imagine you were recounting the story of salvation to someone who had not heard the Good News of Jesus Christ. Where would you begin? What would you say?

SECTION 2
Celebrating the Sacrament of Baptism

MAIN IDEA

There are separate rites for the initiation of adults and children; however, the essential Rite of Baptism for each group is the same and involves an immersion in or pouring on of water and the pronouncement of the words "in the name of the Father, the Son, and the Holy Spirit."

Every unbaptized person—whether an adult or a child—can be baptized. Since the beginning of the Church, the catechumenate for adults has occupied an important place. In fact, by virtue of living a life of faith, hope, and charity, catechumens are already joined to the Church.

Infant Baptisms have also taken place from the Church's earliest days. In fact, when Peter preached on Pentecost, he said, "Repent and be baptized, every one of you, in the name of Jesus Christ for the forgiveness of your sins; and you will receive the gift of the holy Spirit" (Acts 2:38). Note that Peter said, "every one of you." He added, "For the promise is made to you and to your children and to all those far off, whomever the Lord our God will call" (Acts 2:39).

Several other examples in the New Testament (e.g., Acts 16:15; Acts 16:33; 1 Corinthians 1:16) mention that entire households, which presumably included children, were offered Baptism and converted to Christianity.

Infant Baptisms became more common in the fourth and fifth centuries. Two important factors contributed to this change. First, when Christianity was legalized and then made the official religion of the

NOTE TAKING

Organizing Concepts. Create a chart like the one below to identify the essential elements of the Sacrament of Baptism. Name each element and explain what takes place. List any important signs associated with each element, and tell what they signify.

ESSENTIAL ELEMENT	WHAT TAKES PLACE	WHAT IT SIGNIFIES
1.		
2.		
3.		
4.		
5.		
6.		
7.		
8.		

Roman Empire, the persecution of Christians ended and more and more families, including those with young children, sought Baptism. A second and even more significant factor was that in the fourth and fifth centuries, the doctrine of **Original Sin**—the sin of the first man and woman that is passed on to all people—became more clearly understood through the writings of St. Augustine and other theologians. With this new understanding, a new emphasis was placed on early reception of the Sacrament of Baptism, which takes away Original Sin and all previous personal sins. Since many children of this era did not live to adulthood, the Church emphasized early reception of the sacrament.

The practice of infant Baptism shows that salvation is a pure gift of Christ's grace that does not presuppose anything a human must do to deserve it. Today most Catholics are baptized as infants, through the Rite of Baptism of Children (RBC). Infant Baptism requires postbaptismal Christian formation and catechesis so that the baptismal grace may truly bloom in the baptized person. This formation is entrusted to the parents of the baptized child, in keeping with their role as the nurturers of their children's faith. Godparents, too, have a special role in the Christian formation of the newly baptized. The godmother and godfather, who must be firm believers, are called to enter into the role with a desire to help the newly baptized on the road of Christian life.

The Necessity of Baptism

Jesus said Baptism is necessary for salvation (see John 3:5), and he commanded his disciples to proclaim the Gospel to all nations and to baptize them (see Matthew 28:19–20). Baptism, birth into new life in Christ, is necessary for those who have heard the Good News and have been able to ask for the sacrament. Jesus said upon commissioning his disciples, "Whoever believes and is baptized will be saved; whoever does not believe will be condemned" (Mk 16:16).

Does this mean that no one can be saved without Baptism? The Church clearly teaches that Baptism is absolutely necessary "for those to whom the Gospel has been proclaimed and who have had the possibility of asking for the sacrament" (*CCC*, 1257). However, the *Catechism of the Catholic Church* does add that although "God has bound salvation to the Sacrament of Baptism . . . he himself is not bound by his sacraments" (*CCC*, 1257). Thus, there may be circumstances in which salvation and eternal union with God can occur without Baptism. Three special situations are further acknowledged by the Church.

First, those who suffer death for their faith prior to having received the Sacrament of Baptism are baptized by their death, suffered for and with Christ. This **Baptism of blood** brings about the fruits of Baptism for these Christian martyrs.

Second, catechumens who die a natural death prior to being baptized are also assured of the salvation they were not able to receive through the sacrament because of their "desire to receive it, together with repentance for their sins, and charity" (*CCC*, 1259). They are saved through the **Baptism of desire**. The Church also holds that those who never heard the Gospel, lived a life according to God's will the best they could, and would

Original Sin The personal sin of Adam and Eve, which in an analogous way describes the fallen state of human nature into which all generations of people are born. Christ Jesus came to save the world from Original Sin and all personal sin.

Baptism of blood The belief that martyrs—people who die for their faith in Jesus—who had not yet been baptized by water may receive forgiveness for their sins and experience God's saving mercy.

Baptism of desire The belief that catechumens who died before receiving the Sacrament of Baptism may receive forgiveness for their sins and experience God's saving mercy.

have been baptized if they had known of the necessity can also be saved through the Baptism of desire.

Finally, there is the question of children who have died without Baptism. The Church entrusts them to God's mercy, knowing that God desires all people to be saved. Jesus said, "Let the children come to me; do not prevent them, for the kingdom of God belongs to such as these" (Mk 10:14). The Church also remembers these children in the funeral Mass.

Rite and Symbols of the Sacrament

The meaning and the graces of the Sacrament of Baptism are revealed in the essential rite and other words, gestures, and symbols of the sacrament. The Baptism of adults normally takes place during the Easter Vigil in the presence of the assembly of the faithful. Likewise, the Baptism of infants is typically celebrated during a Sunday Mass to highlight the connection of Baptism with the Eucharist and to other members of the Church. The *Catechism of the Catholic Church* teaches:

> Baptism is the sacrament of faith. But faith needs the community of believers. It is only within the faith of the Church that each of the faithful can believe. (*CCC*, 1253)

The ordinary ministers of Baptism are bishops and priests. In the Western Church, deacons may also administer the sacrament. The exception is made in emergency situations, when *any* person—Catholic, Christian, or not—may baptize if he or she intends to do what the Church does when she baptizes and applies the Trinitarian baptismal formula while pouring water over the person's head.

The sacrament consists of the following elements:

1. *Sign of the Cross.* The priest or deacon imprints a cross on the forehead of the catechumen as a sign that he or she belongs to Christ. This sign also reminds the person of the grace Christ won for him or her by his

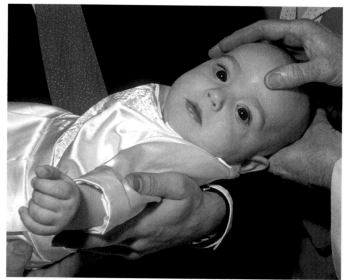

Receiving the Sign of the Cross and wearing a white garment show that the newly baptized belongs to Christ and has put on Christ.

Death on the Cross. Then the minister asks the adult to be baptized (or in the case of infant Baptism, the parents and godparents), "What do you ask of God's Church?" The response is "faith" or "Baptism." Right from the beginning of the celebration, the Church is reminded that "Baptism is the sacrament of faith" (*CCC*, 1253). Faith in Christ Jesus brings you to Baptism, and Baptism strengthens you to live as a faithful member of God's people, the Church.

2. *The Word of God.* The multiple Scripture readings and responsorial psalms from the Easter Vigil teach that God always initiates your relationship with him. For example, some of the options for Gospel readings in the Rite of Baptism of Children are John 3:1–6, Matthew 28:18–20, Mark 1:9–11, and Mark 10:13–16. God calls you and invites you to become his son or daughter. You, in turn, respond in faith by committing yourself to follow his Son, Jesus.

3. *Exorcisms and Profession of Faith.* Because Baptism signifies liberation from sin and from the one who brings about sin, Satan, one or more exorcisms are said over each candidate. The priest asks publicly and authoritatively in the name of Jesus Christ that each person be protected against the power of Satan and the lure of sin. The celebrant then anoints each

candidate with the **oil of catechumens**, or lays hands on him or her, and renounces Satan. Each candidate is thus prepared to confess the faith of the Church, which will be entrusted to the candidate by Baptism.

4. *Blessing of the water.* The celebrant calls on the Holy Spirit to bless the water that will be used for Baptism. In this blessing, "the Church asks God that through his Son the power of the Holy Spirit may be sent upon the water, so that those who will be baptized in it may be 'born of water and the Spirit'" (*CCC*, 1238, quoting Jn 3:5).

5. *Essential Rite of Baptism.* The essential rite of the sacrament is very simple. The celebrant immerses each candidate in the blessed water three times or pours water three times over the candidate's head. At the same time, the celebrant says, "N., I baptize you in the name of the Father, and of the Son, and of the Holy Spirit" (*Christian Initiation of Adults*, 220). "Immersion in water symbolizes not only death and purification, but also regeneration and renewal" (*CCC*, 1262).

6. *Anointing with sacred chrism.* If the celebration of Confirmation does not follow immediately (as in adult Baptism), the celebrant anoints each newly baptized (neophyte) on the crown of the head with consecrated oil known as **sacred chrism**. This anointing symbolizes the coming of the Holy Spirit to the newly baptized. It signifies that a new character, or identity, has been given to the person. He or she now officially belongs to Christ and may be called a Christian. The anointing also brings the baptized person into union with the threefold mission of Christ as priest

The lit candle the newly baptized receive symbolizes the light of Christ and serves as a reminder that Christians are "the light of the world" (Mt 5:14).

(participating in the Church's worship), prophet (proclaiming God's word), and king (humbly serving others in Christ's name). The directives for the *Christian Initiation of Adults* state, "The anointing with chrism after Baptism is a sign of the royal priesthood of the baptized and their enrollment in the fellowship of the people of God" (33).

7. *Receiving or clothing in a white garment.* Each of the neophytes either receives or is dressed in a white robe that "is a symbol of their new dignity" (*Christian Initiation of Adults*, 33). The white robe signifies that the person is now freed from the darkness of sin and has "put on Christ."

8. *Receiving of a lit candle.* The celebrant then gives the newly baptized a small white candle lit from the Easter candle, which was blessed and lit earlier in the Easter Vigil service. The candle symbolizes the light of Christ the newly baptized have received. In the case of infant Baptisms, the light is entrusted to the parents and godparents, who have the responsibility to keep the light of Christ burning bright in the life of the child. For neophytes, the candle not only symbolizes the light of Christ they have received but also their responsibility to bring that light into the world. "The lighted candle shows their vocation of living as befits the children of light" (*Christian Initiation of Adults*, 33).

---

oil of catechumens Olive oil that is blessed by a bishop at the Chrism Mass on or around Holy Thursday and used to anoint those preparing for Baptism.

sacred chrism Perfumed oil consecrated by the bishop and used for anointing in the Sacraments of Baptism, Confirmation, and Holy Orders.

Adults who are being initiated at the Easter Vigil usually proceed directly with the celebration of the Sacrament of Confirmation. This is then followed by the Liturgy of the Eucharist and the reception of First Communion. In the Western Church, the baptismal rite for babies concludes with a solemn blessing of the newly baptized, along with their parents and the entire assembly.

SECTION ASSESSMENT

NOTE TAKING

Refer to the chart you created to help you complete the following items.

1. Describe the essential Rite of Baptism.
2. Name and explain three elements of the Sacrament of Baptism.
3. Name and explain two symbols associated with the Sacrament of Baptism.

COMPREHENSION

4. Who can be baptized?
5. Name some evidence from Scripture for infant Baptism.
6. What does it mean to say that God "is not bound by his sacraments"?

VOCABULARY

7. Define *Baptism of blood* and *Baptism of desire*.

REFLECTION

8. Tell at least two ways you have "put on Christ" in your own life.

The Graces of the Sacrament of Baptism

MAIN IDEA
Two primary graces or effects of the sacrament are forgiveness of sins and a rebirth to new life.

The immersion in water in the Rite of Baptism, discussed in the preceding section, signifies two primary graces of the sacrament: death to the old way of sin as well as a new birth in the Holy Spirit. These and other effects of the sacrament are explained in more detail in the following sections.

Death to Sin

In Baptism, sin is overcome. Baptism forgives both Original Sin and personal sins. Of course, suffering and death remain, as does the human inclination to sin, called **concupiscence**.

Original Sin—the sin by which the first humans disobeyed God's commands, choosing to follow their own will rather than God's will—is an essential truth of the faith. However, Original Sin can be fully understood only through the long journey of Revelation and salvation history that culminates in the Death and Resurrection of Jesus Christ. As the *Catechism of the Catholic Church* teaches, "We must know Christ as the source of grace in order to know Adam as the source of sin" (*CCC*, 388).

The sin of Adam and Eve wounded human nature and is transmitted to all generations. It destroyed the **original holiness and original justice** in which God created the first humans. By Adam's *personal sin*, all human nature was affected and took on a fallen state. From then on, humankind was subject to conflict and to concupiscence. Harmony with creation was broken. Death entered the world.

Although because of Original Sin you have a weakened human nature and are prone to sin, the Sacrament

NOTE TAKING

Identifying Main Ideas. Create an outline like the one below to help you organize the content in this section. Sample main topics have been provided for you, but you should further adjust main topics and subtopics based on the text. Add any remaining subtopics as you read. Provide one or more sentences explaining each topic and subtopic.

I. Effects of Baptism
    A. Death to sin
    B. New life as an adopted child of God

II. Baptism calls for ongoing conversion

III. The Church reminds Catholics of Baptism in her liturgies and practices

concupiscence The human inclination toward sin, caused by Original Sin.

original holiness and original justice The original state of human beings in their relationship with God before sin entered the world.

In speaking of the Church, Pope Benedict XVI once said, "The Church is not self-made; she was created by God and she is continuously formed by him. This finds expression in the sacraments, above all in that of Baptism: I enter into the Church not by a bureaucratic act but through the sacrament."

of Baptism grants you the life of Christ's grace, erases Original Sin, and turns you back to God. Baptism does not restore original justice, but it exceeds in restoring the gift of original holiness. Those who receive this grace of Christ at Baptism receive a holiness that is an even greater blessing than original holiness. Although you are still weak and still inclined to sin, Christ's grace gives you the strength to resist temptation. Christ's sacrifice on the Cross is the source of your salvation. St. Paul's Letter to the Romans reminds the Church, "For just as through the disobedience of one person the many were made sinners, so through the obedience of one the many will be made righteous" (Rom 5:19). Thus, because of Christ, victory over sin and salvation can be yours.

New Life as an Adopted Child of God

Baptism makes you an adopted son or daughter of God, a "new creature" ransomed by Christ. You are no longer a slave to sin. St. Paul's Letter to the Galatians helps explain this:

> But when the fullness of time had come, God sent his Son, born of a woman, born under the law, to ransom those under the law, so that we might receive adoption. As proof that you are children, God sent the spirit of his Son into our hearts, crying out, "Abba, Father!" So you are no longer a slave but a child, and if a child then also an heir, through God. (Gal 4:4–7)

As a child of God, you become a partaker in the divine life and a temple of the Holy Spirit. The Blessed Trinity gives you sanctifying grace, by which your sins are forgiven, you are made holy, and your friendship with God is restored. Sanctifying grace enables you to believe in God, hope in him, and love him. It gives you the power to live and act under the prompting of the Holy Spirit through the gifts he gives you, and allows you to grow in goodness and virtue.

Incorporation into the Church

In his catechesis on the Sacrament of Baptism, Pope Francis said, "[Baptism] makes us members of the Body of Christ and of the People of God." Quoting St. Thomas Aquinas, he went on to say, "Whoever receives Baptism is incorporated in Christ, almost as one of his own limbs, and becomes aggregated to the community of the faithful" (General Audience, January 15, 2014).

Through Baptism, Christians are no longer alone but are "members of one another" (Eph 4:25). You no longer belong to yourself but to Christ, who died and rose for you. As a member of the Body of Christ, you have rights and duties that flow from your Baptism in Christ:

- You are called to be subject to others, to serve others in the communion of the Church, and to respect and obey and follow Church leaders.

- You are also called to spread the Gospel message through apostolic and missionary work.

- Baptized into the common priesthood of Christ, you are called to worship with other Catholics, especially on Sundays and holy days, and to guide and support one another in your life of discipleship. A particular application is to follow the **precepts of the Church**.

In return, among the rights you receive as a member of the Church are the right to receive the sacraments, the right to be nourished with the Word of God, and the right to take part in and be sustained "by the other spiritual helps of the Church" (*CCC*, 1269).

Unity with Other Christians

Baptism grants a "sacramental bond of unity" (*CCC*, 1271) among all those who are reborn through it. Therefore, through Baptism, you are also united with all those who have been baptized, even those not yet in full communion with the Catholic Church. Justified by faith in Baptism, these fellow Christians are incorporated into Christ. In Christ's name, Catholics are brothers and sisters with these other Christians.

The Sacramental Character of Baptism

When you receive the Sacrament of Baptism, you are sealed with an indelible spiritual mark or character that configures you to Christ, marks you as "belonging" to Christ (*CCC*, 1272), and "consecrates" you for Christian worship (*CCC*, 1273). That is why Baptism is given only once and is not repeated when a member of another ecclesial community seeks full communion with the Catholic Church. Even sin cannot erase the mark, although sin can prevent a baptized person from gaining the rewards of salvation.

The sacramental character of Baptism not only consecrates you for Christian worship, but it also enables and commits you to serve God by participating in the liturgy, living a holy life, and serving others with charity. If you remain faithful to your baptismal calling, you can live with the hope that you will share eternal life with God one day.

Living the Sacrament of Baptism

Speaking about Baptism, Pope Francis reminded Catholics not to lose the memory of "that which the Lord has done in us, the memory of the gift that we received," and not to consider it only an event that happened in the past (General Audience, January 8, 2014).

> **precepts of the Church** Basic rules that bind Catholics who belong to Christ's Body. These are the minimal obligations for members to be in good standing in the Catholic Church. (See page 324 for a list of the precepts.)

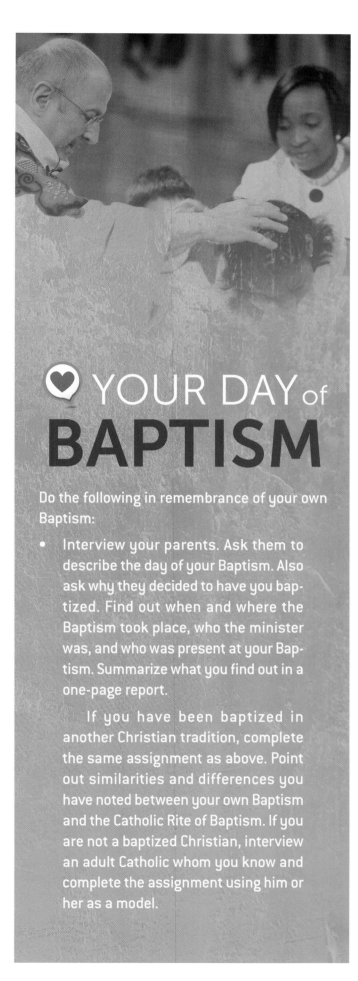

YOUR DAY of BAPTISM

Do the following in remembrance of your own Baptism:

- Interview your parents. Ask them to describe the day of your Baptism. Also ask why they decided to have you baptized. Find out when and where the Baptism took place, who the minister was, and who was present at your Baptism. Summarize what you find out in a one-page report.

    If you have been baptized in another Christian tradition, complete the same assignment as above. Point out similarities and differences you have noted between your own Baptism and the Catholic Rite of Baptism. If you are not a baptized Christian, interview an adult Catholic whom you know and complete the assignment using him or her as a model.

Indeed, Baptism is not a one-time occurrence, something that only happened in your past. Baptism calls you to ongoing conversion, to a daily commitment to share in the Death and Resurrection of Christ and to strive to be an imitator of God as his beloved child (see *CCC*, 1694). Because humans are wounded by Original Sin, it is not always easy to live up to our call to be followers of Christ. As the *Catechism of the Catholic Church* teaches, "The way of perfection passes by way of the Cross. There is no perfection without spiritual battle" (*CCC*, 2015). Yet Christ's gift of salvation offers you the grace you need to persevere in this battle.

Through Baptism, you are aided on your journey to holiness by the Blessed Trinity, who gives you the sanctifying grace of justification. The grace of the Holy Spirit has the power to justify you and to communicate to you the righteousness of God through faith in his Son, Jesus. You are also assisted by Christ's teachings, especially in the Sermon on the Mount, which offers you "the perfect way of the Christian life" and all the principles you need to shape it. But the graces or effects of Baptism remain stagnant unless you put them to use. In his Letter to the Ephesians, St. Paul implored the faithful to "be imitators of God, as beloved children, and live in love, as Christ loved us and handed himself over for us as a sacrificial offering to God for a fragrant aroma" (Eph 5:1–2).

Baptism is an essential sacrament because it "clothes" you with Christ (see Galatians 3:27). In Baptism, you enter into communion with Christ's Death, are buried with him, and rise with him. Baptism introduces you into the intimacy of the Trinitarian life: it allows you to participate in the grace of Christ, to call God "Father" as his adopted child, and to receive the life of the Holy Spirit, who breathes charity in you and purifies, justifies, and sanctifies you.

Awakening the Memory of Baptism

There are several ways Catholics remember their Baptisms on a weekly or daily basis. This is essential according to Pope Francis, who said, "We must awaken the memory of our Baptism!" (General Audience, January 8, 2014). The Church offers several reminders of your Baptism in both her liturgies and her practices. These include the following:

- Even as you enter a church, you are invited to bless yourself with holy water from the font placed near the entrance. This blessing, accompanied by the Sign of the Cross, is a sacramental that reminds you of your unity with the Blessed Trinity. A similar holy water font may also be used in the home.

- The liturgy also provides reminders. For example:

  - *Reading of the creation account at the Easter Vigil.* The celebration of new life in Christ begins with a reading from the creation account. Creation is the foundation of all of God's saving plans. When God saw everything he created, he found it very good.

  - *Blessing of the baptismal water at the Easter Vigil.* The Church remembers the events of salvation history that prefigure the mystery of Baptism. The celebrant prays:

    > Father, you give us grace through sacramental signs,
    > which tell us of the wonders of your unseen power.
    > In Baptism we use your gift of water, which you have made a rich symbol of the grace you give us in this sacrament. (Easter Vigil 42, Blessing of Water, *Roman Missal*)

  - *Renewal of the baptismal promises at the Easter Vigil.* "For all the baptized, children or adults, faith must grow *after* Baptism. For this reason the Church celebrates each year at the Easter Vigil the renewal of the baptismal promises." (*CCC*, 1254)

- You are also reminded of Baptism in your personal prayer life. Catholics are called to prayerful reflection on the meaning of Baptism. One way to do so is through contemplative prayer. This form of silent prayer helps you gain real union with the prayer of Christ. You are encouraged to contemplate the mystery of Baptism especially as it helps you to follow Christ and grow closer to him. Through the power of the Holy Spirit and with your participation in the sacraments, you take part in Christ's Passion and his Resurrection by being born to a new life.

Baptism confers sanctifying grace, the grace of justification. This grace has the power to cleanse you from your sins and to help you grow in holiness and goodness. Baptism is your first step on the Way of the Cross. This path, taken by Christ, is the way to perfection. The graces conferred on you at Baptism give you the strength to undertake this journey in your life each day as you turn away from sin and seek union with the Blessed Trinity.

SECTION ASSESSMENT

NOTE TAKING

Refer to the outline you created to help you answer the following questions.

1. What are the two primary graces, or effects, of the Sacrament of Baptism?
2. What are two other effects of Baptism?
3. What does it mean that Baptism calls a Catholic to ongoing conversion?
4. Who or what aids in this conversion?
5. What are three reminders of the Sacrament of Baptism at the Easter Vigil?
6. What are two other reminders of Baptism in the Church's liturgy and practices?

COMPREHENSION

7. What are the effects of Original Sin today?
8. Explain the "sacramental bond of unity" (*CCC,* 1271) with other Christians that Baptism grants to Catholics.
9. Describe the sacramental character of Baptism.

REFLECTION

10. Explain the following Scripture verse as it relates to Baptism: "I live, no longer I, but Christ lives in me" (Gal 2:20).

Section Summaries

Focus Question

How does the Sacrament of Baptism make you a child of God and a sharer in the Paschal Mystery?

 Complete one of the following:

- Make a collage incorporating words and images that represent how Baptism makes Catholics adopted children of God.

- Write a one-page essay explaining how you share in Christ's Paschal Mystery through your Baptism.

- Review the readings for the Easter Vigil liturgy (see page 82). Create a timeline depicting the events of salvation history the readings present. Write a paragraph explaining how the Death and Resurrection of Jesus are the culmination of the long journey of salvation history.

INTRODUCTION (PAGES 75–76)
Saying No to Sin

A person rejects several sinful parts of his or her life when baptized. A person's rejection of sin is also a rejection of cultural values that promote moral relativism. In Baptism, you also affirm your belief in the life offered by the Blessed Trinity— Father, Son, and Holy Spirit.

 Define *moral relativism*, and tell how popular culture sometimes encourages or promotes this approach to moral judgment.

SECTION 1 (PAGES 77–84)
Understanding the Sacrament of Baptism

The Old Testament prefigures Baptism, especially in the accounts of creation, the Great Flood, and the Israelites' crossing of the Red Sea. Although Jesus was without sin, he went to St. John the Baptist to be baptized. Your own Baptism is connected with the Paschal Mystery of Christ, and it unites you with the Body of Christ, the Church.

 Read about Moses leading the Israelites across the Red Sea in Exodus 14:10–31, and tell how this Old Testament passage prefigures the Sacrament of Baptism.

SECTION 2 (PAGES 85–89)

Celebrating the Sacrament of Baptism

"The Church does not know of any means other than Baptism that assures entry into the eternal beatitude" (*CCC*, 1257), but because God himself is not bound by his sacraments, God is able to save apart from sacramental Baptism. There are separate rites for the initiation of adults and children; however, the essential Rite of Baptism for each is the same and involves an immersion in or pouring on of water and the pronouncement of the words "in the name of the Father, the Son, and the Holy Spirit."

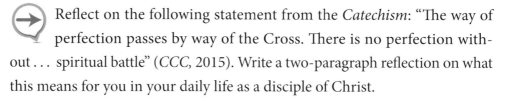 Give an example of a circumstance in which salvation and eternal life with God may be possible without Baptism. Write a paragraph explaining how this is so.

SECTION 3 (PAGES 90–95)

The Graces of the Sacrament of Baptism

The primary graces or effects of the Sacrament of Baptism—forgiveness of both Original Sin and all personal sin and new birth in the Holy Spirit—are both indicated by the immersion in water. Other graces of the sacrament are incorporation into the Church, unity with other Christians, and the granting of the indelible character that configures the baptized to Christ. Baptism calls you to ongoing conversion—that is, a daily commitment to share in the Death and Resurrection of Christ.

Reflect on the following statement from the *Catechism*: "The way of perfection passes by way of the Cross. There is no perfection without . . . spiritual battle" (*CCC*, 2015). Write a two-paragraph reflection on what this means for you in your daily life as a disciple of Christ.

Chapter Assignments

Choose and complete at least one of the following three assignments assessing your understanding of the material in this chapter.

1. Presenting Pope Francis's Catechesis on Baptism

Read Pope Francis's teaching on Baptism at his Wednesday audiences in January 2014. (You can find the text at www.vatican.va.) Develop a multimedia presentation that captures the essential points of his teaching. Your presentation should feature a minimum of twelve slides and should include direct quotations from Pope Francis as well as your own statements and some images related to Baptism. In the notes section of your presentation, provide commentary that connects the pope's teaching to what you have learned in this chapter.

2. Researching Christian Persecution in the Modern World

Speaking about the Catholic Church in Japan, which survived despite intense persecution in earlier centuries, Pope Francis said, "They maintained, even in secret, a strong communal spirit, because their Baptism had made of them one single body in Christ" (General Audience, January 15, 2014). Research Christian communities in the world today who suffer persecution for their faith. Prepare a multimedia or written presentation about one of these communities. Your presentation should provide the following information:

- Who is the group being persecuted? Is the group predominantly Catholic (Eastern or Latin Rite) or part of another ecclesial community?

- In what part of the world (in which country or region) does the group live?

- How large is this Catholic community (in overall numbers and as a percentage of the overall local or national population)?

- When did persecutions begin or become particularly intensified?

- Have these Catholics been able to continue to participate in the liturgy and sacraments?

After you have addressed the above and similar questions, conclude your report with a one- to two-paragraph summary citing examples to prove the thesis: Because their Baptisms make them one single Body in Christ, Catholics maintain a communal spirit.

3. Interviewing an RCIA Candidate

Ask the coordinator of adult faith formation or another person responsible for RCIA at your parish or a neighboring parish to connect you with a parishioner who has entered into full communion with the Church through the RCIA. Explain that you will be interviewing the person.

Arrange for the interview, and prepare questions in advance. Your questions should address the person's journey of faith leading up to his or her entry into the catechumenate, through the RCIA process, and following his or her reception of the Sacraments of Christian Initiation. Following your interview, write a two-page report summarizing your interviewee's faith journey and ways in which it reflects the RCIA process as described in this chapter. Your completed assignment should also include an attachment with the interview questions you prepared along with the answers from your interview session.

Faithful Disciples

The Martyrs of Nagasaki

The twenty-six martyrs of Nagasaki are depicted in bronze at the Twenty-Six Martyrs Museum and Monument in Nagasaki, Japan.

The Christian faith was first proclaimed in Japan in the sixteenth century by St. Francis Xavier (1506–1552). He and later missionaries converted thousands of Japanese people to the faith, and by 1587, around two hundred thousand Japanese people had entered the Church. However, over time the missionaries came to be seen by Japanese rulers as agents of foreign power, and suspicion against them grew. In 1597, an intense persecution of Christians began, lasting into the seventeenth century. Thousands of Christians—priests and laypeople alike—who would not renounce their faith were martyred. Crucifixion and burning at the stake were common forms of execution.

One of the best-known Japanese martyrs was St. Paul Miki, who was studying to join the Jesuit order. Paul Miki was among a group of twenty-six sentenced to death in 1597. Even as this group undertook their month-long, six-hundred-mile march to Nagasaki, where they would be executed, they offered a strong witness to their faith by preaching to the crowds that had come to jeer at them. As they were led to the place where they would be crucified, the group continued to sing songs of praise to God.

Paul Miki's last act of evangelism took place as he hung on his cross. To the gathered crowds he announced, "The only reason for my being killed is that I have taught the Gospel of Christ. I thank God that it is for this reason that I die. . . . I hope my blood will fall on my fellow men like fruitful rain." Paul Miki and his companions were executed on February 5, 1597.

Despite the persecution of the Catholic Church in Japan, the faith continued to be practiced underground and endured, so that—as Pope Francis explained—when missionaries returned to Japan again, "thousands of Christians stepped out into the open and the Church was able to flourish again." How was this so? Pope Francis went on to say, "They survived by the grace of Baptism! This is profound: the People of God transmits the faith, baptizes her children, and goes forward. And they maintained, even in secret, a strong communal spirit, because their Baptism had made of them one single body in Christ" (General Audience, January 15, 2014).

Reading Comprehension

1. How did the Christian faith come to Japan?

2. What led to the persecution of Christians in sixteenth-century Japan?

3. How did St. Paul Miki and his companions show courage in the face of persecution?

Writing Task

- Research Catholicism in Japan. Write two or three paragraphs that explain how the Catholic faith survived in Japan after the persecutions of the late sixteenth and seventeenth centuries.

Explaining the Faith

What does it mean to be a member of the common priesthood of the faithful?

Through Baptism, you share in the priesthood of Christ and are joined to Christ, who is Priest, Prophet, and King. This is called the common priesthood of the faithful. The call to participate in Christ's priesthood is expressed when the celebrant anoints the person with sacred chrism and says, "As Christ was anointed Priest, Prophet, and King, so may you live always as a member of his Body, sharing everlasting life" (*Rite of Baptism*). So what does it mean to live the baptismal call to follow Christ by being priest, prophet, and king?

- *Priest.* By virtue of your Baptism, you share in the priesthood of Christ. You live this baptismal call by ministering to the needs of others through prayer or by making sacrifices to serve them.

- *Prophet.* A prophet proclaims the Gospel message and is a witness to God's saving love in the world. You live the baptismal call to be prophet by being a witness to your Christian faith through your words and actions.

- *King.* To be king requires selfless service to others, following Jesus' example. You live this baptismal call by being selfless in your love for others and by putting the needs of others ahead of your own.

Further Research

- Read paragraph 1546 of the *Catechism of the Catholic Church*. Explain the meaning of the phrase "each according to his own vocation" as it relates to your baptismal priesthood.

Prayer

You Called Us by Name

God, our Father,
in Baptism you called us by name,
making us members of your people,
the Church.
We praise you for your goodness.
We thank you for your gifts.
We ask you to strengthen us
to live in love and service to others
after the example of your Son, Jesus.

Father, look upon your Church with love
and bless your people
with generous single men and women,
with loving husbands and wives,
with understanding parents,
with trusting children,
with dedicated priests, sisters,
deacons, and brothers.
Help us to see our vocations
as a journey toward you.
You have called us,
not to set us apart,
but to bring us together
with others who need our love.

Make us faithful signs of your
presence in their midst.

We ask you through Christ, our Lord.
Amen.

—Prayer for Vocations #33,
United States Conference of Catholic Bishops

THE SACRAMENT OF CONFIRMATION

A Breath of NEW LIFE

Nicole and Tanya had been friends with Kate since fourth grade. By the time they were in eighth grade, their friendship circle had grown, but the three were still close. That was until Kate started to act differently.

Nicole and Tanya noticed that she began cancelling plans suddenly. When they questioned her, Kate shrugged them off with an excuse about being tired. She was also quiet and showed little enthusiasm for the activities she had always enjoyed.

When Nicole and Tanya asked Kate what was wrong, she apologized for not being a good friend and told them she felt like they might be better off without her. She was bored with everything, she said, and wasn't sure she would ever feel better. The girls assured Kate that they still considered her a great friend. They made plans to go to the movies together.

Kate cancelled at the last minute. She refused to give a reason why. Later that night, Nicole received a call from Kate's mother saying Kate was in the hospital. She had taken an overdose of over-the-counter pain medication. She was okay physically but would need psychiatric treatment for what Kate admitted had been a suicide attempt.

The following are feelings of a teen who may be at risk for suicide:

- hopelessness—feeling like things are bad and won't get any better
- fear of losing control, going crazy, or harming oneself or others
- helplessness—a belief that there's nothing that can make life better
- worthlessness—feeling useless and of no value
- self-hate, guilt, or shame
- extreme sadness or loneliness
- anxiety or worry

These feelings may be accompanied by some, or all, of the following actions:

- drug or alcohol abuse
- talking or writing about death or destruction
- aggression
- recklessness

These feelings or actions are warnings—cries for help. Talking to a person in such a situation may not be enough. If they could help themselves or "get over it," they would. It's as though they've fallen in a well—and they need your help.

If *you* are in the well, reach out to someone who can pull you up and out.

(Based on Maureen Underwood and John Kalafat, *Lifelines: A Suicide Prevention Program* [Center City, MN: Hazelden, 2009]; and an online article from Hazelden, "Preventing Teen Suicide.")

FOCUS QUESTION

How does the Sacrament of Confirmation help you **ASSUME THE RESPONSIBILITIES** of Christian life?

INTRODUCTION
The Sacrament of the Holy Spirit

The Holy Spirit hovers over such chaos as alluded to in the story of Kate and her suicide attempt. In difficult times, he is there, just as he was at creation, breathing new life into humankind. Confirmation, the subject of this chapter, is a sacrament closely associated with the Holy Spirit. In cases like depression that might lead to suicide, ask the Holy Spirit to lead you and guide you to do the right thing for a friend.

Pope Francis has preached on the Sacrament of Confirmation:

> Dear brothers and sisters, let us remember that we have received Confirmation! All of us! Let us remember it, first in order to thank the Lord for this gift, and then to ask him to help us to live as true Christians, to walk always with joy in the Holy Spirit who has been given to us. (General Audience, January 29, 2014)

Pope Francis emphasized a key word in understanding the meaning of the sacrament: *gift*. Much of the instruction around preparation for Confirmation focuses on learning about how the sacrament is a "gift of the Holy Spirit." Also, candidates are often asked to commit to memory the seven gifts of the Holy Spirit imparted at Confirmation. This chapter will share both information about these gifts and reasons why it is important, as Pope Francis said, to express gratitude for them.

Baptism, Confirmation, and Eucharist constitute the Sacraments of Christian Initiation. All three are necessary for your initiation into the Church to be complete. At Baptism, you are reborn as a son or daughter of God and called to publicly profess the faith you have received from the Church. Confirmation increases and deepens the grace you receive at Baptism; it unites you more firmly to Christ and makes your bond with his Church more perfect. It also gives you a special strength of the Holy Spirit to spread and defend the faith. Eucharist is the culmination of Christian initiation.

NOTE TAKING

Capturing Key Concepts. As you read through this section, summarize the key points associated with each of the following concepts.

- Sacraments of Christian Initiation
- the Holy Spirit as the source of holiness
- Profession of Faith as it relates to Baptism, Confirmation, and Eucharist
- the Holy Spirit at work in your life

Pope Francis is cheered by the faithful as he arrives for his weekly General Audience in St. Peter's Square at the Vatican.

The Holy Spirit is the source of holiness and love in the Church and the bond of unity among all Christians. As Pope Francis explained, without Confirmation your journey toward membership into the Church remains unfinished and at a "midpoint":

> It is important to take care that our children, our young people, receive this sacrament. We all take care that they are baptized and this is good, but perhaps we do not take so much care that they are confirmed. Thus they remain at a midpoint in their journey and do not receive the Holy Spirit, who is so important in the Christian life since he gives us the strength to go on. (General Audience, January 29, 2014)

The Holy Spirit Is at Work in Your Life

Confirmation conforms those who receive it into the image of Christ. Pope Francis further explained the effect of Confirmation:

> Confirmation, like every sacrament, is not the work of men but of God, who cares for our lives in such a manner as to mold us in the image of his Son, to make us capable of loving like him. He does it by infusing in us his Holy Spirit, whose action pervades the whole person and his entire life, as reflected in the seven gifts that Tradition, in light of the Sacred Scripture, has always highlighted. (General Audience, January 29, 2014)

During the Rite of Confirmation, as the bishop begins the rite of the sacrament—the laying on of hands, the anointing with sacred chrism, and the words "Be sealed with the Gift of the Holy Spirit"—he faces the candidates and the rest of the gathered faithful and prays,

> My dear friends:
> In Baptism God our Father gave the new birth
> of eternal life
> to his chosen sons and daughters.
> Let us pray to our Father
> that he will pour out the Holy Spirit
> to strengthen his sons and daughters with his gifts
> and anoint them to be more like Christ the Son
> of God.

After a short time of silent prayer, the bishop asks God the Father, through his Son, Jesus Christ, to send the Holy Spirit to help and guide the candidates: "Give them the spirit of wisdom and understanding, the spirit of right judgment and courage, the spirit of knowledge and reverence. Fill them with the spirit of wonder and awe in your presence" (*Rite of Confirmation*, 41, 42).

The gifts of the Holy Spirit, which you will learn about in more detail in Section 3, enable you to live as a disciple of Christ in all aspects of your life. These gifts are not magically infused into you. However, if you are open to receiving these gifts, they have several benefits. The gifts of the Spirit enrich and strengthen your prayer life and your communion with the Blessed Trinity. They give you the courage to always act with moral integrity and to reject choices that wound your holiness and virtue. They give you wisdom to lead others to holiness and virtue by your words and example. They help you use the talents and gifts that God has given you to honor and serve him. They help you say yes to God's will always, to give him greater glory, and to attain for yourself eternal life with the Blessed Trinity.

Of course, newly given gifts are often not used on the spot. Think of gifts received on Christmas morning. They may be opened before breakfast but then overlooked until the festivities are over or until an even later time. But any valuable gift will eventually find use. The graces of the Sacrament of Confirmation work like that. Over time, the evidence of the Holy Spirit's power and gifts can be dramatic.

This chapter will cover more about the effects of the Sacrament of Confirmation. You will also consider the origins of Confirmation, how it is celebrated, and ways the gift of the Holy Spirit and the particular seven gifts of the Spirit transform those who receive them.

SECTION ASSESSMENT

NOTE TAKING

Use your notes on the key points of the main concepts of this section to help you complete the following items.

1. Briefly describe each of the three Sacraments of Christian Initiation.
2. How does the Holy Spirit strengthen the Church?

COMPREHENSION

3. What is the source of the Church's understanding of the seven gifts of the Holy Spirit?
4. What did Pope Francis mean when he said that those who do not receive Confirmation remain at a "midpoint" in their Christian initiation?

REFLECTION

5. If you have made your Confirmation, what were your reasons for doing so? If you haven't made your Confirmation, what would be some reasons you might seek out this sacrament for yourself?

SECTION 1
Understanding the Sacrament of Confirmation

MAIN IDEA
Christ instituted the Sacrament of Confirmation, which has been celebrated since apostolic times. Later, different traditions emerged in the way the sacrament was celebrated in the Eastern and Western Churches.

The Holy Spirit's connection with God's Chosen People and the promised Messiah has been present from the beginning. Since Old Testament times, the Spirit of the Lord has been associated with the hoped-for Messiah and his saving mission. The Holy Spirit perfects your mission, as a disciple of Christ and intimately united with him through Baptism, to share the Good News of Jesus with all.

In the Old Testament, the Book of Isaiah foretold that the Holy Spirit would rest on the Messiah. That prophecy was fulfilled in the Holy Spirit's descent upon Jesus at his Baptism (see Luke 3:21–22). Early in his public ministry, as recorded in Luke 4:16–22a, Christ quoted Isaiah 61:1 regarding his own mission:

> The spirit of the Lord GOD is upon me,
> because the LORD has anointed me;
> He has sent me to bring good news to the afflicted,
> to bind up the brokenhearted,
> To proclaim liberty to the captives,
> release to the prisoners. (Is 61:1)

The Spirit that descended upon Jesus at his own Baptism was communicated to all who heard and accepted his message. This fulfilled the words of the prophet Ezekiel: "I will give you a new heart, and a new spirit I will put within you. I will remove the heart

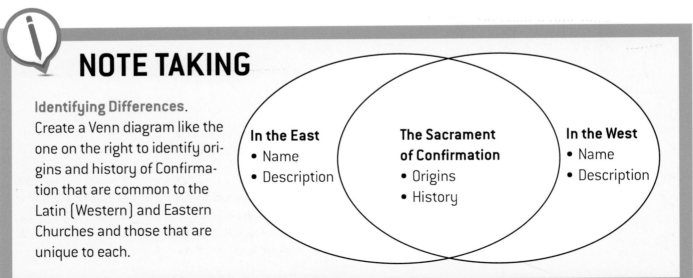

NOTE TAKING

Identifying Differences.
Create a Venn diagram like the one on the right to identify origins and history of Confirmation that are common to the Latin (Western) and Eastern Churches and those that are unique to each.

In the East
- Name
- Description

The Sacrament of Confirmation
- Origins
- History

In the West
- Name
- Description

of stone from your flesh and give you a heart of flesh" (Ez 36:26).

Throughout his public ministry, Jesus promised his followers the outpouring of the Holy Spirit:

- While preaching to his disciples about facing persecution, he said, "When they take you before synagogues and before rulers and authorities, do not worry about how or what your defense will be or about what you are to say. For the holy Spirit will teach you at that moment what you should say" (Lk 12:11–12).

- In answering the question of the Pharisee Nicodemus about how a person who is grown can be "born again," Jesus said, "The wind blows where it wills, and you can hear the sound it makes, but you do not know where it comes from or where it goes; so it is with everyone who is born of the Spirit" (Jn 3:8).

- At the Last Supper, Jesus promised that after he returned to the Father he would send the Advocate: "If I do not go, the Advocate will not come to you. But if I go, I will send him to you" (Jn 16:7).

Jesus' promise was fulfilled on Pentecost, when the Holy Spirit descended upon the Apostles, with Mary in their midst:

> When the time for Pentecost was fulfilled, they were all in one place together. And suddenly there came from the sky a noise like a strong driving wind, and it filled the entire house in which they were. Then there appeared to them tongues as of fire, which parted and came to rest on each of them. And they were all filled with the holy Spirit and began to speak in different tongues. (Acts 2:1–4)

The Holy Spirit helped the Apostles bear true witness to Jesus, just as he had assured them before his Ascension: "You will receive power when the holy Spirit comes upon you, and you will be my witnesses in Jerusalem, throughout Judea and Samaria, and to the ends of the earth" (Acts 1:8).

Origins of the Sacrament of Confirmation

Once the Holy Spirit came upon the Apostles, the effect was permanent. The Advocate that Jesus had sent was with them always. He "remains with you, and will be in you" (Jn 14:17). From the time of Pentecost, the Apostles imparted on the newly baptized the gift of the Holy Spirit by the laying on of hands. The imposition of hands completed the graces of Baptism and is "rightly recognized by the Catholic tradition as the origin of the Sacrament of Confirmation, which in a certain way perpetuates the grace of Pentecost in the Church" (*CCC*, 1288, quoting Pope Paul VI).

The laying on of hands has been a sign of the descent of the Holy Spirit since the time of Pentecost. This action transmits the grace of Pentecost in the Church. The Letter to the Hebrews describes the laying on of hands as one of the basic teachings of the Apostles (see Hebrews 6:2). When the Apostles laid their hands on the newly baptized, they were giving a divine blessing and imparting the gift of the Holy Spirit. For example, Peter and John went to Samaria to pray and lay hands on those who had accepted the Word of God and already been baptized: "Then they laid hands on them and they received the holy Spirit" (Acts 8:17). The same thing happens in Confirmation today. When the bishop extends his hands over, or

> **Advocate** A name for the Holy Spirit, who will live in you and guide you to truth.
>
> **laying on of hands** A gesture that is part of the essential rite and origin of the Sacrament of Confirmation. Acts 19:1–6 tells the story of a new group of disciples who, after being baptized, received the Holy Spirit when St. Paul laid hands on them.

imposes his hands on, candidates for Confirmation, the Holy Spirit rests upon them and comes to dwell within them.

Very early in the development of the Sacrament of Confirmation, an anointing with perfumed oil called *sacred chrism* was added to the laying on of hands. This anointing highlights the name "Christian," which means "anointed" and is derived from the name of Christ himself, the "anointed one." As Pope Francis explained in his teaching on Confirmation, "through the oil we are conformed, in the power of the Spirit, to Jesus Christ, who is the only true 'anointed one,' the 'Holy One of God'" (General Audience, January 29, 2014).

Chrism is a mixture of olive oil (which by its rich and abundant nature symbolizes the Holy Spirit's overflowing outpouring of grace) and balsam (a fragrant perfume—sometimes referred to as "the balm of Gilead"—used in healing and preservation from corruption). The balsam symbolizes the sweet "odor" of Christianity, found in virtuous living and imitation of Christ (see 2 Corinthians 2:15). Those who are anointed with sacred chrism have a new identity—that of Christians, who share in Christ's mission and have the special duty of proclaiming his Gospel to the world. Oil is a sign of abundance; it cleanses and limbers; it is a sign of healing; and it suffuses those who are anointed with beauty, health, and strength (see *CCC,* 1293).

Anointing with sacred chrism has been part of the Rite of Confirmation since the early Church in both the East and West. The name for Confirmation in the Eastern Church, *Chrismation*, specifically recalls this anointing. In the Western Church, the name *Confirmation* affirms that this sacrament confirms and strengthens the graces of Baptism.

> **Chrismation** The name in the Eastern rites for the Sacrament of Confirmation. It comes from the chrism used as part of the sacrament.

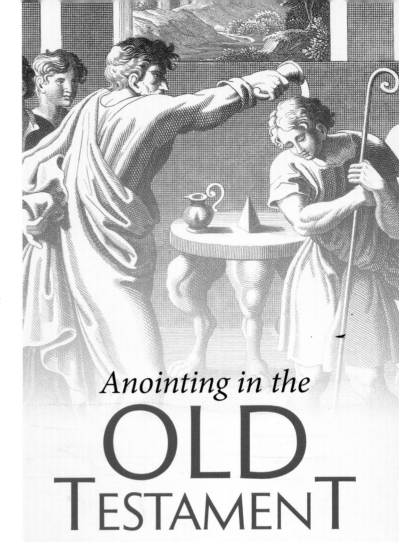

Anointing in the OLD TESTAMENT

The anointing with consecrated oil that takes place in the Rite of Confirmation can be traced back to the Old Testament, where both objects and people were anointed to dedicate them to special service to God.

- Among the objects anointed in the Old Testament were the Ark of the Covenant, the tent of meeting, and the furniture of the tent (see Exodus 30:22–33).
- Among the people anointed were priests and kings. For example, when God selected David to be king of Israel, he was anointed by the prophet Samuel: "Then Samuel, with the horn of oil in hand, anointed [David] in the midst of his brothers, and from that day on, the spirit of the Lord rushed upon David" (1 Sm 16:13).

Confirmation in the East and in the West

Two traditions of the Sacrament of Confirmation emerged in the East and the West. Recall that Christian initiation is accomplished in the three Sacraments of Christian Initiation: Baptism (which confers new life), Confirmation (which strengthens that new life), and the Eucharist (which nourishes the Christian life through the Body and Blood of Christ).

In the early centuries of the Church, Confirmation was generally part of one single celebration with Baptism. St. Cyprian (ca. AD 200–258) called the celebration a "double sacrament." This "double sacrament" was administered by the bishop. Over time, however, as the number of infant Baptisms increased and Christianity spread out over a growing number of rural parishes in ever-larger dioceses, it became increasingly difficult for bishops to be present at each baptismal celebration. The bishop began to limit his visits to parishes to either annual or biannual frequency. This practical reality led to the development of two traditions for celebrating the Sacrament of Confirmation, one in the East and one in the West.

In the West, the practice of the double anointing that took place after Baptism—first by the priest,

Confirmation, whether it is celebrated with Baptism or some years later, recalls a person's Baptism and completes the graces of Baptism. The Rite of Confirmation highlights the intimate connection between Confirmation and Baptism. For example:

1 The Rite of Christian Initiation for Adults calls for all converts to celebrate Baptism, Confirmation, and the Eucharist at the same Easter Vigil.

2 Each **confirmand** (plural is *confirmandi*) is encouraged to use his or her baptismal name as a Confirmation name. This is usually the name of a canonized saint or Christian hero who inspires the person to be a good Christian.

3 The Church encourages baptismal godparents also to act as Confirmation sponsors (see *Code of Canon Law*, 893 § 2 and *CCC*, 1311). It is the sponsor's duty "to see that the confirmed person acts as a true witness of Christ and faithfully fulfills the obligations connected with this sacrament" (*Code of Canon Law*, 892).

4 The Rite of Confirmation, if celebrated separately from Baptism—as is the practice in the Roman Catholic Church—includes a public renewal of baptismal promises and a profession of faith. This shows that Confirmation follows Baptism.

In Confirmation, you remember that you are Christ's own possession. You also remember how the Holy Spirit has been working in your life since your Baptism to make you a stronger and more committed Christian.

> **confirmand** A candidate for Confirmation.

signifying that the person baptized participates in the prophetic, priestly, and kingly offices of Christ, and then by the bishop—facilitated the development of the practice of separate celebrations for the Sacraments of Baptism and Confirmation. The Roman Church (in the West) sought to maintain the explicit connection between the Sacrament of Confirmation and the bishop. This connection with the bishop signifies that the Church is one, catholic (universal), and apostolic, because every bishop—through the laying on of hands in the Sacrament of Holy Orders—traces his authority back to the Apostles. Recall that this is called apostolic succession. Thus, in the West the celebration of the two sacraments was separated, with Baptism taking place in infancy, with the priest as the ordinary minister. Confirmation was delayed until the bishop could be present. This remains the practice of the Roman Catholic Church today.

In the East, the Sacraments of Christian Initiation remained united, emphasizing the unity of Christian initiation. Like Baptism, Confirmation (or Chrismation) is conferred by the priest, using sacred chrism (called *myron*, a Greek word) consecrated by the bishop, thus expressing the apostolic unity of the Church. Today, in the Eastern Churches, Baptism is immediately followed by Confirmation and the reception of the Eucharist (including for infants).

SECTION ASSESSMENT

NOTE TAKING

Use your Venn diagram to help you complete the following items.

1. Summarize the origins of the Sacrament of Confirmation. Include at least one reference from the Old Testament.

2. Summarize the history of the celebration of the Sacrament of Confirmation in the early Church.

3. Describe ways in which the celebration of Confirmation differs between the Churches of the East and West. Provide details of how such differences emerged.

COMPREHENSION

4. Explain the significance of the laying on of hands in Confirmation.

5. Explain the significance of anointing with sacred chrism during the Rite of Confirmation.

CRITICAL THINKING

6. Jesus said to Nicodemus: "The wind blows where it wills, and you can hear the sound it makes, but you do not know where it comes from or where it goes; so it is with everyone who is born of the Spirit" (Jn 3:8). Write a paragraph explaining how Jesus' statement applies to the Sacrament of Confirmation.

Celebrating the Sacrament of Confirmation

MAIN IDEA

The celebration of Confirmation ordinarily takes place at Mass. Essential elements of the Rite of Confirmation include the laying on of hands and anointing with sacred chrism, accompanied by the words, "Be sealed with the Gift of the Holy Spirit."

The Sacrament of Confirmation actually begins before the date of the sacrament. The beginning of the celebration can be traced to the **Chrism Mass** that occurs during the Holy Week that precedes Confirmation. At the Chrism Mass, the bishop consecrates the sacred chrism and the other oils used in the diocese throughout the year. Only the bishop can bless the sacred chrism. Thus, whenever it is used in a sacrament (Baptism, Confirmation, or Holy Orders) in parishes

> **Chrism Mass** An annual Mass, celebrated in a diocesan cathedral on or near Holy Thursday, in which the bishop consecrates the sacred chrism and other oils that will be used in the diocese throughout the year.

throughout his diocese, the sacred chrism reminds Catholics of the authority and approval of the bishop as the official successor of the Apostles. In some Eastern Churches, this consecration is reserved to the *patriarch* (a leading bishop).

The celebration of Confirmation itself ordinarily takes place at Mass to emphasize the fundamental connection of this sacrament with all of Christian initiation, which reaches its culmination in the Eucharist (see *Rite of Confirmation*, 13). As does every other liturgy, the Sacrament of Confirmation begins with the Introductory Rites of the Mass; candidates, sponsors, and families gather with the assembly, and the Mass proceeds in its regular order.

The Rite of Confirmation

The Rite of Confirmation takes place during the Liturgy of the Word portion of Mass. The Rite of Confirmation

NOTE TAKING

Summarizing Main Ideas. Create an outline like the one below to identify the parts of the Confirmation liturgy and summarize what takes place during each part. Two items have been started for you.

A. Rite of Confirmation
  1. Scripture Readings
    a. Special emphasis is placed on the Word of God because through it the Holy Spirit flows out upon the Church.
    b.
  2. The Presentation of the Candidates
    a. After the Gospel, a catechist, deacon, or priest presents the candidates for Confirmation to the bishop.
    b.

stresses that special focus should be given to the celebration of God's Word because through the Word of God the Holy Spirit flows out upon the Body of Christ and all the baptized. The parts of the rite are explained in the next sections.

The Presentation of the Candidates

After the Gospel, a catechist, deacon, or priest presents the candidates for Confirmation to the bishop. If possible, each candidate's name is read aloud, and the person comes forward individually to meet the bishop.

Homily

In the homily that follows, according to some local customs, the bishop may conduct a question-and-answer dialogue with the confirmandi to make sure they understand the meaning of Confirmation.

Renewal of Baptismal Promises

After the homily, the candidates publicly renew their baptismal promises, promising to reject Satan and professing their faith in the Blessed Trinity and in the Church. The bishop confirms their profession of faith by proclaiming the faith of the Church with these words: "This is our faith. This is the faith of the Church. We are proud to profess it in Christ Jesus the Lord." The entire assembly responds: "Amen" (*Rite of Confirmation*, 23).

Invocation of the Outpouring of the Spirit

After the Profession of Faith, the bishop extends his hands over the whole group, praying for the outpouring of the Holy Spirit. He prays:

> All-powerful God, Father of our Lord Jesus Christ,
> by water and the Holy Spirit

Confirmation READINGS

The following are three Scripture passages that may be read at the Confirmation liturgy. Read all three; then write a two- or three-paragraph reflection on their meaning, especially what they might mean for a confirmand.

FIRST READING
Isaiah 61:1–3a, 6a, 8b–9

SECOND READING
Romans 5:1–2, 5–8

GOSPEL
John 14:15–17

> you freed your sons and daughters from sin
> and gave them new life.
> Send your Holy Spirit upon them
> to be their helper and guide.
> Give them the spirit of wisdom and understanding,
> the spirit of right judgment and courage,
> the spirit of knowledge and reverence.
> Fill them with the spirit of wonder and awe in
> your presence.
> We ask this through Christ our Lord. Amen.

(*Rite of Confirmation*, 25)

The Laying on of Hands and Anointing with Sacred Chrism

The laying on of hands by the bishop accompanies the anointing with sacred chrism. The laying on of hands communicates the grace of the Holy Spirit and continues the laying on of hands by the Apostles to those who were newly baptized. From the Church's origins, the laying on of hands was understood to impart the gift of the Holy Spirit and complete the graces of Baptism.

A bishop and priest pose with newly confirmed teenagers after confirmation ceremonies.

The anointing is the essential rite of Confirmation. It is often a deacon who brings the sacred chrism to the bishop as each candidate comes forward with his or her sponsor. The sponsor gives the candidate's name to the bishop and places his or her right hand on the candidate's right shoulder. The bishop dips his right thumb in the chrism and then makes the Sign of the Cross with his thumb on the forehead of the person being confirmed. Simultaneously,

> he says: "N., be sealed with the Gift of the Holy Spirit."
>
> The newly confirmed responds: "Amen."
>
> The bishop says: "Peace be with you."
>
> The newly confirmed responds: "And with your spirit." (*Rite of Confirmation,* 27)

> **particular judgment** The individual judgment of every person right after death, when Christ will rule on his or her eternal destiny in heaven (after purification in Purgatory, if needed) or in hell.

The Sign of Peace signifies unity with the bishop and with all the faithful.

In the Eastern Churches, the forehead, eyes, nose, ears, lips, chest, back, hands, and feet are anointed with *myron.* Each anointing is accompanied by the words "The seal of the Holy Spirit."

The anointing at Confirmation likewise signifies and imprints a spiritual seal, a grace or effect of the sacrament (see pages 121–128) on those already incorporated into Christ by Baptism. This seal is a sign of identity and ownership. Just as God the Father set his seal on Jesus (see John 6:27), so God puts his seal on those who are confirmed through the anointing by the bishop. Christian discipleship is truly authenticated by the Sacrament of Confirmation: "This seal of the Holy Spirit marks our total belonging to Christ, our enrollment in his service for ever" (*CCC,* 1296). The spiritual seal also gives the newly confirmed the promise of divine protection at the time of his or her death and **particular judgment.**

General Intercessions

After all the candidates have been confirmed, the **General Intercessions** are prayed. These prayers are for the newly confirmed, their sponsors, and their families. The prayers also ask God to help everyone in the Church to be open to the gifts of the Holy Spirit and give witness to the Gospel of Jesus (see *Rite of Confirmation*, 30).

The celebration continues with the Liturgy of the Eucharist. The Creed is omitted because the Profession of Faith was made by the candidates in their renewal of baptismal promises. Some of the newly confirmed may join in bringing the gifts to the altar. Special importance is attached to the praying of the Lord's Prayer because it is the Holy Spirit who moves the Church to pray. It is only in the Holy Spirit that you can call God "Father" (see *Rite of Confirmation*, 13).

After Communion, the bishop prays a special blessing over the newly confirmed and all the assembled people, asking the Blessed Trinity—Father, Son, and Holy Spirit—to watch over them with fatherly love, bless them and give them courage, and keep them one in faith and love, that they might know the joy of God's kingdom (see *Rite of Confirmation*, 33).

Who Can Be Confirmed?

Every baptized person who is not yet confirmed can and should receive the Sacrament of Confirmation. Because Baptism, Confirmation, and the Eucharist form a unity, all three sacraments are essential for Christian initiation to be complete. Without Confirmation and the Eucharist, Baptism is certainly valid and efficacious, but Christian initiation remains unfinished.

Along with having been baptized, to be eligible for Confirmation a candidate must have attained the **age of reason** (also called the "age of discretion"), be in a state of grace and have received the Sacrament of Penance and Reconciliation, profess the faith, and commit to live as a disciple of Jesus Christ.

In the Roman Catholic Church, the age of reason has been used for centuries as the reference point for receiving Confirmation (see *CCC*, 1307). The Rite of Confirmation allows the bishops of individual nations to name the appropriate age for Confirmation. In the United States, the age of Confirmation varies from diocese to diocese; the local bishop can designate it anywhere from the age of reason to about age sixteen. According to these age guidelines, reception of the Sacrament of Confirmation follows that of First Eucharist, which usually takes place around age seven. If a child is in danger of death, however, the child should be confirmed even if he or she has not attained the age of reason.

Of course, it's important to remember that, although Confirmation has been called "the sacrament of Christian maturity," a mature faith is not necessarily commensurate with chronological age. As St. Thomas Aquinas said, "Age of body does not determine age of soul." Nor is baptismal grace a gift you earn; instead, it is a free, unmerited gift of God, given to you out of love.

Some dioceses have adopted the "restored order" for the Sacraments of Christian Initiation. In the restored order, Baptism is followed by Confirmation rather than by the Eucharist. Thus, a baptized child who has reached the age of reason will receive Confirmation followed by First Eucharist in the same liturgy, usually around second grade.

Preparing for Confirmation

The Church requires adequate preparation and instruction for reception of Confirmation. Preparation

> **General Intercessions** Also called the Prayer of the Faithful; prayers of petition for the sake of others.
>
> **age of reason** Also called the "age of discretion," the age (typically the end of the seventh year) at which a person becomes capable of moral reasoning.

This image, Confirmation Mass *by Giulio Rosati, shows how the entire Church is involved in confirming new members.*

should aim at leading a Christian to "a more intimate union with Christ and a more lively familiarity with the Holy Spirit" (*CCC,* 1309). The preparation time should encourage a greater participation and belonging in the life of the universal Church and the parish community.

The candidate should also commit to more intense prayer in order to be prepared to receive and act on the graces of the Holy Spirit. To help in the preparation, candidates seek the spiritual help of a sponsor. To be qualified to be a Confirmation sponsor, a person must have received all three Sacraments of Christian Initiation, be at least sixteen years old, and lead "a life in harmony with the faith and the role to be undertaken" (*Code of Canon Law,* 874; see *CCC,* 1311). To emphasize the unity with Baptism, the sponsor appropriately could be one of the baptismal godparents.

The Minister of the Sacrament

In the Latin Church, the "ordinary minister" of the Sacrament of Confirmation is the bishop. Bishops are successors of the Apostles. They have received the fullness of the Sacrament of Holy Orders. Their personal administering of Confirmation clearly demonstrates that the effect of the sacrament is to unite those who receive it more closely to the Church, to the Apostles, and to the mission of bearing witness to Christ.

There are circumstances when a priest may confer Confirmation. As already mentioned, a priest (using the sacred chrism consecrated by the bishop) is typically the minister of Confirmation for adults who receive all three Sacraments of Christian Initiation at the Easter Vigil. Also, a priest can confer Confirmation if a person is in danger of death.

In the Eastern Churches, the priest is the ordinary minister of Confirmation and confers the sacrament immediately after Baptism. However, recall that in the East, the unity with the bishop is preserved in this sacrament especially through the sacred chrism, which has been consecrated by the bishop or patriarch, thus expressing the apostolic unity of the Church.

SECTION ASSESSMENT

NOTE TAKING

Use the outline you created to help you answer the following questions.

1. Why is special emphasis placed on the Word of God during the Confirmation liturgy?
2. When does the renewal of baptismal promises take place during the Confirmation liturgy?
3. What does the bishop say when he anoints a person with sacred chrism at Confirmation?
4. What does this anointing symbolize?

COMPREHENSION

5. What is the essential rite of Confirmation?
6. Why can it be said that the celebration of Confirmation begins before the conferring of the sacrament?
7. How does the sacred chrism used in Confirmation remind Catholics of the authority of the bishop as a successor of the Apostles?

CRITICAL THINKING

8. In the United States, dioceses may set the age for the Sacrament of Confirmation between the age of reason and age sixteen. Name some positive reasons for the celebration of Confirmation at each of the following ages: second grade, junior high, and high school.

SECTION 3
The Graces of the Sacrament of Confirmation

MAIN IDEA
Confirmation imprints your soul with an indelible spiritual mark, or character, that is the sign that Jesus has marked you with the seal of his Spirit. Through Confirmation, you are called and strengthened to live as a Gospel witness in all that you do.

The graces received in Confirmation must be discussed together with those received at Baptism. Confirmation completes Baptism and perfects baptismal grace. It also

- helps you become a more perfect image of Christ;
- makes you a more complete member of his Body;
- strengthens you to live as a Gospel witness in all that you do; and
- intensifies your relationship with the Holy Spirit, who lives within you and helps you to be more receptive, more open, to his gifts.

Through Baptism, you die to sin and rise to new life with the Blessed Trinity. You become God's adopted son or daughter. You become a brother or sister of Jesus Christ. And you become a temple of the Holy Spirit. You are united with the Trinity. You breathe in divine grace and love. You share in God's own life.

Like the blood that flows through your body to keep it functioning in a healthy way, Confirmation keeps you spiritually functioning throughout life. Confirmation helps you grow and mature in faith. That is why St. Thomas Aquinas once said that Confirmation is to Baptism what growth is to generation (see *Summa Theologica* 3.72.6). Confirmation helps you grow as part of the Body of Christ and develop spiritually.

Like Baptism, Confirmation is given only once, since it, too, imprints on your soul an indelible spiritual mark, or character. Confirmation perfects the common priesthood of the faithful, received in Baptism, and allows you to testify to your faith in Christ. Yet although you receive the sacrament only once, receiving the gift of the Holy Spirit is not a one-time, fleeting event. Instead, Confirmation acts continuously within you, providing you with the necessary spiritual gifts needed to grow closer to God.

NOTE TAKING

Connecting Concepts. Create a word web around the concepts Gifts of the Holy Spirit and Effects of Confirmation. To make a word web, draw lines from the circle to key words and phrases that will help you understand the meaning of the concept.

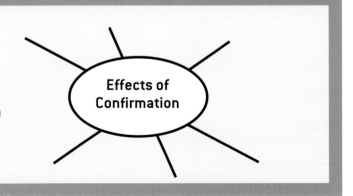

Effects of Confirmation

The greatest effect of Confirmation is the special outpouring of the Holy Spirit, much in the same way the Holy Spirit once came to the Apostles at Pentecost. And just as the coming of the Holy Spirit imparted upon the Apostles both gifts and responsibilities, Confirmation communicates to you both gifts, or effects, and their corresponding responsibilities.

The Effects of the
Sacrament of Confirmation

- You are rooted more deeply in the *divine filiation*—that is, in your adoption as a child of God.

- You are united more firmly to Christ.

- The gifts of the Holy Spirit are increased in you.

- Your bond with the Church is strengthened.

- You are given a special strength of the Holy Spirit to spread and defend the faith by word and action as a true witness of Christ, to confess the name of Christ boldly, and never to be ashamed to call yourself a Christian. (See *CCC*, 1303.)

Each of these effects of the Sacrament of Confirmation is covered in more detail in the next sections.

You Are Able to Live as a Child of God

Your Baptism helps you experience what being a son or daughter of God means. St. Paul's Letter to the Romans teaches, "Those who are led by the Spirit of God are children of God. For you did not receive a spirit of slavery to fall back into fear, but you received a spirit of adoption, through which we cry, 'Abba, Father!'" (Rom 8:14–15).

Being a child of God is an intimate part of your identity. When you have truly experienced God as your Father, you are more firmly established as a member of his family. You have a firsthand experience, a familiarity, with the Blessed Trinity.

You Are United to Christ

Confirmation "unites [you] more firmly to Christ" (*CCC*, 1303). It helps you "more perfectly become the image" of Christ (Christian Initiation 2, General Introduction, *The Rites*). The Holy Spirit comes to you in the sacrament and helps you pray always and continually renew and deepen your relationship with Christ. St. Paul explained that "the Spirit too comes to the aid of our weakness; for we do not know how to pray as we ought, but the Spirit itself intercedes with inexpressible groanings" (Rom 8:26). The grace you receive at

Confirmation also nurtures your faith and helps you remain faithful to Christ.

You Receive the Gifts of the Holy Spirit

Confirmation "increases the gifts of the Holy Spirit in us" (*CCC*, 1303). The Church has traditionally defined these seven gifts as wisdom, understanding, counsel, fortitude, knowledge, piety, and fear of the Lord. The scriptural source of these gifts of the Holy Spirit is Isaiah 11:2–3. These gifts were perfectly present in the person of Jesus. They work within you and help you grow in holiness, faith, and union with the Blessed Trinity. They help you listen more closely to God's Word and act on that Word in daily life. Consider the effects of each gift.

GIFT	SOME ADDITIONAL DETAILS	HELPS OR ENABLES YOU TO . . .
Wisdom 	The word *wisdom* comes from a German word (*wissen*) and is long associated with prudence and self-control.	value what is most important in life and keep your priorities straight. seek God's Kingdom first (see Matthew 6:33) and make everything else less important. see yourself, others, and God clearly—as God does.
Understanding 	This gift can help with the larger mysteries of life.	see "the bigger picture" and the real meaning or truth, not just the way things seem on the surface. see "the spirit" behind God's laws and not just "the letter of the laws." put yourself "in the shoes" of others, so that you can empathize with them and show compassion.

GIFT	SOME ADDITIONAL DETAILS	HELPS OR ENABLES YOU TO . . .
Counsel 	Counsel is also called *right judgment*. It relies on the virtue of prudence.	make good decisions, based on the desire to do God's will. seek advice from trusted others. give good advice to others as they try to live their Christian faith.
Fortitude 	Fortitude is also called *courage*.	stand up for your beliefs and remain true to them even in the face of hardship. overcome obstacles that arise in the practice of your faith. use your God-given talents bravely. reach out to others in loving service.
Knowledge 	This gift allows you both to know God and to be known in more unique ways.	open yourself to be known by God in a deeper way. learn more about him and about the faith of the Church.
Piety 	The word *piety* means "faithful obedience and love." It is also called *reverence*.	give God true worship and praise. show proper respect for God and for everything he has made. put your trust in God and not only listen to but also follow his Word.
Fear of the Lord 	Fear of the Lord is also called *wonder and awe*.	be receptive to God's loving presence in your life. never underestimate God or think you have him completely figured out. fear offending God.

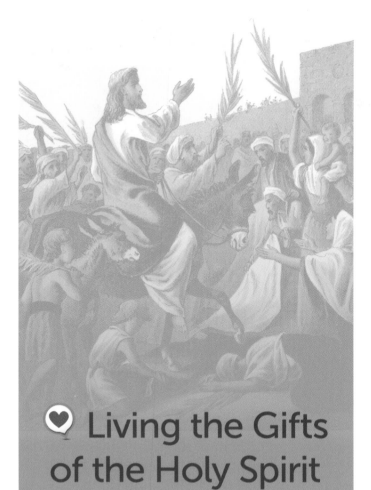

♥ Living the Gifts of the Holy Spirit

All of Jesus' earthly life embodied the gifts of the Holy Spirit. As a child and an adolescent, he grew in wisdom; later he expressed that wisdom in his parables. Jesus understood the poor and the sick as well as the true motives of the people who came to him. Jesus always used right judgment, even when some perceived his actions as a violation of the Law. He courageously went to Jerusalem knowing he would be arrested and crucified. As God's Son, Jesus had special knowledge of the Father. Jesus never took the world or people for granted. He loved all of nature.

Select one of the gifts of the Holy Spirit. Find an example from the Gospels showing how Jesus expressed this gift in his life and actions. Then write a paragraph, poem, or prayer about how you could express this gift in your own life and actions.

You Form a Deeper Bond with the Church

The Sacrament of Confirmation strengthens your bond with the Church. It helps you become a member of the Church, the Body of Christ. The Second Vatican Council taught that "[the baptized faithful] are more perfectly bound to the Church by the sacrament of Confirmation, and the Holy Spirit endows them with special strength so that they are more strictly obliged to spread and defend the faith, both by word and by deed, as true witnesses of Christ" (*Lumen Gentium*, 11). Because of the Holy Spirit's presence and work within you, when you receive this sacrament you are *confirmed* as a member of the People of God, of the Church.

How can others tell you are a disciple of Christ and member of his Church? They can see in you the same gifts of the Spirit that Jesus had. They can see, by your attitude and actions, that you are a person of wisdom, understanding, counsel, fortitude, knowledge, piety, and fear of the Lord. Just as a gardener can judge a tree as good or bad by the fruit it produces, so people can judge you by the "fruit" you produce. The twelve **fruits of the Spirit** are charity, joy, peace, patience, kindness, goodness, generosity, gentleness, faithfulness, modesty, self-control, and chastity. When people see these virtues in you, they know that the Holy Spirit dwells in you. You are the one who hears the Word of the Lord and accepts it so that it bears fruit "thirty and sixty and a hundredfold" (Mk 4:20).

> **fruits of the Spirit** Perfections that result from living in union with the Holy Spirit.

You Receive a New Character

The spiritual character or mark you receive at Confirmation is a different one than you receive at Baptism. It is this indelible character that helps you to spread and defend the faith as a witness of Christ and to never be ashamed of the Cross. In other words, it enables you to know that you are a vital member of Christ's Body. As God's anointed, you share more completely in the mission of Jesus to spread the Gospel message (see *CCC*, 1294).

Catholics who have received Confirmation are subsequently required to live "in God's Spirit." As St. Paul told the Ephesians, "you should put away the old self of your former way of life, corrupted through deceitful desires, and be renewed in the spirit of your minds, and put on the new self, created in God's way in righteousness and holiness of truth" (Eph 4:22–24). The *Catechism of the Catholic Church* explains that Confirmation confers "a sacramental *character* or 'seal' by which the Christian shares in Christ's priesthood" (*CCC*, 1121). This character perfects the common priesthood of the faithful, received in Baptism, and confers on the confirmed person the power to profess faith in Christ publicly. Once you are sealed with the Holy Spirit, you are forever changed. It is for this reason that a person may be confirmed only once (see *CCC*, 1317).

Yet because the *effect* of Confirmation is continual and ongoing, its grace and gifts continue to strengthen your faith. Just as the human body grows and develops, so your spiritual life must also grow in grace and develop. Faith is not static or unchanging. It is not a "lump sum" quantity that you get once, and that is it. Instead, living faith is dynamic, evolving, and constantly changing. Faith grows as you grow emotionally, intellectually, socially, and physically. As faith evolves and matures, it becomes more sophisticated, more internalized. At the same time, it grows stronger, more unshakable. You believe less and less in worldly "idols" such as wealth, power, popularity, or possessions. Instead, you put your faith in what truly matters: the love of the Blessed Trinity—Father, Son, and Holy Spirit.

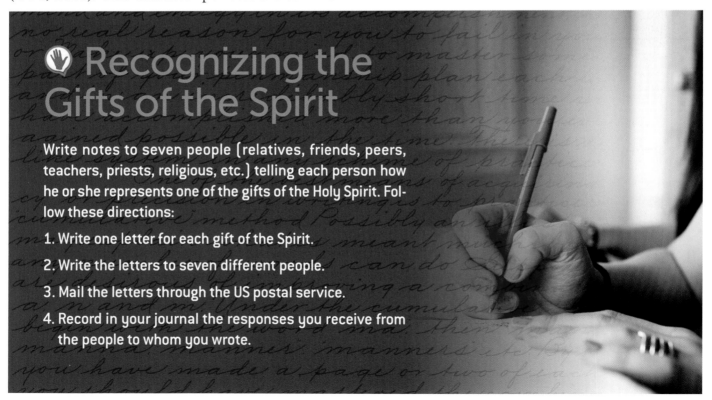

Recognizing the Gifts of the Spirit

Write notes to seven people (relatives, friends, peers, teachers, priests, religious, etc.) telling each person how he or she represents one of the gifts of the Holy Spirit. Follow these directions:

1. Write one letter for each gift of the Spirit.

2. Write the letters to seven different people.

3. Mail the letters through the US postal service.

4. Record in your journal the responses you receive from the people to whom you wrote.

THE GIFT OF SPEECH

Soeren Palumbo was confirmed at St. Theresa Catholic Church in Palatine, Illinois, when he was in eighth grade. Four years later, as a senior at Fremd High School, he gave the speech of a lifetime to his peers at a student assembly.

Palumbo spoke out against the use of the word *retard*, as teens and adults use it disrespectfully. Soeren's younger sister Olivia has an intellectual disability. Soeren told the audience that "your mockery of [the disabled]—it's nothing but another form of hatred." He explained in his speech:

Soeren Palumbo and his sister, Olivia

So why am I doing this? Why do I risk being misunderstood and resented by this school's student body and staff? I'm doing this because I know how much you can learn from people, from all people, even—no, not even, especially—the mentally handicapped.

I know this because every morning I wake up and I come downstairs and I sit across from my sister, quietly eating her Cheerios. And as I sit down, she sets her spoon down on the table and she looks at me. Her strawberry blonde hair hanging over her freckled face almost completely hides the question mark–shaped scar above her ear from her brain surgery two years ago.

She looks at me, and she smiles. . . . It lights up her face. Her front two teeth are faintly stained from the years of intense epilepsy medication, but I don't notice that anymore. I lean over to her and say, "Good morning, Olivia." She stares at me for a moment and says quickly, "Good morning, Soeren," and goes back to her Cheerios. . . .

She finishes her Cheerios and grabs her favorite blue backpack and waits for her bus driver, Miss Debbie, who like clockwork arrives at our house at exactly seven o'clock each morning. She gives me a quick hug goodbye and runs excitedly to the bus, ecstatic for another day of school.

And I watch the bus disappear around the turn, and I can't help but remember the jokes. The short bus. The retard rocket. No matter what she does, no matter how much she loves those around her, she will always be the butt of some immature kid's joke. She will always be the butt of some mature kid's joke. She will always be the butt of some adult's joke.

continued on next page

continued from previous page

By no fault of her own, she will spend her entire life being stared at and judged. Despite the fact that she will never hate, never judge, never make fun of, never hurt, she will never be accepted. That's why I'm doing this. I'm doing this because I don't think you understand how much you hurt others when you hate.

The student body and staff didn't misunderstand or resent Soeren. Instead they gave him a standing ovation. A YouTube broadcast of his speech attracted attention worldwide. The local television news and newspaper came to interview him about the speech. Months afterward the speech was still being talked about.

His mom, Kristen Palumbo, said, "Soeren loves his sister. He's protective of her. It's been a good thing. She is a gift." Of the feeling he got from giving the speech, Soeren recalled, "It was such a rush. I was crying at the end of it. But to look out and see everyone stand up and the other people wiping their eyes . . . to see all the warm acceptance that came with it was just out of this world."

The Holy Spirit brings those who are confirmed into conformity with Christ and enables them to spread Christ's presence to all. All in God's time.

SECTION ASSESSMENT

NOTE TAKING

Use the word web you created to help you complete the following items.

1. Name and briefly describe each of the effects of Confirmation.
2. Name the seven gifts of the Holy Spirit and describe two of them.

COMPREHENSION

3. How is Confirmation intimately connected with Baptism?
4. Why can a person be confirmed only once?

CRITICAL THINKING

5. Choose one of the gifts of the Holy Spirit. Write two paragraphs about how a person you know lives out that gift.
6. What does the indelible character you receive in Confirmation help you do?

REFLECTION

7. Write a paragraph telling how Confirmation helps a person to become a more complete and perfect image of Christ.

Section Summaries

Focus Question

How does the Sacrament of Confirmation help you assume the responsibilities of Christian life?

Complete one of the following:

 Write a prayer to the Holy Spirit in which you ask for guidance in helping a friend or another person experiencing challenges.

 If you have already celebrated the Sacrament of Confirmation, write a reflection about how the grace of the sacrament helps you live a life of Christian discipleship.

 Write a poem or song lyrics about one or more of the gifts of the Holy Spirit.

INTRODUCTION (PAGES 107–109)
The Sacrament of the Holy Spirit

Confirmation, a sacrament strongly associated with the Holy Spirit and the showering of his gifts on the confirmed, is the work of God, who cares for you and molds you in the image of his Son, to make you capable of loving like him. He accomplishes this by infusing in you his Holy Spirit. Without Confirmation, Christian initiation remains incomplete.

 Read paragraph 1285 of the *Catechism of the Catholic Church*. Summarize the paragraph in your own words, and use quotations from Pope Francis cited in this chapter's Introduction to support your summary.

SECTION 1 (PAGES 110–114)
Understanding the Sacrament of Confirmation

The Holy Spirit was at work in the lives of the Chosen People. At Jesus' Baptism, the Holy Spirit descended upon him, signaling that he was the long-awaited Messiah. At Pentecost, the Holy Spirit descended upon the Apostles. The Sacrament of Confirmation, instituted by Christ, has been celebrated since apostolic times. Over time, different traditions emerged in the way the sacrament was celebrated in the Eastern and Western Churches.

 Read three Scripture passages quoted or cited in Section 1, and explain what they communicate about the work of the Holy Spirit and about Confirmation.

SECTION 2 (PAGES 115–120)

Celebrating the Sacrament of Confirmation

The celebration of Confirmation begins at the Chrism Mass with the bishop's blessing of the sacred chrism. The Rite of Confirmation itself ordinarily takes place at Mass. Essential elements of the Rite of Confirmation include the laying on of hands and anointing with sacred chrism, accompanied by the words, "Be sealed with the Gift of the Holy Spirit."

 Name the parts of the Confirmation liturgy, starting with the Liturgy of the Word and ending with the Blessing, and briefly describe each.

SECTION 3 (PAGES 121–128)

The Graces of the Sacrament of Confirmation

Confirmation may be received only once because it marks you with an indelible character, which helps you spread and defend the faith as a witness of Christ. Among the graces of Confirmation is an infusion of the gifts of the Holy Spirit—wisdom, understanding, counsel, fortitude, knowledge, piety, and fear of the Lord.

 Explain the indelible character Confirmation imparts and its effects on those who receive the sacrament.

Chapter Assignments

Choose and complete at least one of the following three assignments assessing your understanding of the material in this chapter.

1. The Coat of Arms of the Bishop and Your Coat of Arms

Each bishop has his own coat of arms to represent who he is as a witness for Christ. Even Pope Francis, as bishop of Rome, has his own coat of arms. Research the seal of your own diocesan bishop. Then do the following:

- Either reproduce a copy of the coat of arms or draw a copy yourself. Draw lines from several parts of the coat of arms to caption boxes. In the caption boxes, write what the images, words, shapes, and colors tell about the bishop and the diocese.

- Design a coat of arms for yourself as a disciple of Christ following the pattern of the bishop's seal. Include at least five elements that depict something about your Christian faith. Label these with a number key. On a separate sheet of paper, write an explanation of what each numbered item stands for.

2. The Holy Spirit in Scripture

Both the Old and New Testaments tell of the working of the Holy Spirit, bringing life and hope to replace death and despair. Read the following Scripture passages, then complete the assignment that follows.

- Exodus 13:17–22 (the crossing of the Red Sea)

- Isaiah 11:1–9 (the Messiah will possess wisdom and understanding)

- Ezekiel 37:1–13 (the vision of dry bones)

- Acts of the Apostles 2:1–13 (the coming of the Holy Spirit)

- Galatians 5:13–26 (live by the Spirit)

Write a one- to two-page essay telling about who the Holy Spirit is and describing his work in the lives of God's People. Explain whether the Holy Spirit takes an active or a passive role and how the gifts he gives can help you in different circumstances. Cite specific examples from the Scripture passages to support your explanations.

Accompany your essay with an artistic portrayal of one of the key points about the work of the Holy Spirit as presented in one or more of the Scripture passages. Your artwork can be hand-drawn or -painted or can be a digital creation.

Optional: Put together a two- to three-minute audio track of what you think the Holy Spirit might sound like. Use sounds from nature, percussion rhythms, or various other musical instruments to make an original composition.

3. Confirmation Multimedia Presentation

Create a multimedia presentation about the Sacrament of Confirmation. Your presentation should address the following: the relationship between Baptism and Confirmation, the celebration of the sacrament, the signs of the sacrament, the effects of the sacrament, and the differences in the celebration of the sacrament between the Eastern and Western Churches. Your presentation should include text and images and at least two of the following:

- Scripture quotations

- quotations from the *Catechism of the Catholic Church* (see paragraphs 1285 to 1321)

- one or more quotations from Pope Francis's catechesis on Confirmation (search the Vatican website for the pope's January 29, 2014, General Audience)

- a test on the Sacrament of Confirmation that your classmates should be able to successfully complete

Faithful Disciple

St. Kateri Tekakwitha

Statue of St. Kateri Tekakwitha, the first Native American to be beatified, outside the cathedral basilica of St. Francis of Assisi.

St. Kateri Tekakwitha, the daughter of a Mohawk warrior, was born in 1656 in what is now upstate New York. "Tekakwitha" was her Native American name. It means "she who bumps into things"!

When European settlers arrived in North America in the sixteenth century, they inadvertently brought with them deadly diseases, including smallpox. These diseases often spread among Native American populations, killing countless people. Tekakwitha's parents were among those killed by smallpox; they died when she was just four years old. Tekakwitha also contracted the disease. Although she survived smallpox, she was left badly disfigured and with impaired eyesight. Orphaned and sickly, she was taken in by relatives who tended to her care.

In 1667, when Tekakwitha was around eleven years old, Jesuit missionaries arrived in her village. Tekakwitha's uncle forbade her to have any contact with them. He did not want her to convert to Christianity. Over time, however, as she learned more about Jesus and his message of compassion and love, she was drawn to the Catholic faith. On Easter Sunday, in 1676, when she was twenty years old, Tekakwitha was baptized and received into the Church. It was then that she took the name Kateri, which is Mohawk for Catherine.

Many members of Kateri's tribe opposed her conversion and treated her with cruelty. Kateri faced this treatment with patience and courage. Eventually, Kateri left her village and went to live among other Christians, where she could freely practice her faith. She lived a life dedicated to prayer and to the care of the sick and aged, and she had an intense devotion to the Eucharist.

When Kateri was twenty-four years old, she became ill and quickly died. Moments after her death, her body was transformed. Her scarred complexion was replaced by beautiful radiance. There were many witnesses to this occurrence.

After her death, Kateri became known as the "Lily of the Mohawks." Because of her example, many Native Americans were baptized. Kateri was beatified in 1980 and canonized by Pope Benedict XVI in 2012.

 ## Reading Comprehension

1. What were the circumstances of Kateri's birth and early childhood?

2. How did Kateri learn about the Catholic faith?

3. What disease did Kateri contract as a child, and what were its lasting consequences?

 ## Writing Task

- Review the fruits of the Holy Spirit (see page 125), and write a two- to three-paragraph essay describing one or more of those fruits that were expressed in St. Kateri's life.

Explaining the Faith

How can a person be sure that he or she is following the will of the Holy Spirit in his or her life?

You likely want to be faithful to God's will for your life, but at times you may wonder if a thought, wish, ambition, desire, or seeming answer to prayer is really coming from God or if it is just your imagination or some other source. Here are four ways you can learn to keep yourself open to the voice of the Holy Spirit:

1. *Read Sacred Scripture.* Don't just skim the Bible, but read carefully to gain a really close knowledge of it. Dive into it; let it fill your thoughts; let it guide your prayers. In the words of St. Jerome, "ignorance of Scripture is ignorance of Christ," and ignorance of Christ will keep you at a distance from his Spirit.

2. *Live the sacraments.* Liturgy is the work of Christ and an action of the Church. Participating in the liturgy will produce great results for your life, new life in the Spirit, and involvement in the Church's mission; it will encourage your service to strengthen the Church's unity. Attend Mass every Sunday, and receive Jesus in the Eucharist with love. Run to him in the Sacrament of Penance when you feel troubled or discouraged. Support friends and family who are preparing to receive Baptism, First Communion, Confirmation, Holy Orders, or Matrimony. Consider attending a parish celebration of the Anointing of the Sick. Know that each time you participate in the sacraments, you are encountering the power of the Holy Spirit. The Holy Spirit enlightens your faith and inspires you to respond. He unites you with the Church and helps you to live the life of the Risen Christ.

3. *Love the Church.* While individual Catholics are imperfect, the Church is the Bride of Christ, who is beautiful and radiant (see Revelation 21:2, 17). The Spirit and the Church are so closely intertwined that, outside of the Church, you cannot be sure that you are in touch with the Holy Spirit anymore. Stay close to the Church that you know Christ established.

4. *Pray.* That might seem obvious, but it is surprisingly easy to forget that thinking about prayer isn't the same as actually praying. Each morning and evening, sit quietly with God. Even a few moments will do at first. The Holy Spirit will use that time to move your mind and heart in the right direction.

Finally, many spiritual writers say that to know the will of God, you don't need to go searching off in the distance. Start where you are, doing what you already know you must do today. Do all those things as well and completely as you can. In doing them, you will begin to see the next steps you need to take.

Further Research

*   Read paragraph 688 of the *Catechism of the Catholic Church*. Write a brief summary stating how the Holy Spirit helps you to be aware of God's presence and promptings in your life.

Prayer

A Meditation on Following God's Will

God has created me to do him some definite service; he has committed some work to me which he has not committed to another. I have my mission—I may never know it in this life, but I shall be told it in the next. . . . I am a link in a chain, a bond of connection between persons. He has not created me for naught. I shall do good, I shall do his work; I shall be an angel of peace, a preacher of truth in my own place, while not intending it, if I do but keep his commandments and serve him in my calling.

Therefore, I will trust him. Whatever, wherever I am, I can never be thrown away. If I am in sickness, my sickness may serve him; in perplexity, my perplexity may serve him; if I am in sorrow, my sorrow may serve him. . . . He does nothing in vain. . . . He knows what he is about. He may take away my friends, he may throw me among strangers, he may make me feel desolate, make my spirits sink, hide my future from me—still he knows what he is about.

—Bl. John Henry Newman, *Meditations on Christian Doctrine*

THE SACRAMENT
OF THE EUCHARIST

An Athlete Who Practices His *Faith*

Do you feel that it's hard for you to get to Mass? Think about Catholic professional athletes in any of the major sports who play games on Sundays. Have you ever wondered if, and how, these Catholic athletes are able to set aside time on Sunday for going to Mass in the midst of preparing for and playing an important, high-pressure game?

One person who did this successfully is Andre Ethier, an outfielder who recently played for the Los Angeles Dodgers. A native of Phoenix, Arizona, Andre has revealed in interviews that his Catholic faith has played an important part in his life. Andre says, "It's developed me into the person I am. And to shun away from that just because you're supposed to be more vanilla in certain areas, it wouldn't be me. I'm always trying to portray myself as who I really am, so that's definitely part of me—the faith part."

Because Sunday is a game day, Sunday Mass takes a little planning ahead for the Major League Baseball player. Andre explains, "People ask me, 'On Sundays, why do you always come dressed up?' It's because either I've come from church or I am going to go to church following the game." Occasionally, for home games, the Dodgers provide a team chaplain to say Mass in a room adjacent to the team's clubhouse.

Andre finds that Sunday Mass is "a great time to be able to clear your mind and think about where you're at in general. Sometimes things get out of perspective pretty quickly. So no matter what happens, good or bad, you gotta keep steady in that faith."

When asked, "How hard is it, being in professional sports, to practice your faith?" Andre answers, "For me it starts probably with the most basic and simple—going to Mass every Sunday, and making a point to do that." Andre continues, "The faith won't lead you wrong. It's led me right the whole way, and I still go to church every Sunday. I love it, and I'm glad to be involved and I'm glad to be a part of that Catholic community."

(Based on Tom Murray, "Dre's Anatomy," *Los Angeles Times Magazine*, August 2010.)

FOCUS QUESTION

Why is the Eucharist the "SOURCE AND SUMMIT" of the Christian life?

INTRODUCTION
Source and Summit

In his catechesis on the sacraments, Pope Francis put forward the following questions about the Eucharist: "Now let us ask ourselves several questions that spring from the relationship between the Eucharist that we celebrate and our life, as a Church and as individual Christians. *How do we experience the Eucharist?* When we go to Sunday Mass, how do we live it? Is it only a moment of celebration, an established tradition, an opportunity to find oneself or to feel justified, or is it something more?" (General Audience, February 12, 2014).

How would you answer these questions? How do you live the Eucharist? How does your understanding of this sacrament lead you to the "something more" that Pope Francis spoke of?

The Eucharist is the most important and special sacrament. It is called the "source and summit of the Christian life" (*CCC*, 1324, quoting *Lumen Gentium*, 11). This sacrament is the culmination of Christian initiation, and all of the other sacraments and works of the Church are bound up with and oriented to it because Christ himself is contained in it.

The term *Eucharist*, which comes from a Greek word meaning "to give thanks," has two principle understandings. First, it refers to the entire Mass, the

NOTE TAKING

Creating a Cluster Diagram. Create a diagram like the one to the right, with the word *Eucharist* in the center circle. In the surrounding circles, write key terms or phrases from the section that support your understanding of the Eucharist. Add as many outer circles as you need. Write a sentence or two clarifying each term or phrase.

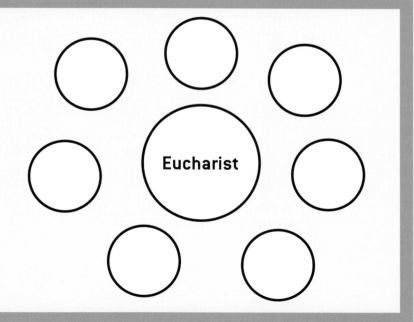

Church's central act of divine worship. In the Eucharist, you give God thanks and praise for all his blessings as you are sent out into the world, especially for the gift of Jesus and the salvation he won for humankind. Second, the word *Eucharist* refers to the consecrated species of wheat bread and grape wine—the Body and Blood of Christ—that you receive at Holy Communion.

Your being "sent forth" from the Eucharist reminds you that *Eucharist* can also be a verb (an action), rather than a noun (a thing). It describes what you become—the Body of Christ—when you receive the Body and Blood of Jesus in the form of the consecrated species of bread and wine. It describes your own transformation into the hands and feet of Christ in today's world, as well as your actions—how you continue Jesus' work of spreading the Good News of God's love to others.

Recall from the preceding chapters that because Baptism and Confirmation confer a spiritual mark or character, you may receive these sacraments only once. Eucharist, on the other hand, is like the daily food the physical body needs to maintain its strength and health. Jesus said, "My flesh is true food, and my blood is true drink" (Jn 6:55). The Eucharist feeds your soul and renews your commitment as a member of the Church, the Body of Christ. Just as the human body needs food each day, so you are encouraged to receive the Eucharist often.

The Eucharist is intimately connected to Jesus, the sacrament of God's love, and to the Church, the sacrament of Jesus. It is the sacrament of the sacrifice of Jesus on the Cross that makes Jesus, in his Death and Resurrection, present to you today. This presence is called **Real Presence**; in the Eucharist it exists through the consecration at Mass, in which the reality

> **Real Presence** The doctrine that Jesus Christ is truly present in his Body and Blood under the form of bread and wine in the Eucharist.

The Sacrament of Holy Eucharist has many names,

as its richness is truly inexhaustible (see *CCC*, 1328–1332).

For example, it is called

the **LORD'S SUPPER** because of its connection with the supper Jesus shared with his disciples on the night before his Passion;

the **BREAKING OF BREAD**, by which the communion of the faithful with Christ and others is indicated;

the **EUCHARISTIC ASSEMBLY** because the Mass is celebrated with faithful Catholics and is a visible expression of the Church;

the **MEMORIAL** of the Lord's Passion and Resurrection;

the **HOLY SACRIFICE** because it makes present the one sacrifice of Christ the Savior and includes the Church's offering;

the **HOLY AND DIVINE LITURGY** because the Church's whole liturgy centers on the celebration of this sacrament;

HOLY COMMUNION because the Eucharist unites Catholics in one Body after receiving the Body and Blood of Christ; and

MASS because it concludes with a "sending forth" (*missio*) of the faithful so that they may fulfill God's will in their daily lives.

(substance) of the wheat bread and grape wine changes into the reality of Jesus—his risen, glorified Body and Blood. Also, the Eucharist is the sacrament of communion with the Church. It nourishes the union of all Catholics with one another and strengthens their identity as Church. Again, these understandings speak to the sacrament's inexhaustible and mysterious meaning.

Ven. Archbishop Fulton J. Sheen, a dynamic speaker and evangelizer who had his own television program in the 1950s, once tried to explain the inexhaustible meaning of the Holy Eucharist:

> By a beautiful paradox of Divine love, God makes his cross the very means of our salvation and our life. We have slain him; we have nailed him there and crucified him; but the love in his eternal heart could not be extinguished. He willed to give us the very life we slew; to give us the very good we destroyed; to nourish us with the very bread we buried, and the very blood we poured forth. He made our very crime into a happy fault; he turned a Crucifixion into a redemption; a consecration into a communion; a death into life everlasting.

In this chapter, you will trace the origins of the Eucharist found in Sacred Scripture, explore the grace and effects of the sacrament, and examine the celebration of the Eucharist in the Sacrifice of the Mass. All of this information is intended to lead to your overall deeper understanding and appreciation of the Eucharist.

SECTION ASSESSMENT

NOTE TAKING

Use the cluster diagram you created to help you answer the following questions.

1. What does it mean to say that the Eucharist is the "source and summit of the Christian life"?

2. What does the word *Eucharist* mean?

3. What are some other names for the Eucharist?

COMPREHENSION

4. Why is the Eucharist called "Holy Communion"?

REFLECTION

5. How is the opportunity to participate at Mass important to you?

6. Which description of Eucharist best resonates with your understanding of the sacrament? Why do you feel this way?

7. Which description of Eucharist are you least familiar with?

SECTION 1
Understanding the Sacrament of the Eucharist

MAIN IDEA

At the Last Supper, Jesus instituted the Sacrament of the Eucharist as a memorial of his Death and Resurrection, ensuring his presence in the Church for all ages.

invocation A call, request, or supplication for God's help.

You are probably very familiar with artistic depictions of the Last Supper. After all, Leonardo da Vinci's *Last Supper* is among the most famous works in Western art. You have also witnessed the consecration at Mass many times. Although these images and actions might seem routine in their familiarity, what they represent and signify is anything but routine.

Just as he did at the Last Supper, at every Mass, Jesus gives himself to the Church under the species or appearances of bread and wine. At Mass, by the words of Christ and the **invocation** of the Holy Spirit, bread and wine become the Body and Blood of the Lord. The signs of bread and wine signify the goodness of God's creation. In the Offertory at Mass, the priest remembers the blessing of bread and wine that God has bestowed on the Church:

> Blessed are you, Lord God of all creation, for through your goodness we have received the bread we offer you: fruit of the earth and work of human hands, it will become for us the bread of life.
>
> Blessed are you, Lord God of all creation, for through your goodness we have received the wine we offer you: fruit of the vine and work of human hands, it will become our spiritual drink.

NOTE TAKING

Identifying Main Ideas. Create a two-column chart like the one to the right to help you name main questions about the Eucharist. Fill in the second column with answers to the questions found in this section. Add as many rows as necessary to list your questions.

HOW IS THE EUCHARIST . . .	ANSWER
connected to Passover?	
structured?	
a sacrifice to God?	
the Real Presence of Christ?	

When Abraham met with the king-priest Melchizedek of Salem (which may be the same place as Jerusalem) and offered him gifts, Melchizedek in turn brought out bread and wine. Later, in the New Testament, Jesus is described as a priest "according to the order of Melchizedek" (see Hebrews 5:1–10). The bread and wine offered by the Church are the fulfillment of Melchizedek's offering under the old Law.

Both signs have roots in Scripture. In the Old Testament, bread and wine were offered in sacrifice among the first fruits of earth. They received new meaning in the Exodus. The manna the Israelites ate in the desert commemorated their liberation from Egypt and taught them always to rely on the Word of God for sustenance.

In the New Covenant, the "cup of blessing" at the end of the Jewish Passover added to the joy of the celebration. Jesus' public ministry had already given new meaning to the significance of bread, wine, and the common sharing of a meal. For example, Jesus' multiplication of the loaves to feed thousands is recorded in the Gospels using Eucharistic language:

> He ordered the crowd to sit down on the ground. Then he took the seven loaves and the fish, gave thanks, broke the loaves, and gave them to the disciples, who in turn gave them to the crowds. (Mt 15:35–36)

Jesus' conversion of water to wine at the Cana wedding announced his glorious Resurrection and Ascension and made present the wedding feast in the Father's Kingdom, where all will share in the fruits of God's love. Jesus mentioned this feast at the Last Supper:

> Amen, I say to you, I shall not drink again the fruit of the vine until the day when I drink it new in the kingdom of God. (Mk 14:25)

When Jesus first announced the Eucharist to his disciples, his explanation shocked and divided them. He told them they must eat his flesh and drink his blood in order to gain eternal life. At the end of his discourse on the Bread of Life, Jesus clearly announced:

> I am the living bread that came down from heaven; whoever eats this bread will live forever; and the bread that I will give is my flesh for the life of the world. (Jn 6:51)

He added:

> Amen, amen, I say to you, unless you eat the flesh of the Son of Man and drink his blood, you do not have life within you. Whoever eats my flesh and drinks my blood has eternal life, and I will raise him on the last day. For my flesh is true food, and my blood is true drink. (Jn 6:53–55)

Many of the disciples protested: "This saying is hard; who can accept it?" (Jn 6:60). In fact, some of them left Jesus and returned to their former way of life. Jesus wondered if the Apostles were planning to leave also. Peter responded:

> Master, to whom shall we go? You have the words of eternal life. We have come to believe and are convinced that you are the Holy One of God. (Jn 6:68–69)

Understanding and accepting the meaning of the Eucharist remains a challenge today. Many are challenged by the truth that Jesus' Body and Blood are truly present under the appearances of wheat bread and grape wine. Jesus' question to the Apostles, "Do you also want to leave?" (Jn 6:67), is asked of you, too. Just as Peter did, you will discover the Good News that only Jesus has the words of eternal life and that receiving the gift of Eucharist is receiving the Lord himself.

The Institution of the Eucharist

Jesus instituted the Eucharist as a memorial of his Death and Resurrection. You learn about the institution of the

Eucharist in three of the four Gospels, as well as in the writings of St. Paul. On the night before he died, Jesus took bread, said the blessing, broke the bread, and gave it to his disciples, saying, "This is my body, which will be given for you; do this in memory of me." He then took the cup and said, "This cup is the new covenant in my blood, which will be shed for you" (Lk 22:19–20).

By this action, Jesus gave the Jewish Passover its ultimate meaning and anticipated the final Passover of the Church into the glory of his Kingdom. By giving his Apostles the power to do what he had done—change bread and wine into his Body and Blood—Jesus ensured the presence of the Eucharist in the Catholic Church for all ages.

From the beginning, the Church has been faithful to Jesus' call to celebrate the Eucharist in his memory. When the Church offers Mass, she blesses God for the great events of salvation—from creation, to the Exodus, to the Death and Resurrection of Jesus and the coming of the Holy Spirit, to the **second coming of Christ** and the establishment of a new heaven and a new earth. As the Church proclaims these events, she is caught up in them. In the Eucharist, Christ's redeeming act of freeing you from sin and death is made present once again in its fullness and leads you to freedom. The Holy Spirit moves in your life. In the Eucharist, you are caught up in the new creation in which all tears are wiped away. In other words, when the Church celebrates the Eucharist, the entire Body of Christ—Head and Body—praises God for the life and salvation that Christ has given, and you experience that life and salvation in the present moment. In the Eucharist, the time of liberation, the time of redemption, and the time of new creation are all *now*.

> **second coming of Christ** Also known as the Parousia, the time when Jesus will return to earth, the Kingdom of God will be fully established, and victory over evil will be complete.

The Eucharist through the Age of the Church

At the Last Supper, Jesus commanded the Apostles to "do this in memory of me" (Lk 22:19). In the early Church, Christians "devoted themselves to the teaching of the apostles and to the communal life, to the breaking of bread and to the prayers" (Acts 2:42). It was especially on the first day of the week, Sunday, the day of the Lord's Resurrection, that the first Christians met to "break bread." St. Justin Martyr, writing in the second century, provides an eyewitness account of Eucharistic celebrations in the early Church:

> On the day we call the day of the sun, all who dwell in the city or country gather in the same place.
>
> The memoirs of the apostles and the writings of the prophets are read, as much as time permits.
>
> When the reader has finished, he who presides over those gathered admonishes and challenges them to imitate these beautiful things.
>
> Then we all rise together and offer prayers for ourselves . . . and for all others, wherever they may be, so that we may be found righteous by our life and actions, and faithful to the commandments, so as to obtain eternal salvation.
>
> When the prayers are concluded we exchange the kiss.
>
> Then someone brings bread and a cup of water and wine mixed together to him who presides over the brethren.
>
> He takes them and offers praise and glory to the Father of the universe, through the name of the Son and of the Holy Spirit and for a considerable time he gives thanks (in Greek:

The Tridentine Mass, also known as the extraordinary form of the Roman Rite of Mass, is still celebrated today.

eucharistian) that we have been judged worthy of these gifts.

When he has concluded the prayers and thanksgivings, all present give voice to an acclamation by saying: "Amen."

When he who presides has given thanks and the people have responded, those whom we call deacons give to those present the "eucharisted" bread, wine and water and take them to those who are absent. (*CCC*, 1345, quoting St. Justin, *First Apology*, 65–67)

From these early liturgical celebrations, the Church has continued the celebration of the Eucharist following the same fundamental structure, as a *memorial* of

> **Confiteor** From the first word in Latin meaning "I confess," a prayer used during the Penitential Rite at the beginning of Mass and at other times to prepare to receive grace.

Christ, of his life, of his Death, of his Resurrection, and of his intercession in the presence of God the Father. The Eucharist remains the center of Church life.

In the early Church, every local church community followed the same order of the celebration. However, over time, different liturgical rites began to develop. The pattern of the Eastern liturgy (with centers in Jerusalem, Constantinople, Antioch, and Alexandria) did not change much after the sixth century. In the West (Rome), the pattern of the Eucharist continued to evolve until the sixteenth century, when the Council of Trent (1545–1563) established one uniform way for the celebration of Mass in the Roman Catholic Church. This Mass is known as the Tridentine Mass and was standard for the Church for five hundred years until the Second Vatican Council. It was said in Latin and followed this general structure:

- Prayers by the priest (in Latin) at the foot of the altar: Sign of the Cross, Psalm 42, the **Confiteor**

- Prayers by the priest at the altar: **introit**, opening prayer, Kyrie (Lord, Have Mercy), Gloria, and **collect**

- Scripture readings (in Latin): epistle reading, prayer response, Alleluia, Gospel reading, and homily or sermon

- Profession of Faith: **Nicene Creed** in Latin

- Offertory: preparation of wine in the chalice and of the host on a plate called a *paten*, washing of priest's hands, and the offertory prayer

- The Canon: preface, Sanctus (Holy, Holy, Holy), prayers for the living and for the universal Church, Words of Institution, prayers for the dead, and Amen

- Communion Rite: Pater Noster (Our Father), Agnus Dei (Lamb of God), Communion of the priest, Communion of the people, and post-Communion prayer

- Closing Rite: dismissal, final blessing, and reading from John 1:1–14

Sacrosanctum Concilium (*Constitution on the Sacred Liturgy*), the first document issued by the Second Vatican Council, reformed the Church's liturgy and allowed for Mass to be celebrated in the *vernacular* (the local language). The Council Fathers were moved by a desire that "all the faithful should be led to take full, conscious, and active part in liturgical celebrations" (*Sacrosanctum Concilium*, 14). These changes did not alter the fundamental structure of the Eucharistic celebration, "which has been preserved throughout the centuries down to our own day" (*CCC*, 1346). This structure continues to be made up of the Liturgy of the Word (readings, homily, and General Intercessions) and the Liturgy of the Eucharist (presentation of the bread and wine, consecration, thanksgiving, and Communion). Together the Liturgy of the Word and Liturgy of the Eucharist form "one single act of worship."

In 2002, the third edition of the *Roman Missal* was published in Latin. The English translation of this edition was released in 2011. In 2007, Pope Benedict XVI issued a *motu proprio* allowing for the celebration of the Tridentine Mass alongside the Missal of Pope Paul VI (the ordinary form of the Mass) with the desire for "interior reconciliation in the heart of the Church."

Understanding the Eucharist as a Sacrifice

In the Eucharist, the Church both remembers and proclaims the great works God has done. The events of salvation become present and actual. In the Eucharist, Christ's sacrifice on the Cross is re-presented—that is, "made present again." The Eucharist is a sacrifice because in it, Christ gives the Church the very Body he gave up on the Cross and the very Blood he "shed on behalf of many for the forgiveness of sins" (Mt 26:28). The Eucharist is a sacrifice of the Church; as a sacrifice it is offered for the sins of the living and the dead "so that they may be able to enter into the light and peace of Christ" (*CCC*, 1371).

The sacrifice of Christ on the Cross and the sacrifice of the Eucharist are one single sacrifice. As the Council of Trent taught, "The victim is one and the same: the same now offers through the ministry of priests, who then offered himself on the cross; only the manner of offering is different" (*CCC*, 1367).

Jesus continues to offer the one and only sacrifice of himself each time the Eucharist is offered. Each

introit An antiphon, usually from a psalm, that is sung when the priest enters the church and approaches the altar.

collect The prayer appointed for the day or feast that concludes the Introductory Rites before the Liturgy of the Word begins.

Nicene Creed The formal Profession of Faith recited at Mass. It came from the first two ecumenical councils, at Nicaea in AD 325 and Constantinople in AD 381.

motu proprio Literally "of his own accord," a papal document promulgated on the pope's own initiative.

POPE FRANCIS'S CATECHESIS ON THE SACRAMENTS

In his catechesis on the sacraments, Pope Francis said the following about the Eucharist:

> What we see when we gather to celebrate the Eucharist, the Mass, already gives us an intuition of what we are about to live. At the center of the space intended for the celebration there is an altar, which is a table covered with a tablecloth, and this makes us think of a banquet. . . .
>
> [But] the Eucharistic Celebration is much more than simple banquet: it is exactly the memorial of Jesus' Paschal sacrifice, the mystery at the center of salvation. "Memorial" does not simply mean a remembrance, a mere memory; it means that every time we celebrate this Sacrament we participate in the mystery of the passion, death and resurrection of Christ. (General Audience, February 5, 2014)

Eucharist is not a new sacrifice. Rather, each Eucharist makes present the *one eternal sacrifice* that Jesus made on the Cross nearly two thousand years ago. As the *Catechism of the Catholic Church* explains,

> In order to leave them a pledge of this love, in order never to depart from his own and to make them sharers in his Passover, he instituted the Eucharist as the memorial of his death and Resurrection, and commanded his apostles to celebrate it until his return; "thereby he constituted them priests of the New Testament." (*CCC*, 1337, quoting the Council of Trent)

The Eucharist is a sacramental sacrifice in three ways: as (1) thanksgiving and praise to the Father, (2) the sacrificial memorial of Christ and his Body, and (3) the presence of Christ by the power of his Word and of his Spirit.

Thanksgiving and Praise to the Father

The Eucharist is a sacramental sacrifice to God the Father as an act of gratitude for his blessings on creation, our redemption, and our sanctification. Recall that the word *Eucharist* means "thanksgiving." Above all, the Eucharist thanks the Father for the gift of his Son. Pope Francis explained:

> Jesus' gesture at the Last Supper is the ultimate thanksgiving to the Father for his love, for his mercy. "Thanksgiving" in Greek is expressed as "eucharist." And that is why the Sacrament is called the Eucharist: it is the supreme thanksgiving to the Father, who so loved us that he gave us his Son out of love. This is why the term Eucharist includes the whole of that act, which is the act of God and man together, the act of Jesus Christ, true God and true Man. (General Audience, February 5, 2014)

At Mass, the **doxology** of the Eucharistic Prayer reminds the assembled that all praise and glory are due the Father in the name of all creation so that this sacrifice is offered *through* Christ and *with* him, to be accepted *in* him (see *CCC*, 1361).

Sacrificial Memorial of Christ

In 1562, the Council of Trent defined the Eucharist as "an unbloody sacrifice." What this means is that the Eucharist is really the *sacrament of the sacrifice of Jesus*. There is only one sacrifice—that of Jesus. For this reason, the *Catechism of the Catholic Church* teaches that "the sacrifice of Christ and the sacrifice of the Eucharist are *one single sacrifice*" (*CCC*, 1367). The Eucharist "re-presents" and perpetuates "the sacrifice of the cross throughout the ages until [Christ] should come again" (*CCC*, 1323). At every Mass, then, you are joined to Christ himself, who is present, offering his Body and Blood to God for your salvation. The Eucharist doesn't just recall or memorialize the sacrifice of Jesus; rather, it makes his sacrifice present. As the *Catechism of the Catholic Church* teaches,

> The Eucharist is the memorial of Christ's Passover, the making present and the sacramental offering of his unique sacrifice, in the liturgy of the Church which is his Body. . . .
>
> The Eucharist is thus a sacrifice because it *re-presents* (makes present) the sacrifice of the cross. (*CCC*, 1362, 1366)

The Eucharist is also a sacrifice of the Church. The Church offers herself with Christ by giving to the Father all praise, suffering, prayer, and work united with those of Christ. This means your sacrifices gain new value whenever you participate in the Eucharist. Also, the whole Church is united as one Body in communion with the whole Church—with the pope and with the bishop in the place where the Mass is being offered. Again, in the Eucharistic Prayer, the priest prays,

> Remember, Lord, your Church spread throughout the world, and bring her to the fullness of charity together with N. our Pope and N. our Bishop and all the clergy.

The Eucharist is offered not only for those faithful on earth but also, in communion with those who are already in heaven, for "the faithful departed 'who have died in Christ but are not yet wholly purified'" (*CCC*, 1371, quoting the Council of Trent).

St. Augustine of Hippo wrote of the sacrifice offered at Mass: "The Church continues to reproduce this sacrifice in the sacrament of the altar so well-known to believers wherein it is evident to them that in what she offers she herself is offered" (*City of God*, 10, quoted in *CCC*, 1372).

Christ's Presence in the Eucharist

Although Christ is present to the Church in many other ways—in the minister of the sacraments, in the community that has gathered in his name, and in the Holy Scriptures that are read—his presence in the Eucharist is unique. In the Eucharist, the Body and Blood of Christ, "*the whole Christ is truly, really, and substantially* contained" (Council of Trent, quoted in *CCC*, 1374). This presence is "Real Presence" not because the other ways Jesus is present in the world are not real but because it is his presence in the fullest sense.

The term **transubstantiation** is used to express how the reality (substance) of bread and wine changes into the

---

doxology A prayer of praise to the Blessed Trinity. The Eucharistic Prayer ends in a doxology.

transubstantiation What happens at the consecration of the bread and wine at Mass when their entire substance is turned into the entire substance of the Body and Blood of Christ, even though the appearances of bread and wine remain. The Eucharistic presence of Christ begins at the moment of consecration and endures as long as the Eucharistic species subsist.

WHY GO TO *Mass*

The Sunday Eucharist is the foundation and confirmation of all Catholic practice. The Third Commandment—"Keep holy the Lord's day" (see Exodus 20:8–11)—obliges you to attend and participate in the Eucharistic celebration on Sundays and holy days of obligation. The "Sunday obligation" is also the first precept of the Church: "You shall attend Mass on Sundays and on holy days of obligation and rest from servile labor" (*CCC*, 2042). Thus, those who deliberately skip Mass on those days without a serious reason or a dispensation from their pastor fail in this duty and commit a grave sin. The third precept of the Church requires Catholics to receive the Sacrament of the Eucharist during the Easter season at a minimum. While all this is true, you shouldn't attend Mass only because of what you avoid (that is, sin). Instead, you should cultivate a genuine desire to be present at Mass. Good reasons to attend Mass include the following:

- I need Jesus' presence in my life.
- It helps me live a good Christian life.
- I want to keep my baptismal vows.
- I love God and want to please him.
- Jesus asked me to do this to remember him.
- I want to be a good example to others.

> **Viaticum** The Eucharist received by a dying person. This is a Latin term that means "food for the journey."

- I want to go to heaven.
- I belong to the Catholic Church and want to be a part of her life and worship.

Your participation at Mass and receiving Holy Communion is synonymous with being Catholic. It is essential to your spiritual development, in the same way food is essential to your physical development. As Cardinal Joseph Bernardin of Chicago once explained,

> Liturgy is not an option nor merely an obligation, not a bonus, but a need—like food and drink, like sleep and work, like friends. We need to gather, listen, give praise and thanks, and share communion. Otherwise we forget who we are and whose we are; and we can have neither the strength nor the joy to be Christ's body—present in the world today.

Thus, communion with the flesh of the Risen Christ, "given life and giving life through the Holy Spirit" (*CCC*, 1392), sustains you. It preserves, increases, and renews the life of grace you receive at Baptism. It is the bread for your earthly pilgrimage until the moment of death, when it will be given to you one last time as **Viaticum**.

reality of Jesus—his risen, glorified Body and Blood. The Church Fathers affirmed the Church's faith in the power of the words of Christ and of the action of the Holy Spirit to bring about this conversion. One fourth-century Church Father, St. John Chrysostom, declared,

> It is not man that causes the things offered to become the Body and Blood of Christ, but he who was crucified for us, Christ himself. The priest, in the role of Christ, pronounces these words, but their power and grace are God's. This is my body, he says. This word transforms the things offered.

The Council of Trent in the sixteenth century summarized this belief:

Because Christ our Redeemer said that it was truly his body that he was offering under the species of bread, it has always been the conviction of the Church of God, and this holy Council now declares again, that by the consecration of the bread and wine there takes place a change of the whole substance of the bread.

It makes perfect sense that Jesus would want to remain present in the Church in this unique way. He desires to express for all Catholics the same privileges of friendship, blessing, and love that he first afforded his disciples who walked the earth with him many years ago.

SECTION ASSESSMENT

NOTE TAKING

Refer to the questions and answers you recorded to help you answer the questions listed below.

1. How were the Eucharistic signs of bread and wine prefigured in the Old Testament?
2. What does it mean to say that the fundamental structure of the Eucharistic celebration has not changed over time?
3. What are three ways that the Eucharist is a sacramental sacrifice?
4. What is the Eucharist a memorial of?

COMPREHENSION

5. When did Jesus institute the Sacrament of the Eucharist?
6. What is the Tridentine Mass?

REFLECTION

7. Describe what Christ's presence in the Eucharist means to you personally.

Celebrating the Sacrament of the Eucharist

MAIN IDEA

A gathering of the People of God is normal for the celebration of the Eucharistic liturgy, or Mass. The Mass has two main parts: the Liturgy of the Word and the Liturgy of the Eucharist.

Since the days of the early Church, when the disciples gathered for the breaking of the bread and for prayer (see Acts 2), a gathering of the People of God has been a normal part of the Eucharistic celebration, though a priest may sometimes celebrate Mass alone if there is a just cause. At the head of the People of God, the Church, is Christ himself. As the High Priest of the New Covenant, it is Christ himself who presides invisibly over every Eucharistic celebration (see *CCC*, 1348).

The original meaning of the term *liturgy* refers to "public work" or "service done on behalf of people." The primary meaning of *liturgy* is the participation of the Church in the "work of God" (see *CCC*, 1069). This work involves people with each of these roles:

- The priest or bishop represents Christ, acting in the person of Christ the Head. The priest or bishop is the presider who speaks after the readings, receives the offerings, and says the Eucharistic Prayer.

- All in the assembly have their own active parts to play in the celebration. Some are altar servers, others are readers, some bring up the gifts, and others give Communion. The whole people respond "Amen"—"I agree"—to bring their participation to life.

An explanation of the order of the Mass follows.

Introductory Rites

The Mass begins with Introductory Rites, whose purpose is to help the assembled people become a worshipping community and to prepare them for listening to God's Word and celebrating the Eucharist. As the priest and ministers process to the altar, the

NOTE TAKING

Summarizing Material. Create an outline like the one below in your notebook to name and explain what takes place during the various parts of the Mass. *Note*: Only some of the outline is filled in for you.

I. Introductory Rites
    A. Greeting
    B.
    C.

II. Liturgy of the Word
    A. First reading
    B.

III. Liturgy of the Eucharist
    A. Presentation of the Gifts
    B. Eucharistic Prayer

IV. Concluding Rites

congregation sings an entrance song. At the end of the song, the priest greets the people.

> Priest: In the name of the Father, and of the Son, and of the Holy Spirit.
>
> People: Amen.
>
> Priest: The grace of our Lord Jesus Christ, and the love of God, and the communion of the Holy Spirit be with you all.
>
> People: And with your spirit.

Next, there is either a rite of blessing and sprinkling of holy water or a **Penitential Rite**. The priest invites the people to repent of their sins and prepare themselves "to celebrate the sacred mysteries" (Penitential Act, *Roman Missal*). The Penitential Rite may consist of the Confiteor ("I confess") and/or the Kyrie ("Lord, have mercy"). The Gloria is said or sung, except on the Sundays of Advent and Lent and on weekdays that are not feasts or solemnities. Then the priest prays an opening prayer.

Liturgy of the Word

The Liturgy of the Word includes "the writings of the prophets"—that is, the Old Testament—and "the memoirs of the apostles" (their letters and the Gospels) (see *CCC*, 1349). The Old Testament is proclaimed in the first reading. The cantor then leads the people in a **responsorial psalm**. A second reading (on Sundays and holy days) is proclaimed, usually from the New Testament letters. An Alleluia or Gospel acclamation is sung by all as a reminder of the joy and hope the faithful have because of the Good News of Jesus. The priest

> **Penitential Rite** Part of the Introductory Rites at Mass when the priest invites people to repent of their sins and prepare themselves to encounter Christ in the Eucharist.
>
> **responsorial psalm** A psalm sung or said at Mass in response to the first Scripture reading.

or deacon then reads a passage from one of the four Gospels. Then, in the homily, he explains the Word of God and exhorts those assembled to be open to it and accept it.

If catechumens are present, they are dismissed after the homily. Then all the baptized members of the assembly say the Nicene Creed or renew their baptismal promises. General Intercessions (the Prayer of the Faithful) follow.

Liturgy of the Eucharist

The second part of Mass, the Liturgy of the Eucharist, outlined on the next page, follows a general structure that is discussed in the following sections.

Presentation of the Gifts and Preparation of the Altar

The Presentation of the Gifts is also called the Offertory. A monetary collection for the maintenance of the parish and the needs of the poor is taken. This

Liturgical Signs and Symbols

When you attend Mass this coming Sunday, take note of three signs or symbols of the liturgical celebration whose meaning you don't fully understand. Examples include the color of the celebrant's vestments and the altar cloth, the use of sacred vessels, or the use of incense. Write a brief report providing the following information for each: the element of the liturgical celebration; a description of how the element figures in the Mass; and an explanation, based on research you conduct, of the significance of that element in the liturgical celebration.

THE ORDER OF MASS

The Eucharistic celebration is the center of the Church's life. From the time of the early Christians through today, the celebration of the Eucharist has been continued so that today it is celebrated everywhere in the Church with the same fundamental structure. The Mass always includes the following elements:

- the proclamation of God's Word
- thanksgiving to God for all his gifts, including the gifts of creation, but especially the gift of his Son, Jesus
- the consecration of the bread and wine
- the assembly's participation in the liturgical meal in the reception of Holy Communion

The two main parts of the Mass are the Liturgy of the Word and the Liturgy of the Eucharist. They are surrounded by the Introductory Rites and Concluding Rites. Here is an outline of the Sunday liturgy. This is called the Order of Mass.

INTRODUCTORY RITES

- Entrance
- Greeting
- Penitential Rite
- Kyrie (Lord, Have Mercy)
- Gloria (Glory to God)
- Collect (Opening Prayer)

LITURGY OF THE WORD

- First reading
- Responsorial psalm
- Second reading
- Gospel acclamation (Alleluia)
- Gospel
- Homily
- Profession of Faith (Nicene Creed)
- Universal Prayer (Prayer of the Faithful)

LITURGY OF THE EUCHARIST

- Presentation of the Gifts and Preparation of the Altar
- Prayer over the Offerings
- Eucharistic Prayer
  - Preface
  - Holy, Holy, Holy (Sanctus)
  - First half of prayer, including consecration
  - Memorial Acclamation (Anamnesis)
  - Second half of prayer, ending with doxology
- Communion Rite
  - The Lord's Prayer
  - Rite of Peace
  - Lamb of God (Fraction Rite)
  - Communion
  - Prayer after Communion

CONCLUDING RITES

- Greeting and blessing
- Dismissal

Celebrating the Eucharist is one way Catholics "continually offer God a sacrifice of praise" (Heb 13:15).

practice goes back to the first days in the Church when those assembled for liturgy brought gifts of food and money for the Apostles and also gave generously to other Christians in need (see 1 Corinthians 16:1–4, Romans 15:26–29, 2 Corinthians 8–9). The congregation sings a song as the collection takes place.

When the collection is completed, it is usually taken to the altar, along with the gifts of bread and wine. The bread and wine not only symbolize all the gifts of creation God has generously given the Church; they also symbolize each person assembled. With the gifts of bread and wine, you offer God the sacrifice of yourself, in union with the sacrifice of Jesus, sharing in his universal sacrifice.

At the altar, the priest—acting in the person of Jesus and in the name of the entire assembly—pours wine into the chalice. He adds a drop of water, which symbolizes the human nature of Jesus that coexists with his divinity. He also places the hosts that are to be consecrated on the paten or in the ciborium that rests on the *corporal* (white cloth). When the altar has been readied, he sings or says the following prayer: "Pray, brethren (brothers and sisters), that my sacrifice and yours may be acceptable to God, the almighty Father." All respond, "May the Lord accept the sacrifice at your hands for the praise and glory of his name, for our good, and the good of all his holy Church." Only validly ordained priests can preside at the Eucharist and consecrate the bread and wine so that they become the Body and Blood of Christ (see *CCC*, 1411).

Eucharistic Prayer

The **Eucharistic Prayer** is the Church's great prayer of praise and thanksgiving to God. It is the high point of the Liturgy of the Eucharist and of the Mass itself. There are four main Eucharistic Prayers in the Roman

Rite. There are also Eucharistic Prayers for Masses with Children and for Masses of Reconciliation. Although each of these prayers is different in length and content, each one has the same basic structure.

The Eucharistic Prayer begins with the Preface, which is a prayer of thanksgiving to the Father, through Christ and in the Holy Spirit, for his work of creation, redemption, and sanctification. The Eucharistic Prayer is known by another name in the Eastern Church: the *anaphora*, meaning "offering." After the priest says a prayer of thanksgiving and praise to God, everyone says or sings the Sanctus, the Holy, Holy, Holy. The whole community thus joins in the unending praise that the Church in heaven—the angels and all the saints—sings to the thrice-holy God.

The **epiclesis**—a Greek word that means "calling down upon" or "invocation"—is the next part of the Eucharistic Prayer. Here the priest asks the Father to send the Holy Spirit to sanctify the gifts of bread and wine. The essential signs of the Sacrament of the Eucharist are wheat bread and grape wine. The wheat bread is unleavened in the Roman Catholic Church, leavened in the Eastern Churches. The bread must be recently made and in no danger of spoiling. The wine must be natural from the vine and not spoiled.

Eucharistic Prayer The Church's great prayer of praise and thanksgiving to God that takes place during the Liturgy of the Eucharist. There are four main Eucharistic Prayers in the Roman Rite.

epiclesis The prayer that petitions God to send the Holy Spirit to transform the bread and wine offered at the Eucharistic liturgy into the Body and Blood of Jesus Christ. This term also applies to the prayer said in every sacrament that asks for the sanctifying power of the Holy Spirit.

Words of Institution The words said by Jesus over the bread and wine at the Last Supper. The priest repeats these words over the bread and wine at Mass as they are changed into the Body and Blood of Christ.

The bread and wine will become the Body and Blood of Christ—not through the holiness of the priest or the assembled Church but through the power of the Holy Spirit. The priest prays the epiclesis: "Make holy, therefore, these gifts, we pray, by sending down your Spirit upon them like the dewfall, so that they may become for us the Body and Blood of our Lord Jesus Christ" (Eucharistic Prayer II, *Roman Missal*).

In the **Words of Institution**, or institution narrative, the priest repeats the words of Jesus at the Last Supper:

> At the time he was betrayed
> and entered willingly into his Passion,
> he took bread and, giving thanks, broke it,
> and gave it to his disciples, saying:
> "Take this, all of you, and eat of it,
> For this is my body,
> Which will be given up for you."
> In a similar way, when supper was ended,
> he took the chalice
> and, once more giving thanks,
> he gave it to his disciples, saying:
> "Take this, all of you, and drink from it,
> For this is the chalice of my blood,
> The blood of the new and eternal covenant,
> Which will be poured out for you and for many
> For the forgiveness of sins.
> Do this in memory of me."
> (Eucharistic Prayer II, *Roman Missal*)

In the institution narrative, the power of the words and actions of Christ and the power of the Holy Spirit make Christ's Body and Blood, and his sacrifice on the Cross, sacramentally present under the species of bread and wine. As the Council of Trent clearly taught, "By the consecration of the bread and wine the whole substance of the bread is changed into the substance of the body of Christ our Lord, and the whole substance of the wine is changed into the substance of his blood" (*Eucharist,* 4). It is forbidden for the priest to consecrate one matter (the bread or the wine) without the other or to consecrate them outside of the Mass.

Immediately after the Words of Institution, the assembled Church "calls to mind the Passion, resurrection, and glorious return of Christ Jesus" (*CCC*, 1354). This is called the *anamnesis*—a Greek word that means "memorial"—or the memorial acclamation. The congregation says, "We proclaim your Death, O Lord, and profess your Resurrection until you come again," or another one of the memorial acclamations.

Following the anamnesis are the intercessions, which consist of prayers for the entire Church, living and dead. Depending on which Eucharistic Prayer is selected, there are intercessions for the following:

- *All those gathered for the Eucharist.* The priest prays that the faithful may be nourished by the Eucharist, be filled with the Holy Spirit, and become "one body, one spirit in Christ."

- *The pope, the bishop, and all the clergy.* The priest prays for the Church's ordained leaders as a reminder that the Church is a universal Church.

- *Catholics in need.* The priest prays that God will hear and answer "the prayers of the family you have gathered here before you."

- *The faithful deceased.* The priest prays that God will "welcome into your kingdom our departed brothers and sisters, and all who have left this world in your friendship."

These intercessory prayers should remind you of two important beliefs regarding the Eucharist. First, the Church offers this sacrificial meal in the hope that "the whole human race may be brought into the unity of God's family" (Christian Initiation 2, General Introduction, *The Rites*). Second, at each Eucharist, you join with the whole Church—all living members, those present and absent, those near and far, as well as the faithful dead—in celebrating the offering and the intercession of Christ.

The Eucharistic Prayer ends with a doxology, a reminder that every Eucharist strengthens your initiation into the life of the Trinity. The Church offers every Mass to praise the Trinity. It is a "sacrifice of praise to the Father . . . offered *through* Christ and *with* him, to be accepted *in* him" (*CCC*, 1361). So too, everything Catholics do aims at praising the Blessed Trinity. United with Christ, you give glory and honor to the Blessed Trinity. The priest says, or sings, the following prayer while holding up the Body and Blood of Christ:

> Through him, and
> with him, and
> in him; O God, almighty Father;
> in the unity of the Holy Spirit;
> all glory and honor is yours;
> for ever and ever.

The people respond by saying or singing the **Great Amen**. The word *amen* means "so be it" or "I agree." The Great Amen is your yes to all that has been said in the Eucharistic Prayer. It professes your belief that the Risen Jesus is truly among the gathered faithful.

The Communion Rite

The Communion Rite readies the faithful to receive the Lord, the "Bread of Life" and the "Chalice of Eternal Salvation." The Communion Rite is made up of the Lord's Prayer, the Rite of Peace, the Fraction Rite, the reception of Communion, and the prayer after Communion.

The Lord's Prayer is another name for the Our Father. It is the prayer Jesus taught his Apostles (see Matthew 6:9–13, Luke 11:2–4). This prayer acknowledges your identity as God's adopted son or daughter, as a brother or sister of Jesus and of one another. As

Great Amen The affirmation by the faithful of the entire Eucharistic Prayer.

WHO CAN RECEIVE THE EUCHARIST?

If you turn to the inside cover of the worship book or the back of the bulletin when you're at Mass, you will see a paragraph with a title such as "Guidelines for the Reception of Holy Communion." It's important to know that this paragraph is not there in order to turn anyone away. All are welcome at Mass, always. But only baptized Catholics in a state of grace who have already received their First Communion can receive the Eucharist because receiving the Eucharist is a sign of full unity with the Church. Those who belong to other ecclesial communities, as well as those Catholics who may have fallen into mortal sin, lack this full unity.

Receiving the Eucharist is also a sign of belief in the Real Presence of Jesus in the Eucharist. So even though many Protestant Christians may share a wide range of other beliefs with Catholics, they still may not receive the Eucharist at Mass. If they did so, they would be making a false statement, since they do not believe Jesus is present in the Eucharist in the same sense that Catholics believe this. Because of apostolic succession and the priesthood, the Holy Eucharist in the Catholic Church is the Body and Blood of Christ. Churches without apostolic succession do not have the gift that makes the consecration of bread and wine into the Body and Blood of Christ possible.

Likewise, it would be a false statement for a Catholic to receive communion at a Protestant worship service, since Catholics believe that Jesus is only present when the bread and wine are consecrated by a validly ordained priest. This division is saddening, but it is hoped that one day it will be a thing of the past: "The more painful the experience of the divisions in the Church which break the common participation in the table of the Lord, the more urgent are our prayers to the Lord that the time of complete unity among all who believe in him may return" (*CCC*, 1398).

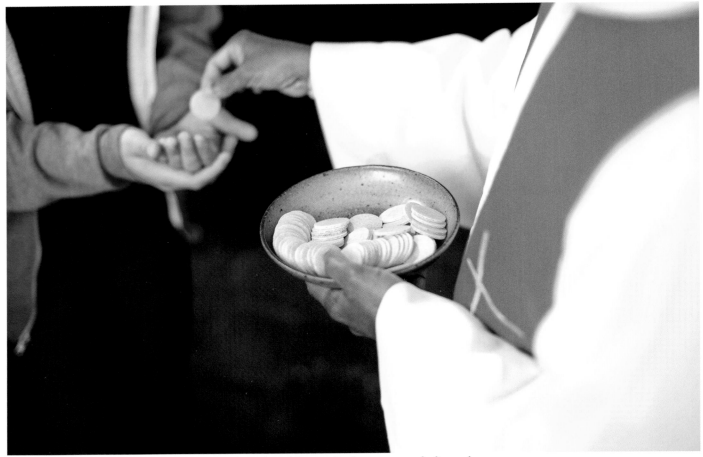

Catholics are encouraged to receive Communion devoutly and frequently whenever properly disposed.

the *Catechism of the Catholic Church* states, "When we pray to the Father, we are *in communion with him* and with his Son, Jesus Christ" (*CCC*, 2781).

> We can adore the Father because he has caused us to be reborn to his life by *adopting* us as his children in his only Son: by Baptism, he incorporates us into the Body of his Christ; through the anointing of his Spirit who flows from the head to the members, he makes us other "Christs." (*CCC*, 2782)

> **Fraction Rite** The time during the Communion Rite when the priest breaks the Body of Christ. He puts a piece of the consecrated bread into the chalice containing the Blood of Christ to signify the unity of the Body and Blood of Christ.

In the Rite of Peace, the "Church asks for peace and unity for herself and for the whole human family" (*General Instruction of the Roman Missal*, 82). The gathered people exchange a Sign of Peace as an expression of their communion with one another.

During the **Fraction Rite**, the priest repeats the action of Jesus at the Last Supper: he breaks the blessed bread. He puts a piece of the consecrated host into the chalice of wine to "signify the unity of the Body and Blood of the Lord in the work of salvation" (*GIRM*, 83). Meanwhile, the people sing the Lamb of God.

The reception of Communion follows. The priest is first to receive the Body and Blood of Christ. Then he and the Eucharistic ministers distribute Holy Communion to the people. In the Western Church, Catholics may receive the host on the tongue or in the hand, as they wish. Communion under both species (wheat bread and grape wine) is "more complete" since this is the way it was first shared at the Last Supper. However, because Christ is sacramentally present under each of the species, you receive all the grace of the Eucharist when you receive Communion under the species of bread alone.

After receiving Holy Communion, people spend time in private prayer as the cantor or choir sings an appropriate Communion song or a time of silence is observed. At the end of this time, the priest concludes the Communion Rite with a prayer after Communion.

Nourished by the Body and Blood of Christ, the faithful are then sent out into the world in the Concluding Rites, with an exhortation to serve Christ and to be Christ for others.

SECTION ASSESSMENT

NOTE TAKING

Draw from your outline to help you complete the following items.

1. What are the two main parts of the Mass?
2. What takes place during the Liturgy of the Word?
3. Explain the *epiclesis*.
4. What is the meaning of *anamnesis*? What is the anamnesis at Mass?

COMPREHENSION

5. From where are the three Scripture readings for a Sunday Mass usually taken?
6. What is the basis in Scripture for bringing gifts of money to the altar?
7. What is the high point of the Mass?
8. What are two important beliefs regarding the Eucharist that the intercessory prayers following the anamnesis remind you of?

APPLICATION

9. How might your increasing understanding of the Eucharistic liturgy influence your understanding and participation in the liturgy the next time you attend Mass?

SECTION 3
The Graces of Holy Communion

MAIN IDEA
Unity with Christ, forgiveness of venial sins, incorporation into the Church, and being Eucharist for others, especially the poor, are among the graces you receive from Holy Communion.

As you have learned, the Eucharist is the source and the summit of the Church's life. In the Eucharist, Christ unites the Church and all her members with his sacrifice on the Cross. Thus, when you receive the Eucharist, your relationship with Christ and the Church is strengthened. Consider what happened to two of Jesus' disciples shortly after the Crucifixion.

The two disheartened disciples were walking from Jerusalem to Emmaus. Along the way, a stranger joined them. He began to tell them about the meaning of the Scriptures, of Jesus' true identity as a "Suffering Servant"— that is, a Messiah who had to die for the sins of others. Later that day, when the disciples shared bread with this stranger, "their eyes were opened and they recognized him" as the Risen Jesus (Lk 24:31). This incredible experience of communion renewed the disciples and set their hearts aflame. They said to each other, "Were not our hearts burning [within us] while he spoke to us?" (Lk 24:32). They were immediately moved to go back to Jerusalem and tell everyone Jesus had risen and had appeared to them (see Luke 24:1–35). From their experience of Jesus in the figurative breaking open of God's Word and the literal breaking of the bread, they were empowered to go out and share Christ's love with others.

Likewise, your participation in the Eucharist and reception of Holy Communion will renew you and set you aflame with Christ's compelling love (see *Sacrosanctum Concilium*, 10). It strengthens your relationship not

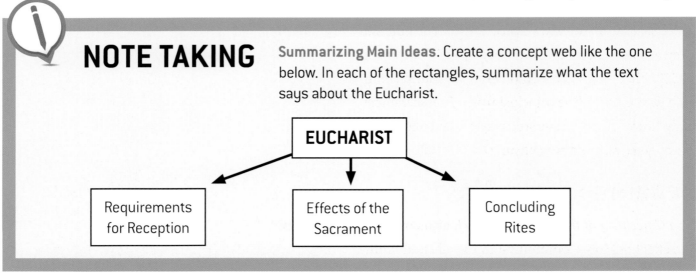

NOTE TAKING Summarizing Main Ideas. Create a concept web like the one below. In each of the rectangles, summarize what the text says about the Eucharist.

EUCHARIST

- Requirements for Reception
- Effects of the Sacrament
- Concluding Rites

only with Christ but also with others in his name, especially the poor. You become more generous, compassionate, and selfless. You are strengthened to love others because you know with certainty that God has first loved you (see 1 John 4:10). You also see the intimate connection between love of God and love of others. You know *in your heart* the truth contained in the First Letter of John:

> If anyone says, "I love God," but hates his brother, he is a liar; for whoever does not love a brother whom he has seen cannot love God whom he has not seen. This is the commandment we have from him: whoever loves God must also love his brother. (1 Jn 4:20–21)

The Eucharist does not only enable you to love others *in imitation of* Christ; it also enables you to be so united with Christ that he reveals himself to others through you. The *Catechism of the Catholic Church* describes several particular fruits, or effects, of your participation in the Eucharist and reception of Holy Communion in more detail. Brief descriptions of these effects follow.

Unity with Christ

The *Catechism of the Catholic Church* teaches, "The celebration of the Eucharistic sacrifice is wholly directed toward the intimate union of the faithful with Christ through communion. To receive communion is to receive Christ himself who has offered himself for us" (*CCC,* 1382). This communion is so intimate that Christ becomes a part of you and you become a part of him. You deepen your identity as his very body (see 1 Corinthians 12:27). That Holy Communion expands your relationship with Christ is the principal fruit of the sacrament. Holy Communion "preserves, increases, and renews the life of grace received at Baptism" (*CCC,* 1392).

Separation from Sin

The *Catechism of the Catholic Church* also compares the effect of Holy Communion to the effect of bodily nourishment on a weakened body: "As bodily nourishment restores lost strength, so the Eucharist strengthens our charity, which tends to be weakened in daily life; and this living charity *wipes away venial sins*" (*CCC,* 1394). In other words, the Eucharist separates

♥ Christian LOVE

The first encyclical of Pope Benedict XVI, *Deus Caritas Est,* was about Christian love. The pope cited Mary, the Mother of Jesus, as an example of someone who is so united with Christ that others see Christ in her. The pope ended his encyclical with the following prayer:

> Holy Mary, Mother of God, you have given the world its true light, Jesus, your Son—the Son of God. You abandoned yourself completely to God's call and thus became a wellspring of the goodness that flows forth from him. Show us Jesus. Lead us to him. Teach us to know and love him, so that we too can become capable of true love and be fountains of living water in the midst of a thirsting world. (42)

ASSIGNMENT

- Write your own prayer, poem, or song to Christ in the Eucharist, asking that you may be so united with him that others may see him in you and through your actions. Pray for the increased ability to love others as Christ himself loved others. Be prepared to share what you have written at the prayer service at the end of this chapter.

you from sin and cleanses your soul of venial sins. Also, by drawing you closer to Christ's Passion and Resurrection, the Eucharist enables you to "share the life of Christ and progress in his friendship" and makes it "more difficult . . . to break away from him by mortal sin" (*CCC*, 1395). Yet although the Eucharist protects you from future mortal sins, it is not intended for the forgiveness of past mortal sins. Instead, God grants you this forgiveness through the Sacrament of Penance and Reconciliation.

Becoming United with Others

Just as the Eucharist deepens your relationship with Christ, it also unites you to your brothers and sisters in the Church. Every celebration of the Sacrament of the Eucharist helps those who are united through Baptism to form and build the Church. You act *as a member of the Church* whenever you participate in the Eucharist. Each Mass unites you with the whole Church through your bishop and your local community. As a Sacrament of Initiation, the Eucharist both incorporates you more completely into the Church and nourishes you spiritually so that you actually become united with other Catholics.

Strengthened by the Eucharist, you can express and "portray to others the mystery of Christ and the real nature of the true church" (*Sacrosanctum Concilium*, 2). What are some ways you can do this in your everyday life? Here are some examples:

1. You can participate actively in the entire life of the local parish.

2. You can contribute money, time, and/or goods to the missionary activity of the Church in rural areas or in other countries.

3. You can "animate" your family, school, and workplace with "the spirit of Christianity" through your attitude and example (see *Gaudium et Spes*, 43).

4. You can engage in **evangelization**—spreading the message of Jesus to others through your daily words and actions.

5. You can build community with the members of your parish.

6. You can help strengthen the unity of all Christians through prayer.

evangelization Bringing the Good News of Jesus Christ to others.

Becoming a Source of Sustenance for Those in Need

Another fruit of the Eucharist is that it transforms your relationship with the poor and all those who suffer. The *Catechism of the Catholic Church* points out that "the Eucharist commits us to the poor. To receive in truth the Body and Blood of Christ given up for us, we must recognize Christ in the poorest, his brethren" (*CCC,* 1397). This unity with the poor has been bound to the celebration of the Eucharist since the time of the early Christians. These Christians held all things in common until there was no distinction between rich and poor (see Acts 2:44–45).

The Eucharist is both a sacrifice and a heavenly meal that facilitates communion of the faithful with the Blessed Trinity, with other Catholics, and with those outside of the Church. The Eucharist is also a foretaste of the heavenly banquet you will one day experience in union with the Blessed Trinity. Through the Eucharist, you become a source of sustenance for others in need. Through the Eucharist, you sacrifice your own needs, as Jesus himself did, in service to others.

Receiving the Eucharist

Before receiving Holy Communion at Mass, you pray, "Lord, I am not worthy that you should enter under my roof, but only say the word and my soul shall be healed" (*Roman Missal*). In spite of this unworthiness to receive his Body and Blood, Christ desires deep union with you. For this reason, the Church encourages frequent reception of this sacrament. The *Catechism of the Catholic Church* states,

> It is in keeping with the very meaning of the Eucharist that the faithful, if they have the required dispositions, *receive communion when they participate in the Mass.* (*CCC,* 1388)

The Second Vatican Council describes the reception of Holy Communion at Mass as the "more perfect form of participation in the Mass" (*Sacrosanctum Concilium*, 55).

Yet although receiving Communion is desirable, you must, as the *Catechism* explains, have the required disposition. To find out what *required disposition* means, read and answer for yourself the following two questions.

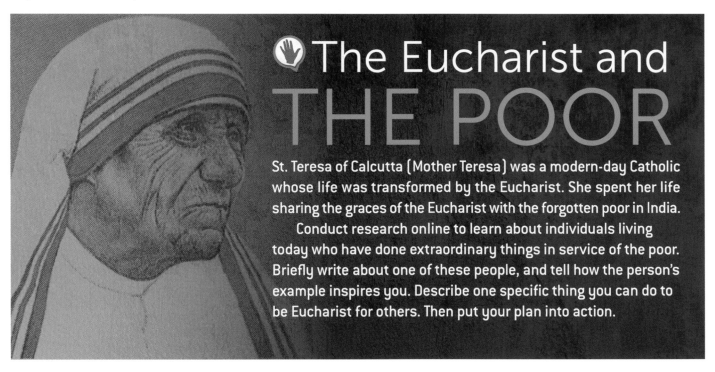

The Eucharist and THE POOR

St. Teresa of Calcutta (Mother Teresa) was a modern-day Catholic whose life was transformed by the Eucharist. She spent her life sharing the graces of the Eucharist with the forgotten poor in India. Conduct research online to learn about individuals living today who have done extraordinary things in service of the poor. Briefly write about one of these people, and tell how the person's example inspires you. Describe one specific thing you can do to be Eucharist for others. Then put your plan into action.

This means you are free from grave or mortal sin. If you answered yes, go on to question 2. If you answered no, you must receive absolution in the Sacrament of Penance before approaching the Sacrament of the Eucharist. (Note that the second precept of the Church requires that all Catholics confess their grave sins at least once a year in the Sacrament of Penance.)

2. Have you prepared by fasting (for one hour in the Roman Catholic Church, from midnight in the Eastern Churches)?

This fast reminds you that the Eucharist is not ordinary food. It also reminds you to abstain from words and deeds that undermine your unity with Christ and his Church. If you answered yes to this question as well, you have the required disposition to receive Holy Communion.

Also remember that your outward appearance (your clothing, your words, and your actions) are to convey the respect, solemnity, and joy of this great gift. This means you should celebrate the Eucharist dressed in your "Sunday best"—that is, in neat, modest clothing, dressier than everyday clothing, that speaks to your own dignity and shows respect for Christ. Your words and actions should similarly reflect your own dignity and your position as a disciple of Christ. Do you meet all these standards as well?

As you anticipate this coming Sunday's Mass, prepare by examining your conscience, celebrating the Sacrament of Penance if needed, and making sure your outward appearance (clothing, words, actions) shows reverence for Christ in the Eucharist.

To prepare yourself for such a great and holy moment as reception of Holy Communion, you should heed St. Paul's call to examine your conscience:

> Therefore whoever eats the bread or drinks the cup of the Lord unworthily will have to answer for the body and blood of the Lord. A person should examine himself, and so eat the bread and drink the cup. For anyone who eats and drinks without discerning the body, eats and drinks judgment on himself. (1 Cor 11:27–29)

Church law requires members to "take part in the Divine Liturgy on Sundays and feast days . . . and to receive the Eucharist at least once a year, if possible during the Easter season" (*CCC*, 1389). Further, because the Eucharist nourishes Catholics spiritually and strengthens their bond of friendship with God, the Church "strongly encourages the faithful to receive the holy Eucharist on Sundays and feast days, or more often still, even daily" (*CCC*, 1389). You are also permitted to receive the Eucharist a second time on the same day, as long you do so within the celebration of a Mass you attend.

Based on the Gospel story in which Jesus said, "Let the children come to me" (Mk 10:14), St. Pius X lowered the age for First Communion to seven years in 1910 as part of a liturgical movement that viewed reception of Holy Communion as an integral part of the Mass.

In addition to obeying the Church's rules regarding the reception of Communion, it is important to desire to be one with God in Jesus and the Holy Spirit.

You Are Sent

When you participate in the communal celebration of the Sunday Eucharist, you give testimony to your belonging to, and being faithful to, Christ and his Church. You also give witness to your faithfulness to Christ by your communion in faith and charity. As a community, you and the other recipients of Holy

Communion testify to God's holiness and your hope of salvation. You strengthen one another under the guidance of the Holy Spirit.

You continue this witness in your daily life after the liturgy concludes. In the Concluding Rites at Mass, the priest or deacon commissions and sends you to go out into the world and spread the Gospel. Just as Jesus commissioned and sent his Apostles to teach the entire world about him and his message (see Matthew 28:19–20), so the Church sends you forth from the Eucharist to share your communion with the Blessed Trinity, the Church, and others, especially the poor.

The Concluding Rites are short and simple. The priest or deacon may say one of the following:

- "Go forth, the Mass is ended."
- "Go and announce the Gospel of the Lord."
- "Go in peace, glorifying the Lord by your life."
- "Go in peace."

You reply: "Thanks be to God" (*Roman Missal*).

The message of the Concluding Rites, then, is that because of the Eucharist you have just celebrated, the Lord is both with and within you. His sanctifying grace empowers you to go forth and *to be Eucharist* for others—at home, at school, at work, in your neighborhood, and in your country. You have an important mission—not only to spread the Good News of Jesus but to be Christ in today's world.

This is one of the reasons the Second Vatican Council clearly stated that the Eucharist is "the source and summit of the Christian life" (*Lumen Gentium*, 11). In the Eucharist, Christ associates his Church and all her members with his sacrifice of praise and thanksgiving offered to his Father. By this sacrifice, offered on the Cross for all people, Christ pours out the graces of salvation on his Body, the Church. You need the Eucharist to nourish you and keep you connected more closely to Jesus, the Bread of Life and the True Vine. At the same time, Christ, through the Eucharist,

Worshippers leaving Sunday Mass at St Joseph's Church in Stone Town, Zanzibar.

renews, strengthens, and deepens your membership in the Church that was already achieved at Baptism. You are to continue his work in today's world.

Pope John Paul II explained that incorporation into Christ is "constantly renewed and consolidated by sharing in the Eucharistic sacrifice"; that, when you celebrate Eucharist, you become "a 'sacrament' for humanity . . . the light of the world and the salt of the earth . . . for the redemption of all" (*Ecclesia de Eucharistia*, 22). The Eucharist sends you out into the world ready to love more completely. Moreover, it sends you out not only as a loving individual, but also with others as a loving community. The Eucharist strengthens the bonds between all who receive it and makes it possible for you to demonstrate to yourself, among others, the love you are to share with the world.

SECTION ASSESSMENT

NOTE TAKING

Use the concept web you created to complete the following items.

1. Name the fruits or effects of the Sacrament of the Eucharist.

2. What type of sin is forgiven in the Sacrament of the Eucharist?

3. Name two ways reception of Holy Communion helps Catholics "be Eucharist" for others.

4. How can participation in the Eucharist encourage charitable actions—especially to the poor?

5. What does it mean to have the proper disposition to receive Holy Communion?

COMPREHENSION

6. How did Pope John Paul II relate incorporation into Christ to receiving the Eucharist?

REFLECTION

7. Choose one fruit of Holy Communion and describe it in more detail.

Section Summaries

Focus Question

Why is the Eucharist the "source and summit" of the Christian life?

Complete one of the following:

 Create a photo collage that captures the essence of the statement "source and summit" as it relates to the Eucharist. Include six to eight photos.

 Write a poem or prayer expressing the importance of the Eucharist in your life.

 Research the life of a saint who is known for special devotion to the Eucharist. Write two or three paragraphs about the saint and his or her devotion.

INTRODUCTION (PAGES 141–143)
Source and Summit

The term *Eucharist* refers both to the Mass and to the consecrated species of bread and wine. The Sacrament of the Eucharist has many other names because its richness is truly inexhaustible.

 Imagine that you must explain the Eucharist to a non-Catholic. Choose three names for the Eucharist noted in your text and write a one- or two-paragraph explanation of each term addressed to a non-Catholic.

SECTION 1 (PAGES 144–152)
Understanding the Sacrament of the Eucharist

Christ instituted the Eucharist as a memorial of his Death and Resurrection. Through the Eucharist, he redeems people from sin and leads them to freedom. By the words of Christ and the invocation of the Holy Spirit, bread and wine become the Body and Blood of the Lord at Mass.

Read paragraphs 1341 to 1343 of the *Catechism of the Catholic Church*. Write a one-sentence summary for each of these paragraphs.

SECTION 2 (PAGES 153–161)

Celebrating the Sacrament of the Eucharist

The Mass is divided into two parts: the Liturgy of the Word and the Liturgy of the Eucharist. The Eucharistic Prayer is the high point of the Liturgy of the Eucharist and of the Mass itself.

→ Identify the Scripture readings for an upcoming Sunday. Write a three-paragraph "mini-homily" that highlights the common theme of the First Reading and the Gospel while mentioning something from the Second Reading as well. Also list the Sunday you have chosen, its cycle in the Lectionary, and the Scripture references. (You can find the readings for the coming Sunday—and the whole liturgical year—at www.usccb.org/bible/readings.)

SECTION 3 (PAGES 162–168)

The Graces of Holy Communion

Catholics are obliged to attend and participate at Mass on Sundays and other holy days of obligation. Grace from the Eucharistic liturgy is a source of unity with Christ and with other Catholics. The grace also brings about a cleansing from venial sin and a commitment to others, especially the poor.

→ Review the requirements for reception of Holy Communion (see pages 165–166). Write a two- or three-paragraph reflection on the meaning of those requirements and how they enrich your faith life and devotion to the Eucharist.

Chapter Assignments

Choose and complete at least one of the following three assignments assessing your understanding of the material in this chapter.

1. A Video Interview on the Eucharist

→ Create a "man on the street" type of question-and-answer video by asking questions about the Eucharist to several people in your school community (e.g., classmates, teachers, campus minister, coaches, administrators, etc.). You may also choose to substitute random parishioners as your subjects. (If you choose this option, consider taping the interviews outside the church after Sunday Mass.) Here are some possible questions to ask your subjects. You can also add your own.

- Define the word *Eucharist*.
- How do you understand Christ's Real Presence in the Eucharist?
- Why do you think the Church describes the Eucharist as the "source and summit" of Christian life?
- Why is the Eucharist central to your life as a Catholic?

Edit your video around common questions or themes. Download your video to a public media site available for viewing at your school, and arrange to play it for your teacher and classmates.

2. A Children's First Communion Book

→ Using your own drawings, photos, and some written words, create a Mass book for young children of First Communion age. Represent each of the main parts of the Mass (see page 155) with images children can understand. Follow these guidelines:

- Create a front cover, a back cover, a title page, and sixteen to twenty inside pages.
- Cite the main parts of the Mass (Introductory Rites, Liturgy of the Word, Liturgy of the Eucharist, and Concluding Rites) and all of the elements that fall under each part.
- Include at least one quotation from a saint or a pope.
- Use both text and images, remembering that the text should be written at about second-grade reading level. However, the names for the parts and elements of the Mass should not be changed.

Develop your Mass book digitally or in print. After it has been graded, refer to the material in this chapter to offer a "closing commentary" that corrects any erroneous answers. Arrange to give the book to a family member or parishioner who is preparing for First Communion.

3. Gospel Reflections on the Eucharist

Read each of the following Gospel passages, which foreshadow Jesus' gift of himself in the Eucharist. Copy the title of each passage and the Scripture passage onto a piece of paper. Under the title, draw your own image or copy an image from another source that represents the passage. Next, copy the boldfaced question and one of the other two questions onto your paper and write a response of at least three sentences to each.

Gospel Passages and Questions

The Wedding at Cana (John 2:1–11)

- What is something you did only because a parent wanted you to?

- How do your parents treat you when you are with them in a social gathering with their friends?

- **How did this miracle preview what Jesus would do at the Last Supper? How would you have reacted to it if you had been there?**

Jesus Feeds the Thousands (Mark 6:30–52 and 8:1–10)

- When was a time you were overwhelmed by a crowd and wanted to send them away or to get away yourself?

- **What verses sound like "Eucharistic language" in each of the passages? What posture, attitude, and response do you have when you hear these words at Mass?**

- How does what Jesus wants to do with the crowds differ from what his disciples wish to do? What would you have done?

The Bread of Life Sermon (John 6:22–69)

- **Many listeners had difficulty accepting Jesus' words "I am the bread of life" and his charge to eat his flesh and drink his blood. What are some of the things you think they found hard about this teaching? What do you find hard about this teaching?**

- Recall your understanding of the Eucharist when you made your First Communion. How is your understanding different today?

- Some of Jesus' disciples left him on hearing this teaching. The Twelve remained. Peter gave his reason for remaining with Jesus. Why do you remain his follower? Give one specific, personal reason.

Faithful Disciple

St. Katharine Drexel

By the end of her life, St. Katharine Drexel had established 145 missions as well as sixty-two schools.

If you won a five-million-dollar lottery, what would you do with the money?

In 1885, a young woman in Philadelphia, Pennsylvania, was left nearly that much money (worth many times more than that today) at her father's death. Her name was Katharine Drexel. She came from a wealthy Catholic family—a family who lived their faith by generously giving to all in need. The family did not flaunt their generosity or condescend to those with whom they shared. As Katharine's mother used to say, "Kindness may be unkind if it leaves a sting behind."

At about age twenty-five, Katharine took a trip out West that exposed her to the extreme poverty of the Native American peoples and changed the course of her life. Katharine used some of her inheritance to found a school for Native Americans in Santa Fe, New Mexico, in 1887. She was also concerned about African Americans, who suffered from discrimination and lack of opportunity.

During a vacation trip to Rome, Katharine had an audience with Pope Leo XIII. She expressed her concerns and asked the pope to send missionaries to the United States. The pope in turn asked her, "But why not be a missionary yourself, my child?"

Katharine answered this question by joining the Sisters of Mercy, with the aim of founding a new religious community. The community's special mission would be to work among the Native American and African American people in the United States. By the time she died, St. Katharine and her community had founded sixty schools. Among them was Xavier University in New Orleans, the only African American Catholic college in the United States.

Mother Katharine Drexel had a special love for the Eucharist, and this love was reflected in the name she chose for her new community: the Sisters of the Blessed Sacrament. At the end of her life, when she was afflicted with paralysis, she spent long hours in prayer before Jesus in the Eucharist. St. Katharine desired that everyone come to a love of the Blessed Sacrament. Pope John Paul II canonized St. Katharine Drexel on October 1, 2000.

Reading Comprehension

1. What was one of the first things Katharine did with her inheritance?

2. Who urged her to consider a vocation as a missionary?

3. What did Katharine call her new community, and why?

Writing Task

- Write a letter to a Sister of the Blessed Sacrament. Ask her how her vocation and ministry have drawn inspiration from St. Katharine Drexel. Mail your letter.

Explaining the Faith

How do Catholics show reverence for and devotion to the Eucharist?

Because Jesus himself, in his Body and Blood, is truly present in the Eucharist, Catholics express reverence for the Eucharist. They do so in different and important ways.

First, Catholics show reverence for the Eucharist through gestures such as bowing deeply and genuflecting when they approach the altar or the tabernacle, where the Body of Christ under the species of unleavened bread—called the Blessed Sacrament—is reserved. The Church recommends that the tabernacle be located in an especially worthy place in every church. When the Blessed Sacrament is in repose in the tabernacle, a light is kept burning next to it at all times as a symbol of Christ's presence.

Second, Catholics honor and worship Christ in the Blessed Sacrament through *Eucharistic Exposition*. In Eucharistic Exposition, the Blessed Sacrament is placed in a sacred vessel called a *monstrance* and set on the altar so the faithful can contemplate the presence of Christ in quiet prayer, or adoration. Many parishes offer weekly times for Eucharistic Adoration. Some parishes or religious communities even offer Perpetual Adoration, in which members of the parish or community take hours of adoration before the exposed Blessed Sacrament throughout the day and night for a set period of time (days, weeks, or perpetually).

Catholics honor and worship Christ even when the Blessed Sacrament is in the tabernacle and not exposed. The next time you are in church, pay special attention to the tabernacle. In addition to bowing or genuflecting in reverence, why not also stop for some quiet prayer? Also take time to learn about your own, or another local parish's, times for Eucharistic Adoration, and make time to participate and visit with Jesus in silent prayer. As Pope Paul VI wrote in his encyclical *Mysterium Fidei* (*Mystery of Faith*), "to visit the Blessed Sacrament is a proof of gratitude, an expression of love, and a duty of adoration toward Christ our Lord" (66).

 Further Research

- Check your parish's website or weekly bulletin for times when Eucharistic Adoration is offered, and attend. Write a reflection about your experience.

Prayer
Prayer before Communion

I believe, O Lord, and I confess that Thou are truly the Christ, the Son of the living God, who came into the world to save sinners, of whom I am first. I believe also that this is truly Thine own most pure Body, and this is truly Thine own precious Blood. Therefore, I pray Thee: have mercy upon me and forgive my transgressions both voluntary and involuntary, of word and of deed, committed in knowledge or in ignorance. And make me worthy to partake without condemnation of Thy most pure Mysteries, for the remission of my sins and unto life everlasting. Amen.

Of Thy Mystical Supper, O Son of God, accept me today as a communicant; for I will not speak of Thy Mystery to Thine enemies, neither like Judas will I give Thee a kiss; but like the thief will I confess Thee: Remember me, O Lord, in Thy Kingdom.

May the communion of Thy holy Mysteries be neither to my judgment, nor to my condemnation, O Lord, but to the healing of soul and body. Amen.

—An Eastern Catholic prayer

THE SACRAMENT OF PENANCE AND RECONCILIATION

6

MAKING THING$ RIGHT

In a cemetery in Bethany, Oklahoma, Tona Herndon was visiting the grave of her recently deceased husband. Since his burial, Tona had come to visit daily.

As she knelt to place flowers at the grave, she felt a violent tug at her shoulder. Her purse was torn from her, with money, keys, and personal information inside. She saw the man running away. Because the suspect tried to use her credit card, the police identified him and put his photo on the local news.

A fifteen-year-old named Christian Lunsford saw a picture of the suspect on television and recognized him. The man was his father, who had a history of petty crime and was often in and out of jail. The two had only occasional contact, but Christian thought of the $250 his father had recently given him to pay for band camp. Could the money have come from that widow's purse? Christian didn't know for sure, but he knew that, in good conscience, he could not keep the money.

Christian phoned Mrs. Herndon and asked to meet with her. She agreed, and the two arranged to meet in a church parking lot. Christian apologized to the seventy-eight-year-old widow in the name of his father.

Then he gave Mrs. Herndon the $250. Mrs. Herndon graciously accepted his apology and the money but then immediately returned the money to him, saying, "I want you to take your band trip."

Later, Christian told CBS News, "It needed to be done. She needed an apology from somebody. If I didn't apologize, who would?"

(Based on two articles from *The Blaze*, an online newspaper, dated August 21, 2013, and September 29, 2013.)

FOCUS QUESTION

Why do Catholics CONFESS THEIR SINS in the Sacrament of PENANCE AND RECONCILIATION?

INTRODUCTION
A Marvelous Reality

MAIN IDEA
When you approach the Sacrament of Penance in faith, you are cleansed of your sins and restored to grace.

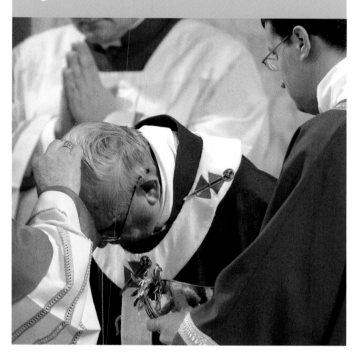

Jesus Christ, as "physician of our souls and bodies" (*CCC*, 1421), left the Church two sacraments—the Sacrament of Penance and Reconciliation and the Sacrament of the Anointing of the Sick—that bring both healing and sanctification. The subject of Chapter 6 is the Sacrament of Penance and Reconciliation, or in short form, the Sacrament of Penance. In Chapter 7, you will learn about the Sacrament of the Anointing of the Sick.

You are probably familiar with the Sacrament of Penance. How often do you go to confession? How do you decide when it is time for you to go? The second precept of the Catholic Church calls you to confess your sins at least once a year by receiving the Sacrament of Penance. Doing so helps you recognize that "individual, integral confession and absolution remain the only ordinary way for the faithful to reconcile themselves with God and the Church, unless physical or moral impossibility excuses from this kind of confession" (*CCC*, 1484).

This truth is not always accepted today. You may even have heard people say, mistakenly, that you

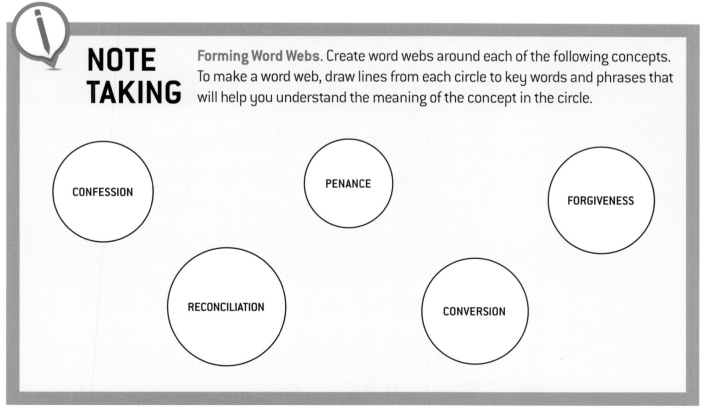

NOTE TAKING **Forming Word Webs**. Create word webs around each of the following concepts. To make a word web, draw lines from each circle to key words and phrases that will help you understand the meaning of the concept in the circle.

CONFESSION

PENANCE

FORGIVENESS

RECONCILIATION

CONVERSION

only need to go to confession if you have committed an extremely serious sin, like murder. Some people believe that you don't have to go to confession at all.

Catholics who do not participate in the Sacrament of Penance are missing a great deal. After Baptism, it is only through this sacrament that your soul can be cleansed of serious sin. The sacrament provides great riches of grace if you approach it in humility and love. It is nothing less than, in the words of Pope Benedict XVI, "a spiritual rebirth, which transforms the **penitent** into a new creature. . . . This is a marvelous reality that the Lord gives us" (Address to clergy of the Diocese of Rome, February 6, 2008).

Pope Francis has also spoken of this renewal: "When one is in line to go to Confession, one feels all these things, even shame, but then when one finishes Confession one leaves free, grand, beautiful, forgiven, candid, happy. This is the beauty of Confession!" (General Audience, February 19, 2014).

As you know, *sacraments* are "efficacious signs of grace, instituted by Christ and entrusted to the Church, by which divine life is dispensed to us" through the work of the Holy Spirit (*CCC,* 1131). When Jesus forgave sinners, his actions anticipated four dimensions of the Sacrament of Penance:

Memorial	The sacrament recalls the many times God welcomed the Israelites back to the Covenant and the many times Jesus forgave sinners.
Celebration	The sacrament reflects great joy at the forgiveness and mercy of God.
Communion	The sacrament restores your fellowship with God, others, and yourself.
Transformation	The sacrament offers a rebirth of sorts as the result of God's sanctifying grace.

Today, this sacrament of healing is called by many names, depending upon what part of the sacrament is being emphasized. It is sometimes called the *sacrament of conversion* because in it Catholics resolve to turn away from sin and return to God's grace. Other times, it is called the *sacrament of confession* because it involves telling your sins to a priest. It is also called the *sacrament of penance* because it makes holy your personal efforts and efforts within the Church of conversion, penance, and satisfaction. It is called the *sacrament of forgiveness* because through the sacrament, God forgives your sins. And finally, it is called the *sacrament of reconciliation* because through this sacrament, Catholics are reunited with God and the Church.

The Need for This Sacrament

A world without sin would not need the Sacrament of Penance. Your initial conversion as a son or daughter of God through the Sacraments of Christian Initiation would have transformed you into a perfect follower

penitent A person who admits his or her sins, is truly sorry for having sinned, and wishes to be restored to relationship with God and the Church.

of Jesus Christ. Remember, too, that Baptism wipes Original Sin from your soul. Unfortunately, *concupiscence*, the inclination to sin that can lead even baptized believers to fall into daily sin, remains.

When Jesus began his public ministry, he called people to "repent, and believe in the gospel" (Mk 1:15). He also commissioned his disciples to baptize people of all nations (see Matthew 28:19). Jesus knew that conversion is a lifelong process. Everyone is continually tempted to sin, and sometimes people deliberately sin. You continually need God's grace and forgiveness. The Sacrament of Penance is a sign of God's willingness to extend this forgiveness as often as you need it, showing a love that is truly a "marvelous reality."

SECTION ASSESSMENT

NOTE TAKING

Use the word webs you created for this section to help you complete the following questions.

1. How do the different names for the Sacrament of Penance show the different aspects of the sacrament?
2. Which names emphasize recognizing your own sins?
3. Which names emphasize the mercy and love of God?

COMPREHENSION

4. Name the four dimensions of the Sacrament of Penance that are anticipated by Jesus' actions in the Gospels.
5. Why do Catholics need the Sacrament of Penance?

REFLECTION

6. Recall your last visit to the Sacrament of Penance. How did it help you remember or celebrate God's forgiveness, return to a state of communion, or find transforming grace?

SECTION 1
Understanding the Sacrament of Penance and Reconciliation

MAIN IDEA

Jesus established the Sacrament of Penance and Reconciliation as a way for you to access God's forgiveness and continue your conversion of heart after Baptism; although the format of the sacrament has changed over time, the purpose remains the same.

Jesus instituted the Sacrament of Penance as a call to continuing conversion after Baptism. The sacrament is rooted in Jesus' own forgiving actions and in his command to the Apostles after the Resurrection: "Receive the Holy Spirit. Whose sins you forgive are forgiven them, and whose sins you retain are retained" (Jn 20:22–23).

Only God forgives sins (see *CCC*, 1441, 1444). During his public ministry, Jesus forgave sinners. In addition to the paralytic who was lying on a stretcher (see Matthew 9:1–7, Mark 2:1–12, Luke 5:17–26), he forgave the woman who washed his feet with her tears (see Luke 7:36–50), the tax collector who repented of cheating people (see Luke 19:1–10), and the soldiers who nailed him to the Cross (see Luke 23:34). Jesus' forgiveness engendered the wrath of the Pharisees; they thought he was committing blasphemy in making himself God's equal. But that is exactly the point: Jesus forgives sins because he is the Son of God, the Second Person of the Blessed Trinity. And because he is God, he is also able to empower his Church to forgive sins.

The Incarnation proved the Father's love for you. Jesus became human in order to atone for the sins of humans once and for all. Because of Christ, you are

NOTE TAKING

Chronicling the Development of the Sacraments. Draw a horizontal line to show the progression of time from the early Church to today. On it, mark these different stages of the development of the Sacrament of Penance. Write down some features of the sacrament at each stage to help you recall when each development took place.

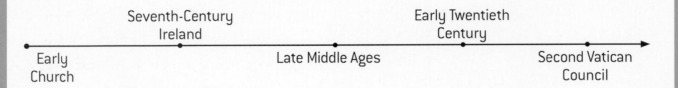

Seventh-Century Ireland   Early Twentieth Century

Early Church   Late Middle Ages   Second Vatican Council

no longer *only* a sinner. You are a sinner *who has been forgiven.* Through Jesus you have hope; you have a way back to reconciliation with the Father (see John 14:6).

The Sacrament of Penance shows that God is infinitely merciful and kind, that followers of Jesus are called to continual conversion, and that the reconciliation Jesus won for the world is offered to you through the Church.

God's Infinite Mercy

The Sacrament of Penance and Reconciliation reminds Catholics of what in Hebrew is known as *hesed*—that is, God's infinite mercy. God continuously calls you to friendship with him—not because you deserve it but because of his great love for you.

If you want to be on good terms with your friends, you allow friendship to grow over time. And you do not expect to keep a friend if you cause hurt without making amends. This also applies to your relationship with God. "We cannot be united with God unless we freely choose to love him" (*CCC*, 1033). Sin damages or destroys this love, but the Sacrament of Penance offers an opportunity for you to repair the relationship.

Sacred Scripture is the story of God's seeking friendship with humans, not the other way around. In the Old Testament, God is compassionate and merciful, and he saves his people in times of trouble. In the New Testament, Jesus reveals God as "Abba," a Father of love and forgiveness. The New Covenant focuses on your relationship with God, as the Old Testament prophet Jeremiah foretold:

> I will place my law within them, and write it upon their hearts; I will be their God, and they shall be my people. They will no longer teach their friends and relatives, "Know the LORD!" Everyone, from least to greatest, shall know me . . . for I will forgive their iniquity and no longer remember their sin. (Jer 31:33–34)

Nineteenth-century French artist Jean Alphonse Roehn's portrait Confession.

Jesus wants you to know that the Father seeks an intimate relationship with you. The New Covenant with God is written on your heart. It fulfills, and surpasses, the Old Covenant and brings it to perfection.

Ongoing Conversion

When Jesus called people to "repent, and believe in the gospel" (Mk 1:15), he knew this call would take a lifetime. As the *Catechism of the Catholic Church* explains, "Christ's call to conversion continues to resound in the lives of Christians. . . . A 'contrite heart' [is] drawn and moved by grace to respond to the merciful love of God who loved us first" (*CCC*, 1428). To Jesus, sin is equated with "hardness of heart." It cuts you off from God's invitation to love.

You can understand the kind of relationship God wants with you by recalling that Jesus told the Apostles

A Brief History of the
Sacrament of Penance

The first clear reference to a sacramental rite of healing after Baptism appears in the writings of the Church Fathers in *The Shepherd of Hermas* (AD 140–150). Early Christians who committed serious sins after Baptism (such as idolatry, murder, or adultery) were admitted into the Order of Penitents, in which they performed very

rigorous penances, sometimes for years. During this time, the sinners could not receive Holy Communion or socialize with other Christians. Only after they successfully completed the required penance did the bishop forgive their sins and readmit them to communion with the Church. Because of its public nature and difficulty, very few Christians enrolled in the Order of Penitents and received the Sacrament of Penance. Those who did typically did so only once in their lives.

In the seventh century, because no bishop was available to absolve people completing the Order of Penitents, Irish missionaries began to hear private confessions. Sinners confessed their sins, expressed sorrow, and performed a penance before receiving **absolution**. This practice eventually spread throughout the Church. Over time, priests began to give absolution to penitents at the time of confession, with the understanding that the penitents would complete the assigned penance afterward.

Procession of the Penitents Blancs at Puy-en-Velay on Good Friday *by Aime Olivier*

At one time, books called **penitentiaries** were common; they told confessors exactly what penances to give for each sin. Some people began to look at the sacrament as a matter of mathematics and formulas. They believed that God kept "score" of the times they had been good and bad. This view overemphasized justice at the expense of God's merciful love. Penitentiaries are no longer in use.

By the end of the Middle Ages, common advice encouraged confession before each reception of Holy Communion, so many people avoided receiving the Eucharist except on rare occasions. To confess and

> **absolution** The prayer by which a priest, through the power given to the Church by Jesus Christ, pardons a repentant sinner in the Sacrament of Penance.
>
> **penitentiaries** Books for confessors in the past that listed sins with corresponding penances.

Pope Pius X

receive more often was seen as unusual. In the early twentieth century, Pope Pius X promoted more frequent Communion for laypeople, and many more Catholics began to go to confession often, sometimes weekly. One of the things that contributed to the promotion of frequent Communion was a clear emphasis on the fact that only *mortal* sin debarred a person from Communion.

The new Rite of Penance, called for by the Second Vatican Council, emphasizes the call to an ongoing covenant of love and friendship with God and the Church. It focuses on celebrating the mercy of God, who continually calls you back to union with him.

In all eras, the Sacrament of Penance has given Catholics both God's forgiveness and the grace they need for lifelong conversion. The sacrament helps you maintain a good relationship with the Blessed Trinity. You are a *forgiven sinner*, not just a sinner.

they were his friends, not his servants or inferiors. "I no longer call you slaves, because a slave does not know what his master is doing. I have called you friends" (Jn 15:15). Jesus also proved what real friendship is about by dying on the Cross for the sins of others. "No one has greater love than this, to lay down one's life for one's friends" (Jn 15:13). Jesus wants you to be his friend.

If you truly love God and desire friendship with him, you will work to stay close to him. You will prove your sorrow for your sins "in visible signs, gestures and works of penance" (*CCC*, 1430). Even more important, you will try your best not to sin at all. "You are my friends if you do what I command you" (Jn 15:14). You will strive to obey the commandments.

Following divine law, though, does not mean placing rules before love. The Pharisees criticized Jesus when he disobeyed their strict interpretation of the Sabbath laws. These laws forbade work on the Sabbath, and yet Jesus let his disciples pick grain and prepare food on the Sabbath (see Matthew 12:1–8). He also performed miracles on the Sabbath (see Mark 3:1–6, Luke 13:10–17, Luke 14:1–6, John 5:1–18). Jesus showed that love, generosity, and self-sacrifice are more important than simply obeying laws. Just as God is merciful toward you, so you should be merciful toward others.

Yet Jesus did not give people license to abandon religious laws altogether. Instead, he said:

> Do not think that I have come to abolish the law or the prophets. I have come not to abolish but to fulfill. Amen, I say to you, until heaven and earth pass away, not the smallest letter or the smallest part of a letter will pass from the law, until all things have taken place. Therefore, whoever breaks one of the least of these commandments and teaches others to do so will be called least in the kingdom of heaven. But whoever obeys and teaches these

Tracing the HISTORY

Throughout the history of the Church, the Sacrament of Penance has taken many forms, but certain features have remained the same. Read paragraphs 1446 to 1448 of the *Catechism of the Catholic Church*. Then write one paragraph explaining how both the actions of the penitent and the actions of God through the Church are essential to this sacrament.

commandments will be called greatest in the kingdom of heaven. I tell you, unless your righteousness surpasses that of the scribes and Pharisees, you will not enter into the kingdom of heaven. (Mt 5:17–20)

Jesus was teaching you that your motive for following the commandments is vitally important. If you are truly a friend of God, you will nurture that friendship by keeping the commandments.

The Church and the Sacrament of Penance

When Jesus won the Father's forgiveness for humankind, he also chose to give access to that forgiveness to those who believed through his Apostles and their successors. He gave the Church the power to forgive sins in his name, as the following Scripture passages teach:

And so I say to you, you are Peter, and upon this rock I will build my church, and the gates of the netherworld shall not prevail against it. I will give you the keys to the kingdom of heaven. Whatever you bind on earth shall be bound in heaven; and whatever you loose on earth shall be loosed in heaven. (Mt 16:18–19)

And when he had said this, he breathed on them and said to them, "Receive the holy Spirit. Whose sins you forgive are forgiven them, and whose sins you retain are retained." (Jn 20:22–23)

The Apostles did not absolve sinners by their own authority. Rather, Christ acted through them to forgive the sins of others. In other words, Jesus delegated his authority to forgive sinners. "He entrusted the ministry of reconciliation to the Church, in the person of the Apostles" (*Decree by Sacred Congregation for Divine Worship, Rite of Penance*). Because of this act of trust, "*reconciliation with the Church is inseparable from reconciliation with God*" (*CCC*, 1445).

The Church's ministers of the sacrament are bishops and priests. As such, they must remain faithful to Church teaching, lead the people to moral healing and spiritual maturity, pray and do penance themselves for penitents, and encourage everyone to confess their sins. Priests must make themselves readily available for confession, establishing regular schedules for the sacrament in their parishes. Through these efforts, they help to bring people back into communion with the Church.

SECTION ASSESSMENT

NOTE TAKING

Use the timeline you created for this section to help you complete the following questions.

1. How was the Sacrament of Penance celebrated in the early Church?
2. How did private celebration of the Sacrament of Penance arise?
3. What development in the practice of this sacrament did Pope Pius X promote?
4. What aspect of the sacrament does the new Rite of Penance emphasize?

VOCABULARY

5. What purpose did a *penitentiary* once serve?

COMPREHENSION

6. Name one example of how Jesus forgave sinners in his public ministry.
7. What does the Sacrament of Penance teach about God's infinite mercy?
8. Who are the ministers of the Sacrament of Penance?

CRITICAL THINKING

9. What are some logical outcomes of the belief that God keeps a strict, unforgiving tally of your good and bad actions? What harm could this error cause?

SECTION 2

Celebrating the Sacrament of Penance and Reconciliation

MAIN IDEA

Through three main acts of the penitent—contrition, confession, and penance—and one act of the priest, namely absolution, the Sacrament of Penance and Reconciliation restores Catholics to a state of grace.

The Rite of Penance allows for three ways to celebrate the sacrament. These three ways are detailed here:

1. *Private individual confession.* This is the "only ordinary way" for Catholics to be reconciled with God after a mortal sin (see *CCC*, 1484). You may confess your sins anonymously behind a screen to a priest, or you may join the priest in a reconciliation room for face-to-face confession.

2. *Communal celebration with individual confession and individual absolution.* This practice is common in parishes during Advent and Lent. Parishioners come together to prepare themselves for the sacrament through a Liturgy of the Word, a common **examination of conscience**, and a communal request for forgiveness. This is followed by personal confession of sins to a priest and individual absolution. Finally, the sacrament ends with communal prayer (see *CCC*, 1482).

NOTE TAKING

Understanding Main Ideas. Create a two-column chart like the one below to help you recall what takes place at each stage of the Sacrament of Penance. Fill in the second column with relevant details.

STAGE	ACTIONS
Preparation	
Contrition	
Greeting	
Liturgy of the Word	
Confession	
Act of Contrition	
Absolution	
Penance	

3. *Communal celebration with general confession and general absolution.* Because no individual confession and absolution occurs here, this form of the sacrament is reserved for rare cases of grave necessity, at the discretion of the diocesan bishop (see *CCC*, 1483).

In any form, the Sacrament of Penance is a liturgical action. As you will usually experience it, the sacrament consists of several parts, including three essential acts of the penitent. These acts are contrition, confession of sins, and penance or satisfaction. Before these actions take place, the priest gives you a greeting and blessing. He welcomes you as Christ welcomed sinners. If you do not know the priest, you might take a moment to tell him your situation in life and about how long it has been since your last confession. Then the following dialogue takes place:

> PENITENT:
> *In the name of the Father, and of the Son, and of the Holy Spirit. Amen.*
>
> PRIEST:
> *May God, who has enlightened every heart, help you to know your sins and trust in his mercy.*
>
> PENITENT:
> *Amen.*

The Sign of the Cross connects this sacrament to Baptism, the original sacrament of forgiveness.

Like all sacramental rites, the Rite of Penance may include one or more readings from Scripture. The purpose of this Liturgy of the Word is to help you recognize not only your sins but also God's abundant mercy. No sin is too terrible for God to forgive. The priest may give a few words relating the Scripture reading to Christian life today.

Preparation of the Priest and Penitent

Before celebrating the Sacrament of Penance, both the celebrant and the penitent should prepare. As the *Rite of Penance* explains, the confessor "should call upon the Holy Spirit so that he may receive enlightenment and charity" (Intro, *Rite of Penance*, 15). You, as a penitent, also have preparation to do. You should make time for an honest examination of conscience so that you can acknowledge any sins you have committed since your last confession and pray for God's mercy.

Contrition

Following the examination of conscience, the first and most important act of the penitent is **contrition**. Contrition begins before the penitent arrives at the sacrament. You will be more able to have real contrition if you have a clear understanding of what sin is.

Sin is an offense against God as well as against reason, truth, and one's right conscience. Every sin hurts your relationship with God and the Church. Personal sins, or actual sins, are sins "in thought, word, deed, or omission" (*CCC*, 1853). For example, it is sinful to wish someone were harmed or killed, or to plot revenge (thoughts). It is sinful to spread false rumors (words) or to steal or commit murder (deeds). It is also sinful to refuse to act when you should (omission).

---

examination of conscience An honest self-assessment of how well you have lived God's covenant of love, leading you to accept responsibility for your sins and to realize your need for God's merciful forgiveness.

contrition Heartfelt sorrow for sins committed, along with the intention of sinning no more. This most important act of penitents is necessary for receiving absolution in the Sacrament of Penance.

Mortal sin destroys, or kills, your relationship with God and the Church. If not repented and forgiven by God, mortal sin removes you from God's Kingdom and leads you to hell. **Venial sin** weakens your relationship with God and the Church. A thorough examination of conscience will consider all the ways in which you may have hurt your relationship with God and the sins for which you are sorry and need his forgiveness.

Of course, the Sacrament of Penance is not an automatic removal of sin that you can obtain by merely going through the motions. It is not like a car wash, with drive-through cleaning. You need sincere contrition for your sins, which includes a firm desire for amendment—to try your best not to sin again. Contrition is much more than saying, "I'm sorry." *Perfect contrition* (also known as "contrition of charity") is sorrow for sin because you love God and want to be in relationship with him. *Imperfect contrition* (or "attrition") is sorrow for sin because you fear punishment or perceive the ugliness of sin. Imperfect contrition, as long as it's authentic, is sufficient for the valid celebration of the Sacrament of Penance (see *CCC*, 1453). Another name for contrition is *repentance*.

Confession of Sins

After expressing contrition by saying words such as "Forgive me, Father, for I have sinned," you then confess your sins. This second act of the penitent is an essential part of the Sacrament of Penance. To be forgiven, you must confess all mortal sins that you are aware (after making a serious examination

> **mortal sin** A serious, deadly violation of God's law of love that destroys sanctifying grace in the soul of the sinner. Mortal sins involve grave matter, full knowledge of the evil done, and full consent of the will.
>
> **venial sin** A sin that weakens and wounds your relationship with God but does not destroy grace in your soul.

CONDITIONS FOR MORTAL SIN

Mortal sin effectively destroys your relationship with God and kills your ability to love. Mortal sins cannot be committed by accident. For a sin to be mortal, three conditions must exist:

1 The moral object must be of grave or serious matter. Grave matter is specified in the Ten Commandments (e.g., do not kill, do not commit adultery, do not steal, etc.)

2 The person must have full knowledge of the gravity of the sinful action.

3 The person must completely consent to the action. It must be a personal choice.

Ignorance can reduce or even remove the responsibility for mortal sin. "But no one is deemed to be ignorant of the principles of the moral law, which are written on the conscience of every man" (*CCC*, 1860). The most serious mortal sins are those committed through malice, by deliberately choosing evil.

Some confessionals, such as this one in Bolivia, blend in with the church's architecture.

of conscience) of having committed since your last confession.

Your inner examination of conscience, which is an honest assessment of the times and ways you have broken God's law of love, and your exterior confession of sin are made in light of God's mercy. You admit you cannot live without God's love and generosity. Confessing your sins is an open statement that you need God, that you can't "go it alone" in the spiritual life.

Confession initiates conversion and creates a new life for you in the Church. When you confess your sins to a priest, you admit the harm you have caused to others. You admit that your sin affected the entire Body of Christ. You express your belief in the goodness of the Church that will welcome you back.

moral object A term for the material or content of a moral action, whether good, evil, or neutral. If the moral object of an act is evil, the act itself is evil.

sacramental seal The secrecy priests are bound to keep regarding any sins confessed to them.

The graces you receive from a good confession (see pages 196–202) are many. Often, you feel as if a physical burden has been lifted from you through naming your sins and declaring your sorrow. When you confess all mortal sins that you remember, you place them before God's mercy for pardon. A penitent who knowingly withholds a mortal sin from the priest in confession cannot receive remission of his or her sins. The Council of Trent, quoting St. Jerome, compared this to a sick person's being too ashamed to show his wound to the doctor: "The medicine cannot heal what it does not know."

Although confession of venial sins is not strictly required, the Church encourages you to confess these sins as well, as a way to come to full knowledge of yourself and admit your need for God's grace and mercy.

All sins confessed to the priest are protected by the **sacramental seal**. Out of respect for the individual and recognizing the importance of the ministry, the Church declares that every priest who hears confession is bound under severe penalties to keep absolute secrecy regarding the sins confessed to him, without exception.

Satisfaction

Have you ever apologized to a friend or family member for something hurtful you did, only to hear the person respond, "Saying I'm sorry is not enough"? When and why might such a response be fair? Depending on the circumstances, the response may be not only fair but also fitting. Perhaps you wronged your friend at other times and apologized, only to repeat your same errors again. In this case it wouldn't be shocking for your latest apology to fall on deaf ears. Your friend would rather be *satisfied* that your "I'm sorry" is for real.

Or think about a person who gossiped or spread untruths about someone else. Besides saying "I am sorry" for the actions, the person must work to repair the harm. This might involve going back to the people who were told the gossip or the lies, admitting the untruths, and correcting them with truth. Similarly, someone guilty of stealing should do more than apologize. The person must make things right by returning the stolen goods. Justice requires efforts as well as words.

In the same way, sacramental absolution does not remove all penalties for what you have done. So the confessor imposes a penance in line with the gravity and nature of the sins committed. It may be one of the following:

- prayer
- an offering
- works of mercy
- service to neighbor
- voluntary self-denial
- sacrifices

Completing this penance, the third and final act of the penitent in this sacrament, helps to "configure [you] to Christ" (*CCC*, 1460) as you suffer with him.

Absolution of Sin

Absolution is the priest's essential action in the sacrament. In celebrating the Sacrament of Penance, the priest fulfills the ministry of Jesus Christ, the Good Shepherd, who seeks out those who are lost (see John 10:11–15); the Father who awaits his prodigal son and welcomes and forgives him when he returns (see Luke 15:11–32); and the impartial judge who rules with both justice and mercy (see Luke 18:9–14).

When the priest senses that a person's conversion is genuine and hears the person pray an **Act of Contrition** (see page 328), he extends his hands over that person and pronounces the words of absolution:

> God, the Father of mercies, through the Death and the Resurrection of his Son has reconciled the world to himself and sent the Holy Spirit among us for the forgiveness of sins; through the ministry of the Church may God give you pardon and peace, and I absolve you from your sins in the name of the Father, and of the Son, and of the Holy Spirit.
>
> The penitent responds: Amen. (*Rite of Penance*, 46)

When the priest says the words beginning with "I absolve you," he makes the Sign of the Cross over the penitent. This formula expresses the work of the Blessed Trinity in the Sacrament of Penance. God the Father, who is the source of all mercy, forgives. Jesus Christ, the Son, reconciles the sinner to himself through the Paschal Mystery—his work of salvation. The Holy Spirit makes forgiveness and conversion possible. It is in the name of the Blessed Trinity that the Church offers this sacrament.

The priest, the minister of the sacrament, receives the *power* to absolve sins in the Sacrament of Holy

> **Act of Contrition** A prayer that expresses sorrow for sins.

Orders and the *faculties*—that is, the right or privilege—to be the minister of the sacrament from his bishop, his religious superior, or the pope. The priest unites himself to the intention and love of Christ.

After granting absolution, the priest says something such as "The Lord has freed you from your sins. Go in peace." Like the Dismissal Rite at Mass, this dismissal gives you a mission to complete. You are challenged to complete your penance, to live a life in communion with God the Father and the Church, to grow in holiness, and to show mercy to others as God has shown mercy to you.

♥ Peace Be with You

In the words of absolution, the priest grants you God's "pardon and peace." True peace comes only through forgiveness. Think about a time in your life when you truly felt forgiven for a sin. Write about this experience in your journal; creatively express the feeling of peace you found as a song, prayer, poem, etc.

SECTION ASSESSMENT

NOTE TAKING

Use the chart you created for this section to help you complete the following questions.

1. When does a penitent's contrition begin?
2. What does the priest say as the Sacrament of Penance begins?
3. What information does the penitent give the priest at this point?
4. What type of sins must always be confessed?
5. What other type of sin is it also a good idea to confess?
6. How does a penitent make satisfaction for his or her sins?

COMPREHENSION

7. What are three ways to celebrate the Sacrament of Penance?
8. Explain the three conditions for a sin to be a mortal sin.

VOCABULARY

9. Explain the difference between *mortal sin* and *venial sin*.
10. Define *perfect contrition* and *imperfect contrition*.

CRITICAL THINKING

11. What do you think would be an appropriate penance for someone who lied to a friend? Cheated on a test? Missed Mass deliberately?
12. With regard to the priest's role in the Sacrament of Penance, the *Catechism of the Catholic Church* says he is "not the master of God's forgiveness, but its servant" (*CCC*, 1466). What do you think this means?

SECTION 3

The Graces of the Sacrament of Penance and Reconciliation

> **MAIN IDEA**
> The Sacrament of Penance brings you back into communion with God, the Church, and yourself and helps to heal the effects of sin in your life, your relationships, and society.

The graces of the Sacrament of Penance and Reconciliation are directly related to the effects of sin. Sin is harmful because it weakens or breaks your connection with God and others. The Sacrament of Penance repairs these rifts, reconciles you to God, gives you peace of conscience, brings you spiritual consolation, and restores grace and blessings to your life.

When Jesus described himself as "the true vine" and his followers as "the branches" (Jn 15:1–5), he was saying that he is the source of all life and happiness. In order to remain spiritually alive and happy, you need to stay connected to him. The Body of Christ is like the human body. Every part of the physical body lives because it is connected to the heart by blood vessels.

If blood vessels are severed or impaired, the body part they nourish can no longer receive oxygen and food. As a result, the part dies. Sin is like that. It cuts you off from Jesus, the vine; then you spiritually wither and die.

The Nature of Reconciliation

The Sacrament of Penance does not focus just on sin. It is also concerned with repairing the damage and restoring the bonds that were weakened or broken. Just as it takes time for the human body to heal from a broken bone, so the process of repair and reconciliation after sin takes time. Small wounds heal quickly, but major breaks may require months or even years before healing is completed.

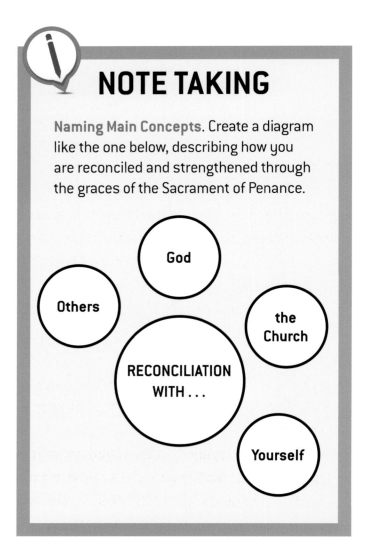

NOTE TAKING

Naming Main Concepts. Create a diagram like the one below, describing how you are reconciled and strengthened through the graces of the Sacrament of Penance.

God

Others

the Church

RECONCILIATION WITH . . .

Yourself

In the parable of the prodigal son (see Luke 15:11–32), the younger son was able to be reconciled to his father only after he had repented his actions and returned home.

The word *reconciliation* comes from a Latin word that means "to restore to union, to rejoin, to put together again." That is exactly what happens as a result of the sacrament: you are restored to communion with God, the Church, others, and yourself. This is not the same as forgetting the sin that took place. Nor does it mean you accept the sin as now "okay." Instead, reconciliation indicates your desire to be in relationship again. The relationship is so important to you that you are forgiven what happened, learn from that experience, and focus on building a new life with the person you harmed.

You know the saying, "To err is human, to forgive divine." Reconciliation is much like resurrection. It is God's gift of new, restored life to you when you accept his grace. Without the graces of the Sacrament of Penance, no one could fully bring broken relationships back to life.

The Sacrament of Penance brings about forgiveness of sins, which in turn makes communion with God possible. "The whole power of the sacrament of Penance consists in restoring us to God's grace and joining us with him in an intimate friendship" (*Roman Catechism*, II, V, 18, quoted in *CCC*, 1468). The sacrament also brings the sinner back into communion with all members of Christ's Mystical Body. Pope John Paul II taught that the "forgiven penitent is reconciled with himself in his inmost being, where he regains his innermost truth" (*CCC*, 1469).

Reconciliation with God

"Reconciliation with God is . . . the purpose and effect of this sacrament" (*CCC*, 1468). Jesus' parable of the prodigal son (Luke 15:11–32) offers a good description of what reconciliation with God is like. In the story, the younger son demands his inheritance and then squanders it selfishly. Only when he is penniless, jobless, and hungry does he repent of his sins. He decides to go home, beg his father's forgiveness, and ask to work for his father as a hired servant. The father, however, rejoices the minute he sees his son returning. He embraces the boy, adorns him with new clothes and jewelry, and then orders the servants to prepare a banquet in his honor. Their relationship has been restored.

This same rejoicing occurs in heaven when one sinner returns to God. Not only does the sinner rejoice at being forgiven but God rejoices to have him or her back! The prophet Isaiah describes this reality:

> In an outburst of wrath, for a moment
> I hid my face from you;
> But with enduring love I take pity on you,
> says the LORD, your redeemer. . . .
> My love shall never fall away from you
> nor my covenant of peace be shaken,
> says the LORD, who has mercy on you. (Is 54:8, 10)

God calls you to return home to him. No matter what you have done, he still loves you.

Reconciliation with the Church

Grave sin not only destroys a person's relationship with God; it also destroys his or her relationship with the Church. Persons in grave sin put themselves outside the faith community; they "excommunicate" themselves from the group of believers. Grave sins that incur automatic **excommunication** from the Church include

- procuring an abortion;
- engaging in apostasy, heresy, or schism;
- a confessor's violating the seal of confession; and
- physically attacking the pope.

In most cases, receiving absolution in the Sacrament of Penance restores a person to fellowship and communion with the Church. In rare cases of grave public sin, the Church has, throughout history, formally excommunicated individual sinners. In such cases, the sinner can be reconciled to the Church only

> **excommunication** A serious penalty that means a baptized person is no longer "in communion" with the Catholic Church.

GAINING AN Indulgence

The *Catechism of the Catholic Church* teaches that "through indulgences the faithful can obtain the remission of temporal punishment resulting from sin for themselves and also for the souls in Purgatory" (*CCC*, 1498). *Indulgence* is defined as "a partial or total wiping away of punishment due for sins that have been forgiven."

Try this practice yourself. First, choose an action or prayer that the Church has linked with an indulgence. Check with your teacher to determine an appropriate online site that lists indulgences. Do the action or pray the prayer. If you are trying for a plenary indulgence, then—within a week before or after—go to confession, receive Communion at Mass, and say an Our Father, Hail Mary, and Glory Be for the pope's special intentions. (Do an online search for "pope's special intentions," or look for the pope's monthly intention on the Vatican website.)

by the pope, the bishop of the place, or priests authorized by them (see *CCC,* 1463).

During his public ministry, Jesus not only forgave sinners but also brought them back into the community of the People of God. An example of this is when he invited the tax collector Zacchaeus to share a meal with him (see Luke 19:1–10). In the same way, although grave sin destroys not only your relationship with God but also your relationship with the Church, through the Sacrament of Penance Jesus reconciles you with God and with the Church. Reconciled with the Communion of Saints, you are also strengthened in living a life of virtue and avoiding sin. You can receive Holy Communion because you are, in fact, united with other Church members who are truly trying to live as followers of Jesus.

Reconciliation with Self

You may have experienced a sense of inner peace and serenity of conscience after you have celebrated the Sacrament of Penance. Why? Sin wounds human dignity. When you choose to sin, you let yourself down. You fail to be the person God intended you to be. The Sacrament of Penance can bring about a profound sense of spiritual consolation. Because you are assured of God's ongoing love and forgiveness, you can learn to forgive yourself for your wrongdoing. You can develop inner peace of mind, true serenity of conscience. Pope John Paul II, in his 1984 apostolic exhortation *Reconciliatio et Paenitentia* (*Reconciliation and Penance*), explained this effect of Penance: "The forgiven penitent is reconciled with himself in his inmost being, where he regains his own true identity" (31.V).

> **Purgatory** Purification after death for those who died in God's friendship but still need to be purified from past sins before entering heaven.

Forgiving yourself is often much harder than forgiving others. But self-forgiveness is a gift of God's redemption. God has really saved you from sin. Jesus has truly taken away your guilt. You are now free to return to life as a child of God, to once again take your place at the Eucharistic table.

Finally, your conversion and absolution from mortal sin removes the one obstacle that would prevent you from entering heaven. "For it is now, in this life, that we are offered the choice between life and death, and it is only by the road of conversion that we can enter the Kingdom, from which one is excluded by grave sin" (*CCC,* 1470). The sacrament restores the graces belonging to a baptized Catholic. Forgiveness of mortal sin brings a remission not only of eternal punishment but also, at least in part, of punishment in this world as well. Through works of charity and penance (e.g., prayer, fasting, works of mercy, patient suffering), as well as through gaining indulgences, the grace of the sacrament allows you to be cleansed of the remaining punishment and healed of the effects of sin. This process of purification may continue after death in **Purgatory**, but here on earth, you participate consciously in it by cooperating with God's grace. In the process, you put away your old self and become new. You find the spiritual strength to live a Christian life and to resist temptation.

You Are Changed by God's Forgiveness

In the Sacrament of Penance, God's forgiving love heals you. Healing is meant to spark permanent change. Whenever Jesus forgave someone, he also called the person to transform his or her life. For example, Jesus told the paralytic, "Rise, pick up your stretcher, and go home" (Mt 9:6)—to rebuild a loving relationship with his family. To the woman who washed his feet with her tears, Jesus said, "Go in peace" (Lk 7:50)—to reconcile with her husband. Likewise, Jesus told the

Ways the Sacrament of Penance
TRANSFORMS YOU

As a rainfall transforms and invigorates a parched garden, the Sacrament of Penance transforms Catholics, energizing and bringing new life. The sacrament strengthens you and renews your commitment to living your baptismal commitment to be a disciple of Christ.

The changes that result are tangible. Examine some of the changes that may come about as a result of going to confession, being absolved of your sins, and receiving God's peace in your heart.

Commitment to PRACTICING DISCIPLINE

The Sacrament of Penance helps you discipline yourself so that, in the future, you avoid temptation and refrain from sin.

- **FASTING**, or controlling, in a healthy way, what and how much you eat, represents conversion in relation to yourself. It shows that you are willing to orient yourself toward God's love rather than to your own passions and selfishness.
- **PRAYER** represents conversion in relation to God. You realize that you need God's grace and that you can't save yourself by your own efforts.
- **ALMSGIVING** expresses conversion in relation to others. You realize your connection to others as brothers and sisters of Christ, as creatures made in God's image, and as people with inherent dignity.

Ability to FORGIVE

Your experience of God's forgiveness encourages you to be forgiving toward others, following Jesus' admonition to Peter to forgive not seven times but seventy-seven times (see Matthew 18:21–22).

Strength to REFRAIN FROM ANGER AND SEEKING REVENGE

True forgiveness means letting go of anger. Jesus told us, "If you bring your gift to the altar, and there recall that your brother has anything against you, leave your gift there at the altar, go first and be reconciled with your brother, and then come and offer your gift" (Mt 5:23–24). This means that if someone has hurt you or your loved ones, you do not seek to "get even" but instead love and forgive as God does.

Fortitude to **PURSUE JUSTICE AND PEACE**

It takes courage to approach someone with whom you are angry. It also takes a great deal of humility to forgive someone who hasn't apologized. But Jesus has called you to be an ambassador of reconciliation: "If your brother sins (against you), go and tell him his fault between you and him alone. If he listens to you, you have won over your brother. If he does not listen, take one or two others along with you, so that 'every fact may be established on the testimony of two or three witnesses.' If he refuses to listen to them, tell the church" (Mt 18:15–17). Thus, just as God never gives up on you, so you are not to give up on achieving peace with others.

Grace to **RESPOND TO THE CALL TO PERFECTION**

In the Gospel story of the rich young man (see Matthew 19:16–30), the disciples ask Jesus, "Who then can be saved?" (Mt 19:25). Jesus' answer is enlightening: "For human beings this is impossible, but for God all things are possible" (Mt 19:26).

It is impossible for humans to be perfect as God is perfect, to forgive as God forgives, to love as God loves. But with the grace God gives the Church in the Sacrament of Penance, all things are possible. You are not alone in your journey of conversion and repentance. God truly does give you the strength "to begin anew" (*CCC*, 1432). The Holy Spirit, who "brings sin to light, . . . also . . . gives the human heart grace for repentance and conversion" (see *CCC*, 1433). Therefore, when you avail yourself of the Sacrament of Penance and of its transforming graces, your life becomes truly fruitful.

adulterous woman, "Go, [and] from now on do not sin any more" (Jn 8:11). Being forgiven is meant to lead to a "profound change of the whole person by which one begins to consider, judge, and arrange his life according to the holiness and love of God, made manifest in his Son in the last days and given to us in abundance" (*Rite of Penance*, 6a).

This type of life transformation is the final step of conversion. You are called to be a new creation (see 2 Corinthians 5:17). As the *Catechism of the Catholic Church* explains, Catholics are to "form our conscience, fight against evil tendencies, let ourselves be healed by Christ and progress in the life of the Spirit" (*CCC*, 1458). In other words, we are to work on developing habits of thought, speech, and action "befitting a disciple of Christ" (*CCC*, 1494). Think about some ways you can do this.

SECTION ASSESSMENT

NOTE TAKING

Use the diagram you created for this section to help you complete the following questions.

1. How does the Sacrament of Penance reconcile you with God?
2. How does the grace of the sacrament help you to be at peace with yourself?
3. How is forgiveness toward others a grace of the Sacrament of Penance?

COMPREHENSION

4. What did Jesus mean when he said he was the "true vine" and his followers "the branches"?
5. How is it possible for human beings to achieve perfection?

CRITICAL THINKING

6. How are conversion, forgiveness of others, and personal transformation all linked together?

REFLECTION

7. Which do you find more difficult, forgiving yourself or forgiving others? Why?
8. What prayers or actions have helped you to remove the consequences of sin from your life?

Section Summaries

Focus Question

Why do Catholics confess their sins in the Sacrament of Penance and Reconciliation?

Complete one of the following:

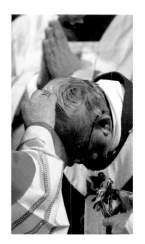

Briefly list the advantages of sacramental confession as a way of overcoming sinfulness. Feel free to list benefits discussed in the chapter as well as any others you can think of.

Create an examination of conscience specifically for teenagers. Use it to prepare for your next visit to the Sacrament of Penance.

Write a poem, story, song, or short essay reflecting your understanding of what ongoing conversion means.

INTRODUCTION (PAGES 181–183)

A Marvelous Reality

When you approach the Sacrament of Penance in faith, you are cleansed of your sins and restored to grace. This sacrament is the only ordinary means by which your soul can return to grace after Baptism. It points to the marvelous reality of God's love, which constantly calls you to conversion of heart and deeper relationship with him.

Write three paragraphs about a time when you have felt called to move beyond a particular sin, mistake, or bad habit and into a deeper relationship with God.

SECTION 1 (PAGES 184–189)

Understanding the Sacrament of Penance and Reconciliation

Jesus instituted the Sacrament of Penance by his forgiveness of sinners and his gift to the Apostles of the power to forgive sins. The sacrament is a sign of God's infinite mercy and love and of his desire to be in relationship with you. The practice of the Sacrament of Penance has changed throughout the life of the Church, but its purpose remains the same: to help you maintain a loving relationship with the Blessed Trinity in and through the Church.

Read paragraphs 8 through 11 of Pope John Paul II's document *Reconciliatio et Paenitentia*. Summarize in one paragraph how the Church is both reconciled to God and charged with the task of reconciling others to him.

SECTION 2 (PAGES 190–195)

Celebrating the Sacrament of Penance and Reconciliation

The Sacrament of Penance can be celebrated in three different ways: individually; as a communal liturgy with individual confessions; and in rare, grave circumstances, as a communal liturgy with a communal absolution. In its normal form, it involves three actions of the penitent—contrition, confession, and penance—as well as absolution granted by the priest. The act of penance performed by the penitent helps to restore justice and heal any damage caused by the sins confessed. To receive forgiveness, a person must confess all mortal sins he or she can remember.

 Make a list of different penances that could help penitents heal the ill effects of sin in their own, and others', lives.

SECTION 3 (PAGES 196–202)

The Graces of the Sacrament of Penance and Reconciliation

The Sacrament of Penance brings you to reconciliation with God, others, the Church, and yourself. It gives you the grace you need for ongoing conversion: to apply self-discipline, to forgive others, to refrain from anger and revenge, to pursue justice and peace, and to answer Jesus' call to perfection. Although this call is beyond your natural abilities, the sacrament reassures you that you are never without the help of God's grace and love.

 With a partner, take turns describing a time when you felt called to forgive someone, and how your experience of being forgiven by God helped you to do that.

Chapter Assignments

Choose and complete at least one of the following three assignments assessing your understanding of the material in this chapter.

1. Radio Spot Promoting the Sacrament of Penance

Imagine that your bishop has charged you with promoting the sacrament through a radio advertisement. The diocese has purchased a one-minute slot on a station popular with teens. Create an advertisement geared to that audience. Remember, good marketing is all about promoting the benefits, so be sure your ad provides factual information but also answers the audience's question: "What's in it for me?" Keep in mind that your answer to this question should include theology as well as practical reasons for celebrating the sacrament. Your goal is to encourage more Catholic teens to celebrate this sacrament on a regular basis.

Your completed project should include a one-minute audio recording. Save your recording on a social media site that has an audio and/or video recording option. Submit the link to this site to your teacher for grading, along with your script and a storyboard showing how you developed the concepts for the ad. Arrange to play the audio recording and share your storyboard with your class.

2. Reconciliation Brochure

Imagine that your parish has asked you to develop a four-page brochure to help parishioners learn about the Sacrament of Penance and make a renewed commitment to this sacrament. Develop a brochure with the following content:

Page 1: General information about the Sacrament of Penance, covering both theology and practice.

Page 2: FAQs about the sacrament, focusing on questions or confusion people might have that may keep them from celebrating the sacrament.

Page 3: Information about your parish (name, address, name of pastor and other priests, and so forth) and the days and times when the sacrament is celebrated (both communally and individually).

Page 4: Any additional content you think would encourage your fellow parishioners to celebrate the Sacrament of Penance. Be creative in choosing or creating content for this page.

Other guidelines:

- Include at least one quotation about the Sacrament of Penance and Reconciliation from Pope Francis or another recent pope.

- Use text and images.

- Develop the brochure to appeal to a family audience.

Submit your brochure (either in print or digitally) with a one-page written reflection on what you learned and how your own understanding and appreciation of the sacrament were strengthened through this assignment.

3. Report on the Sacrament of Penance

Choose from this chapter a topic related to the Sacrament of Penance and Reconciliation (forgiveness of sin or conversion, for example), and write a four- to five-page report on the subject that builds on, and goes deeper into, the chapter content. Your essay should include the following:

- at least three quotations from primary sources such as Church documents,

- at least one quotation from Pope Francis or another recent pope, and

- at least two Gospel references or quotations.

Be sure to use proper citations for all quoted material.

Conclude your report with a two- to three-paragraph reflection on your growing understanding and appreciation of the gift of God's forgiveness and the healing offered to you in the sacrament.

Faithful Disciple

St. John Vianney

St. John Vianney

Without a good education, it is very difficult to succeed in life. St. John Vianney found that his lack of education (barely at what you might call the eighth-grade level) almost prevented him from becoming a priest. But he never gave up. After several attempts to pass the seminary entrance exams, he was finally admitted. He still struggled, especially with Latin, and failed the ordination examinations more than once. But he kept trying and was ordained in 1815 at the age of twenty-nine.

Perhaps his own struggles prepared him to help others in their struggles. Assigned to a poor parish in the town of Ars, France, he found that the people there had given up the practice of their faith. Fr. John Vianney began his ministry with those most in need: those who were sick or housebound. He helped destitute girls by gathering them together into an orphanage called Providence. His catechism lessons and lectures to the girls became so popular that parishioners came to hear them, and eventually, they had to be moved to the church.

Fr. John Vianney encouraged his parishioners to pray, reminding them that God loved them and wanted to hear from them. He also encouraged them to receive the Sacrament of Penance often:

> My children, we cannot comprehend the goodness of God towards us in instituting this great Sacrament of Penance . . . which heals the wounds of our soul. If we thought seriously about it, we should have such a lively horror of sin that we could not commit it.

> It is said that many confess, and few are converted. I believe it is so, my children, because few confess with tears of repentance.

> Put yourself on good terms with God; have recourse to the Sacrament of Penance; you will sleep quietly as an angel. You will be glad to waken in the night, to pray to God; you will have nothing but thanksgiving on your lips; you will rise towards heaven with great facility, as an eagle soars through the air.

His own example of a prayerful life encouraged the people, and many from all over the country came to him for confession—so many that, to accommodate the visitors, the French railroad opened a special ticket office in Lyons (the nearest city) just for tickets to Ars. Nearly twenty thousand people a year came to Ars because it became known that Fr. John Vianney could "read hearts" and also had the gift of healing. For the last ten years of his life, St. John Vianney spent nearly eighteen hours a day hearing confessions.

St. John Vianney died in 1859, and his body has remained incorrupt—that is, completely preserved as it was in life. He is the patron saint of parish priests and confessors. His feast day is August 4.

Reading Comprehension

1. What obstacle did St. John Vianney overcome on his road to the priesthood?

2. What two groups in his parish did St. John Vianney help first?

3. How did St. John Vianney show an exceptional commitment to the Sacrament of Penance?

Writing Task

• Interview a priest in your parish or diocese. Ask him how his ministry has drawn inspiration from St. John Vianney.

Explaining the Faith

Why should you seek God's forgiveness through the Sacrament of Penance and Reconciliation rather than just approaching God directly in prayer?

While humans are bound by Church law and the sacraments, God's grace transcends all limits. He can forgive you however and whenever he wants. But God also knows human nature, and he knows what is best for you. In the Sacrament of Penance and Reconciliation, he gives you the basis for total confidence that your grave sins can be forgiven. He wants the Church to be the "sign and instrument" (*CCC*, 1442) of the forgiveness Jesus has already won for you. He wants you to know for certain that, through the apostolic ministry of the Church, his mercy is always ready to welcome you again and again.

You can easily see why you need this certainty. At times, you may feel afraid that your contrition is not good enough—that you are not really as sorry as you say you are—especially if you commit the same sin over again as you struggle to overcome it. If you are not yet able to stop sinning, how can you be sure God forgives you? At other times, you might have trouble facing up to the reality of sin, being tempted to deny it or gloss over it. If you have done nothing wrong, what is there to forgive? Confessing your sins directly to a priest helps to solve both these problems. When you must say aloud what you have done, you own your mistakes and are challenged to take action to make things right. At the same time, when you hear the words of absolution spoken by the priest, you open yourself to God's great gift of comfort and reassurance, pardon and peace. You can rest assured that if you approach this sacrament in honesty and good faith, God will always extend his forgiveness to you through it.

That said, there are times when prayer remits sins. Specifically, receiving Holy Communion wipes away venial sins. An act of perfect contrition can also remove guilt for venial sins—and even for mortal sins, if you seriously intend to sacramentally confess them as soon as possible. However, you should never receive the Eucharist if you are conscious of a mortal sin. In that case, you always need to confess first since you are not really in union with the Church, and to receive Communion as if you were would not be honest.

 Further Research

- Read the "In Brief" section at the end of the *Catechism of the Catholic Church* chapter on the Sacrament of Penance (paragraphs 1485–1498). Write a paragraph explaining, in your own words, why this sacrament is so important to your spiritual life.

Prayer
The Confiteor

I confess to almighty God

and to you, my brothers and sisters,

that I have greatly sinned

in my thoughts and in my words,

in what I have done

and in what I have failed to do,

through my fault,

through my fault,

through my most grievous fault;

therefore I ask blessed Mary ever-Virgin,

all the Angels and Saints,

and you, my brothers and sisters,

to pray for me to the Lord our God.

—*New Roman Missal*, third edition

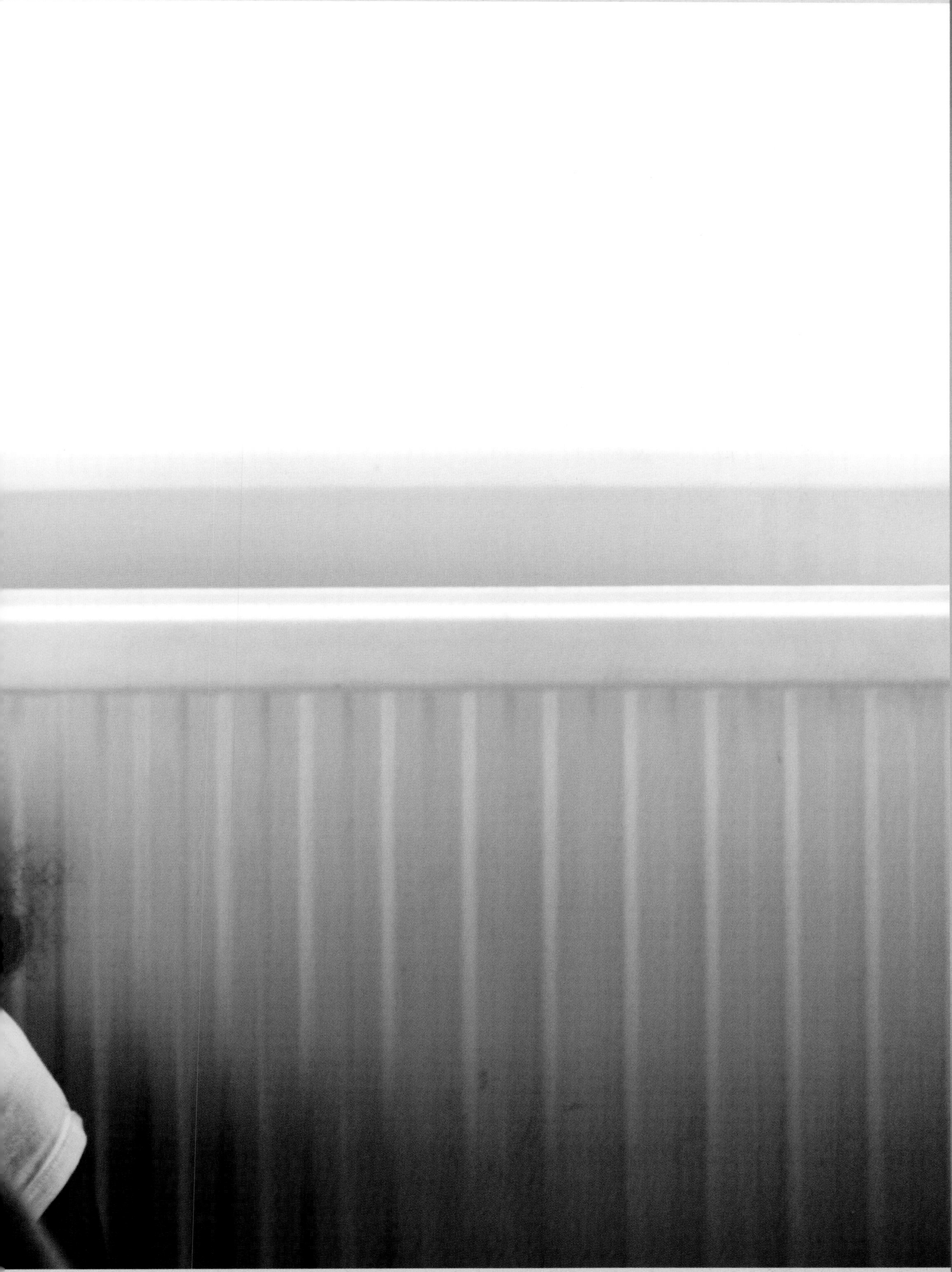

THE SACRAMENT

OF THE ANOINTING OF THE SICK

GIVING UP FEAR

From the time he was a little boy, Macklin Swinney of Indianapolis loved summer days and all that came with them. He loved hanging out with friends, especially at the lake. "Once it hit summertime, I never had my shirt on. Sunscreen wasn't a big deal for me. Early twenties, you're invincible," he said.

In 2010, at age twenty-four, Macklin discovered that he had stage IV melanoma, a skin cancer. The prognosis for recovery was not good. While Macklin was struggling with his illness, he was also seeking God. Macklin pursued becoming a Catholic through the Rite of Christian Initiation of Adults, and just before Easter of 2013, Fr. Richard Nagel, a priest he had been meeting with, arranged an emergency Baptism for him. Immediately after his Baptism, Macklin received the Sacrament of the Anointing of the Sick.

Since it was still Lent, Macklin told Fr. Nagel, "I'm going to give up fear." He later explained, "Without fear, I didn't have the anxiety that loomed around all the time. It took a lot of things out of the equation. It let me focus on my life."

Fr. Nagel recalled, "In all my years in the church, that was a new one for me— to give up fear. I think we should all give up fear." Macklin Swinney died on Good Friday, 2014.

(Based on Yvonne Man, "Local Man Gets Another Fighting Chance with Cancer Treatment," Fox59. com, June 19, 2013; and John Shaughnessy, "Faith Leads Young Man with Cancer to Resolve to Live Life to the Utmost," *National Catholic Reporter* online, April 12, 2014.)

FOCUS QUESTION

What does it mean to be PHYSICALLY and SPIRITUALLY HEALED?

INTRODUCTION
"Is Anyone among You Suffering?"

MAIN IDEA
Illness and suffering are indirect consequences of Original Sin; the Sacrament of the Anointing of the Sick helps to heal the spiritual and, sometimes, the physical suffering a person encounters due to illness.

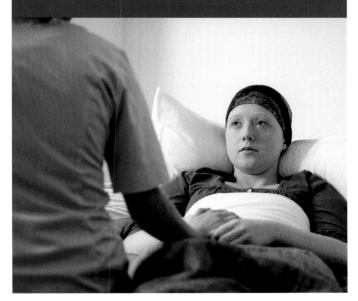

If the question on the left (posed by the Apostle James in James 5:13) were posed in any family or community, the answer would return in the affirmative. There are people in every place who are sick. "Illness and suffering have always been among the gravest problems confronted in human life" (*CCC*, 1500).

When people face illness and suffering, they often turn inward to self-absorption, anguish, and sometimes even despair, and they revolt against God. They ask the most difficult questions, which usually begin with the word *why*. They wonder:

- Why me?
- Why do I suffer?
- Why is there illness and suffering in the world?
- Why does God permit such pain?

These questions have answers, even if they are not immediately clear. Suffering can lead a person to seek and return to God. It can remind someone of what in life is really important and what is not.

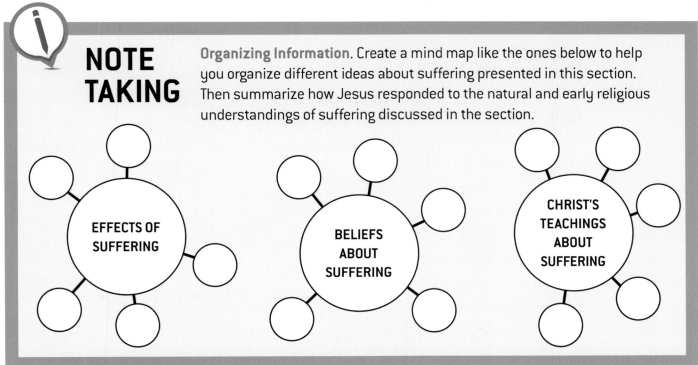

NOTE TAKING

Organizing Information. Create a mind map like the ones below to help you organize different ideas about suffering presented in this section. Then summarize how Jesus responded to the natural and early religious understandings of suffering discussed in the section.

EFFECTS OF SUFFERING

BELIEFS ABOUT SUFFERING

CHRIST'S TEACHINGS ABOUT SUFFERING

Suffering and the Old Testament

In the Old Testament, believers lived their illnesses in the presence of God. People lamented their illness, begged God for healing, and viewed God as the ultimate master of life and death.

Part of the mindset of the Hebrew people was that sickness was a moral condition—in part, a punishment for sin. The suffering and death of Adam and Eve (see Genesis 3:1–19) were viewed as the consequences of their sin. In fact, Adam and Eve not only lost the gifts of original holiness and original justice but transmitted to their descendants their own wounded nature. All humans have inherited Original Sin. As a result, human nature is weakened and inclined to sin. All people are subject to ignorance, suffering, and death.

However, the early Israelites took this belief further, imagining that each instance of suffering directly resulted from a specific sin: a belief called the "law of retribution." They believed that people who were seriously ill or died early in life must have sinned or their families must have done something to offend God. They believed that God blessed "good people" with health, many children, riches, and a long life. Jesus would eventually discredit the law of retribution.

Even prior to Jesus, the mentality forged by the law of retribution was challenged in the Book of Job. This book of the Old Testament tells the story of Job, a faithful, good man who loses everything: first his possessions, then his family, and finally his health. Job wants to know why God is letting these things happen. For what is he being punished? Job does not answer the question so much as he ponders suffering, lives with it, and explores it in depth. Job knows he has not sinned. He understands that God sends trials to those he loves, and he cries out to God for an explanation. God simply reminds Job that, as Creator and Lord of all, he holds the keys to life and death. Although Job

Job's friends believed his sufferings were the result of sin and tried to get Job to repent. After speaking with Job, God rebuked Job's friends for not speaking rightly about him (see Job 42:7–9).

is restored to riches and health at the end of the story, this action is somewhat anticlimactic. It is Job's suffering and his face-to-face encounter with God that truly strengthen his faith.

The answer found in the Book of Job did not seem adequate to some Israelites. After all, many good people who suffer in this life are *not* restored to their riches or good health. So some Israelite writers began to adapt the law of retribution into a new way of thinking known as **apocalyptic** writings. In this genre, God's justice remains intact. If good people do not find justice in this life, then God will give them justice in the next life. Catholics hold some aspects of this view. Catholics continue to believe that at the Final Judgment, each person will be rewarded according to his or her works and acceptance or refusal of grace. The good will be rewarded with eternal life; the evil will

> **apocalyptic** Relating to belief in the enactment of God's justice after death or in an end time when good people will be rewarded and evil people will be punished. In the Bible, the Books of Daniel and Revelation contain examples of apocalyptic writing.

experience everlasting punishment. When people of faith endure their sufferings patiently, one day God will make them whole again in the New Jerusalem. As the prophet Isaiah predicted, "No one who dwells there will say, 'I am sick'; the people who live there will be forgiven their guilt" (Is 33:24).

Throughout the Old Testament, the Israelites lived among peoples of other religions who also looked upon sickness as a moral condition. The sick, the elderly, and the disabled were often considered worthless and shunned or abandoned because it was thought that they might bring God's wrath upon the entire group. These beliefs had particularly cruel consequences in a nomadic society. Many of the sick or disabled were left to die alone in the desert.

With the gift of the Law to Moses, the Israelites began to understand their moral responsibility to help weaker community members. The Fourth Commandment, "Honor your father and your mother" (Ex 20:12), told adults they needed to take care of their sick and elderly parents and not abandon them. The Books of Ruth and Tobit reinforced this message: truly good people take care of their sick parents and other relatives, and God will reward them for doing so.

Christ the Physician

What did Jesus say about the reason people suffer? Jesus did not *say* as much about suffering as he *acted* on suffering. He is known as the Divine Physician because he treated physical illness as well as offered forgiveness for sin. For example, he was moved by the faith of those who lowered a paralyzed man through a hole in the roof to be healed by him. Jesus first forgave the man's sins. When observers accused him of blasphemy, Jesus said to them:

> Why are you thinking such things in your hearts? Which is easier, to say to the paralytic, "Your sins are forgiven," or to say, "Rise, pick up your mat and walk"? But that you may

Those who came to Jesus or brought others to Jesus for healing showed their faith in his power and left with their faith strengthened.

know that the Son of Man has authority to forgive sins on earth . . . I say to you, rise, pick up your mat, and go home. (Mk 2:8–11)

Jesus also rejected the idea that suffering is a punishment for sin. He explicitly addressed this issue before healing a man born blind (see John 9:1–41). When his disciples asked him, "Rabbi, who sinned, this man or his parents, that he was born blind?" Jesus answered, "Neither he nor his parents sinned; it is so that the works of God might be made visible through him" (Jn 9:2–3). It was primarily to strengthen the already living faith of the man he healed, and of his disciples, that Jesus performed this miracle.

In the days of Jesus, people with illnesses and disabilities were still treated as outcasts. They were often isolated from the life of the community—confined to

How Did JESUS HEAL?

When scribes and Pharisees noted that Jesus was eating with tax collectors and sinners, they wondered why. Jesus said, "Those who are well do not need a physician, but the sick do. I did not come to call the righteous but sinners" (Mk 2:17).

Jesus not only forgave sins but he also performed three types of healing miracles:

1 PHYSICAL CURES. All four Gospels record Jesus' ability to restore health to the sick, even those who were paralyzed or had leprosy. "People brought to him all those who were sick and begged him that they might touch only the tassel on his cloak, and as many as touched it were healed" (Mt 14:35–36). Jesus could heal the ill and disabled, restore sight to the blind, and give hearing to the deaf.

2 EXORCISMS. "When it was evening, they brought him many who were possessed by demons, and he drove out the spirits by a word and cured all the sick" (Mt 8:16). Jesus freed some people from the domination of Satan. The exorcisms "anticipate Jesus' great victory over 'the ruler of this world'" (*CCC*, 550).

3 RESUSCITATIONS. Jesus raised from the dead at least three people—the daughter of Jairus (see Matthew 9:18–19, 23–26; Mark 5:21–24, 35–43; Luke 8:40–42, 49–56), the son of the widow at Nain (see Luke 7:11–17), and his friend Lazarus (see John 11:1–44). Jesus resuscitated these people, which means they were restored to life but would eventually die.

their rooms or their homes. Some, especially lepers and the possessed, had to live in the garbage dumps outside the city walls. Many were forced to beg for alms and food in public places. Leviticus 13–14 describes several laws that Jews of Jesus' time observed regarding people with scaly or fungal infections like leprosy. Being unclean meant they could not take part in community worship and prayer unless they underwent certain purification rites.

Jesus, however, embraced the sick and the disabled, and he allowed them to touch him. He laid hands on them, washed them, and even rubbed mud on them, to give them God's healing. They were made whole again, whether their illness was physical, mental, emotional, or spiritual. The healing miracles of Jesus proved the Father's love, echoing his words from Exodus: "I, the LORD, am your healer" (15:26). Importantly, those who were not physically healed were still equally loved. In the parable of the great feast, the servants are ordered to "Go out quickly into the streets and alleys of the town and bring in here the poor and the crippled, the blind and the lame" (Lk 14:21). The sick and the disabled are not outcasts but beloved children of God. They are welcome at God's table.

Jesus Also Taught about Suffering

Jesus' primary response to human suffering was to put an end to it, which he did very directly through his healings. Though teaching about suffering came second to acting to alleviate it, Jesus did make several important points about it:

- Sickness and death are not God's ways of punishing people.
- God loves the sick and disabled just as much as he loves healthy people.
- God's love is stronger than sickness, pain, suffering, and death.

- God does not abandon you when you are sick or suffering. Rather, he shares your suffering, above all through the Cross.
- The sick should not be treated as outcasts; instead, they have an important role to play in the community.

The Gospels do not record whether Jesus ever got a cold or flu, ran a fever, got a toothache, broke a bone, or was in any way sick. The Gospels do reveal that Jesus truly suffered: at times he felt tired, hungry, discouraged, angry, and isolated. He knows what you go through when you feel pain and when you fear death. Ultimately, Jesus demonstrated the meaning of suffering through his own Passion and Death, through which he "took upon himself the whole weight of evil and took away the 'sin of the world,' of which illness is only a consequence" (*CCC*, 1505). Through this act, he showed how much God truly loves people: enough to endure the Cross for our sake. You are invited to take up your cross as his disciple. By this act, you can now unite your sufferings with Jesus' sacrifice, become more like him, and contribute to the redemption of the world. Jesus is with you in your sufferings; he will never abandon or forget you.

Jesus cured the physical ailments of others both because of his compassion for them and to show clearly that he was the Messiah. He told the disciples of John the Baptist, "Go and tell John what you have seen and heard: the blind regain their sight, the lame walk, lepers are cleansed, the deaf hear, the dead are raised, the poor have the good news proclaimed to them" (Lk 7:22). The healings of Jesus and his teaching and example about the meaning of suffering not only showed his divine power but also expressed his heartfelt love for humankind. Jesus truly cared for people who suffered. His healing miracles revealed to people his Father's love and compassion for those who suffer.

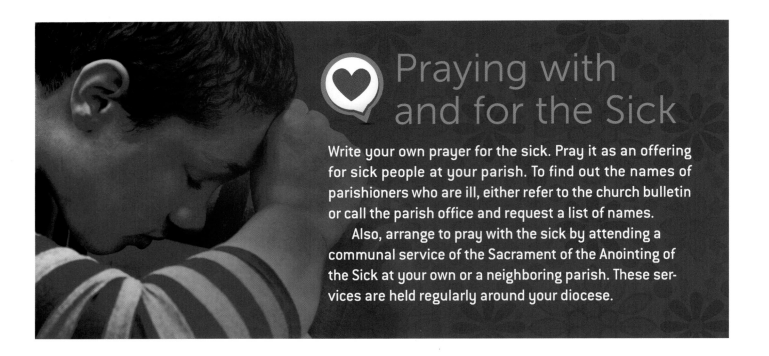

Praying with and for the Sick

Write your own prayer for the sick. Pray it as an offering for sick people at your parish. To find out the names of parishioners who are ill, either refer to the church bulletin or call the parish office and request a list of names.

Also, arrange to pray with the sick by attending a communal service of the Sacrament of the Anointing of the Sick at your own or a neighboring parish. These services are held regularly around your diocese.

SECTION ASSESSMENT

NOTE TAKING

Use the mind maps you created for this section to help you complete the following questions.

1. What are some effects that suffering can have on people?
2. How did the ancient Israelites understand suffering?
3. How did Jesus answer the question about the reason for suffering?

COMPREHENSION

4. Why is Christ known as the Divine Physician?

APPLICATION

5. How do you know that Jesus loves us?
6. How can you unite your sufferings with Jesus' sacrifice?

REFLECTION

7. Have you ever been frightened by an illness or by suffering? When was that?
8. What role did your faith have in helping you feel better and less afraid?

SECTION 1

Understanding the Sacrament of the Anointing of the Sick

MAIN IDEA
The Church has always offered healing for the sick through prayer, anointing with oil, and the laying on of hands in the Sacrament of the Anointing of the Sick.

Do you ever think of suffering as a gift and not a hardship? St. Rose of Lima said, "Without the burden of afflictions it is impossible to reach the height of grace. The gifts of grace increase as the struggles increase." Seen as a gift, suffering helps you align yourself with the Cross of Christ.

Without the help of the Holy Spirit, though, suffering will not free you to love. Instead, it can wear down your spirit and weaken your faith. Suffering can make you feel selfish, angry, irritable, demanding, and impatient. It can cause intense loneliness and even despair. Jesus gave the Church the Sacrament of the Anointing of the Sick to defend people against these negative aspects of suffering. This sacrament helps those who are seriously ill to transform their illnesses into grace that serves the Body of Christ.

The Church Heals the Sick

During his public ministry, Jesus told his disciples to "cure the sick, raise the dead, cleanse lepers, drive out demons" (Mt 10:8). They were to continue to heal the sick while preaching the saving words of the Good News. Following Jesus' instruction, the Twelve "drove out many demons, and they anointed with oil many who were sick and cured them" (Mk 6:13). The Church continues to respond to this command of Christ. She

NOTE TAKING **Chronicling Stages of Development.** Draw a horizontal timeline, and mark it as shown to represent the different stages of development of the Sacrament of the Anointing of the Sick. Write down at least one or two distinctive features of the sacrament at each stage to help you recall when each development took place.

Early Church   Middle Ages   Council of Trent   Second Vatican Council

takes care of the physical and spiritual needs of the sick. Christ's presence as Divine Physician is witnessed in the sacraments, especially the Eucharist, in which the Body and Blood of Christ offer eternal life and are connected with bodily health (see 1 Corinthians 11:30).

When the Apostle James asked, "Is anyone among you suffering?" he was prepared with an answer to suffering in the name of the Church. His answer is evidence of Christ's institution of, and desire for, the Sacrament of the Anointing of the Sick:

> Is anyone among you suffering? He should pray. . . . Is anyone among you sick? He should summon the presbyters of the church, and they should pray over him and anoint [him] with oil in the name of the Lord, and the prayer of faith will save the sick person, and the Lord will raise him up. If he has committed any sins, he will be forgiven. (Jas 5:13–15)

Realizing that it was sacramental—a sign of healing in which God was truly present—the Church took up the practice of having **presbyters** lay hands and anoint with oil, in imitation of Jesus and the Apostles.

A Brief History of the Sacrament

Both during Jesus' life and after his Ascension to heaven, his disciples anointed and laid hands on those who were sick in order to heal them. From the second through seventh centuries, whenever a person was seriously ill, other Christians would gather around and pray for him or her and then rub oil that had been blessed by a bishop on whatever parts of the body needed healing. For the anointing to be sacramental, it was necessary for the oil to be blessed by a bishop and for either the bishop or presbyter to administer it.

By the Middle Ages, the sacrament had come to be practiced only when someone was close to death. It became linked to a final reception of the Sacraments of Penance and the Eucharist, which necessitated a priest's presence.

Changes after the Second Vatican Council

The Fathers of the Second Vatican Council faced a challenging task in updating the rite of the sacrament. As they sought to renew the sacramental practice in light of the best traditions, they considered whether they should follow the practice of the early Church, which celebrated the Anointing of the Sick as a sacrament of healing and faith in God's presence in suffering, or follow the practice of the Church since the Middle Ages, which celebrated the Anointing of the Sick to prepare people for death.

Who Helps the SICK?

Choose and do one of the following:

1. Research and write a two-page report on one or more religious communities whose primary apostolate, or focus, is to care for the sick and suffering.

2. Interview a doctor, nurse, or someone else in the medical profession. Ask his or her opinion about the role of the Spirit in healing the body. Write a two-page report detailing the results of your interview.

presbyters The name for priests or members of the order of priesthood who are coworkers with the bishops and are servants to God's People, especially in celebrating the Eucharist.

ANOINTING OF THE SICK THROUGH THE YEARS

ca. AD 215: *The Apostolic Tradition* of Hippolytus described how, at Mass, a bishop blessed the **oil of the sick** (olive or another plant oil), praying that the oil would bring strength to all anointed with it. Christians regarded their blessed oil as an especially effective remedy and a sign of God's presence.

ca. 416: Pope Innocent I described in a letter how blessed oil was used for the Sacrament of the Anointing of the Sick.

428: St. Cyril of Alexandria warned Christians not to turn to pagan magicians and sorcerers when they were sick. Instead, they were to turn to God's healing through the bishop and presbyters of the Church.

1551: The Council of Trent affirmed that "only priests (bishops and presbyters) are ministers of the Anointing of the Sick" (*CCC*, 1516).

1965: The Second Vatican Council wrote that "'Extreme Unction,' which may also and more fittingly be called 'Anointing of the Sick,' is not a sacrament intended only for those who are at the point of death. . . . As soon as any of the faithful begins to be in danger of death from sickness or old age, this is already a suitable time for them to receive this sacrament" (*Sacrosanctum Concilium*, 73).

oil of the sick Olive or another plant oil that is blessed by a bishop at a Chrism Mass or, in case of necessity, by any priest at the time of anointing. Anointing with the oil of the sick is an efficacious sign of healing and strength that is part of the Sacrament of the Anointing of the Sick.

Extreme Unction A term from the Latin for "last anointing." It once referred to the reception of the Sacrament of the Anointing of the Sick just before death. It is accompanied by Viaticum.

In the end, the Council embraced both meanings of the sacrament. The new Rite of the Anointing of the Sick, approved in 1974, emphasizes God's concern for the sick, Christ's healing love, and the Church's prayers for the sick person's recovery to health—both physically and spiritually. Any baptized person of any age who has a serious or life-threatening illness or is about to undergo major surgery may receive the sacrament.

SECTION ASSESSMENT

NOTE TAKING

Use the timeline you created for this section to help you complete the following questions.

1. Briefly explain how the Sacrament of the Anointing of the Sick was practiced in the early Church.

2. What understanding about the sacrament changed during the Middle Ages?

3. What statement did the Council of Trent make about the minister of the sacrament?

4. How did the Second Vatican Council embrace both the emphasis on healing and the preparation for death in its revision of the Rite of the Anointing of the Sick?

COMPREHENSION

5. What is the first written evidence of the Sacrament of the Anointing of the Sick being practiced in the Church?

6. What was St. Cyril's warning to Christians about remedies for illness?

APPLICATION

7. How can you apply St. Rose of Lima's words (see page 221) to help you deal with a situation of suffering in your life?

SECTION 2

Celebrating the Sacrament of the Anointing of the Sick

MAIN IDEA
The rite of the Sacrament of the Anointing of the Sick focuses on bringing spiritual strength and peace in the midst of suffering, whether in preparation for death or in the hope of recovery.

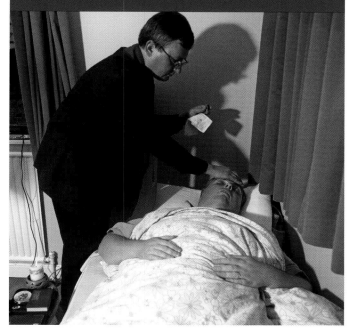

Knowing some of the requirements and details about the Rite of the Sacrament of the Anointing of the Sick is helpful for understanding how the sacrament can unite a person to the Passion and Death of Jesus Christ.

A priest, as representative of the Church, is the minister of the sacrament. The introduction to the Church's instruction on the sacrament, the *Pastoral Care of the Sick: Rites of Anointing and Viaticum*, asks that the priest visit the sick and show personal acts of kindness.

The Letter of James states that anointing should be given to a sick person to "save the sick person" and "raise him up" (see Jas 5:15). It is up to the individual

or family in most cases to decide when an illness is serious. The following types of people are encouraged to receive the sacrament:

- those who are dangerously ill due to sickness or old age;

- those whose illness recurs or becomes more serious;

- those about to undergo serious surgery;

- those who are growing weaker due to old age, even if no serious illness is present;

- children who have reached the age of reason and who are seriously ill; and

- sick people who have lost consciousness or the use of reason but who would have asked for the sacrament if they were able to do so.

When a priest is called to administer the sacrament to someone who has already died, he prays that God will forgive the person's sins and welcome him or her into the Kingdom, but he does not administer the sacrament. If he is unsure whether the person is dead, he may administer the sacrament conditionally.

The matter for the sacrament is always the same: olive oil blessed by a bishop. (In necessary cases, other vegetable oils are allowed, and the priest may bless the

NOTE TAKING

Summarizing Material. Create an outline in your notebook like the one started below. As you read the section, use the outline to help you summarize the material.

 A. Who should receive the sacrament?
  1. The dangerously ill
  2. Those facing surgery
 B. What are the parts of the sacrament?
  1.
 C. What is Viaticum?
  1.

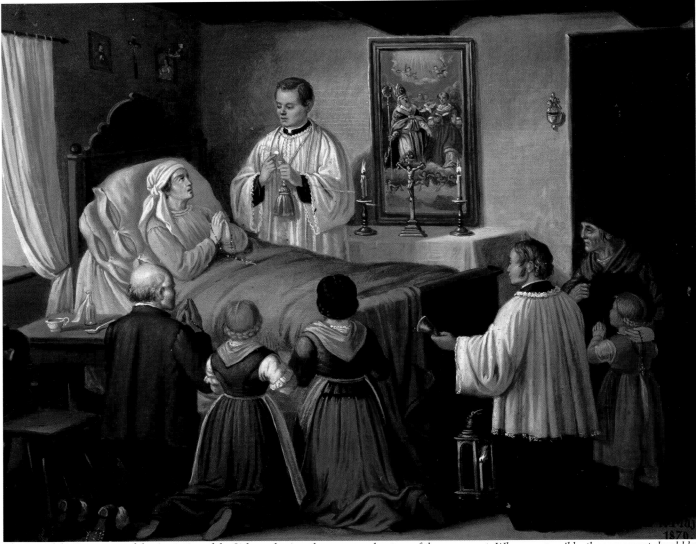

The Rite of the Sacrament of the Anointing of the Sick emphasizes the communal nature of the sacrament. Whenever possible, the sacrament should be observed as a community.

oil.) As with the other liturgical oils, the bishop blesses the oil of the sick at the Chrism Mass.

Rite of Anointing

The Sacrament of the Anointing of the Sick, given during sickness or immediately before death, is a true celebration of God's faithful and healing love. The sacrament is intended to be celebrated in a communal setting because sickness and death affect the entire Church. Family members, friends, and parishioners are strongly encouraged to surround the sick person in his or her moment of need. The sacrament may take place in the family home, a hospital, a convalescent home, a hospice, or a parish church. The sacrament may be for a single sick person or a group of sick people, depending on need (see *CCC*, 1517).

In keeping with a celebration that evokes Christ's Resurrection, the priest or bishop usually wears white vestments. If the Rite of the Anointing of the Sick takes place during Mass, it occurs after the homily. The sick person(s) and all those present are encouraged to take part in the Sacrament of Penance before Mass and to receive Communion during Mass. If the Rite of the Anointing of the Sick takes place outside Mass, those who are to be anointed are encouraged to celebrate the Sacrament of Penance first.

The essential Rite of the Anointing of the Sick consists in the anointing of the forehead and hands of the sick person (in the Roman Rite) or other parts of the body (in the Eastern Rite) while the celebrant prays for the special grace of the sacrament. The new Rite of the Anointing of the Sick consists of eight parts: Introductory Rites, Liturgy of the Word, Litany or Prayer of the Faithful, Laying on of Hands, Blessing of Oil, Prayer of Thanksgiving, Anointing with Oil of the Sick, and Prayer after Anointing.

Introductory Rites

The priest or bishop greets the sick person(s) and gathered assembly. Then he explains what will happen:

> Priest: The grace of our Lord Jesus Christ and the love of God and the fellowship of the Holy Spirit be with you all.
>
> All: And with your spirit.
>
> Priest: Lord God, you have told us through your Apostle James: "Is there anyone sick among you? Let him call for the elders of the Church, and let them pray over him and anoint him in the name of the Lord. This prayer, made in faith, will save the sick man. The Lord will restore his health, and if he has committed any sins, they will be forgiven." Gathered here in your name, we ask you to listen to the prayer we make in faith: in your love and kindness protect our brother (sister) N. in his (her) illness. Lead us all to the peace and joy of your kingdom where you live for ever and ever.
>
> All: Amen.

A Penitential Rite follows. Those who are sick may receive the Sacrament of Penance at this time by individual confession. If there is no sacramental confession, or if it has taken place earlier, the priest invites everyone present to join in the Penitential Rite, which is similar to the one you hear at Mass on Sundays.

Liturgy of the Word

The Liturgy of the Word also mirrors the one you hear at Mass. It may consist of a first reading (usually from the Old Testament), a responsorial psalm, a second reading (usually from the New Testament), a Gospel acclamation, a Gospel reading, and a homily given by the presiding priest or bishop. In cases of necessity (such as impending death), the Liturgy of the Word may be shortened considerably. The *Catechism of the Catholic Church* explains the purpose of this part of the rite: "The Liturgy of the Word, preceded by an act of repentance, opens the celebration. The words of Christ, the witness of the apostles, awaken the faith of the sick person and of the community to ask the Lord for the strength of his Spirit" (*CCC*, 1518).

The homily should invite deeper faith in God's healing presence and faithful love. It should also remind everyone that the prayers of the community can have a healing effect on those who are sick.

Litany (Prayer of the Faithful)

Again, just as at Mass, there are prayers of petition for the needs of those gathered. These prayers may be adapted for the particular situation. Here are some options:

> Priest: My brothers and sisters, with faith let us ask the Lord to hear our prayers for our brother (sister) N. Lord, through this holy anointing, come and comfort N. with your love and mercy.
>
> All: Lord, hear our prayer.
>
> Priest: Free N. from all harm.
>
> All: Lord, hear our prayer.
>
> Priest: Relieve the sufferings of all the sick.
>
> All: Lord, hear our prayer.
>
> Priest: Assist all those dedicated to the care of the sick.
>
> All: Lord, hear our prayer.
>
> Priest: Free N. from sin and all temptation.

All: Lord, hear our prayer.

Priest: Give life and health to our brother (sister) N. on whom we lay our hands in your name.

All: Lord, hear our prayer.

Laying on of Hands

In imitation of Jesus, who healed many sick people by touching them or laying his hands on them, the priest lays his hands on the head of the sick person(s). In silence, the priest prays over the sick in the faith of the Church. The *Catechism of the Catholic Church* explains that "this is the epiclesis proper to this sacrament" (*CCC,* 1519). (*Epiclesis*, recall, is a prayer that calls upon the Holy Spirit to act in, and through, the sacraments.) The priest, in the name of the whole Church, calls on God to come and fill the sick person with his healing presence.

Blessing of Oil

If necessary, any priest who administers Anointing of the Sick may bless the oil as part of the sacrament. However, as pointed out previously, this blessing usually happens only once a year, at the Chrism Mass for the diocese. During this special Mass, before the end of the Eucharistic Prayer or at the end of the Liturgy of the Word, representatives from each parish process to the sanctuary with the oil of the sick, sacred chrism, and oil of catechumens. The bishop blesses the oils, praying in part, "Make this oil a remedy for all who are anointed with it; heal them in body, in soul, and in spirit, and deliver them from every affliction" (*Sacramentary*, 919). If a priest needs to bless oil in an emergency, he uses the same words of blessing as the bishop at the Chrism Mass.

Prayer of Thanksgiving

Using the blessed oil of the sick, the priest prays a prayer of praise to the Trinity. Then, just before anointing the sick person, he asks God to "ease his (her) sufferings and strengthen him (her) in his (her) weakness."

Anointing with Oil of the Sick

In the Roman Rite, the priest (or bishop) anoints the forehead of the sick person(s), saying, "Through this holy anointing, may the Lord in his love and mercy help you with the grace of the Holy Spirit." Then he anoints the hands of the sick person, saying, "May the Lord who frees you from sin save you and raise you up." The person being anointed answers "Amen" to both prayers. This is the essential rite of the sacrament.

Prayer after Anointing

After all the anointings have taken place, the priest says a final prayer:

Priest: Lord Jesus Christ, you shared in our human nature to heal the sick and save all mankind. Mercifully listen to our prayers for the physical and spiritual health of our sick brother (sister) whom we have anointed in your name. May your protection console him (her) and your strength make him (her) well again. Help him (her) find hope in suffering, for you have given him (her) a share in your passion. You are Lord for ever and ever.

All: Amen.

No matter what the setting, the rite for the sacrament emphasizes its communal nature and the responsibility of all the faithful to care for the sick. Also, the sick person is encouraged to pray when he or she is alone or with family, friends, or those who care for him or her. The prayer should draw on the parts of Scripture that speak of the mystery of human suffering in Christ. Priests are encouraged to help the sick with this prayer.

Bottles of sacramental oils—oleum infirmorum (oil of the sick), sacrum chrisma (sacred chrism), and oleum sanctorum (oil of catechumens)—in a Roman Catholic Church.

Viaticum

The Sacrament of the Anointing of the Sick is for all who are seriously ill. Viaticum is a separate liturgical rite for those who are dying. Recall that the term *Viaticum* means "food for the journey." It is the person's last reception of the Eucharist. The gift of the Lord's Body and Blood near the time of death strengthens the person and reminds him or her of Christ's promise of resurrection.

All Catholics who can receive Holy Communion are bound to receive Viaticum when in danger of death. When possible, Viaticum should be received within Mass, under both species, to emphasize the meal symbolism of the Eucharist as a preparation for the heavenly banquet. If the dying person cannot receive Jesus' Body in the form of the consecrated bread, he or she may receive his Blood under the species of consecrated wine.

Outside of Mass, the ordinary minister of Viaticum is a priest. If no priest is available, Viaticum may be brought to the sick by a deacon or another member of the parish, a man or woman who by authority of the Church has been appointed by the local bishop to distribute the Eucharist to the faithful.

A distinctive feature of the reception of the Eucharist as Viaticum is the renewal of baptismal vows by the person who is dying. Also, before a person receives Viaticum, he or she should participate in the Sacrament of Penance, if possible, and in the Sacrament of the Anointing of the Sick. Penance, Anointing of the Sick, and Viaticum are the "last rites" for Catholics on their way to God. They mark the end of a person's earthly pilgrimage and prepare him or her to enter eternal life (see *CCC,* 1525).

BASIC KIT FOR GIVING VIATICUM

STOLE
A simple white stole is ideal if a priest is not able to bring vestments.

PYX

This small, round box holds the Eucharist for those who can't attend Mass.

OILS
The priest carries these with him in a small travel container.

TEXT
The priest brings a copy of the prayers of the ritual.

SECTION ASSESSMENT

NOTE TAKING
Use the outline you created for this section to help you complete the following questions.

1. Name six categories of people who should receive the Sacrament of the Anointing of the Sick.

2. Name the eight parts of the Rite of the Anointing of the Sick.

3. What is Viaticum, and how does it relate to the Sacrament of the Anointing of the Sick?

COMPREHENSION

4. Who is the minister of the Sacrament of the Anointing of the Sick?

5. What happens if a priest is called to administer the Sacrament of the Anointing of the Sick and he is not sure whether the person is alive or dead?

VOCABULARY

6. What does the word *Viaticum* mean, and who should receive Viaticum?

CRITICAL THINKING

7. How does the suffering of an individual affect the entire Church?

SECTION 3
The Graces of the Sacrament of the Anointing of the Sick

MAIN IDEA
In the Sacrament of the Anointing of the Sick, those who suffer receive the graces to accept their suffering, unite themselves with Jesus' redemptive sacrifice, serve the Church, and prepare for the end of life.

When you consider the effects of the Sacrament of the Anointing of the Sick, you have to remember that you don't necessarily celebrate the sacrament and then find an immediate release from all of your ailments. It's true that in rare cases people are miraculously cured of their cancers or healed of their disabilities. But in most cases, this does not happen. And obviously, many people who receive the sacrament do so right before they die.

So what is to be said about the effects of the sacrament? Is the Sacrament of the Anointing of the Sick just wishful thinking? Of course not. Jesus' healing power is real, and it is still active in the Church.

Healing always takes place as a result of the sacrament, although emotional or spiritual healing cannot always be seen or measured. It is often only in looking back that people can trace the long-term effects of interior healing they have experienced, yet these effects are

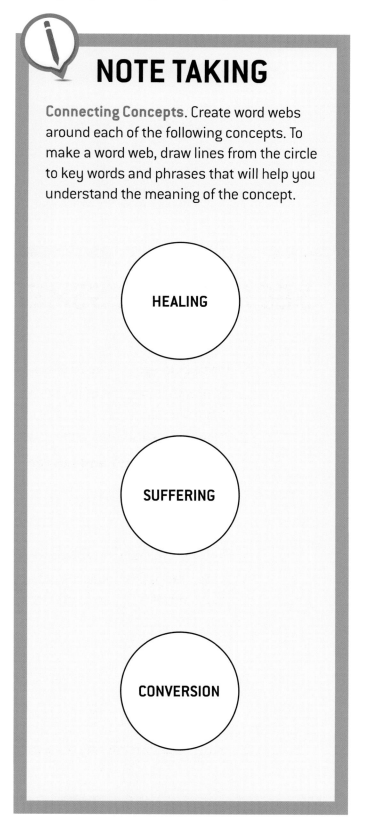

NOTE TAKING

Connecting Concepts. Create word webs around each of the following concepts. To make a word web, draw lines from the circle to key words and phrases that will help you understand the meaning of the concept.

HEALING

SUFFERING

CONVERSION

tangible and real. The *Catechism of the Catholic Church* lists four main effects of the sacrament:

1. The sacrament is a particular gift of the Holy Spirit.

The first grace a person experiences is to be able to accept the trials of being sick. The sacrament gives the person strength, peace, and courage to get through a serious illness or the effects of old age. Through the assistance of Jesus, through the power of the Holy Spirit, the person's soul is healed. The body is healed, too, if it is God's will and helps toward his or her salvation. Also, a person's sins are forgiven through the sacrament in conjunction with the Sacrament of Penance, and eternal punishment is remitted with only imperfect contrition (see *CCC*, 1520).

2. The sacrament unites the person with the Passion of Christ.

The sacrament unites those who participate in it to Christ more closely in illness and approaching death. Suffering, a result of Original Sin, is given new meaning when a person shares in the saving work of Jesus (see *CCC*, 1521).

3. The sacrament is grace for the Church.

When she cares for the sick and dying, the Church serves Christ himself and participates in his ministry. Likewise, people unite themselves to the Passion of Christ when they are sick. In doing so, they witness to the truth of Christ's redemption and provide an opportunity for the Church to live as the Body of Christ. Those who are sick can still serve the rest of the Church by reminding everyone they are in contact with to be grateful for the gifts of health and life as well as by witnessing to the faith in times of difficulty (see *CCC*, 1522).

4. The sacrament is preparation for the final journey.

A person is given the supernatural strength to complete "our conformity to the death and Resurrection of Christ, just as Baptism began it" (*CCC*, 1523). When the sacrament is received at the end of life, it is also called *sacramentum exeuntium* ("the sacrament of those departing"). In addition, near the time of death, the Church offers Viaticum as "the seed of eternal life and the power of resurrection" (*CCC*, 1524).

The Sacrament of the Anointing of the Sick is there to help you face illness and death with courage and dignity. You come to accept your situation as Jesus accepted his on the night before he died, when he prayed in the Garden of Gethsemane, "My Father, if it is possible, let this cup pass from me; yet, not as I will, but as you will. . . . My Father, if it is not possible that this cup pass without my drinking it, your will be done!" (Mt 26:39, 42).

The Sacrament of the Anointing of the Sick reminds you of your faith through its connection with the Sacraments of Baptism and Confirmation. In both Baptism and Confirmation, you were also anointed with oil. These anointings changed your very character. The oil of catechumens exorcised you from the power of evil. It strengthened you in your resolve to turn away from sin and orient your life toward God. The sacred chrism consecrated you as a child of God. It bound you to him in a covenant relationship that sickness and death cannot destroy.

Being anointed with the oil of the sick has similar effects. It communicates that your life has meaning and purpose, even when you are sick or in pain. The sacrament strengthens you and helps bring about spiritual, and sometimes physical, healing.

Transformation through the Sacrament

The Sacrament of the Anointing of the Sick helps transform the lives of those who receive it by helping them look at their suffering in a new way, as a participation in the saving works of Christ. Practically, this grace helps those who are sick and suffering within their own lives as they move from self-centeredness to God-centeredness. It also transforms them and the entire Church by helping them develop compassion and concern for others who suffer, prompting them to reach out. Jesus explicitly said that Christians must care for those who are sick. Doing so, he said, is equivalent to caring for the Lord himself. In the parable of the sheep and the goats, Jesus taught,

> Then the righteous will answer him and say, "Lord, when did we see you hungry and feed you, or thirsty and give you drink? When did we see you a stranger and welcome you, or naked and clothe you? When did we see you ill or in prison, and visit you?" And the king will say to them in reply, "Amen, I say to you, whatever you did for one of these least brothers of mine, you did for me." (Mt 25:37–40)

From Self-Centeredness to God-Centeredness

People struggling with sickness or pain very often get locked into their own worlds. They may act angry, impatient, and unreasonably demanding. They may complain because no one seems to help enough, no one responds fast enough, or no one takes care of the problem in exactly the right way.

Job himself (see pages 216–217) at one point became trapped in self-pity. He spent a great deal of time wondering why he was afflicted with suffering and illness. The answer to Job's problems was conversion. Job was challenged to put himself in God's place—to see the world and everyone in it from the Lord's perspective. Of course, Job could not do this alone, because he was only human and not divine. Instead, Job came to accept his limitations and inability to understand the mind of God. He took up the challenge to trust in God's loving plan for all creation; he found God in the midst of his suffering. He believed that good somehow came out of his bad situation.

The Sacrament of the Anointing of the Sick facilitates this type of conversion. Sickness is not a punishment. Instead, the sacrament helps a person see sickness and suffering as opportunities for growth in holiness. You can become holy by becoming more and more like Jesus and having the same attitude he had toward suffering and death. As St. Paul wrote,

> Have among yourselves the same attitude that is also yours in Christ Jesus,
> > Who, though he was in the form of God, did not regard equality with God something to be grasped.
> > Rather . . . he humbled himself, becoming obedient to death, even death on a cross. (Phil 2:5–8)

Some of the Church's greatest saints knew what it meant to unite themselves with the suffering of Jesus. St. Thérèse of Lisieux, for example, longed to be a missionary—in particular, someone who traveled to different parts of the world to share the Good News. Instead, she contracted tuberculosis as a young woman and was confined to bed. In her suffering, she slowly learned, through God's grace, to change her natural willfulness—especially her impetuous bad temper—into patient endurance. She called this her "little way" and described her efforts like this:

> Miss no single opportunity of making some small sacrifice, here by a smiling look, there by a kindly word; always doing the small thing right and doing it all for love. . . . Remember

St. Ignatius of Loyola

that nothing is small in the eyes of God. Do all that you do with love. (*Story of a Soul*, quoted in *Quotable Saints*, 117)

St. Thérèse died at age twenty-four, but the autobiography she left behind became a spiritual classic, encouraging many others to use their suffering as an opportunity for spiritual growth. Although she never left her convent, St. Thérèse is one of the Church's patron saints for missionaries.

Another saint whose life was affected by his own suffering was St. Ignatius of Loyola. St. Ignatius came from a rich family and started his career as a brilliant soldier, but then he was seriously wounded in battle and had to spend many months in bed recovering. During this time, St. Ignatius came to know the Blessed Trinity as never before. Once he was strong enough, he did not return to the army. Instead, he founded the Society of Jesus as a spiritual army to bring God's love to others. As he wrote,

Few souls understand what God would accomplish in them if they were to abandon themselves unreservedly to him and if they were to allow his grace to mold them accordingly. (*Spiritual Exercises*, quoted in *Quotable Saints*, 164–165)

These two saints, like many others throughout the Church's history, learned to identify with Jesus through their suffering. The title *Christ* means "God's anointed one." When you are anointed with the oil of the sick in the Sacrament of the Anointing of the Sick, you are challenged to unite yourself with Christ so completely that you also become "the anointed one." Your suffering, united with Christ's suffering, becomes truly redemptive.

From Self-Centeredness to Other-Centeredness

Transformation into "God's anointed one" means you willingly sacrifice yourself for the good of others. Like Jesus, you bring healing to others in today's world. In the words of Henri Nouwen—a Dutch Catholic priest who spent the last years of his life ministering with mentally disabled people at the L'Arche community in Toronto, Ontario—you allow yourself to become a "wounded healer." You can heal others because you know what it is like to suffer and to be healed by God's love. St. Paul explained this transformation from self-centeredness to other-centeredness in his Second Letter to the Corinthians:

Blessed be the God and Father of our Lord Jesus Christ, the Father of compassion and God of all encouragement, who encourages us in our every affliction, so that we may be able to encourage those who are in any affliction with the encouragement with which we ourselves are encouraged by God. (2 Cor 1:3–4)

YOUR Healing Ministry

All Catholics are called to continue the healing ministry of Jesus. You do this whenever you actively promote life, faith, hope, and love—in other words, when you follow the example of the Good Samaritan (see Lk 10:29–37). Being a minister of healing can be as simple as doing ordinary acts of kindness such as the ones below. Read the list. Then write a journal entry that tells three other ways you can be a minister of healing to others.

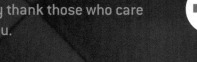 When you are sick, you sincerely thank those who care for you.

When you are sick, you faithfully take the medicine or treatment prescribed.

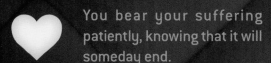 You bear your suffering patiently, knowing that it will someday end.

If you are not sick, you visit family members who are ill. You brighten their day with flowers, a magazine, or cheerful conversation.

You hold open the door for a person on crutches or in a wheelchair.

You contribute money to, or raise funds for, medical research institutes.

 You volunteer to help in hospitals, convalescent homes, retirement homes, and hospices.

 You run errands for those who are confined to their beds or homes.

 You pray for those who are sick, either privately or at Mass.

 You attend the Sacrament of the Anointing of the Sick in your parish to pray for and support those who are sick.

 You offer consolation and comfort to the families of people who have recently died.

In short, you can simply *be present* to others. Henri Nouwen wrote,

> My own desire to be useful, to do something significant, or to be part of some impressive project is so strong that soon my time is taken up by meetings, conferences, study groups, and workshops that prevent me from walking the streets. . . . But I wonder more and more if the first thing shouldn't be to know people by name, to eat and drink with them, to listen to their stories and tell your own, and to let them know in words, handshakes, and hugs that you do not simply like them but you truly love them. (*Gratias*)

The comfort you are able to offer others comes not from pious platitudes or tired clichés. Instead, your words of faith are based on firsthand experience. You have been on the receiving end of God's compassionate love and encouragement. Thus, you can profoundly encourage others to have faith too. This grace of being more Christ-like may be the most important effect of the Sacrament of the Anointing of the Sick.

SECTION ASSESSMENT

NOTE TAKING

Use the word webs you created for this section to help you complete the following questions.

1. How does the Sacrament of the Anointing of the Sick bring about spiritual healing?
2. How does the sacrament promote conversion?
3. What happens to your suffering when it is united to the Passion and Death of Christ in this sacrament?

COMPREHENSION

4. Name and explain the four main effects of the Sacrament of the Anointing of the Sick.
5. How does the Sacrament of the Anointing of the Sick remind Catholics of Baptism and Confirmation?
6. Briefly describe the lessons St. Thérèse of Lisieux and St. Ignatius of Loyola learned about suffering.
7. What did Henri Nouwen mean by the term "wounded healer"?

CRITICAL THINKING

8. How is sickness an opportunity to grow in holiness?
9. How can you serve those who are sick?

Section Summaries

Focus Question

What does it mean to be physically and spiritually healed?

Complete one of the following:

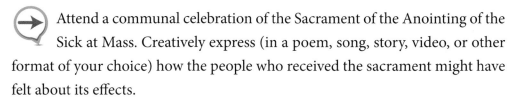

→ Attend a communal celebration of the Sacrament of the Anointing of the Sick at Mass. Creatively express (in a poem, song, story, video, or other format of your choice) how the people who received the sacrament might have felt about its effects.

→ Visit a Catholic cemetery, which is considered sacred ground. Spend some time praying for the souls and families of those who have died. Ask for God's help in accepting his will for your life, including whatever suffering may come to you. Take photos of the place you visited, and write a three-paragraph reflection on the experience.

→ Write a three-paragraph profile of someone you know or someone in the news who fits the definitions offered in this chapter of a person who has been spiritually healed.

INTRODUCTION (PAGES 215–220)
"Is Anyone among You Suffering?"

Human nature is weakened by the effects of Original Sin, so people are inclined to sin and are subject to illness, suffering, and death. The Sacrament of the Anointing of the Sick helps Catholics to accept suffering and transform it into a participation in the redemptive sacrifice of Jesus Christ. The sacrament is rooted in the healing power of Jesus, which he showed on earth through his miracles of physical and spiritual healing. These miracles, like the sacrament, prove the love and care that God has for each person.

→ Write about a time when you suffered from illness or injury. Write a prayer thanking Jesus for the grace you received to accept and overcome your pain.

SECTION 1 (PAGES 221–224)

Understanding the Sacrament of the Anointing of the Sick

The Sacrament of the Anointing of the Sick has been practiced since the earliest days of the Church, when blessed oil was used to anoint any baptized person who became ill. This oil of the sick was always blessed by the bishop, and the sacrament was always administered by a bishop or presbyter. As centuries passed, the sacrament was more associated with those who were at the point of death, and it was most often administered along with the Sacraments of Penance and the Eucharist. The Second Vatican Council restored the practice of offering anointing to believers suffering from serious illness while also retaining the sacrament's link to a safe passage out of this world.

Read paragraphs 73 to 75 of *Sacrosanctum Concilium*, which can be found at www.vatican.va. Write a paragraph explaining what the Second Vatican Council wanted to emphasize in the Church's practice of the Sacrament of the Anointing of the Sick.

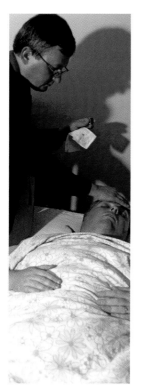

SECTION 2 (PAGES 225–230)

Celebrating the Sacrament of the Anointing of the Sick

The updated Rite of the Sacrament of the Anointing of the Sick focuses on the healing grace of the Holy Spirit to give spiritual strength and peace. The structure of the sacrament recalls the structure of the Mass, with a Penitential Rite, a Liturgy of the Word, and finally the anointing and the healing prayer, which are the sacrament's essential rite. When a person is in danger of death, the sacrament is often offered along with the Sacrament of Penance and a final reception of the Eucharist, known as Viaticum, or "food for the journey."

Consider the role of a priest who has been asked to pray with a suffering person. What is something consoling a priest might say to this person? Is there anything he should avoid saying? In a one-page report, write down your responses to these questions along with three Scripture verses the priest can suggest to the person for meditation.

SECTION 3 (PAGES 231–236)

The Graces of the Sacrament of the Anointing of the Sick

The Sacrament of the Anointing of the Sick offers graces that help a sick person to accept his or her suffering, unite it with the Passion and Death of Christ, serve the Church, and if necessary, prepare for death. At times, the sacrament offers physical healing as well, if physical healing would help toward the person's salvation. When you strive to accept the will of God even in times of suffering, your suffering can help bring about your deeper conversion, keeping you oriented toward God and others.

→ Research stories of people who received the Sacrament of the Anointing of the Sick and were physically or spiritually healed. Take notes on one of the stories you find, and share the story with classmates in a three- to five-minute presentation.

Chapter Assignments

Choose and complete at least one of the following three assignments assessing your understanding of the material in this chapter.

1. Understanding the Anointing of the Sick in Scripture

 Read one of the following Scripture passages and answer the corresponding question. Write a three- to five-sentence response to each question.

- John 9:1–41 (the man born blind). How does this passage show that sickness and death are not God's way of punishing us?

- Luke 14:15–24 (parable of the great feast). How does this parable show that God loves the sick and disabled just as much as he loves healthy people?

- Matthew 6:25–34 (dependence on God). How does this passage show that God's love is stronger than sickness, pain, and death?

- Matthew 8:14–15 (Jesus cures Peter's mother-in-law). How does this passage show that the sick have an important role to play in the community?

- Matthew 25:35–46 (the Last Judgment). How does this passage show that Catholics have a moral responsibility toward the sick, disabled, and dying?

2. A Response to "The Little Match Girl"

 "The Little Match Girl" is a famous short story by Dutch author and poet Hans Christian Andersen (1805–1875). It is the story of a child dying from poverty and cold while at the same time holding on to her hopes and dreams. Look up and read the story online; then complete a written report that includes all of the following elements.

- Write one paragraph summarizing the plot.

- Answer each of the following questions about the story: (1) Why was the little girl afraid to go home? (2) What did the little girl's grandmother say about the meaning of the falling star? (3) What happens to the girl at the end of the story?

- Locate a story in the news about a child or children who suffer. Write two paragraphs summarizing the story.

- Write one suggestion of something an individual could do to help children like those in "The Little Match Girl" and the child(ren) in your news story avoid suffering.

- Write one suggestion of something society could do to help children like those in "The Little Match Girl" and the child(ren) in your news story avoid suffering.

- Write a short prayer for children who suffer.

3. How Other Religions View Suffering

"Why do people suffer?" is a universal question that has been asked in every generation. All major religions have attempted to answer the question. For example, Buddhists believe, according to the first of two major Noble Truths, that all life is suffering caused by reliance on worldly possessions and attachments. This reliance can take the form of greed, hatred, and ignorance, which, unless they are alleviated, can return to the person in the form of karma, the principle of cause and effect whereby a person's intent and actions influence the person's future. Do all of the following:

- Ask a Catholic priest or religious the question "Why do people suffer?" Record and comment on the response.

- Research the ways the following religions view suffering: Hinduism, Islam, and Judaism. Write a one-paragraph response for each religion that answers the same question about suffering.

Faithful Disciple

St. Teresa of Calcutta

St. Teresa of Calcutta cared for the very old and the very young, two groups that are especially affected by poverty.

St. Teresa of Calcutta once said, "The fruit of faith is love, and the fruit of love is service. . . . Unless a life is lived for others, it is not worthwhile." Mother Teresa embodied this belief in her life and work.

Born Agnes Gonxha Bojaxhiu in Macedonia in 1910, Mother Teresa entered the Sisters of Loreto at the age of eighteen, and in 1929 arrived in India to teach at a school run by her religious order. She made her final vows in 1937 while she was teaching in eastern Calcutta. Mother Teresa was greatly disturbed by the poverty she saw on the streets of that city. Many poor people were living and dying on the streets, and no one seemed to care.

One day Mother Teresa heard God tell her to help these dying people herself. In 1948 she left the Sisters of Loreto to minister to the destitute and the starving on her own. She opened a school in the slums to teach the children of the poor. She got an education in medicine and gradually began to visit the homes of the sick and minister to them. She then began to go into the city streets and minister to the dying men, women, and children she found there who had been rejected by the local hospitals.

In 1950, Mother Teresa founded the Missionaries of Charity in Calcutta. The apostolate, or mission, of this religious community, she explained, was to care for "people that have become a burden to the society and are shunned by everyone."

In 1952, Mother Teresa opened the first Home for the Dying in Calcutta. People brought to the home received medical attention and were given the opportunity to die with dignity according to their religious faith, whether they were Muslim, Hindu, or Catholic. Mother Teresa and her sisters next opened a hospice for people suffering from leprosy; the sisters tended to the lepers' wounds, applied medication and bandages, and provided food. "The miracle is not that we do this work, but that we are happy to do it," Mother Teresa recalled later.

In 1955, Mother Teresa opened her first orphanage for homeless youth. Repeatedly, when she spoke in public, she talked of the need for strong family love. "The poor you may have right in your own family," she advised others. "Find them. Love them. Speak tenderly to them. Let there be kindness in your face, in your eyes, in your smile, in the warmth of your greeting. Always have a cheerful smile. Don't only give your care, but give your heart as well."

Mother Teresa was awarded the Nobel Peace Prize in 1979 for her selfless and courageous work. She used her $192,000 award to support her community's work.

At the time of her death in 1997, the Missionaries of Charity (which had grown to four thousand sisters, three hundred brothers, and more than one hundred thousand laypeople) were operating more than six hundred missions in 123 countries.

Pope Francis approved a miracle attributed to the intercession of Mother Teresa in December 2015, advancing her cause for sainthood. She was canonized by Pope Francis on September 4, 2016.

 ## Reading Comprehension

1. What is the name of the religious order Mother Teresa started?

2. What is the order's primary apostolate?

3. What are some of the ministries St. Teresa of Calcutta's religious community is involved in?

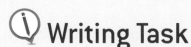 ## Writing Task

•   Research the work of the Missionaries of Charity in the United States. What is the closest ministry to you? Write a brief report about how teens can get involved in this ministry.

Explaining the Faith

How do laypeople participate in the Sacrament of the Anointing of the Sick?

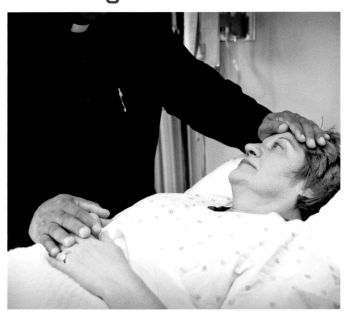

As you read in this chapter, in the early Church, all Christians were permitted and encouraged to use blessed oil in the context of healing prayer. Today the Church teaches that "in no instance may the non-ordained perform anointings either with the oil of the sick or any other oil" ("On Certain Questions," 9 § 1). While some actions belong only to the ordained priesthood, laypeople can and must participate actively in the life of the Church in their own way. (See Section 3 of this chapter for many ways the prayer and actions of laypeople can serve those who are sick and suffering.)

Pope Francis has drawn a positive picture of the family and the priest fulfilling their roles together in this sacrament: "The priest and those who are present during the Anointing of the Sick represent the whole Christian community that, like one body, clings around those who suffer and their relatives, nourishing faith and hope in them, and sustaining them with prayer and fraternal warmth. But the greatest comfort derives from the fact that it is the Lord Jesus Himself who is present in the Sacrament" (General Audience, February 26, 2014).

Further Research

- Read Article 9 of the 1997 instruction "On Certain Questions . . ." (available at www.vatican. va). Write a one-page report explaining the role of the lay faithful around the Sacrament of the Anointing of the Sick.

Prayer
A Prayer of Faith for the Sick

My brothers and sisters, in our prayer of faith let us appeal to God for our brother/sister N.

Come and strengthen him/her through this holy anointing: Lord, have mercy.

R. Lord, have mercy.

Free him/her from all harm: Lord, have mercy. (R.)

Free him/her from sin and all temptation: Lord, have mercy. (R.)

Relieve the sufferings of all the sick: Lord, have mercy. (R.)

Assist all those dedicated to the care of the sick: Lord, have mercy. (R.)

Give life and health to our brother/sister N., on whom we lay our hands in your name:
   Lord, have mercy. (R.)

—from The Rites of the Catholic Church

THE SACRAMENT OF
HOLY ORDERS

"MY BIT IN GOD'S HANDS"

Fr. Michael Doyle is a priest in Camden, New Jersey, a city of seventy-seven thousand people located across the Delaware River from Philadelphia, Pennsylvania. It is a town that has fallen on hard times. The city is plagued by high unemployment, a thriving drug trade, and widespread violence. In recent years, Camden has had the dubious distinction of being one of the most dangerous places to live in America, based on the rate for violent crimes.

Since 1995, Fr. Doyle has been celebrating a special memorial Mass for those who, in the past year, have been murdered in Camden. These Masses have honored 788 victims since 1995. Most of the victims have been young people. Fr. Doyle says the high concentration of poverty in Camden is the root cause of most of this violence and murder.

Fr. Doyle, as pastor of Sacred Heart parish, has also worked to do something about the poverty. The parish sponsors a food sharing and prayer service on Saturday mornings. Free food is given away to women, who take it home to their families. The parish also funds the tuition at its school for two hundred children. Fr. Doyle solicited local business leaders to help pay their tuition.

Fr. Doyle is also one of the founders of the Heart of Camden project, which purchases and refurbishes abandoned homes, then sells them at reduced rates. Purchasers are given a schedule of monthly payments, and the percentage of payment is almost 100 percent.

Fr. Doyle summarizes his priestly work this way: "Even when Jesus was here, he cured ten lepers, and nobody asked him, 'How many lepers are in the quarries?' So I always go by that principle. My bit in God's hands is enough. I do that little bit, that's all I can do. So I don't take all of Camden into my head, or my heart. I just take a bit of it."

(Based on Lucky Severson, "Camden Priest," *Religion & Ethics Newsweekly* television program, PBS.org, January 17, 2014.)

FOCUS QUESTION

How does the Sacrament of Holy Orders SERVE CHRIST and THE CHURCH?

INTRODUCTION
Becoming a Priest

MAIN IDEA

Diverse, talented men continue to answer God's call to the priesthood, being formed to follow Christ more deeply and serve the Church in a more comprehensive way.

The Sacrament of Holy Orders and the Sacrament of Matrimony are two sacraments whose primary purpose is to create, build, and maintain the Church community. That is why these two sacraments are called Sacraments at the Service of Communion. They do so in different ways. Holy Orders concerns the governance of the Church, providing ordained Church leaders. Matrimony (the subject of Chapter 9) emphasizes the service of the common priesthood of the faithful, especially by producing more Catholics and educating them in the faith.

The leaders the Sacrament of Holy Orders provides are ordained ministers who "feed the Church in Christ's name with the word and the grace of God" (*Lumen Gentium*, 11). The sacrament includes three degrees: episcopacy, presbyterate, and diaconate—that is, bishops, priests, and deacons. The word *order* is from the Latin *ordo*, which described an established civil body. *Ordination* is incorporation into an order. Deacons do not share the priestly ministry; they are ordained for service.

The service that priests, deacons, and bishops provide to the Church is a "service to the common priesthood" (*CCC*, 1547)—that is, the priesthood of all believers that unites all who are baptized. Ordained men minister to Catholic men and women who are not

NOTE TAKING

Identifying Concepts. Create word webs around each of the following concepts about the priesthood. To make a word web, draw lines from the circle to key words and phrases that will help you understand the meaning of the concept.

SACRAMENTAL ROLE

REQUIREMENTS

PREPARATION

ordained—the laity—in order to strengthen them in turn for their work of bringing Christ to the world. The role of those in Holy Orders is to nourish the Church by the word and grace of God.

This job description may give you a picture of the kind of man who could be ordained; he may seem stronger, more selfless, or different than others. Yet despite their amazing sacramental powers (which are unmerited gifts from God), priests are simply human. Consider a recent survey by the Catholic bishops of the United States. In it, men who were about to be ordained to the priesthood shared the following responses to complete the phrase "People would be surprised to know that I . . ." Their answers included:

- played guitar in a rock-and-roll band;
- flew fighter jets;
- was called "Killer" on the football field;
- was a successful lawyer;
- was an atheist;
- built my own home and was once engaged to be married; and
- once owned a townhouse, a BMW, and a Rolex watch.

The response of these men who are priests today parallels the response of the first disciples to Jesus' call: "Come after me, and I will make you fishers of men" (Mt 4:19, Mk 1:17). Simon (later called Peter) and his brother Andrew were fishermen. They left their fishing nets to follow Jesus. Likewise, James and his brother John, sons of Zebedee, were on their fishing boat when Jesus approached them. They not only left their nets and boat to follow Jesus—they left their father too. This radical commitment of discipleship is a strong element of the priesthood.

In many parts of the world, the Church has recently struggled to fill seminaries and ordain sufficient numbers of men to the priesthood. However, good men are still listening for, and accepting, God's call to this vitally necessary ministry. Here are several common reasons why men respond to the call to serve the Church in ordained ministry:

First, many men are attracted to the priesthood because of the essential sacramental role the priest has in the Church. The priest has these absolutely unique gifts: to consecrate the Eucharist into the Body and Blood of Jesus Christ, to offer absolution for sins in God's name, and to bring healing in the Sacrament of the Anointing of the Sick. Many men desire to be Christ for the world in this way.

Next, priests are inspired by priests. Almost all seminarians recall when a priest they knew invited them to consider the priesthood. Fr.

John Regan recalls one Saturday afternoon when he was a senior in high school. His pastor said to him, "John, if you ever think about being a priest, I think you would be good." These simple words of invitation encouraged Regan to **discern** more seriously the call to priesthood.

Inner experiences of devotion can also spark the desire to be a priest. From a very young age,

a boy may recognize that God is calling him to a different kind of life. He may think of himself as a leader. He may have compassion for others and empathy for the larger problems of the world. He may feel a deep connection with God and an attraction to the Gospel of Jesus Christ. He is likely devoted to Jesus in the Blessed Sacrament and feels great comfort from participating at Mass. He may also find himself inspired by a great person, such as a pope, or by a special experience like World Youth Day.

Just as he once called Peter, Andrew, James, John, and the other leaders of the early Church, the Lord continues to call men today—in many ways, from many different paths of life—to receive the Sacrament of Holy Orders. A common prayer heard throughout the Church today is that more young men will hear Christ's call and accept this life of ministry, service, and leadership.

Who Can Be Ordained?

The *Catechism of the Catholic Church* teaches that "no one has a *right* to receive the sacrament of Holy Orders. Indeed no one claims this office for himself; he is called to it by God" (*CCC*, 1578).

Reception of the Sacrament of Holy Orders is reserved for baptized males only. Some view this reservation as unjust, usually pointing to the fundamental equality of men and women and the proven capability of women to be successful in many of the same careers as men. Although women and men certainly have equal dignity and ability, women and men are not identical. Thus, the Church's teaching that only men can be priests is not rooted in injustice. Your gender is not incidental; it is an essential part of who you are. It has an impact on how you relate to others, including God and the Church.

The main reason ordination of women is not possible, however, is that the Church is bound to the choice made by the Lord himself. Jesus chose twelve men to be his Apostles, who in turn chose men to be their successors. The pope and bishops today are responsible for

> **discern** To perceive differences between more than one option. In the context of faith, to discern means to listen for the voice of the Holy Spirit when considering different options for action.
>
> **Deposit of Faith** The body of saving truth entrusted by Christ to the Apostles and handed on by them to be preserved and proclaimed by the Church's Magisterium.

Only baptized men can be candidates for ordination.

maintaining the apostolic nature of the Church, making the Twelve Apostles an "ever-present and ever-active reality until Christ's return" (*CCC*, 1577). Jesus' choice of only men as Apostles did not merely reflect the societal norms of his day. Jesus was countercultural in every way, including in his interactions with women. He had many friends who were women at a time when it was unusual for men and women to interact socially at all. He taught women; many sat at his feet as disciples. Still, he did not include them among the Twelve. When the Apostles had to replace Judas among the Twelve, they did not choose a woman. Even Mary, the Mother of God and the most perfect disciple, was not chosen by Jesus or the Twelve to be an Apostle.

In 1995, Pope John Paul II stated that the Catholic practice of ordaining only men to the priesthood cannot be changed because it is part of the Church's **Deposit of Faith**. As such, it must be accepted in faith. In this context, the Church stresses the equality of women and the significance of motherhood. Like ordination, motherhood can be received only as an unmerited gift. Also, motherhood is ordered primarily for the good of the child, just as priesthood is ordered primarily for the service of others. Finally, both priesthood and motherhood are more than jobs, careers, or roles. They have their roots in a person's identity as male or female.

More Requirements for the Reception of Holy Orders

With the exception of married men who are ordained to the permanent diaconate, men who are normally chosen for ordination in the Latin Church pledge to live a life of **celibacy** for the sake of God's Kingdom. In the Eastern Church, bishops must be celibate, while married men can be ordained as priests and deacons; however, unmarried men who are ordained to the priesthood must remain celibate. Pope John Paul II did approve in some circumstances the ordination in the Latin Rite of married men who had been ordained in another ecclesial community (usually Anglican). See Explaining the Faith on page 283 for more information on priestly celibacy.

A priest also pledges humility, obedience, and, particularly in the case of religious-order priests, voluntary poverty of worldly goods.

Answering the Call to Serve

A candidate for ordination must be a mature male who has completed Christian initiation, who willingly and knowingly wishes to be ordained, and who has undergone a review by Church authorities. Most importantly, the candidate must be called by God to this vocation, recognize the call, and respond to it. Pope John Paul II wrote,

> The history of every priestly vocation, indeed of every Christian vocation, is the history of an inexpressible dialogue between God and human beings, between the love of God who

calls and the freedom of individuals who lovingly respond to him. (*Pastores Dabo Vobis*, 36)

While each man called by God to priesthood is responsible for saying yes, other Catholics must encourage and facilitate the call. No one should have to determine his or her vocation in isolation. Everyone relies on the support, prayers, and discernment of others. This means that if you think God may be calling a young man you know to the priesthood, you should tell him so.

Men whom the Church calls to ordination spend a long time preparing to receive the sacrament. First, each candidate undergoes a psychological assessment to ensure his mental and emotional health. If there are concerns, therapy may be suggested, and admission to the seminary may be postponed or denied.

When a candidate is ready, he enters the **seminary**, a communal environment that fosters an important priestly quality: fraternal love and communion among those who will become brother priests. Together, the seminarians experience formation in four important areas:

- *Human formation* helps the candidate learn to relate well to others.
- *Spiritual formation* cultivates an intimate friendship with Jesus Christ, expressed in a lifelong commitment to personal prayer and devotion.

celibacy The renunciation of marriage for more perfect observance of chastity made by those who receive the Sacrament of Holy Orders. Celibacy also extends to consecrated life and to those who forgo marriage for some honorable end.

seminary The place where the training of candidates for the priesthood takes place. The Council of Trent instructed the bishops in each diocese to set up a seminary college to train men for the priesthood.

- *Intellectual formation* involves studies in theology and philosophy, leading to a deeper understanding of what it means to be human and to seek God.

- *Pastoral formation*—the goal of the whole process—makes candidates into shepherds of souls in imitation of Jesus Christ, the Good Shepherd.

Above all, seminarians are entering into a relationship of discipleship with Christ, which, as priests, they will model for the faithful. The word *disciple* means "learner." Discipleship takes a conscious decision; it cannot rest on others' choices. Discipleship cannot be about following rules without deeper reflection on their meaning. Discipleship means asking over and over: "What do I believe? Why do I believe? How does this belief impact my life and the lives of others?" Priests answer these questions and seek to help others answer them, too. Most importantly, they follow Christ by bringing his grace to the Church through the sacraments.

SECTION ASSESSMENT

NOTE TAKING

Use the word webs you created for this section to help you answer the following questions.

1. What are some sacramental roles of the priest?
2. What are other requirements of the priesthood besides celibacy?
3. How is a priest a disciple of—that is, a learner from—Christ?

COMPREHENSION

4. What are some reasons men today are drawn to the priesthood?
5. Why are only men able to receive the Sacrament of Holy Orders?
6. Name the four areas of formation for a candidate for priesthood.

REFLECTION

7. What does it mean to say that no one has the right to choose ordination?
8. What could you do to encourage a classmate who feels called to the priesthood?

SECTION 1
Understanding the Sacrament of Holy Orders

MAIN IDEA

The priesthood established by Jesus has deep roots in the history of the Jewish people. The ministerial priesthood shares in the unique priesthood of Christ.

Since the beginning of the Church, the Sacrament of Holy Orders has been conferred in three degrees: the episcopate, presbyterate, and diaconate. These ordinations lead to the ministries of bishop, priest, and deacon. The *orders* of bishop and priest enable the one who is ordained to act in the Person of Christ, the Head of the Body, in celebration of the sacraments. Deacons are ordained to help and serve priests and bishops in their work. Priests and bishops are configured to Christ so they can act as the head of Christ's Body, the Church. Deacons are configured to Christ that they might serve as he served. Bishops, priests, and deacons are irreplaceable for the structure of the Church; in fact, without them, one cannot speak of the Church.

Tracing the priesthood in the Old and New Testaments is helpful for understanding how the modern orders of bishop, priest, and deacon are related to the priesthood of Israel, fulfilled in the High Priesthood of Christ.

Priesthood in the Old Testament

There was no ordained priesthood in early Israel. The father of a family or the head of a clan acted as the group's priest. He performed spiritual duties and taught his children about God. Around the time of the Exodus,

NOTE TAKING

Highlighting Key Times. Draw a horizontal line across a piece of paper to show the progression of time from the Old Testament to today. Mark it as shown to represent the different stages of development of the priesthood. Write down at least one or two distinctive features of the priesthood at each stage to help you recall when each development took place.

Apostolic Times		Fourth Century		Council of Trent	
Old Testament	Early Church		Middle Ages		Second Vatican Council

the clan of Aaron and the tribe of Levi were set aside as priests (see Exodus 28–29, 32:25–29). Sometimes the men were anointed with oil before they assumed their sacred duties (see Leviticus 8–9). Most of these priests were married, and they passed the priesthood on to their sons.

During the Exodus from Egypt, Moses selected seventy elders to aid him in discerning God's will and leading the twelve tribes (see Numbers 11:24–25). These elders were mature men known for their administrative skills, moral character, and loyalty to the Law. The elders are referred to in a prayer in the Church's ordination rite for priests.

After the construction of the first Jerusalem Temple, the main role of the priests was Temple duty—offering sacrifices to God on behalf of the people. When the second Temple was destroyed in AD 70, the Jewish priesthood effectively ended. However, the priesthood of the Old Testament has much deeper significance as it prefigures the priesthood of Christ and the Church he founded.

The Priesthood of Christ

Jesus was not a Temple priest. Rather, Jesus is the High Priest of the New Covenant, acting as both priest and victim in his sacrifice on the Cross to the Father. The ministerial priesthood shares in the unique priesthood of Christ. St. Thomas Aquinas wrote, "Only Christ is the true priest, the others being only his ministers." The Letter to the Hebrews explains further:

> But when Christ came as high priest of the good things that have come to be, passing through the greater and more perfect tabernacle not made by hands, that is, not belonging to this creation, he entered once for all into the sanctuary, not with the blood of goats and calves but with his own blood, thus obtaining eternal redemption. (Heb 9:11–12)

Jesus Christ handing the keys to the Kingdom to St. Peter.

Through Baptism and Confirmation, all Catholics share in the common priesthood. The ministerial, or hierarchical, priesthood of bishops and priests, however, "confers a sacred power for the service of the faithful" (*CCC*, 1592). Though both priesthoods are "ordered to one another," they are not the same. The common priesthood is an unfolding of baptismal grace—living a life of faith, hope, and love, according to the graces of the Holy Spirit. The ministerial priesthood serves the common priesthood. Through it, Christ builds up the Church.

Because Jesus himself is present to the Church in the ordained minister as "Head of his Body, Shepherd of his flock, high priest of the redemptive sacrifice" (*CCC*, 1548), Jesus is the perfect Mediator between God and humanity. He called the Twelve Apostles to continue his work (see Matthew 10:1–42; Mark 1:17, 3:13–19), consecrating them at the Last Supper (see John 17). He made of these Apostles a Church—a permanent assembly—with Peter as their head (see Matthew 16:18–19, John 21:15–17). Their mission was to be his witnesses to the ends of the earth and, through the power of the Holy Spirit, to make all people his disciples (see Matthew 28:16–20; Mark 16:15; Luke 24:45–48; Acts 1:8, 2:1–36).

The Twelve Apostles soon realized they needed others to help them in their rapidly expanding ministry of spreading the Good News and celebrating the Eucharist. They chose seven men—Stephen, Philip, Prochorus, Nicanor, Timon, Parmenas, and Nicholas of Antioch—to serve as deacons, or ministers (see Acts 6:6). Deacons attended to the internal needs of the community—both at the Eucharistic table and elsewhere. They read aloud the Scriptures, administered Communion, taught catechumens, ministered to the sick, and distributed food and clothing to the poor, especially widows and orphans.

The Apostles chose men to be presbyters, or elders, of each local Church: "They appointed presbyters for them in each church and, with prayer and fasting, commended them to the Lord in whom they had put their faith" (Acts 14:23). The Apostles invested these men through a ritual involving prayer and the laying on of hands. Decisions affecting the entire Church were made at general councils by the Apostles acting together with presbyters (see Acts 15). Eventually, the Apostles selected men to be their successors and to continue their work after their deaths. The recorded Greek name for the successors was *episcopoi*, or bishops.

Brief History of the Sacrament to the Present

By the early second century, St. Ignatius of Antioch had repeated an established tradition that only a bishop or his appointee could preside at the Eucharist or baptize. In the early Church, the community as a whole chose

bishops. A man was chosen as bishop because of the apparent presence of the Holy Spirit within him. After his election, a bishop received the imposition of hands from another bishop. He was ordained to proclaim the Word, forgive sins, preside at the Eucharist, and supervise the work of presbyters and deacons. The bishop ordained presbyters, and other presbyters joined in the laying on of hands at the Rite of Ordination. Deacons were ordained by the bishop alone, specifically to assist the bishop in his ministry.

In the fourth century, after Christianity became the official state religion of the Roman Empire, the **clergy** gained a more privileged status. The desire of the people to elect a particular person as bishop was no longer enough to guarantee he would become bishop; the state attempted to approve the choice of bishops. Still, the Council of Chalcedon (AD 451) stated that priests were to be called by the people of a particular parish and ordained for work within that parish. Any other ordination was considered null and void.

During the Middle Ages, bishops increasingly needed priests who could celebrate Mass. Deacons

clergy From a Greek word for "lot," a term for ordained men.

Even today, monks follow the Rule of St. Benedict of Nursia, which includes the phrase "ora et labora" (meaning "pray and work").

did not have that power. So the diaconate declined, becoming a step on the way to priesthood.

Also during this time, an increase in monastic life influenced the priesthood. Though most monks were not priests, many priests adopted monastic habits, prayers, study, and disciplines, including celibacy, which had already been practiced for centuries. In 1125, the Church legislated against priests being married. Before then, priests could be married, though many priests already lived a single, celibate life.

The Protestant reformers of the sixteenth century pointed to some weaknesses in the clergy of that time, including a lack of education. In response, the Council of Trent (1545–1563) required seminary training for priests. The Council also reaffirmed Holy Orders as a sacrament and emphasized priests' power to celebrate the Eucharist and forgive sins in Christ's name.

In the twentieth century, the Second Vatican Council called for the restoration of the permanent diaconate in the West (which happened in 1967). The Council also called for a new Rite of Ordination that recalled the original meaning of ordained ministry. Finally, the Council reminded the Church of the differences between the ministerial, or hierarchical, priesthood and the common priesthood, while also pointing out their interrelation.

The Second Vatican Council acknowledged the authority Jesus gave to his Apostles and their successors to govern the Church. Bishops and priests are entrusted with the sacred power of ministry and service. They are "to serve in the name and in the person of Christ the Head in the midst of the community" (*CCC*, 1591) as visible signs of his presence. In *Lumen Gentium*, the Council reminded people of the real nature of ordination: its service of communion. Bishops and priests are to work for the salvation of others. The Council stated "that bishops, in an eminent and visible way, sustain the roles of Christ Himself as Teacher, Shepherd and High Priest, and that they act in his person" (*Lumen Gentium*, 21). Thus, the revised Rite of Ordination emphasizes how Jesus ministered to others and how he wanted his disciples to do the same.

SECTION ASSESSMENT

NOTE TAKING

Use the timeline you created to help you answer these questions.

1. What was the role of a bishop in the early Church? A priest? A deacon?
2. How did the Apostles practice the Sacrament of Holy Orders?
3. How did monastic life influence the way people viewed the priesthood?
4. What changes did the Council of Trent make to the requirements for ordination?
5. What did the Second Vatican Council teach about the roles of bishops, priests, and deacons in the Church today?
6. Name two changes around Holy Orders brought about by the Second Vatican Council.

COMPREHENSION

7. What is the main significance of the Old Testament priesthood for Christians?
8. Who gave the Apostles and their successors authority to govern the Church?

REFLECTION

9. What examples have you seen of the clergy and laity working together for the good of the Church and the community?

Celebrating the Sacrament of Holy Orders

MAIN IDEA

Bishops, priests, and deacons receive the gifts needed for their ministry through the Rite of Ordination, which is conferred by a validly ordained bishop.

Although Holy Orders is a single sacrament, it is celebrated and exercised in three degrees: episcopacy, presbyterate, and diaconate. All three degrees are conferred by a sacramental act called *ordination*. Only bishops can confer the Sacrament of Holy Orders on deacons, priests, and other bishops (see *CCC*, 1600).

> The *essential rite* [matter and form] of the sacrament of Holy Orders for all three degrees consists in the bishop's imposition of hands on the head of the **ordinand** and in the bishop's specific consecratory prayer asking God for the outpouring of the Holy Spirit and his gifts proper to the ministry to which the candidate is being ordained. (*CCC*, 1573)

The ordination of a bishop, priest, or deacon is vital to the life of the Church. It normally takes place within the celebration of the Eucharist on either a Saturday or a Sunday in the diocesan cathedral so as many people as possible may attend. As explained on pages 251–252, the Church confers the Sacrament of Holy

> **ordinand** A person receiving the Sacrament of Holy Orders at any level: episcopate, presbyterate, or diaconate.

NOTE TAKING

Identifying Differences. Create a two-column chart like the one on the right to help you understand the differences in the ordinations of bishops, priests, and deacons. Fill in the second column with further details.

DEGREE OF ORDERS	DIFFERENCES IN THE RITE
Bishop	
Priest	
Deacon	

Orders only on baptized males "whose suitability for the exercise of the ministry has been duly recognized" (*CCC*, 1598). In the Latin Church, before the candidate is ordained, he is presented to the bishop, and the bishop and the community are assured he has received the necessary training and been chosen for ordination in accordance with the teaching and practice of the Church. The bishop, who has been validly ordained himself, ordains the candidate. The congregation gives assent to the election. Here is a chart showing the basic structure of the Rite of Ordination for all three degrees:

RITE OF ORDINATION		
Bishop	Priest	Deacon
After Gospel: Presentation of Bishop-Elect	After Gospel: Calling of the Candidate, Presentation of Candidate	After Gospel: Calling of the Candidate, Presentation of Candidate
Reading of Mandate from the Holy See	Election by the Bishop	Election by the Bishop
Consent of the People	Consent of the People	Consent of the People
Homily by Principal Bishop	Homily by Bishop	Homily by Bishop
		Commitment to Celibacy (if candidate is not married)
Examination of the Candidate	Examination of the Candidate	Examination of the Candidate
	Promise of Obedience to the Bishop and His Successors	Promise of Obedience to the Bishop and His Successors
Litany of Saints	Litany of Saints	Litany of Saints
Laying on of Hands	Laying on of Hands	Laying on of Hands
Prayer of Consecration	Prayer of Consecration	Prayer of Consecration
Anointing of the Bishop's Head with Sacred Chrism		
Presentation of Book of the Gospels	Investiture with Stole and Chasuble	Investiture with Stole and Dalmatic
Investiture with Ring, Mitre, and Crosier	Anointing of Hands with Sacred Chrism	Presentation of Book of the Gospels
Seating of the New Bishop		
Liturgy of the Eucharist (new bishop concelebrates with other bishops)	Liturgy of the Eucharist (new priest concelebrates with bishop and other priests)	Liturgy of the Eucharist

The Ordination of Bishops

The consecration of a bishop confers the fullness of the Sacrament of Holy Orders, the summit of sacred ministry. Only the pope chooses bishops. Suitable candidates are identified in local dioceses and recommended by a **nuncio** to the Vatican. The appointment of a bishop is formally made in a **mandate**, an apostolic letter from the Holy See. During the Rite of Ordination of a bishop, this mandate is read aloud to the assembly. An ordained bishop is part of an unbroken succession of leadership that can be traced to the Apostles.

Usually, several bishops participate in the ordination of a new bishop to show the collegial nature of the episcopacy. The **ordinary bishop** confers the Sacrament of Holy Orders on the bishop-elect through the laying on of hands and the consecratory prayer. Here is part of that prayer:

> God the Father of our Lord Jesus Christ, Father of mercies and God of all consolation. . . .
>
> You have chosen your servant for the office of bishop. May he be a shepherd to your holy flock, and a high priest blameless in your sight, ministering to you night and day; may he always gain the blessing of your favor and offer the gifts of your holy Church. Through the Spirit who gives the grace of high priesthood grant him the power to forgive sins as you have commanded, to assign ministries as you have decreed, and to loose every bond by the authority which you gave to your Apostles.

> May he be pleasing to you by his gentleness and purity of heart, presenting a fragrant offering to you, through Jesus Christ, your Son, through whom glory and power and honor are yours with the Holy Spirit in your holy Church, now and for ever. Amen. (*Ordination of a Bishop*, 26)

Next, the celebrating bishop anoints the bishop-elect's head with sacred chrism. This is the fourth anointing the bishop has received in his lifetime (Baptism, Confirmation, and priestly ordination are the first three). It signifies the bishop's role as the head of Christ's Body in his diocese. Next, the new bishop is given a Book of the Gospels as a sign of his ministry to proclaim the Word and to witness to the truth. Finally, the new bishop is invested with the ring, the mitre, and the crosier.

nuncio An archbishop who acts as the official Vatican delegate for a nation. He is also called the apostolic delegate.

mandate An official appointment from the pope that says a certain priest has been chosen to be a bishop.

ordinary bishop The name for the diocesan bishop. He is the pastoral and legal representative of his diocese.

THE RING — A sign of his lifelong commitment and fidelity to the Church, the Bride of Christ

THE MITRE — A distinctive type of tall triangular hat; a sign of his authority

THE CROSIER — A sign of the bishop's role as shepherd of the Lord's flock

During the recitation of the Litany of Saints, ordinands lie prostrate to show their unworthiness for the office they are assuming and their dependence on God and the Church's prayers.

The Ordination of Priests

After a candidate for priesthood has been presented to the bishop and the community has given its assent, the candidate is instructed in the nature of the duties he is about to assume and his willingness to accept those duties is examined. Next, the Litany of Saints is recited. The local Church calls on the entire Church in heaven and on earth to pray for the ordinand, who kneels before the bishop for the essential rite of the sacrament. The bishop confers the Sacrament of Holy Orders on the ordinand through the laying on of hands and the consecratory prayer:

> Come to our help, Lord, holy Father, almighty and eternal God; you are the source of every honor and dignity, of all progress and stability. . . .
>
> With the same loving care you gave companions to your Son's Apostles to help in teaching the faith: they preached the Gospel to the whole world.
>
> Lord, grant also to us such fellow workers, for we are weak and our need is greater.
>
> Almighty Father, grant to this servant of yours the dignity of the priesthood. Renew within him the Spirit of holiness. As a co-worker with the order of bishops may he be faithful to the ministry that he receives from you, Lord God, and be to others a model of right conduct. . . .
>
> We ask this through our Lord Jesus Christ, your Son, who lives and reigns with you and the Holy Spirit, one God, for ever and ever. Amen. (*Ordination of a Priest*, 22)

The new priest is invested with a **stole** and a **chasuble**, the liturgical vestments of priesthood.

THE STOLE

Worn over both shoulders; a sign of the priest's authority

THE CHASUBLE

Outer vestment worn at liturgical celebrations

Then the bishop anoints the new priest's hands with sacred chrism. This anointing offers the priest the grace of the Holy Spirit to make his future ministry fruitful. Only ordained priests and bishops may validly consecrate the Eucharist at Mass. Also, only ordained priests and bishops may give absolution in the Sacrament of Penance.

The Ordination of Deacons

This order is given both to *transitional deacons* (those going on to priesthood) and to *permanent deacons*. In the West, transitional deacons must be celibate and promise to remain celibate throughout life, so as "to consecrate themselves with undivided heart to the Lord" (*CCC,* 1579).

The bishop confers the Sacrament of Holy Orders on the ordinands through the laying on of hands and the consecratory prayer:

Almighty God, be present with us by your power. You are the source of all honor, you assign to each his rank, you give to each his ministry. . . . In the first days of your Church under the inspiration of the Holy Spirit, the Apostles of your Son appointed seven men of good repute to assist them in the daily ministry, so that they themselves might be more free for prayer and preaching. By prayer and the laying on of the hands the Apostles entrusted to those chosen men the ministry of serving at tables.

Lord, look with favor on this servant of yours, whom we now dedicate to the office of deacon, to minister at your holy altar.

Lord, send forth upon him the Holy Spirit, that he may be strengthened by the gift of your sevenfold grace to carry out faithfully the work of the ministry.

May he excel in every virtue: in love that is sincere, in concern for the sick and the poor, in unassuming authority, in self-discipline, and in holiness of life. May his conduct exemplify your commandments and lead your people to imitate his purity of life. May he remain strong and steadfast in Christ, giving to the world the witness of a pure conscience. May he in this life imitate your Son, who came, not to be served but to serve, and one day reign with him in heaven.

We ask this through our Lord Jesus Christ, your Son, who lives and reigns with you and the Holy Spirit, one God, for ever and ever. Amen. (*Ordination of a Deacon,* 21)

The new deacon is invested with a stole and a **dalmatic**. He also receives a Book of the Gospels, a sign of his mission to proclaim the Gospel of Christ.

stole A long, narrow band of fabric, like a scarf. A deacon's stole is worn diagonally from one shoulder. A priest's stole is worn straight from the shoulders.

chasuble The outer vestment worn by a bishop or priest at Eucharistic liturgy. Its color follows the liturgical seasons—purple for Advent or Lent; white for Christmas, Easter, and other feasts of Christ; red for Good Friday, Pentecost, and the feasts of martyrs; and green for Ordinary Time.

dalmatic The outer liturgical vestment of a deacon. It may also be worn by bishops under the chasuble and at certain solemn liturgies.

SECTION ASSESSMENT

NOTE TAKING

Use the chart you created to help you respond to the following items.

1. List the special items that bishops, priests, and deacons receive at their ordination. Tell what each one represents.

2. Why is a mandate needed to ordain bishops but not priests or deacons? What special reality does the mandate represent?

3. What does it mean when a bishop is anointed with sacred chrism?

4. What does it mean when a priest is anointed with sacred chrism?

COMPREHENSION

5. Describe the process for selecting candidates to become bishops.

6. What sacramental powers does a priest receive at his ordination?

7. What is the difference between a transitional deacon and a permanent deacon?

REFLECTION

8. Recall a time in your life when you experienced the presence or power of Christ through your interaction with a priest or bishop. Write about the experience.

The Graces of the Sacrament of Holy Orders

MAIN IDEA
Bishops, priests, and deacons live out their vocation by embodying Christ in the Church for the service of the faithful.

Holy Orders conforms the ordained minister even more closely to Christ, giving him an indelible character—one that can never be taken away. Also, through the gift of sanctifying grace, Holy Orders joins the

recipient even more intimately to the Blessed Trinity than he had been after being baptized and confirmed. As the *Catechism of the Catholic Church* explains, the grace of the Holy Spirit in this sacrament configures the ordained minister to Christ as "Priest, Teacher, and Pastor" (*CCC*, 1585). Like Baptism and Confirmation, this share in Christ's office is given once and for all and cannot be repeated or conferred temporarily.

The vocation of bishops, priests, and deacons involves full-time, wholehearted service to the Church. Bishops receive special graces to guide and defend the Church, to proclaim the Gospel, and to inspire others. Priests receive special graces to proclaim the Gospel, to offer the Eucharistic sacrifice, and to absolve sins. Deacons are given special graces to proclaim the Gospel, to assist in the liturgy, and to perform works of charity (see *CCC*, 1588).

Among other graces of the sacrament is the conversion of the man who receives Holy Orders from self-centeredness to God-centeredness, from duty to genuine love, and from pleasure seeking to Kingdom seeking. Each conversion is explained more fully on the following page:

NOTE TAKING

Summarizing Material. Create an outline like the following in your notebook. As you read this section, use the outline to help you summarize the material.

I. Ordained ministers embody Christ
   A. As High Priest
   B.
   C.

II. Ordained ministers serve the Church
   A. The Universal Church
   B.

1 Self-centeredness to God-centeredness.

What motivates a priest in his daily life and work? Is it wealth, power, or fame, or is it a desire to serve the will of God? In fact, although the former factors are a motivator for many, a priest puts aside these earthly desires in order to serve the will of God. The Jesuits call this selflessness *indifference*, meaning the priest is open to going wherever he is most needed and to doing whatever seems best. It is also related to the promise of obedience made to the priest's bishop or religious superior.

2 Duty ("I should do this") to genuine love ("I want to do this because I truly love God and love others").

St. John Vianney (1786–1859) described priesthood as "the love of the heart of Jesus." Priests are called to be genuine and loving people because they have a loving, personal relationship with Jesus.

Fr. Pedro Arrupe, S.J. (1907–1991), former Superior General of the worldwide Society of Jesus, wrote,

> Nothing is more practical than finding God, that is, than falling in love in a quite absolute, final way. What are you in love with, what seizes your imagination, will affect everything. It will decide what will get you out of bed in the morning, what you will do with your evenings, how you will spend your weekends, what you read, who you know, what breaks your heart, and what amazes you with joy and gratitude. Fall in love, stay in love and it will decide everything. (quoted in *My Life with Saints*, 11)

3 Pleasure seeking to Kingdom seeking.

Clearly a life of celibacy in imitation of Christ, modeling God's Kingdom on earth, involves a certain movement from pleasure to *asceticism*—that is, a strict self-denial as means of spiritual discipline. The goal, however, is not just greater self-mastery or self-discipline but a greater capacity to love.

Some ordained men face harsh lives of persecution and suffering following the public commitment made at the Sacrament of Holy Orders. Some are called to be martyrs for their faith, for their love of Jesus, and for their service of others. An example of a bishop who "gave his life for his sheep" (see *CCC*, 1586) is Oscar Romero (1917–1980) of San Salvador in El Salvador. During his ministry, Archbishop Romero had a conversion that led him to speak up courageously for the rights of the poor in his country. Because of his stance on justice, Archbishop Romero was assassinated in 1980 while saying Mass in San Salvador. Archbishop Romero was beatified by Pope Francis on May 12, 2015. Other examples abound, from both the days of the early Church, when St. Stephen (d. AD 34), a deacon, was stoned to death, to today, with recent martyrdoms taking place in Syria, during the civil war, and in Sudan, to name just two places in the modern world where men in ordained ministry, along with lay Christians, are persecuted for their faith.

Acting as Christ the High Priest

In the New Covenant, there is only one sacrifice and one priest. The sacrifice of Jesus replaces the Temple sacrifice of animal offerings described in the Old Testament. Because Jesus offered the perfect sacrifice of himself on the Cross, he is the one and only Mediator

Bl. Oscar Romero

St. Stephen

between God and the human race (see 1 Timothy 2:5). There is no longer any need for a priest "to offer sacrifice day after day, first for his own sins and then for those of the people; [Christ] did that once for all when he offered himself" (Heb 7:27).

Today's priests do not offer a new sacrifice when they preside at the Eucharist. Christ, the eternal High Priest, acts through the ministry of the priests to offer the Eucharistic sacrifice. When a priest offers the Body of Christ to the Father during the Eucharist, it is Christ who is offering himself. Because Christ is offering himself, the whole Church—the whole Body of Christ—also offers herself "'through him, with him, in him,' in the unity of the Holy Spirit" (*CCC*, 1553). The Church is the Body of Christ; therefore, whatever is done in the name of Christ is done in the name of the Church as

well. In the name of the Church, priests ask the Father to send the Holy Spirit to make Christ's sacrifice present to you so that you can share in it and receive its redeeming graces. Their own ministry also draws its strength from this sacrifice.

Bishops and priests act as Christ the High Priest whenever they bring the Mass and sacraments to the community. By the power of the Holy Spirit, through their actions, priests help make the entire Church, the Body of Christ, holy.

Acting as Christ the Teacher

Throughout his public ministry, Jesus used every opportunity—a dinner conversation, a prayer service, a boat ride, a hillside gathering, a chance encounter—to

GLIMPSES OF A
PRIESTLY VOCATION

The Congregation of Holy Cross is a religious order founded in France in 1837 by Bl. Basil Moreau. It is a unique community in that it includes both religious priests and religious brothers, and Moreau also encouraged partnership with a religious community of women. Holy Cross sisters remain active today. The Congregation of Holy Cross came to the United States shortly after its inception. One of its missionary priests, Fr. Edward Sorin, C.S.C., founded the University of Notre Dame, in northern Indiana, in 1842. The Congregation continues to sponsor Notre Dame and five other colleges and fifteen high schools in the United States. There are more than 1,200 fully professed Holy Cross priests and brothers worldwide. Shared below are some brief statements from Holy Cross priests regarding what led them to answer the call to priesthood.

After graduating from Notre Dame Law School and practicing law for two years, **FR. WILLIAM BEAUCHAMP** entered Moreau seminary at age thirty-five.

> I had been involved as a college professor, college administrator, business professional, and lawyer before I entered the seminary. I was happy and successful in all that I had done, but there was always the unsettled feeling that I was supposed to be doing something else.
>
> The priesthood had come up occasionally in my life, but I had never felt it really fit. Marriage, a family, and a professional life in business were what I had "planned." But the professional life I was pursuing never seemed totally right, and as I practiced law, I more and more felt I had to look into the religious life in Holy Cross. The Holy Cross men I had gotten to know when I was a law student, and the life they lived as religious priests—as men committed to doing God's work together, in a community, sharing a common purse and living a life of common prayer and ministry—became more and more attractive to me.

So I entered Moreau Seminary—really surprised that I was "starting over." But almost from the day I arrived at Moreau I felt that I belonged there, that Holy Cross was my home, and I have never regretted the day I made that move.

FR. STEPHEN KOETH, C.S.C., was ordained to the priesthood in 2007.

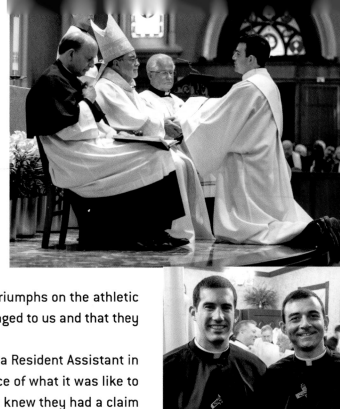

Even from a young age, I recognized that people went to our priests "in situations of suffering, of illness, of death, of problems in the family," but that our priests were also with us when we celebrated our first Sacraments in the Church, our academic achievements in school, and our triumphs on the athletic fields. They were indeed "our priests." We knew they belonged to us and that they allowed us to have a claim on them.

Years later, as a student at Notre Dame, I served as a Resident Assistant in Siegfried Hall. In some small measure I had an experience of what it was like to make myself available in service to others. The students knew they had a claim on me, and they invited me to accompany them in their moments of joy and grief, success and failure.

This experience helped me discern the Lord's call to religious life and priesthood. I knew that there were many ways that I could serve him and others, but I knew of no better way to reach so many different people in every aspect of life.

After some years as a parish priest, **FR. MICHAEL WURTZ, C.S.C.**, is now a doctoral student of liturgy at Sant'Anselmo, Rome.

I was awoken from the not uncommon high school daze when in my junior year I was given the pre-ACT and pre-SAT and a seemingly endless stream of standardized tests all geared toward the future. College was in my future, but I didn't know what my future would hold.

I never avoided the notion of a vocation to religious life or the priesthood. Where others might have been nervous, I was intrigued and when thinking about my future I naturally pondered if priesthood was my calling. It struck me then as it does now that every Catholic youth should instinctually be open to, and not afraid of, a calling to religious life and the priesthood. It is a great life— full of meaning and purpose.

I give praise to God for the gift of my vocation to religious life and the priesthood, which he granted for my salvation and service to the Church. The Congregation of Holy Cross possesses a rich heritage of ministry and sacrifice for the good of the People of God. And there is so much more to do. I am grateful that I might contribute to it. It's what my future holds.

The Congregation of Holy Cross suggests some steps for discernment of a priestly vocation. These steps begin with preparing your heart, which then leads to asking questions and listening to God's call. During this process it is helpful to access aids and help for discernment, as well as to address any and all fears and questions that come up along the way. You may consider these steps of discernment for yourself or suggest them to a male friend you know who might make a good priest. More information is available at the Congregation of Holy Cross website.

teach people about God's saving love. Jesus said, "I am the way and the truth and the life. No one comes to the Father except through me" (Jn 14:6). "For this I came into the world, to testify to the truth. Everyone who belongs to the truth listens to my voice" (Jn 18:37–38).

Jesus commissioned his Apostles to teach the truth to others. "Go, therefore, and make disciples of all nations, baptizing them in the name of the Father, and of the Son, and of the holy Spirit, teaching them to observe all that I have commanded you" (Mt 28:19–20). Jesus sent his Spirit of Truth to the Apostles at Pentecost so that they could fearlessly preach the Gospel and give spiritual nourishment to others. "If you remain in my word, you will truly be my disciples, and you will know the truth, and the truth will set you free" (Jn 8:31–32). Likewise, the contemporary priest acts as Christ the Teacher by sharing the Gospel of Truth.

Bishops and priests are witnesses of the truth, especially in matters of faith and morals. The Second Vatican Council taught specifically about the ministry of bishops: "By virtue, therefore, of the Holy Spirit who has been given to them, bishops have been constituted true and authentic teachers of the faith, pontiffs and pastors" (*Christus Dominus*, 2). The document further stated,

> Bishops should present Christ's teaching in a manner relevant to the needs of the times, providing a response to those difficulties and problems which people find especially distressing and burdensome. They should also safeguard this doctrine, teaching the faithful themselves to defend and spread it. (*Christus Dominus*, 13)

Priests and deacons also share in this teaching work. "It is the first task of priests as co-workers of the

> **diocese** A geographic section of the Church, made up of parishes, that is headed by a bishop.

bishops to preach the Gospel of God to all. . . . Priests owe it to everybody to share with them the truth of the Gospel in which they rejoice in the Lord" (*Presbyterorum Ordinis*, 4). Deacons are "to read the Sacred Scripture to the faithful" and "to instruct and exhort the people" (*Lumen Gentium*, 29).

In short, bishops, priests, and deacons preach the Gospel message by word and behavior. They proclaim the mystery of Christ, explain the Church's faith, and treat contemporary problems in the light of Christ's teaching. "In every case their role is to teach not their own wisdom but the word of God and to issue a pressing invitation to all men and women to conversion and to holiness" (*Presbyterorum Ordinis*, 4).

Acting as Christ the Good Shepherd

Like Jesus, bishops, priests, and deacons are to act as servant leaders. Bishops, especially, are to act as Christ the Good Shepherd (see Jn 10:11–15). As leader of a **diocese**, each bishop is to give his life in service to the spiritual needs of Catholics. Note the following further descriptions:

> The bishops also have been designated by the Holy Spirit to take the place of the Apostles as pastors of souls and, together with the supreme pontiff and subject to his authority, they are commissioned to perpetuate the work of Christ, the eternal Pastor. (*Christus Dominus*, 2)

> Chosen to shepherd the Lord's flock, these pastors [bishops] are servants of Christ and dispensers of the mysteries of God (see 1 Cor 4:1), to whom is entrusted the duty of affirming the Gospel of the grace of God (see Rom 15:16; Acts 20:24), and the glorious service of the Spirit and of justice (see 2 Cor 3:8–9). (*Lumen Gentium*, 21)

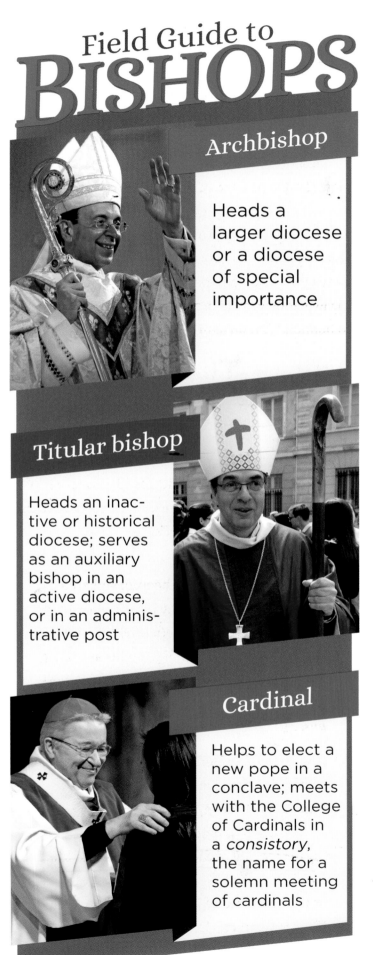

Field Guide to BISHOPS

Archbishop

Heads a larger diocese or a diocese of special importance

Titular bishop

Heads an inactive or historical diocese; serves as an auxiliary bishop in an active diocese, or in an administrative post

Cardinal

Helps to elect a new pope in a conclave; meets with the College of Cardinals in a *consistory*, the name for a solemn meeting of cardinals

Ordination Leads to a Ministry of Service

The Sacrament of Holy Orders requires much of those who receive it, but the graces of the sacrament also strengthen the ordained to live the sacrament. Holy Orders gives special graces of fidelity and, like marriage, is a lifelong vocation. Both of these sacraments *consecrate* the recipients for their vocations. Through them, the Church officially "sets people apart" to serve God. However, "setting apart" does not mean "separating," as the Second Vatican Council emphasized:

> The priests of the New Testament are, it is true, by their vocation and ordination, set apart in some way within the people of God, but this is not in order that they should be separated from that people or from any person, but that they should be completely consecrated to the task for which God chooses them. (*Presbyterorum Ordinis*, 3)

Bishops, especially, take the place of Christ himself in today's Church. Though the term is most associated with the pope, each bishop is the **vicar**, or representative, of Christ. The "bishops by divine institution have succeeded to the place of the apostles as shepherds of the Church, and he who hears them, hears Christ, and he who rejects them, rejects Christ and Him who sent Christ" (*Lumen Gentium*, 20). The bishops are part of an unbroken succession of leadership that can be traced to the Apostles. The Apostles were given a special outpouring of the Holy Spirit by Christ. By the laying on of hands at ordination, they passed on this gift of the Holy Spirit to bishops.

vicar One who serves as a substitute, an agent, or a representative of another. Bishops are vicars of Christ; they take his place in the Church. The pope is the Supreme Vicar of Christ.

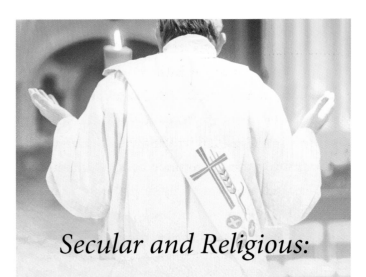

Secular and Religious: WHAT'S THE DIFFERENCE?

Some priests are *secular* or *diocesan* priests who are ordained for a diocese and serve where the bishop places them. Others are *religious* priests, who follow the rule of a religious order or community under the leadership of a religious superior. These priests are also collaborators of the diocesan bishop in his task of evangelization. Some examples of religious priests include Franciscans, Jesuits, and Holy Cross, to name a few.

Most dioceses have both diocesan and religious priests. Diocesan priests usually live and serve at a parish; they have made a promise of lifelong celibacy and obedience to the bishop. Religious priests usually live in communities devoted to a particular charism or spiritual founder. Their religious community may sponsor a parish, high school, or hospital. If so, their priests may live near, or at the site of, their ministry. Like diocesan priests, religious priests promise lifelong celibacy and obedience to their religious superior and to the bishop. They typically add the vow of poverty as well.

Bishops and priests serve the People of God by providing them with means and opportunities to grow in holiness. In general, they do this "by teaching (*munus docendi*), divine worship (*munus liturgicum*) and pastoral governance (*munus regendi*)" (*CCC*, 1592). These tasks are carried out by bishops, who are assisted by priests and deacons, in the universal Church and the local Church.

Service to the Universal Church

Within his diocese, the bishop is the highest Church authority. Bishops "exercise an authority that is proper to them, and are quite correctly called 'prelates,' heads of the people whom they govern" (*Lumen Gentium*, 27). A bishop, however, is not autonomous or totally independent. He cannot make his own rules or interpret Church doctrine in a way that differs from the universal Church. Ordination to the episcopate makes each bishop a member of the **episcopal college**. This assembly of bishops governs the Church in union with the pope, the bishop of Rome, who is its head. "Bishops duly established in all parts of the world [live] in communion with one another and with the Bishop of Rome in a bond of unity, charity, and peace" (*Lumen Gentium*, 22). Individual bishops must build and maintain communion with the universal Church. The bishop of Rome has supreme authority because of the primacy of St. Peter, on whom Christ founded the Church. St. Peter ministered, was martyred, and is buried in Rome.

Regional assemblies of the episcopal college, such as the United States Conference of Catholic Bishops, meet regularly to discuss the needs of the Church in

> **episcopal college** The unity of all ordained bishops in the worldwide Church, in both the East and the West. The pope heads the episcopal college. The episcopal college is also called the "college of bishops."

their region. Two other expressions of the episcopal college are synods of bishops and ecumenical councils. Pope Paul VI established the synod of bishops in 1965. A **synod of bishops** is a representative group of bishops, usually chosen from throughout the world, that comes together to advise the pope on certain Church matters. An **ecumenical council** is an assembly of all (or most) bishops from throughout the world in union with the pope. (The Second Vatican Council was an ecumenical council.) The bishops, in union with the pope, participate in the charism of **infallibility** when they proclaim a definitive doctrine, above all in such an ecumenical council. If it is united with the pope, an ecumenical council is the highest authority in the universal Church when it comes to deciding matters of faith and morals.

The Sacrament of Holy Orders ensures the influence of the Holy Spirit in all decisions made by the Church's Magisterium (pope and bishops acting together), so that it teaches the truth handed down faithfully from Christ and the Apostles. The pope, as head of the college of bishops, also enjoys the charism of infallibility when by virtue of his office as supreme pastor "he proclaims by definitive act a doctrine pertaining to faith or morals" (*CCC*, 891). The pope may also speak a teaching on faith and morals *ex cathedra*—that is, from the chair of St. Peter. The pope rarely declares a statement ex cathedra. The last such statement was made in 1950 by Pope Pius XII, regarding the doctrine of the Assumption of Mary into heaven at the end of her life.

synod of bishops A group of bishops, usually chosen from throughout the world, who come together to advise the pope on certain issues.

ecumenical council An assembly of all (or most) bishops from throughout the world in union with the pope. Such a council is the highest authority in the universal Church when it is conducted in unison with the pope.

infallibility The charism or gift of the Church, offered by the Holy Spirit, in which the pope, and bishops in union with him, can definitively proclaim a doctrine of faith or morals for belief of all the faithful. It is a participation in the fullness of truth in Christ. The pope, as head of the episcopal college, enjoys this gift by virtue of his office. Infallibility is also present in the body of bishops, especially in an ecumenical council, when they teach on matters of faith and morals.

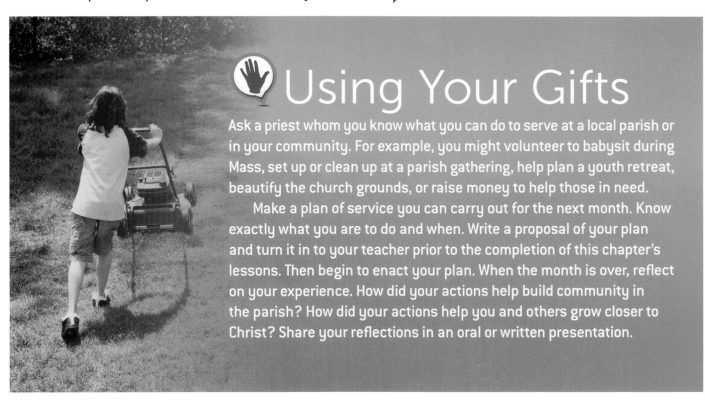

Using Your Gifts

Ask a priest whom you know what you can do to serve at a local parish or in your community. For example, you might volunteer to babysit during Mass, set up or clean up at a parish gathering, help plan a youth retreat, beautify the church grounds, or raise money to help those in need.

Make a plan of service you can carry out for the next month. Know exactly what you are to do and when. Write a proposal of your plan and turn it in to your teacher prior to the completion of this chapter's lessons. Then begin to enact your plan. When the month is over, reflect on your experience. How did your actions help build community in the parish? How did your actions help you and others grow closer to Christ? Share your reflections in an oral or written presentation.

Bishops exercise their teaching role in the Church by their preaching and by establishing catechetical guidelines for their dioceses. They review catechetical books used in Catholic schools and parish religious education programs. The local bishop must give his **imprimatur**, or consent to publish, which says that all contents in the text are free of doctrinal and moral error.

Service to the Local Church

Bishops must also build and maintain communion with the local Church or parishes. "Individual bishops . . . are the visible principle and foundation of unity in their particular churches" (*Lumen Gentium*, 23). "The faithful must cling to their bishop, as the Church does to Christ, and Jesus Christ to the Father, so that all may be of one mind through unity, and abound to the glory of God (see 2 Cor 4:15)" (*Lumen Gentium*, 27).

The Second Vatican Council also strongly recommended that each bishop receive help in his task of teaching, sanctifying, and governing the diocese from synods of priests (sometimes called the priests' senate) and a diocesan council (made up of religious, clergy, and laypeople). To help maintain communion within the diocese, the bishop "should not refuse to listen to his subjects, whom he cherishes as his true sons [and daughters] and exhorts to cooperate readily with him" (*Lumen Gentium*, 27).

Within each diocese, the priests assist the bishop in his tasks of preaching the Gospel, sanctifying the faithful, and governing. In each parish, the priests represent the bishop. In all parish functions, especially the liturgy, priests "make [the bishop] present"

(*Lumen Gentium*, 28). The authority of priests is not autonomous; it comes from their communion with the bishop:

> Priests can exercise their ministry only in dependence on the bishop and in communion with him. The promise of obedience they make to the bishop at the moment of ordination and the kiss of peace from him at the end of the ordination liturgy mean that the bishop considers them his co-workers, his sons, his brothers and his friends, and that they in return owe him love and obedience. (*CCC*, 1567)

Part of a priest's "job description" is to build and maintain communion in the local Church. Priests do this in three main ways: through preaching the Gospel of Christ to all, through the Eucharist and other sacraments, and through pastoral ministry. Here is a brief explanation of each task:

1. *To preach the Gospel to all.* A priest's homily "breaks open" the Word of God. The priest's "role is to teach not [his] own wisdom but the Word of God and to issue a pressing invitation to all men and women to conversion and to holiness" (*Presbyterorum Ordinis*, 4). Priests do this in homilies, in religious education classes at the parish, and in writing. Deacons also preach and teach at the parish level, reading Sacred Scripture to the faithful and giving instruction and exhortation (see *Lumen Gentium*, 29).

2. *To sanctify the People of God by providing the Eucharist and other sacraments.* Through the Sacrament of Holy Orders, priests have the authority to preside at Mass and all the sacraments except Holy Orders. Bishops have the authority to preside at all the sacraments. While bishops are the original ministers of Confirmation, they can delegate this role to priests. Both validly ordained bishops and priests may baptize, reconcile sinners with God and the Church, anoint the sick, consecrate the bread and wine at

imprimatur A bishop's approval to print a religious text or pamphlet because its contents agree with Church teaching.

Mass, and preside at the wedding of a Catholic man and woman or of a Catholic man or woman to a non-Catholic spouse, with the bishop's dispensation or permission. Furthermore, priests must pray the Liturgy of the Hours daily from a liturgical book called the **breviary** (see *Presbyterorum Ordinis*, 5).

Deacons help priests to sanctify the Church. The Second Vatican Council's *Lumen Gentium* states,

> It is the duty of the deacon, according as it shall have been assigned to him by competent authority, to administer baptism solemnly, to be custodian and dispenser of the Eucharist, to assist at and bless marriages in the name of the Church, to bring Viaticum to the dying . . . to preside over the worship and prayer of the faithful, to administer sacramentals, to officiate at funeral and burial services. (*Lumen Gentium*, 29)

3. *To govern the parish through pastoral ministry.* Priests represent the bishop as they govern the parish in collaboration with all its members for its own common good. "A pastoral council is to be established in each parish; the pastor presides over it and through it the Christian faithful along with those who share in the pastoral care of the parish in virtue of their office give their help in fostering pastoral activity" (*Code of Canon Law*, 536). While a parish council may not make decisions without the consent of the pastor, its advice and service promote communion in the local Church.

As St. Paul taught, primarily apostolic ministers (bishops, priests, and deacons) but also all Christians

> **breviary** A liturgical book from which priests and deacons pray the Liturgy of the Hours each day.

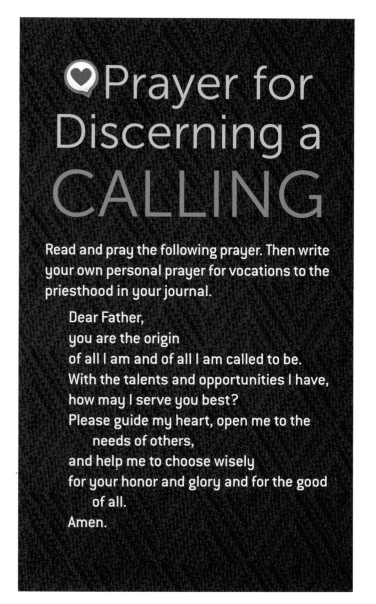

Prayer for Discerning a CALLING

Read and pray the following prayer. Then write your own personal prayer for vocations to the priesthood in your journal.

Dear Father,
you are the origin
of all I am and of all I am called to be.
With the talents and opportunities I have,
how may I serve you best?
Please guide my heart, open me to the
 needs of others,
and help me to choose wisely
for your honor and glory and for the good
 of all.
Amen.

"hold this treasure in earthen vessels, that the surpassing power may be of God and not from us" (2 Cor 4:7). Bishops, priests, and deacons at times make mistakes and commit sin, like all other Catholics. Yet the unworthiness of the ordained minister "does not prevent Christ from acting" through him (*CCC*, 1584). The spiritual powers given by the Holy Spirit in Holy Orders apply to the *sacraments* that the deacon, priest, or bishop administers, not to the *personal or moral character* of the ordained minister himself. This means that any sinfulness of the priest does not affect the validity of the sacrament he has received or offers. Even if a priest sins or harms the Church, Christ still continues to act in, and through, him whenever he baptizes, confirms, celebrates Mass, or grants absolution. The presence of Christ within an ordained man does not preserve him from human error, but it does mean that, even if he sins, the Holy Spirit continues to work through him to bring the real, full grace of the sacraments to all Catholics. In gratitude, you can exercise your role in the common priesthood of believers by praying for bishops, priests, and deacons as they strive to serve the Church faithfully.

SECTION ASSESSMENT

NOTE TAKING

Use the outline you created to help you answer the following questions.

1. How do ordained men act as Christ?
2. How do ordained men grow in holiness?
3. How do ordained men serve the universal Church, the diocese, and the parish?

VOCABULARY

4. Define *infallibility* related to the declaration that Mary was assumed body and soul into heaven.

COMPREHENSION

5. List the special graces that bishops, priests, and deacons receive at ordination.
6. What is the priest's role in the Eucharistic sacrifice?
7. What are the three main ways that bishops and priests serve the People of God?
8. Name three ways a priest builds and maintains communion in the local Church.

CRITICAL THINKING

9. In what ways are priests both set apart from and within the People of God?
10. Why is a bishop not totally independent in decision-making within his diocese?

Section Summaries

Focus Question

How does the Sacrament of Holy Orders serve Christ and the Church?
Complete one of the following:

→ Ask a priest you know why he chose to seek ordination. Write a paragraph reflecting on what he found attractive in priesthood and how that quality speaks to you.

→ Research one of the following ecclesiastically instituted minor orders not mentioned in this text: subdeacon, acolyte, exorcist, lector, and porter. Explain what each did historically and who could join it. Note that these minor orders are not part of the Sacrament of Holy Orders.

→ In a meeting with seminarians, Pope Francis said, "If you are not disposed to follow along this street, it would be better for you to have the courage to seek another path" (Meeting with Seminarians, April 14, 2014). Explain what you think this statement says about the commitment called for in a vocation to ordained ministry.

INTRODUCTION (PAGES 249–253)

Becoming a Priest

The Sacrament of Holy Orders exists to sustain the Church community. Men are drawn to the priesthood for many reasons. No one has a "right" to be a priest; ordination is God's gift. Only baptized men may be ordained. In the Latin Church, except for some permanent deacons and, in some circumstances, married men who had been ordained in another ecclesial community, ordained men promise lifelong celibacy. Those preparing for ordination receive a fourfold formation that leads them closer to Christ.

→ Research and report on information regarding who is eligible to attend a vocations retreat in your diocese, when the next one will be held, and what will be its agenda.

SECTION 1 (PAGES 254–258)

Understanding the Sacrament of Holy Orders

The priesthood of the Old Testament prefigured the High Priesthood of Christ and the ordained ministry of the Church. This ministry exists in three degrees: episcopate, presbyterate, and diaconate. With changes over time, the Sacrament of Holy Orders has existed since the very beginning of the Church, with its roots in Jesus' choice of the Apostles. The Second Vatican Council reinstated the permanent diaconate and reaffirmed the validity and relevance of the Sacrament of Holy Orders.

Read paragraph 3 of the decree *Presbyterorum Ordinis* (*On the Ministry and Life of Priests*) of the Second Vatican Council. It can be found online at the Vatican website. Then explain how priests fit into the whole picture of the People of God.

SECTION 2 (PAGES 259–264)

Celebrating the Sacrament of Holy Orders

All three degrees of Holy Orders are conferred by a sacramental act called ordination, which is performed by a bishop. The Rite of Ordination includes laying on of hands, a prayer of consecration, and anointing with sacred chrism. The episcopate represents the fullness of the Sacrament of Holy Orders.

Look up the names and profiles of men who will be ordained in your diocese in the coming year. Write about one of the men, telling what led him to seek ordination.

SECTION 3 (PAGES 265–276)

The Graces of the Sacrament of Holy Orders

Holy Orders gives an indelible spiritual character, with graces to conform the person of the minister more closely to Christ. The graces of the sacrament allow bishops, priests, and deacons to serve the Church as High Priest, teacher, and Good Shepherd throughout their lives, for the good of the universal and local Church. Even if a priest sins, the Sacrament of Holy Orders remains effective in him, and the sacraments he celebrates still confer the same grace.

 Write a thank-you note to a priest, showing appreciation for the ways his ministry has supported you.

Chapter Assignments

Choose and complete at least one of the following three assignments assessing your understanding of the material in this chapter.

1. Developing a Marketing Campaign for Vocations to the Priesthood

Imagine that you are the vocations director for a large diocese, either your own or another in the country. You are looking for ways to help more young men hear a call to the priesthood. Realizing that men who are called by God to serve him in ordained ministry may often need encouragement and even prompting from others, you determine that a vocations marketing campaign can be of great value. Create a multimedia campaign that includes the following:

- compelling images of seminarians and priests in a variety of pastoral settings,

- a campaign slogan (for example, the Archdiocese of New York uses "The world needs heroes" as its vocations campaign slogan),

- a call to action or some compelling reasons to consider the priesthood,

- quotations from the *Catechism of the Catholic Church* or other Church sources about the importance of the priesthood,

- a quotation from Pope Francis or another recent pope,

- testimonials from men who have answered the call to serve God and the Church in ordained ministry (either seminarians or priests), and

- contact information for the diocesan vocations office and other sources of additional information (your campaign should name an actual US diocese and provide information for that diocese).

Be prepared to present your campaign to your class.

2. Learning about Ordained Martyrs

In this chapter, you read about St. Maximilian Kolbe (see pages 281–282), a priest who was martyred during the Nazi Holocaust. You've also read (in Chapter 3) about the martyrs of Nagasaki, a group of martyrs in sixteenth-century Japan that included a number of seminarians. Even today, bishops, priests, deacons, and seminarians are martyred because of their vocation and their faith. Conduct research to learn about such martyrs. Report on at least six. Prepare an individual report for each that includes

- the bishop's, priest's, deacon's, or seminarian's name, age, and religious order (if he belonged to one);

- the region or place where he was martyred;

- a description of the circumstances that led to his martyrdom; and

- a quotation about the person from the media or another source that helps explain any outstanding qualities the person exhibited during his lifetime or in the circumstances that led to his death.

Other requirements:

- Profile individuals from 1980 or later, with at least two from 2000 or later. Martyrs profiled should be from a minimum of three regions (North Africa, the Middle East, and Europe, for example).

- Each profile should be one page in length. Organize profiles in chronological order. Create a title page for the collection of profiles.

3. Interviewing a Priest, Deacon, or Seminarian

Learn more about the path that leads men to ordained ministry by interviewing someone who has heard and responded to the call to serve God through the Sacrament of Holy Orders. Choose a priest from your parish or diocese and arrange a time for the interview. Ahead of the interview, prepare a series of questions you would like your interviewee to answer. Be sure to schedule sufficient time for an interview that can include some thoughtful discussion. Following the interview, submit the following:

- the list of questions you prepared for the interview,

- your notes from the interview, and

- a one- to two-page journalistic report summarizing what you learned about ordained ministry from your interview.

Be sure to include biographical details about your interview candidate and his ministry, factual information that you learned about serving the Church through the Sacrament of Holy Orders, and anything you learned that was particularly interesting or surprising for you or that you think may be interesting or surprising for others to learn.

Faithful Disciple

St. Maximilian Kolbe

St. Maximilian Kolbe

When a Polish boy named Raymond Kolbe was twelve years old, the Blessed Virgin Mary appeared to him. Her message prepared him for his future. Later, as a priest, Fr. Kolbe described the vision: "I asked the Mother of God what was to become of me. Then she came to me holding two crowns, one white, the other red. She asked if I was willing to accept either of these crowns. The white one meant that I should persevere in purity, and the red that I should become a martyr. I said that I would accept them both."

Raymond's religious name was Maximilian. In his friary near Warsaw, Fr. Kolbe was both superior and director of the friary's publishing company. When the Nazis came to power, Fr. Kolbe criticized them in print, calling them enemies of Jesus. After the Nazis invaded Poland, Fr. Kolbe was arrested but quickly released.

The Nazis also persecuted Polish Jews. After helping refugees, including two thousand Jews, with food and shelter, Fr. Kolbe was arrested again. This time he was sent to Auschwitz, a death camp. There he continued to serve as a priest, teaching about Jesus and the Bible and using smuggled bread and wine to celebrate Mass.

It was at Auschwitz that Fr. Kolbe attained martyrdom. When a prisoner escaped the prison, a group of ten was selected for death by starvation as a lesson to the other prisoners never to attempt escape. Among the group was a young Jewish man who pleaded to be spared. Fr. Kolbe stepped forward and said, "I am a Catholic priest. Let me take his place. I am old. He has a wife and children."

The Nazis agreed. The prisoners were locked into a bunker with no food or drink. Fr. Kolbe prayed the Rosary, sang hymns to Mary, and taught the others about Jesus. After two weeks, Fr. Kolbe was the only prisoner still alive. He was then killed with a lethal injection of carbolic acid.

Franciszek Gajowniczek, the man Fr. Kolbe saved, survived. Until his own death in 1995, he continually told people about Fr. Kolbe's heroic sacrifice.

St. Maximilian Kolbe's feast day is August 14, the eve of the Feast of the Assumption of Mary into Heaven. He is the patron saint of journalists and prisoners. The cell where he died is now a shrine.

Reading Comprehension

1. Describe the vision that the young Raymond Kolbe saw.

2. How did Fr. Kolbe serve as a priest at Auschwitz?

3. How did Fr. Kolbe become a martyr?

Writing Task

- Research the death camp Auschwitz-Birkenau. In addition to more than one million Jews who died there, countless others, including Catholics, were also put to death there. Report on Catholics and others executed at this concentration camp.

Explaining the Faith

Why does the Catholic Church ask men ordained to the priesthood to take a vow of celibacy and not be married?

As you've already read, in the Eastern Church, although bishops must be celibate, married men can be ordained to the priesthood. (However, if a man is unmarried at the time he is ordained to the priesthood, he must remain celibate.) Whether in the Churches in the East or West, celibacy for the ordained in the Church is a discipline, not a doctrine.

Celibacy is a sign of new life and service by which the ordained minister is made holy. It is also a gift to the ordained, supporting his ministry in many ways, such as the following:

- It imitates Christ, who was celibate.

- It allows a priest to dedicate himself more to Christ and the service of the Church: "An unmarried man is anxious about things of the Lord, how he may please the Lord. But a married man is anxious about the things of the world, how he may please his wife, and he is divided" (1 Cor 7:32–34).

- It makes the priest into a sign of the future Kingdom, in which there will be no marriage and Christ will be the Church's only spouse.

- It answers Jesus' charge to give up one's life for his sake and for the Gospel: "And everyone who has given up houses or brothers or sisters or father or mother or children or lands for the sake of my name will receive a hundred times more, and will inherit eternal life" (Mt 19:29).

Further Research

- Read section 29 of Pope John Paul II's apostolic exhortation on the formation of priests, *Pastores Dabo Vobis* (*I Shall Give You Shepherds*). You can find the document at the Vatican website. Write two or three paragraphs telling how the pope's words enrich your understanding of the discipline of celibacy in the priesthood.

Prayer

A Prayer for Priests

Lord Jesus, we your people pray to you for our priests. You have given them to us for *our* needs. We pray for them in *their* needs.

We know that you have made them priests in the likeness of your own priesthood. You have consecrated them, set them aside, anointed them, filled them with the Holy Spirit, appointed them to teach, to preach, to minister, to console, to forgive, and to feed us with your Body and Blood.

Yet we know, too, that they are one with us and share our human weaknesses. We know too that they are tempted to sin and discouragement as are we, needing to be ministered to, as do we, to be consoled and forgiven, as do we. Indeed, we thank you for choosing them from among us, so that they understand us as we understand them, suffer with us and rejoice with us, worry with us and trust with us, share our beings, our lives, our faith.

We ask that you give them this day the gift you gave your chosen ones on the way to Emmaus: your presence in their hearts, your holiness in their souls, your joy in their spirits. And let them see you face to face in the breaking of the Eucharistic bread.

We pray to You, O Lord, through Mary the mother of all priests, for your priests and for ours. Amen.

—Cardinal John O'Connor (1920–2000),
former archbishop of New York

THE SACRAMENT OF MATRIMONY

It Takes a
COMMITMENT

Contrary to a common recent trend of delaying marriage, clinical psychologist Dr. John van Epp points to the benefits for both men and women of marrying in their early twenties. He concludes, "Waiting to get married often leads to more premarital sex, premarital cohabitation, and premarital births, which are all associated with higher rates of marital instability. In addition, there is a small selection pool as you reach your early thirties. (By age thirty, seventy-five percent of the population is married.) At that point, the chances of achieving a quality relationship lower because of the difficulty of finding a suitable partner."

Dr. van Epp further explains that the dating habits of young people have future impact. He cited one study that points out "a clear connection between the number of sexual partners before marriage and the likelihood of marital unfaithfulness; each additional sexual partner before marriage resulted in a significant increase in the risk of having an affair after marriage."

One of Dr. van Epp's clients, a man named Reggie, had realized that his "accumulation of . . . sexually charged relationships had left him feeling empty and alone." In order to think seriously about finding a lasting partner, he decided to delay sexual activity until marriage and to concentrate on building "more serious friendships . . . with his goal of having a fulfilling marriage on his horizon."

When, four years later, he introduced his fiancée, Renee, to Dr. van Epp, his new habits had prepared him to make a marriage commitment. As Dr. van Epp concluded, "There is hope, promised in Scripture and backed by research, for both the Renees and Reggies in the world. But it takes a commitment to attitudes and behaviors beneficial to marriage long before the wedding bells ring."

As Dr. van Epp repeats frequently, "You reap what you sow." Marriage requires a vow of fidelity to one person for a lifetime.

(Based on John van Epp, "Don't Wait for Marriage: Young Adults Should Be Tying the Knot Earlier, Not Later," *U.S. Catholic* 75, no. 9 [September 2010]: 18–22.)

FOCUS QUESTION

What is distinct about a RELATIONSHIP ROOTED in the Sacrament of MATRIMONY?

INTRODUCTION
Helping Each Other Grow in Love

MAIN IDEA
Through the love and grace found in the Sacrament of Matrimony, spouses grow closer to each other, to their families, and to God.

When you think of reasons why people marry, what comes to mind? God himself established marriage for two purposes: for the unity of the husband and wife and for the procreation and education of children. In marriage, a man and a woman form with each other a lifelong covenant. Throughout their lives, they support each other, help each other grow in love, and bring each other closer to God.

Like Holy Orders, the other Sacrament at the Service of Communion, Matrimony focuses on *others*. The effects of the sacrament are directed to the salvation of the spouse and children. If they also contribute to one's own salvation, "it is through service to others that they do so" (*CCC*, 1534).

In faithful, loving marriages, you can see the graces of the sacrament being lived. Consider the story of Joe and Mary Clare Pajakowski. Shortly after their fifty-first wedding anniversary, Mary Clare suffered a debilitating stroke. Though she survived, she needed physical and speech therapy as well as many new medications.

Joe, a retired machine operator, became Mary Clare's primary caretaker. He drove her to therapy, communicated with her doctors, cooked meals,

NOTE TAKING

Sketching a Summary. Divide your paper as shown here. In each segment, illustrate the given characteristic of a holy marriage with a scene from the story of Joe and Mary Clare Pajakowski. (Stick figures are okay!) You can also write any words that come to mind to help the ideas stay with you.

GROWING CLOSER TO GOD	GROWING CLOSER TO EACH OTHER
PUTTING OTHERS' NEEDS FIRST	**RAISING A FAMILY**

Married couples have as their mission the responsibility to reproduce human life and educate their children.

managed her medications, and even helped her get dressed. This was a major reversal from the previous years of their married life. While Joe had focused on his job, working long hours on the second shift, Mary Clare had taken care of the home, supported Joe when he faced difficulties at work, and handled most of the tasks of raising their four children.

Now, Mary Clare's illness provided an opportunity for Joe to do things he hadn't done before. Joe learned patience and a new kind of selflessness. He prayed and went to Mass more often. Joe was also providing Mary Clare an avenue to love in a new way and to grow closer to God, for in depending on Joe for her care, Mary Clare grew to trust more in divine providence. With someone to share in her suffering, she was able to better "lose her life" for the sake of Jesus Christ and the Gospel. She wouldn't have had these same opportunities without her husband.

Mary Clare lived five years after her stroke. Her last four nights were spent in a hospital intensive care unit.

Joe slept in her room in a chair, leaving only to shower. He was with her when she died at 3:15 in the morning on their fifty-sixth wedding anniversary.

An Intimate Communion

From the beginning, God has shared his love with men and women in part by giving them a way of sharing an intimate communion of life and love with each other. Men and women have been created as one, to be one. Original Sin ruptured this original communion between men and women.

The Sacrament of Matrimony gives men and women the grace they need to overcome divisions between the sexes (which result from sin) so that they may be one again, as God intended. When a husband

> **fidelity** From the Latin word *fides*, meaning faith. "Fidelity expresses constancy in keeping one's given word. God is faithful" (*CCC*, 2365).

and wife embrace the grace of the sacrament, they glimpse the unity of the Blessed Trinity. They glimpse the God who is love.

The Sacrament of Matrimony adds a new dimension to natural marriage. Because Matrimony is a sacrament, the baptized man and baptized woman not only pledge to love each other, but they do so *in Christ*. They are one in faith. They find God's presence in their love for one another and for their children. Through daily **fidelity** to their vows, they become a sign to one another and to society of God's faithful love.

Matrimony intensifies Baptism. God calls the bride and groom to share in Christ's mission as priest, prophet, and king. They exercise their common priesthood by offering the daily sacrifices needed to love one another exclusively and to raise a family. They, and their children, grow in holiness and friendship with God. Just as Baptism consecrates all Christians to be a "holy priesthood" (*Lumen Gentium*, 10), so the Sacrament of Matrimony consecrates Christian spouses for "the duties and dignity of their state" (*Gaudium et Spes,* 48). In the wedding ceremony, the bride's white gown symbolizes this consecration. It recalls the white robe of Baptism and the white dress many girls wear for First Communion. It speaks of a bride's desire to leave behind her old life and begin a new life with her husband in Christ.

Sacred Scripture begins in the Book of Genesis with the creation of man and woman as partners in the image of God and concludes with the wedding feast of the Lamb in the Book of Revelation (see Revelation 19:5–8). Marriage mirrors Christ's love for the Church and foreshadows the intimate communion and tremendous joy all people desire, the joy that awaits them in heaven (see *CCC*, 1642).

SECTION ASSESSMENT

NOTE TAKING

Use the sketch notes you created to help you answer the following questions.

1. How is the Sacrament of Matrimony a Sacrament at the Service of Communion?
2. How does the Sacrament of Matrimony help spouses grow in holiness?

COMPREHENSION

3. How does the Sacrament of Matrimony add a new dimension to natural marriage?
4. What does the communion of life and love in marriage foreshadow?

REFLECTION

5. Describe a couple you know who exercise their common priesthood through their vocation to marriage. How do they do this?

SECTION 1
Understanding the Sacrament of Matrimony

MAIN IDEA
God created men and women to live together in loving communion in the context of marriage. In the New Covenant, marriage is a sacrament.

From the beginning of creation, marriage has existed in human society. "The vocation to marriage is written in the very nature of man and woman as they came from the hand of the Creator" (*CCC*, 1603). Genesis 2:4–25 describes Adam's creation and his loneliness at not having a partner with whom to share his life.

The Lord agreed: "It is not good for the man to be alone. I will make a helper suited to him." When Adam saw the woman, he said, "This one, at last, is bone of my bones and flesh of my flesh." The *Catechism of the Catholic Church* teaches,

> The woman, "flesh of his flesh," his equal, his nearest in all things, is given to him by God as a "helpmate"; she thus represents God from whom comes our help. (*CCC*, 1605)

God's Chosen People longed for a vision of loving, lifelong marriage, which God intended from the beginning and which they learned from the Mosaic Law. "Seeing God's covenant with Israel in the image of exclusive and faithful married love, the prophets prepared the Chosen People's conscience for a deepened understanding of the unity and indissolubility of marriage" (*CCC*, 1611).

Marriage is not a purely human institution that must adapt to the corruption of sin. Sacred Scripture teaches that God created man and woman for one another: "That is why a man leaves his father and mother and clings to his wife, and the two of them

NOTE TAKING

Forming a Word Web. Create a word web around the following concept. Draw lines from the circle to key words and phrases that will help you understand the meaning of marriage.

MARRIAGE

become one body" (Gn 2:24). From the beginning, marriage was intended to be unbreakable: "They are no longer two, but one flesh" (Mt 19:6).

As a sacrament, Matrimony is "a covenant by which a man and a woman establish between themselves a partnership of their whole life" (*Code of Canon Law*, 1055; see *CCC*, 1601). The Sacrament of Matrimony recalls, and signifies, God's eternal covenant with humanity. As you know, God established a covenant with Abraham and his descendants, creating a lasting relationship between God and his people. A covenant lasts forever. Unlike a contract, it cannot be dissolved.

Marriage in the Old Covenant

Human sinfulness marks the history of marriage. Marriage in Old Covenant times was primarily a private contract initiated between two male heads of families, much like the buying and selling of property. A father "owned" his daughters and was entitled to any profit they made from working in the fields, sewing, spinning, or cooking. A young man who wanted to marry a girl had to pay her father a "bride price" to compensate him for losing a valuable worker and income producer. Once the bride price was paid, the father escorted the girl to the man's home.

The Law of Moses was clear in protecting the wife from cruelty and domination by her husband. Mosaic Law did permit a decree of **divorce**. Jesus later explained that "hardness of heart," a residue of sin, had allowed divorce; "from the beginning it was not so" (Mt 19:8). **Polygamy** was practiced among the Israelites and even more so by neighboring peoples. Polygamy signaled privilege and wealth; it helped to establish political alliances; it also ensured that a man would have male heirs. In ancient Israel, polygamy was allowed in several cases among patriarchs and

kings and others as well. (Elkanah in 1 Samuel 1–2 is married to both Peninnah and Hannah, and he is not a patriarch or king.) However, Mosaic Law and the teachings of the prophets gradually led toward exclusive and faithful married love far beyond what was being practiced by the Canaanites and other pagans. Mosaic Law also forbade **adultery** because, like divorce and polygamy, it gravely offends the dignity of marriage.

The Old Testament tells how the Israelites repeatedly turned away from their covenant with God to pursue false gods. However, God remained steadfast, faithful, and loving. Hosea, an Old Testament prophet, compared God to a bridegroom who chooses to marry the woman he loves:

> I will betroth you to me forever:
> I will betroth you to me with justice and with
> judgment,
> with loyalty with and with compassion;
> I will betroth you to me with fidelity,
> and you shall know the LORD. (Hos 2:21–22)

Even though Israel turned out to be unfaithful to God, God continued to love her and forgave her:

> The LORD calls you back,
> like a wife forsaken and grieved in spirit. . . .
> With great tenderness I will take you back. (Is 54:6, 7)

---

divorce The dissolution of the marriage contract by the legal system.

polygamy Being married to two or more people at the same time. It is contrary to conjugal love, which is undivided and exclusive.

adultery Infidelity in marriage wherein a married person has sexual intercourse with someone who is not the person's spouse.

Like the covenant between God and Israel, sacramental marriage is indissoluble (*Code of Canon Law*, 1056); it lasts for as long as both spouses live. The permanent nature of the Sacrament of Matrimony is witnessed explicitly by its lifelong quality.

Since the Fall of man, when Original Sin entered the world, marriage has helped couples overcome selfishness and greed while choosing self-giving, openness, and service.

Marriage in the New Covenant

The Old Covenant between God and his people prepared the way for the New Covenant, in which Jesus not only restored marriage to its original state before the Fall but also raised it to a sacrament among the baptized.

Christ clearly taught that marriage is indissoluble: "What God has joined together, no human being must separate" (Mt 19:6; see *CCC*, 1664). While that is a difficult command, Jesus comes into the life of the married couple in the Sacrament of Matrimony to help them keep it. The couple receives the effects of the sacrament throughout their marriage, achieving faithfulness that does not end until death, just as Christ was faithful to his mission until his Death on the Cross. St. Paul explained that the relationship between a husband and wife in the Sacrament of Matrimony reflects the intimacy and union between Christ and the Church (see Ephesians 5:25–26, 31–32). "This grace of Christian marriage is a fruit of Christ's Cross, the source of all Christian life" (*CCC*, 1615).

In the Church's early days, civil marriages were blessed at a later date by priests. As time went on, weddings were held on the church steps, where clergy offered a blessing. From the beginning, the essential rite of the sacrament was the couple's consent to each other. In the thirteenth century, St. Thomas Aquinas

World Meeting of FAMILIES

The World Meeting of Families is a global event held every three years. It was founded by Pope John Paul II in 1992 to bring families from all over the world together in order to strengthen the bond of family life. The 2015 event was held in Philadelphia, Pennsylvania, and was attended by Pope Francis on his first trip to the United States as pontiff.

Often in today's news when the topic is marriage, the focus is on issues such as premarital sex, homosexuality, infertility, and celibacy. Mary Beth Yount, the organizer of the content for the 2015 World Meeting of Families, explained that the topics at the event focused on much more than the act of sex. She said that sexuality "doesn't just mean people having sex. That is a fundamental expression that includes married people, but it also means engaging the world in other ways. It's a self-giving love: married people, people single by choice, and celibacy."

The overriding message of the 2015 World Meeting of Families was how human relationships can help people to love each other and God more deeply. "What are the ways we can live fruitful lives?" was a question Yount said marked the overall theme of the event.

expressed the Church's long-standing opinion that marriage is a sacrament that gives grace to the couple on their journey toward holiness. Franciscan theologian John Duns Scotus (1266–1308) agreed with Aquinas and taught that the bride and groom are the ministers of the sacrament. The priest serves as the official Church witness. This remains the understanding in the Latin Church today: the bride and groom are ministers of the sacrament. In Eastern Churches, the priest is the minister of the sacrament, when he receives the couple's consent on behalf of the Church and then places crowns on their heads as a sign of their marriage covenant.

The Council of Trent (1545–1563) taught that Matrimony is both a sacrament that confers grace and a public commitment for the good of the couple, of society, and of the Church. Thus, when a baptized man and a baptized woman celebrate the Sacrament of Matrimony, they should do so in church during Mass. This continues to be the teaching and practice today:

> It is therefore fitting that the spouses should seal their consent to give themselves to each other through the offering of their own lives by uniting it to the offering of Christ for his Church made present in the Eucharistic sacrifice, and by receiving the Eucharist so that, communicating in the same Body and the same Blood of Christ, they may form but "one body" in Christ. (*CCC*, 1621)

Martin Luther and John Calvin, Protestant reformers of the sixteenth century, did not accept marriage as a sacrament. They believed that it was only a civil reality and, therefore, that divorce was possible. Technically, divorce ends only a civil marriage—a legal contract. Conversely, a **declaration of nullity**, which the Church does permit, says a marriage was never *valid* and never met the requirements for a valid marriage in the Church.

The Church also opposes cohabitation, in which a man and woman live together without marriage. This contradicts the dignity of marriage, weakens fidelity, and uproots the family. The sexual act always belongs within marriage. "Outside of marriage [the sexual act] always constitutes a grave sin and excludes one from sacramental communion" (*CCC*, 2390).

A more recent threat to marriage in America and other developed nations is same-sex marriage, a contractual union between two people with homosexual orientations. The term itself is oxymoronic, in that marriage is intended as a complementary relationship between a man and a woman, with one of its key purposes being procreative.

The Sacrament of Matrimony Today

The Second Vatican Council reiterated that only marriage between baptized Christians can be a sacrament and reaffirmed that Christian marriage is valid when it is contracted in the presence of a priest or deacon and two witnesses. The Council also taught that remarriage of persons divorced from a living, lawful spouse goes against the teaching of Christ. They remain welcome in the Church, but they cannot receive Holy Communion. They are to lead Christian lives, especially by educating their children in the faith.

Christian marriage is meant to help both spouses grow in spiritual perfection (*Code of Canon Law*, 1055 § 1) and to serve the common good. The *Catechism of the Catholic Church* states that "the well-being of . . . both human and Christian society is closely bound up with the healthy state of conjugal and family life"

declaration of nullity The Church's declaration that a particular marriage—whether presumed as a sacramental bond or simply a natural bond—was never valid.

(*CCC*, 1603). Look around, and you will see that this is true. Stable families, even in struggles and trials, nurture healthy and happy individuals who serve the Church and the world.

Also, it is in the family that children are first prepared for marriage. This remote preparation in families allows children to discover their strengths and weaknesses. It is a time when children learn the necessary skills of loving relationships. Parents also help to provide solid catechetical training and formation that witnesses the true vocation of Christian marriage, without excluding the possibility that their children may have a vocation to the priesthood or religious life. Besides parents, the pastors and other faithful Catholics are also vital for transmission of the human and Christian values of marriage.

SECTION ASSESSMENT

NOTE TAKING

Use the word web you created at the beginning of the section to help you answer the following questions.

1. What are the basic characteristics of marriage?
2. What did Jesus teach about marriage?
3. What did St. Paul say about the relationship between a husband and wife?

COMPREHENSION

4. When did human beings begin to practice marriage?
5. Describe the shift in attitudes about marriage from ancient Israel to the time of Jesus.
6. What has always been the essential Rite of the Sacrament of Matrimony?
7. Who are the ministers of the Sacrament of Matrimony in the Latin Church and in the Eastern Churches?
8. When and where does the Church say Catholics should celebrate Matrimony? Why?

REFLECTION

9. What are some virtues that might contribute to a healthy family life?

Celebrating the Sacrament of Matrimony

> **MAIN IDEA**
> When they give their free consent in the Rite of Marriage, spouses receive God's grace to live the Sacrament of Matrimony throughout their lives.

The revised Rite of Marriage contains three rites. Of these, two celebrate the Sacrament of Matrimony: the Rite for Celebrating Marriage during Mass, which is usually used for two baptized Catholics, and the Rite for Celebrating Marriage outside Mass, which celebrates a wedding between a Catholic and a baptized person who is not Catholic. In the latter case, the wedding takes place during a Liturgy of the Word. Finally, the Rite for Celebrating Marriage between a Catholic and an Unbaptized Person marks a nonsacramental marriage. Each option highlights the couple's free consent and exchange of vows.

Recall that the bride and groom are the ministers of Matrimony. They "mutually confer upon each other the sacrament of Matrimony by expressing their consent before the Church" (*CCC*, 1623). Since this consent is so important, many dioceses require engaged couples to enter a marriage preparation program, so that they can better understand the commitment they are making. Such programs touch on issues such as finances, in-laws, family size, children's education, values, preferences, sexuality, and conflict styles. Some programs even help the couple plan their wedding ceremony.

Marriage preparation also addresses the couple's faith. A Catholic who enters into a *mixed marriage* (with a baptized non-Catholic) or a marriage with a *disparity of cult* (with a nonbaptized person) first needs a dispensation or permission from the proper Church authorities (see *Code of Canon Law*, 1124 and 1086). To receive the dispensation, both spouses-to-be

NOTE TAKING

Summarizing Material. Create an outline like the following in your notebook. As you read this section, note what takes place at each stage of the process of getting married. Part of the outline has been started for you.

I. Preparing for the Sacrament of Matrimony

    A. Freedom of consent

    B.

    C.

II. Receiving the Sacrament of Matrimony

    A. Exchanging vows

    B.

    C.

    D.

    E.

must show that they understand, and agree, to what the Church teaches about the purposes and dignity of marriage, and the Catholic spouse must promise that any children born to the couple will be baptized and educated as Catholics.

In the ceremony, the priest or deacon, who acts as the Church's witness, wears white vestments. The Rite of Marriage consists of the couple's consent and exchange of vows. This consent is the essential element that "makes the marriage" (*Code of Canon Law*, 1057). A blessing and an exchange of rings may also take place. When the wedding takes place during Mass, the couple receives a **nuptial blessing** after the Lord's Prayer and a special blessing at the end of Mass. More information on these elements follows.

Free Consent and Exchange of Vows

During the wedding ceremony, the bride and groom express their consent to marry. Without free consent, there is no marriage; it is the indispensable element of the sacrament. Furthermore, each spouse should also sincerely intend to be faithful to the other person and open to children from their union.

The priest or deacon who assists at the wedding receives the consent of the spouses in the name of the Church. The presence of the priest and two other witnesses visibly expresses that the marriage is recognized by the Church. The priest first asks the following questions of the bride and groom:

> Priest: N. and N., have you come here freely and without reservation to give yourselves to each other in marriage?
>
> Bride: Yes.
>
> Groom: Yes.
>
> Priest: Will you honor each other as man and wife for the rest of your lives?
>
> Bride: Yes.
>
> Groom: Yes.
>
> Priest: Will you accept children lovingly from God, and bring them up according to the law of Christ and his Church?
>
> Bride: Yes.
>
> Groom: Yes.

The priest then invites the couple to exchange **marriage vows**:

> Priest: Since it is your intention to enter into marriage, join your right hands, and declare your consent before God and his Church.
>
> Groom: I, N., take you, N., to be my wife. I promise to be true to you in good times and in bad, in sickness and in health. I will love you and honor you all the days of my life.
>
> Bride: I, N., take you, N., to be my husband. I promise to be true to you in good times and in bad, in sickness and in health. I will love you and honor you all the days of my life.

The priest then prays:

> You have declared your consent before the Church.
> May the Lord in his goodness strengthen your consent
> and fill you both with his blessings.
> What God has joined, men must not divide.

---

nuptial blessing A blessing intended for the bride and groom and the marriage covenant that takes place after the couple gives their consent to be married. The word *nuptial* comes from a Latin word that means "wedding."

marriage vows The promises made by the bride and groom to honor one another and to be faithful in good times and in bad, in sickness and in health, throughout their lives. By their consent to one another, the couple establishes a permanent covenant in love.

ARE YOU FREE TO ENTER A
Sacramental
Marriage?

For a sacramental marriage to be valid, the Church sets some conditions that must be true for both spouses. Follow the arrows below to discover when a person can marry sacramentally in the Church.*

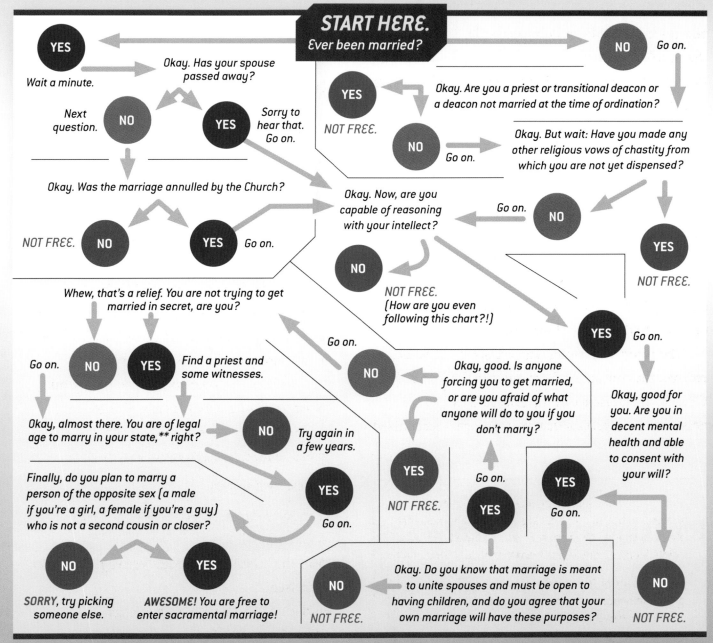

START HERE. Ever been married?

YES — Wait a minute. → Okay. Has your spouse passed away?

NO → Next question. Okay. Was the marriage annulled by the Church?

YES → Sorry to hear that. Go on.

NO → *NOT FREE.*

YES → Go on.

Whew, that's a relief. You are not trying to get married in secret, are you?

NO → Go on.

YES → Find a priest and some witnesses.

Okay, almost there. You are of legal age to marry in your state,** right?

NO → Try again in a few years.

YES → Go on.

Finally, do you plan to marry a person of the opposite sex (a male if you're a girl, a female if you're a guy) who is not a second cousin or closer?

NO → **SORRY,** try picking someone else.

YES → **AWESOME!** You are free to enter sacramental marriage!

NO → Go on.

Okay. Are you a priest or transitional deacon or a deacon not married at the time of ordination?

YES → *NOT FREE.*

NO → Go on. Okay. But wait: Have you made any other religious vows of chastity from which you are not yet dispensed?

NO → Go on.

YES → *NOT FREE.*

Okay. Now, are you capable of reasoning with your intellect?

NO → *NOT FREE.* (How are you even following this chart?!)

YES → Go on. Okay, good for you. Are you in decent mental health and able to consent with your will?

Okay, good. Is anyone forcing you to get married, or are you afraid of what anyone will do to you if you don't marry?

YES → *NOT FREE.*

NO → Go on.

YES → Go on.

Okay. Do you know that marriage is meant to unite spouses and must be open to having children, and do you agree that your own marriage will have these purposes?

NO → *NOT FREE.*

YES → Go on.

NO → *NOT FREE.*

---

* A few of the requirements have been left out. They cover pretty rare situations (like being kidnapped or tricked into marrying a stranger), so you don't need to worry about them for now.

**The Church's age for marriage is sixteen for men, fourteen for women—though a bishops' conference can raise the minimum age, presumably to be in accord with civil law, which varies from one place to another.

Blessing and Exchange of Rings

Many brides and grooms choose to exchange blessed rings. Circles with no beginning or end, rings symbolize the eternal love God has for humans, the eternal commitment of Christ to the Church, and the couple's lifelong faithfulness. Spouses offer the rings to one another as "a sign of . . . love and fidelity" until death (*Rite of Marriage*).

Nuptial Blessing

After the Our Father, the priest faces the couple, who have joined hands, and blesses them. The blessing calls down God's love and grace upon the couple throughout their married life; it asks "that through the sacrament of the Body and Blood of Christ, he will unite in love the couple he has joined in this holy bond."

Holy Communion

Before the wedding, a Catholic bride and groom celebrate the Sacrament of Penance, which prepares them for the celebration of marriage and, of course, to receive Holy Communion. During the wedding liturgy, they are the first to receive Holy Communion under both species, bread and wine. It is appropriate for the man and woman, who have just been joined as one, to drink from the common cup "so that, communicating in the same Body and the same Blood of Christ, they may form but 'one body' in Christ" (*CCC*, 1621). The Holy Eucharist will strengthen and nourish their married life.

Blessing at the End of Mass

Near the end of Mass, the priest again blesses the bride and groom. He prays that God may give them children, peace, friends, happiness, satisfaction in work, and never-ending love, keeping away undue anxiety. He prays that ultimately, after many happy years together,

After the exchange of rings, it used to be common for the priest to wrap the end of his stole around the couple's joined hands to confirm their commitment in the Church's name.

the couple may be welcomed into the eternal Kingdom of Heaven. Imagine receiving such a powerful blessing!

SECTION ASSESSMENT

NOTE TAKING

Use the outline you created to help you answer the following questions.

1. What topics are usually covered in marriage preparation?
2. What must a Catholic do to marry a non-Catholic in the Church?
3. At what point in the ceremony do couples exchange their consent?

VOCABULARY

4. Define *nuptial blessing*.

COMPREHENSION

5. What do wedding rings symbolize?
6. What blessings does the Church pray will be given to newly married couples?
7. Under normal circumstances, why is a priest or deacon and two witnesses necessary for the validity of the sacrament?

REFLECTION

8. If you marry one day, what blessings do you hope to receive in your marriage?

SECTION 3
The Graces of the Sacrament of Matrimony

MAIN IDEA
In their relationship, in their family, in the Church, and in society, the love of a sacramentally married man and woman reflects the love of Christ.

Jesus made every sacramental marriage a sign of God's faithfulness. Loving and faithful relationships between husbands and wives signify the faithful love between Christ and his Church. The love that sustains the Church and makes her one also allows a man and woman to commit themselves totally to one another until death.

Often, people associate the Sacrament of Matrimony only with the wedding day itself. This isn't accurate. The sacrament does not end when the bride and groom leave the church building. The sacrament's graces and effects follow the couple throughout their marriage, helping them grow in love and holiness in their daily life together. The fullness of the sacrament is realized only after years of fidelity and affection.

Sacramental marriage is essentially about communion. The husband and wife share mental, emotional, spiritual, and physical communion, and they are each in relationship with Christ.

There is also a communion between husband and wife and their children—the oneness of family life.

Finally, as a Sacrament at the Service of Communion, Matrimony calls husbands, wives, and children

NOTE TAKING

Creating a Concept Diagram. Create a diagram like the one on the right to describe all the different relationships in which the Sacrament of Matrimony is a Sacrament at the Service of Communion. Then summarize how husbands and wives serve each other and those they encounter.

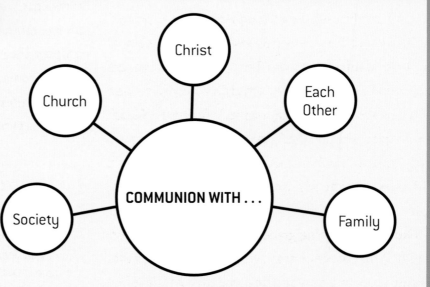

to serve and live in community with the Church and all of society.

Communion between Spouses

The communion between spouses found in marriage helps spouses "to overcome self-absorption, egoism, [and] pursuit of one's own pleasure, and to open oneself to the other, to mutual aid and to self-giving" (*CCC*, 1609). The man and woman place each other first so that they "might no longer live for themselves" (2 Cor 5:15).

To many people, such absolute self-giving to one's spouse can seem awesomely good yet also scary. How could you really say to someone, "I'll love you forever," without knowing any of the details of that forever? How would you feel as the other person ages and changes or if that person becomes ill or disabled? Such unconditional love is very difficult for humans to achieve and sustain. Thus, Christian spouses acknowledge their need for God's continual presence in their marriage, helping them to give support, forgiveness, and acceptance to the other, whatever their feelings may be.

A healthy sexual relationship in marriage is fruitful and exclusive, supports communion and communication, and involves honor and respect between spouses. The Second Vatican Council taught that "the unity of marriage, confirmed by our Lord, is clearly apparent in the equal personal dignity which is accorded to man and wife in mutual and unreserved affection" (*Gaudium et Spes*, 49). St. Paul expressed the same truth more simply: "Each one of you should love his wife as himself, and the wife should respect her husband" (Eph 5:33).

One of the ongoing graces of Matrimony is fidelity. Fidelity is one of the characteristics of God. The more spouses grow in holiness, the more they become like

God: faithful to their promises. The couple is called to "grow continually in their communion through day-to-day fidelity to their marriage promise of total mutual self-giving" (*CCC*, 1644, quoting *Familiaris Consortio*, 19).

Openness to New Life

"Fruitful love" is mutual, productive, and open to new life, as God commanded Adam and Eve: "Be fertile and multiply" (Gn 1:28). In a sacramental marriage, both husband and wife embrace the fertility of their sexual union (see *CCC*, 1664). They recognize their call to become partners with God in creating new life, and they accept children as "the supreme gift of marriage" (*Gaudium et Spes*, 50; see *CCC*, 1664). By the very nature of marriage, married love "is ordered to the procreation and education of the offspring and it is in them that it finds its crowning glory" (*CCC*, 1652, quoting *Gaudium et Spes*, 48, 50).

The Church accepts married couples' attempts to influence the timing of pregnancies, when they have a just reason to do so, through the use of **Natural Family Planning (NFP)**. It is the couple's duty to make sure that their reasons are not selfish, but rather "in conformity with the generosity appropriate to responsible parenthood" (*CCC*, 2368), and that their behavior conforms with the twofold purpose of sexual intercourse: mutual self-giving and procreation. Using NFP, couples observe and chart fertile and infertile times in the woman's reproductive cycle and then decide whether they will try to achieve or to avoid a pregnancy, depending on their family's current situation.

> **Natural Family Planning (NFP)** A Church-approved method for regulating births within marriage; it is in accord with God's will because it is pursued by spouses without external pressure or motives of selfishness and is practiced through natural means of periodic continence and use of infertile periods.

NFP is *not* the "rhythm method," an earlier, nonpersonalized form of cycle charting. Thanks to current advances in medical understanding of fertility, NFP is up to 99 percent effective when used correctly. See Explaining the Faith on page 318 for more about the difference between **contraception** and NFP.

What about those couples who, despite their wishes, are physically unable to have children? The Sacrament of Matrimony calls them to bear fruit in other ways. They can still "radiate a fruitfulness of charity, of hospitality, and of sacrifice" (*CCC*, 1654). They can be open to life in other ways: "For example, adoption, various forms of educational work, and assistance to other families and to poor or handicapped children" (*Familiaris Consortio*, 14). Fruitful love also includes spouses' helping each other in personal growth—for example, supporting a spouse who wants to return to school or take a better job.

The Unity of Marriage

Along with supporting procreation, sacramental marriage supports the mutual growth of husband and wife in holiness through their incarnated love (see *Gaudium et Spes*, 50). It recalls the great mystery of the Incarnation: that God chose to make his love visible in human flesh. Husband and wife encounter God's love through intimacy with one another. They are to love one another unconditionally and completely, body and soul. "In marriage the physical intimacy of the spouses becomes a sign and pledge of spiritual communion" (*CCC*, 2360).

The two purposes of sex in marriage—unitive and procreative—help achieve the twofold end of Matrimony: the joy and pleasure of the couple and the transmission of life. Sex in marriage fosters intimacy, promotes emotional security, and reduces stress and anxiety. It helps the couple reflect mutual, self-giving love.

Communion in Christ

Like every sacrament, Matrimony promotes union with the Blessed Trinity. "The spouses receive the Holy Spirit as the communion of love of Christ and the Church. The Holy Spirit is the seal of their covenant, the ever-available source of their love and the strength to renew their fidelity" (*CCC*, 1624). In this way, spouses are transformed by holiness. Through Matrimony, Christian spouses encounter Christ in one another and can love one another as they know Christ loves them.

The Sacrament of Matrimony uniquely invites husbands and wives into the Paschal Mystery of Christ. Marriage becomes a way of discipleship, of dying to sin and rising to holiness:

> It is by following Christ, renouncing themselves, and taking up their crosses that spouses will be able to "receive" the original meaning of marriage and live it with the help of Christ. (*CCC*, 1615)

Through Matrimony, Christian spouses are able to love each other with Christ's love for his Church. "[Christ] abides with them in order that by their mutual self-giving spouses will love each other with enduring fidelity, as he loved the church and delivered himself for it" (*Gaudium et Spes*, 48).

Jesus' presence at the wedding at Cana (see John 2:1–11) helps communicate his relationship to married couples and to all of humanity. At his mother's request, he performed his first sign, or miracle, at a wedding

contraception Any artificial means (e.g., pills, condoms, diaphragms, surgeries) that deliberately and directly has an outcome of closing off one of the aims of sexual intercourse—the openness to life. Contraception also opposes the unitive aspect of the conjugal act by not allowing for the total self-giving of the couple to one another.

to indicate the goodness of marriage. Forever after, "marriage will be an efficacious sign of Christ's presence" (*CCC*, 1613). Both Sacred Scripture and Sacred Tradition use the analogy of marriage to describe Jesus' relationship with the Church. The Church is "the Bride of Christ" (*CCC*, 796), "the spotless spouse of the spotless Lamb, whom Christ 'loved'" (*Lumen Gentium*, 6, quoting from Revelation 19:7; 21:2, 9; 22:17). Jesus himself is the perfect Bridegroom (see Matthew 9:15, Mark 2:19, Luke 5:34) who will be with his Church always (see Matthew 28:20).

Communion with Christ's Paschal Mystery empowers spouses to make loving sacrifices for one another and enables them to forgive one another for mistakes, failings, and sins. Just as God is gracious, merciful, and "slow to anger, abounding in mercy" (Ps 103:8), so Christian spouses are called to seek peace and reconciliation in times of disagreement and conflict. St. Paul's advice applies in a special way to Christian spouses:

Put on then, as God's chosen ones, holy and beloved, heartfelt compassion, kindness, humility, gentleness, and patience, bearing with one another and forgiving one another, if one has a grievance against another; as the Lord has forgiven you, so must you also do. And over all these put on love, that is, the bond of perfection. And let the peace of Christ control your hearts, the peace into which you were also called in one body. (Col 3:12–15)

Only genuine communion in Christ can enable such actions. That is why, in the Rite of Marriage, the Church prays for all married couples, asking that their love may be unconditional, complete, and unselfish: "May the mystery of Christ's unselfish love, which we celebrate in this Eucharist, increase their love for [God] and for each other" (Prayer over the Gifts, *Mass of Marriage*, 114).

 # The Importance of Friendship

Real friendships help to prepare you for your possible future marriage. Which of the following skills of friendship do you possess?

- I am good at sharing ideas with others.
- I have many interests.
- I am patient with myself and others.
- I can forgive and ask for forgiveness.
- I am growing in self-understanding.
- Jesus is important in my life and relationships.

Together with a classmate, develop a short presentation geared for elementary school students on the importance of friendship with tips for being a good friend. Share the presentation at a school, a religious education class, or an after-school program in your area. Turn in a written report of your presentation to your teacher along with a self-evaluation of how well the presentation resonated with the younger students. Include the name of the place where the presentation took place and the age of the students.

Family Communion

The Sacrament of Matrimony helps the bride and groom form a family—an intergenerational community of faith, hope, and love. Furthermore, the ongoing graces of Matrimony help all family members act as Christ to one another. Just as the Blessed Virgin Mary said yes to God in becoming the Mother of Jesus, and just as St. Joseph said yes to being Mary's faithful partner in raising Jesus, so Christian spouses are called to affirm Jesus in today's world. Many married couples do this by becoming parents and raising their children. They find Christ in their children, and they act as educators in faith, helping their children grow more and more into the image of Christ.

"To be Christ to one another" means striving to build loving relationships. It means showing honor and respect for the dignity and unique needs of each family

> **domestic church** A term for the family as the Church in miniature.

member. It means promoting each person's sense of worth. In short, to act as Christ means to build true Christian community. As Pope John Paul II explained, "The Christian family . . . is the first community called to announce the Gospel to the human person during growth and to bring him or her, through a progressive education and catechesis, to full human and Christian maturity" (*Familiaris Consortio*, 2).

Matrimony helps Christian families mirror the love between Christ and his Church so completely that the family actually becomes a **domestic church**. This term, an ancient expression, has been fleshed out by many Church documents, including the Second Vatican Council's *Lumen Gentium*. The family is the most basic unit of the Church. The *Catechism of the Catholic Church* explains that "the father . . . , mother, children, and all members of the family exercise the *priesthood of the baptized* in a privileged way 'by the reception of the sacraments, prayer and thanksgiving, the witness of a holy life, and self-denial and active charity'" (*CCC*, 1657, quoting *Lumen Gentium*, 10). In addition, "the Christian home is the place where children receive the first proclamation of the faith. For this reason the family home is rightly called 'the domestic church,' a community of grace and prayer, a school of human virtues and of Christian charity" (*CCC*, 1666).

Communion with the Church

Families are the basic units of the Church, but they are not self-contained, self-serving units. Instead, God calls Christian families to transform their love into outward action, sharing in the life and mission of the Church. The *Catechism of the Catholic Church* explains further that Christian families "proclaim the Good News that God loves us with a definitive and irrevocable love, that married couples share in this love, that it supports and sustains them, and that by their own faithfulness they can be witnesses to God's faithful love" (*CCC*, 1648).

How are Christian families to join in the Church's mission? Two ways are shared below:

1. *Christian families promote faith and evangelization, both at home and with others.* The domestic church seeks the sanctification and religious education of all family members. Every Christian family is to be a believing and evangelizing community in dialogue with God. Families worship together at Sunday Mass, participate in the other sacraments, and make time for family prayer and Scripture reflection. Parents set a good example by participating in religious education classes, retreats, and special programs. Groups of families meet regularly to form small Christian communities and to support one another in the faith.

2. *Christian families help serve the needs of the parish.* Most parishes always need volunteers of all ages and talents. Christian families help during the liturgy by bringing up the gifts of bread and wine at Mass or acting as ushers, lectors, altar servers, extraordinary ministers of Holy Communion, or choir members.

They take on special parish projects: cleaning up after Mass, decorating for Christmas, serving at a fish fry, or helping with special events. They visit the sick and elderly in Catholic hospitals and retirement homes. They help collect clothes, food, and furniture for the needy. They give rides to the poor, work with the deaf and the blind, catechize adolescents, console the lonely, and serve on parish councils and diocesan committees.

The family of St. Elizabeth of Hungary was a great example of such service. Elizabeth, queen of Thuringia in the early thirteenth century, gave birth to royal heirs who lived in a luxurious castle. Instead of relishing their riches, though, Elizabeth and her children worked daily to help the poor in their kingdom. They distributed food and clothing, tended the sick, and housed the homeless in their own rooms.

The nineteenth-century American family of St. Elizabeth Seton also modeled holy activity. Widowed with five children, Elizabeth became involved in social work in New York City. She not only educated her own children but she also began the first parochial school in the United States to educate many children in the Catholic faith.

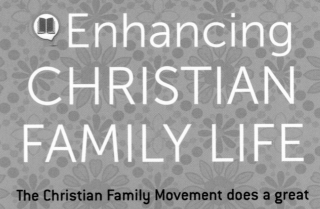

📖 Enhancing **CHRISTIAN FAMILY LIFE**

The Christian Family Movement does a great deal to support family life. Research and report on the mission and functions of this organization. Its website offers more information to support your work on this assignment.

Communion with Society

The Sacrament of Matrimony calls Catholic spouses and their children to become involved in all aspects of society—workplace, marketplace, entertainment, athletics, politics—to help build a world of justice, peace, and love.

Here are three main ways in which Christian families serve society:

1. *Husbands and wives socialize their children.* In the family, children learn to communicate and socialize, to respect others' rights and needs, and to contribute to the common good. "The family is the place where different generations come together to help one another to grow in wisdom and harmonize the rights of individuals with other demands of social life; as such it constitutes the basis of society" (*Gaudium et Spes*, 52). In the family, children learn respect for life, love of the poor, self-control, and good citizenship. As Pope John Paul II wrote, "The fostering of authentic and mature communion between persons within the family is the first and irreplaceable school of social life, an example and stimulus for the broader community of relationships marked by respect, justice, dialogue, and love" (*Familiaris Consortio*, 43).

2. *Christian families participate in politics, promoting and safeguarding family values in society.* The Church encourages laypeople to become involved in politics—as candidates, as voters, as lobbyists—to ensure the rights of every family in society. Some important societal rights for families are the following:

- to marry and establish a family and to have adequate means to support it;

- to act responsibly regarding the transmission of life and the education of children;

- to preserve the intimacy of conjugal love and family life;

- to honor the permanent stability of the marriage bond;

- to believe in, teach, and profess one's faith;

- to bring up children according to one's own values;

- to obtain physical, social, political, and economic security, especially when poor and sick;

- to maintain suitable housing;

- to participate in political expression and representation;

- to form associations with other families;

- to protect minors from substance abuse and pornography;

- to ensure for the elderly a worthy life and a worthy death; and

- to emigrate as a family in search of a better life. (See *Familiaris Consortio*, 46.)

Families can help defend these rights for other families around them. Pope Francis said, "Today, the family is looked down upon and mistreated. We are called to acknowledge how beautiful, true and good it is to start a family, to be a family today; and how indispensable the family is for the life of the world and for the future of humanity" (Speech to the College of Cardinals, February 20, 2014).

3. *Christian families work for justice and peace.* Christian families serve the poor, offer hospitality, and see that no one is neglected or unwanted. Christian families stand for human dignity against racism, sexism, nationalism, and consumerism.

Among the various works of the family apostolate the following may be listed: adopting abandoned children, showing a loving welcome to strangers, helping with the running of schools, supporting adolescents with advice and help, assisting engaged couples to make a better preparation for marriage, taking part in catechism-teaching, supporting married people and families in a material or moral crisis, and, in the case of the aged, providing them not only with what is indispensable but also procuring for them a fair share of the fruits of economic progress. (*Apostolicam Actuositatem*, 11)

Families promote peace by teaching their children to resolve conflict at home and by emphasizing the Christian belief that all humans are created in God's image, with dignity and rights.

Balancing family life with service of others is challenging. Only by being rooted in Christ can Christian families transform their love for one another into a love that also serves the Church and society. Pope Francis spoke of this transformation: "In your journey as a family, you share so many beautiful moments: meals, rest, housework, leisure, prayer, trips and pilgrimages, and times of mutual support. . . . Nevertheless, if there is no love then there is no joy, and authentic love comes to us from Jesus. He offers us his word, which illuminates our path; he gives us the Bread of life which sustains us on our journey" ("Letter to Families," February 2, 2014).

In summary, sacramental marriage is an efficacious sign of Christ's presence; it is the "sacrament of the covenant of Christ and the Church" (*CCC*, 1617). St. Paul wrote, "Husbands, love your wives, even as Christ loved the church and handed himself over for her" (Eph 5:25). The Rite of Marriage reminds all people of this profound unity and includes prayers to strengthen it:

♡ Church of the Home, Church of the Parish

The rhythm of life in a family—the domestic church or "church of the home"—is parallel to the rhythm of life celebrated in a faith community in the parish Church. Write a three- to five-paragraph prayer that tells how the Church of the home and the Church of the parish each fulfill in a loving way these human needs:

- welcomes and initiates new members
- shares meals of unity
- fights and forgives
- heals and comforts one another
- encourages her members to serve others
- nurtures life-giving relationships

PATRON SAINTS of Marriage

There are several patron saints associated with marriage. St. Joseph, the loyal husband of Mary and foster father of Jesus, is foremost. He was present at the key times of Mary's pregnancy, her childbirth, and the early years of Jesus' life. Here are some other patron saints of marriage:

St. Priscilla (first century AD)

Happy Marriages

With her husband Aquila, she was a Christian missionary who lived, worked, and traveled with St. Paul. Her husband was martyred under Emperor Domitian.

St. Monica (322–387)

Married Women

Mother of St. Augustine, she was married to a pagan, Patricius, who was known for a violent temper and licentious lifestyle. Through her prayers, he converted to Christianity near the end of his life.

St. Adelaide of Burgundy (931–983)

Second Marriages

Her first husband, to whom her father had engaged her when she was two, died three years after their marriage. She later married Otto of Germany. Pope John XII crowned them rulers of the Holy Roman Empire.

St. Rita of Cascia (1381–1457)

Difficult Marriages

She was pressured into marriage to a man who proved to be harsh and cruel. After his death, she suffered the death of her two sons. Following their death, she entered religious life.

St. Thomas More (1478–1535)

Difficult Marriages

Literary scholar and lawyer, he was the father of four children. He was beheaded under the orders of King Henry VIII for not supporting the king's divorce from Catherine of Aragon in order to marry Anne Boleyn.

O God, who in creating the human race
willed that man and wife should be one,
join, we pray, in a bond of inseparable love
these your servants who are to be united in the
   covenant of Marriage,
so that, as you make their love fruitful,
they may become, by your grace, witnesses to
   charity itself. (Collect, *For the Celebration of
   Marriage*)

Sacramental marriage also reflects the union between God and humans that awaits all who have been judged worthy by Christ at the end of time:

For the wedding day of the Lamb has come,
   his bride has made herself ready. (Rv 19:7b)

Sacramental marriage, then, is both a sign of Christ's love present to you now and a reminder of the glorious future that awaits you.

SECTION ASSESSMENT

NOTE TAKING

Use the concept diagram you created to help you answer the following questions.

1. How can spouses find communion with one another?
2. Name two ways Christian families join in the Church's mission.
3. Name three ways Christian families can serve society.

VOCABULARY

4. Define *domestic church*.

COMPREHENSION

5. How does marriage promote Christian discipleship for husbands and wives?

CRITICAL THINKING

6. Choose three rights for families named in *Familiaris Consortio* and explain their importance.

Section Summaries

Focus Question

What is distinct about a relationship rooted in the Sacrament of Matrimony?

Complete one of the following:

 Design a set of wedding rings that symbolize the Sacrament of Matrimony for you. Draw and describe in words what the rings look like.

 Research and report on the requirements in your diocese or parish for couples who want to get married in the Church.

 Research divorce statistics in the United States. Look up the percentage of marriages that end in divorce and reasons couples give for divorcing. Share your findings in class.

INTRODUCTION (PAGES 289–291)

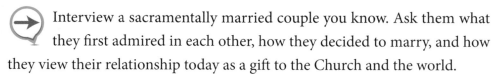

Helping Each Other Grow in Love

In the Catholic Church, the Sacrament of Matrimony is a Sacrament at the Service of Communion. In this sacrament, a baptized man and a baptized woman form a lifelong covenant with each other. Each spouse is meant to help the other, and their children, grow in holiness. Matrimony is an intimate communion of life and love that images God's love.

Interview a sacramentally married couple you know. Ask them what they first admired in each other, how they decided to marry, and how they view their relationship today as a gift to the Church and the world.

SECTION 1 (PAGES 292–296)

Understanding the Sacrament of Matrimony

Since the creation of humanity, marriage has been a part of society. In Old Testament times, the Jewish people developed an understanding of marriage as a unique relationship of tenderness and exclusivity, preparing them to receive Jesus' message about God's plan for marriage. The purpose of marriage is to unite a man and a woman as well as to ensure the procreation and the education of children. In marriage, a man and a woman can grow in holiness together. Love within the Sacrament of Matrimony reflects the love between Christ and the Church.

 Read Ephesians 5:25–33 carefully, dwelling on the actions of love toward the Church that Christ performs. Then write a prayer in your journal thanking Christ for his love for you.

SECTION 2 (PAGES 297–301)

Celebrating the Sacrament of Matrimony

Throughout the history of the Church, the practice of the Sacrament of Matrimony has developed. Today the Rite of Marriage is celebrated in a church and in the presence of a priest or deacon and at least two witnesses to show that it is a communal reality. The spouses' consent to be married is the essential element of Matrimony.

Choose one Old Testament reading, one New Testament epistle, and one Gospel reading that would be appropriate for a wedding Mass.

SECTION 3 (PAGES 302–311)

The Graces of the Sacrament of Matrimony

The Sacrament of Matrimony gives spouses the grace to love each other forever and to help each other and their families reach heaven. A healthy marriage is faithful, fruitful, and exclusive. Families have rights and responsibilities in society, and by fulfilling their mission to serve and evangelize, they help to transform the world in peace and justice.

Choose one of the societal rights for families found on page 308, and research a situation that threatens this right for families in the world today, either in the United States or in another country. Explain why this right is so important and suggest ways it could be better defended in the situation you researched.

Chapter Assignments

Choose and complete at least one of the following three assignments assessing your understanding of the material in this chapter.

1. Understanding Primary Sources on Marriage

➡️ The Church has a wealth of resources and writings on the Sacrament of Matrimony intended to help the faithful prepare for, understand, and live this sacrament. Reading from these documents can deepen your understanding of the sacrament. Many of the documents can be found at www.foryourmarriage.org, a website sponsored by the United States Conference of Catholic Bishops.

- Prepare a report on marriage using three of these documents as primary source material. Your report should focus on the Church's teaching on the sacramental nature of marriage. In addition, you can address other dimensions of the marriage covenant, such as the call to fruitfulness, the sanctity of the family, and so forth. Your report should be a minimum of three pages in length and should include two or more quotations (with proper citations) from each Church document or resource.

2. A Presentation on the Rite of Marriage

➡️ Imagine that you are an adult faith formation minister in your parish and that you have been asked to develop a presentation for engaged couples on the Rite of Marriage. The presentation is intended to help the couples understand and prepare for the marriage ceremony. Develop a presentation that covers the following areas:

- the different forms of the rite;
- an outline of the structure of the rite within Mass;
- when consent is given during the ceremony;
- why consent is so important to the marriage; and
- the exact wording of the vows.

You may wish to refer to www.foryourmarriage.org for information relevant to your presentation. Plan your presentation to last about fifteen minutes. Create a visual element for the presentation using multimedia software. Either share your presentation with your class in person or videotape your presentation, link it to a website approved by your teacher, and provide your teacher with the link to your finished assignment.

3. Profiles of Successful Marriages

Current statistics show that nearly half of all marriages end in divorce. However, what surveys and studies often don't report is that the divorce rate for Catholic marriages is consistently, and appreciably, lower than the national average.

In response to the often negative reports on the state of marriage in the modern world, develop a report profiling successful sacramental marriages. Your report should profile three couples who were sacramentally married in the Church, with at least two of those couples having been married for fifteen years or more. You may interview your parents, grandparents, or other married couples you know for this assignment. Provide the following information on each couple you profile:

- brief biographical details about each spouse (family background, profession, and so forth);

- how the couple met and how they discerned the call to enter into marriage;

- how many children (and grandchildren, if applicable) they have;

- challenges they've overcome in their marriage;

- particularly joyful times they've shared; and

- the importance of their Catholic faith and how it has sustained and strengthened their marriage (support this with a direct quotation from one or both spouses).

You may develop each profile as a written report, a slideshow presentation, or a video presentation. If you choose the written or slideshow format, be sure to include images. Accompany your completed presentation with a one-page reflection on what you have learned about the marriage covenant from this assignment.

Faithful Disciple

St. Margaret of Scotland

St. Margaret of Scotland

You may tend to think of kings and queens as "above it all," living lives of luxury while the other social classes struggle. But a life of glamour was not the life of St. Margaret, Queen of Scotland, who reigned in the eleventh century. Although she was royalty, she is remembered today as a beloved ruler who helped her people, especially the poor.

Yet Margaret did not rule alone. Margaret's husband was King Malcolm III of Scotland. Together, this married couple, who had eight children, demonstrated that marriage is truly a Sacrament at the Service of Communion. Malcolm took pride in Margaret's accomplishments. While he could neither read nor write, Margaret could. Margaret spent much time in prayer and spiritual reading. Malcolm showed his pride in her by having her books decorated with gold and silver. One of these, a pocket Gospel, can be found at the Bodleian Library in Oxford, England.

Margaret's generosity was legendary. She gave alms freely from the king's treasury (and the king never complained). She invited the poor to banquets. She visited the sick in their homes. She founded churches and monasteries and commissioned a ferry to take pilgrims across the river to the Abbey of Dunfermline, which she had founded. This gave the local towns North and South Queensferry their names.

Margaret was also concerned with Church issues. She supported strong ties with the universal Church, such as insisting that the local synod of bishops encourage marriage. She also insisted on the adoption of "the Easter duty" (the reception of Holy Communion at least once a year during the Easter Season) and the forbidding of servile work on Sunday.

On November 13, 1093, King Malcolm and the royal couple's eldest son, Edward, were both killed in a battle against the English. Margaret, upon hearing of their deaths, is reported to have prayed, "I thank you, Almighty God, for sending me so great a sorrow to purify me from my sins." She died four days later from illness at the age of forty-seven. Those who have visited her tomb have reported several miracles.

Pope Innocent IV canonized Margaret in 1249. In 1673 she became the patron saint of Scotland. Her feast day is celebrated on November 16.

Reading Comprehension

1. In what ways was Margaret generous?

2. What was one way King Malcolm showed support for his wife?

3. Name two ways Margaret strengthened Scotland's ties with the universal Church.

Writing Task

- Read more about St. Margaret and her husband. Write a short dialogue between them, in which Margaret and Malcolm discuss Margaret's concern for helping those in need.

Explaining the Faith
Why doesn't the Church allow contraception?

Have you ever considered the deep connection between the use of contraception and **abortion** or deliberate **sterilization**? To some, contraception might seem less problematic since (at least in theory) it is not destroying a life, only preventing it. What most people do not know is that in many cases, contraception can be **abortifacient**. That is, it doesn't prevent new life from being conceived; it stops the fertilized egg from implanting in the womb.

In any case, though, the choice to "disinvite" new life goes against the meaning of the sexual act: a loving embrace of a whole human person, fertility included. Contraception rejects part of another person's identity—their fertility—by using chemicals or implants to alter the body so that it no longer works in harmony with nature. Imagine saying to your spouse, "I love you. I just wish you weren't healthy!" Sterilization rejects a person's fertility in an even more obvious way. It is not hard to see how easily this rejection of part of a person (the spouse) can lead to the rejection of a whole person (the child), whether by preventing life from being conceived or by destroying it. By contrast, Natural Family Planning embraces the whole person, including that person's ability to procreate new life.

 ## Further Research

- Research a method of contraception. Write a paragraph describing what it does to the body. Be sure to list any side effects and possible complications. Then explain how the product prevents pregnancy—is it contraceptive, abortifacient, or both?

abortion The direct and deliberate ending of a pregnancy by killing the unborn child. Direct abortion, willed either as a means or an end, gravely contradicts moral law.

sterilization Any surgical procedure that prevents conception. Sterilization procedures in women include tying or cutting of fallopian tubes, removal of ovaries, and/or removal of the uterus. Sterilization procedures in men include vasectomy (cutting tubes carrying sperm from the testicles) or castration (removing the testicles). Deliberate sterilization is contrary to one of the characteristics of sacramental marriage, the openness to children.

abortifacient A drug that causes an abortion.

Prayer

Prayer to the Holy Family

Jesus, Mary, and Joseph,
in you we contemplate
the splendor of true love,
to you we turn with trust.

Holy Family of Nazareth,
grant that our families too
may be places of communion and prayer,
authentic schools of the Gospel
and small domestic Churches.

Holy Family of Nazareth,
may families never again
experience violence, rejection, and division:
may all who have been hurt or scandalized
find ready comfort and healing.

Holy Family of Nazareth,
may we always be mindful
of the sacredness and inviolability of the family
and of its beauty in God's plan.

Jesus, Mary, and Joseph,
graciously hear our prayer.

—Pope Francis (on the Feast of the Holy Family, 2013)

Beliefs

From the beginning, the Church expressed and handed on her faith in brief formulas accessible to all. These professions of faith are called creeds, because their first word in Latin, credo, *means "I believe." The following creeds have special importance in the Church. The Apostles' Creed is a summary of the Apostles' faith. The Nicene Creed developed from the Councils of Nicaea and Constantinople and remains in common between the Churches of both the East and West.*

Apostles' Creed

I believe in God,
the Father almighty,
Creator of heaven and earth,
and in Jesus Christ, his only Son, our Lord,
who was conceived by the Holy Spirit,
born of the Virgin Mary,
suffered under Pontius Pilate,
was crucified, died, and was buried;
he descended into hell;
on the third day he rose again from the dead;
he ascended into heaven,
and is seated at the right hand of God the
    Father Almighty;
from there he will come to judge the living and
    the dead.

I believe in the Holy Spirit,
the holy catholic Church,
the communion of saints,
the forgiveness of sins,
the resurrection of the body,
and life everlasting. Amen.

Nicene Creed

I believe in one God,
the Father almighty,
maker of heaven and earth,
of all things visible and invisible.

I believe in one Lord Jesus Christ,
the Only Begotten Son of God,
born of the Father before all ages.
God from God, Light from Light,
true God from true God,
begotten, not made, consubstantial with the
    Father;
through him all things were made.
For us men and for our salvation
he came down from heaven,
and by the Holy Spirit was incarnate of the
    Virgin Mary,
and became man.

For our sake he was crucified under Pontius
    Pilate,
he suffered death and was buried,
and rose again on the third day
in accordance with the Scriptures.
He ascended into heaven
and is seated at the right hand of the Father.
He will come again in glory
to judge the living and the dead
and his kingdom will have no end.

I believe in the Holy Spirit, the Lord, the giver
    of life,
who proceeds from the Father and the Son,

who with the Father and the Son is adored and
   glorified,
who has spoken through the prophets.

I believe in one, holy, catholic and apostolic
   Church.
I confess one baptism for the forgiveness of
   sins
and I look forward to the resurrection of the
   dead
and the life of the world to come. Amen.

Deposit of Faith

The Deposit of Faith *is that which is contained in and
transmitted by Sacred Tradition and Sacred Scripture
and handed on from the time of the Apostles, from which
the Church draws all that she proposes is revealed by
God.*

Relationship between Sacred Scripture and Sacred Tradition

The Church does not derive the revealed truths of God
from the holy Scriptures alone. The Sacred Tradition
hands on God's Word, first given to the Apostles by
the Lord and the Holy Spirit, to the successors of the
Apostles (the bishops and the pope). Enlightened by
the Holy Spirit, these successors faithfully preserve,
explain, and spread it to the ends of the earth. The Second Vatican Council Fathers explained the relationship
between Sacred Scripture and Sacred Tradition:

> It is clear therefore that, in the supremely
> wise arrangement of God, Sacred Tradition,
> Sacred Scripture, and the Magisterium of the
> Church are so connected and associated that
> one of them cannot stand without the others.
> Working together, each in its own way, under
> the action of the one Holy Spirit, they all

contribute effectively to the salvation of souls.
(*Dei Verbum*, 10)

Canon of the Bible

There are seventy-three books in the canon of the
Bible—that is, the official list of books the Church
accepts as divinely inspired: forty-six Old Testament
books and twenty-seven New Testament books. (See
the following page for a list of the books.)

THE OLD TESTAMENT

THE PENTATEUCH		THE PROPHETIC BOOKS	
Genesis	Gn	Isaiah	Is
Exodus	Ex	Jeremiah	Jer
Leviticus	Lv	Lamentations	Lam
Numbers	Nm	Baruch	Bar
Deuteronomy	Dt	Ezekiel	Ez
THE HISTORICAL BOOKS		Daniel	Dn
Joshua	Jos	Hosea	Hos
Judges	Jgs	Joel	Jl
Ruth	Ru	Amos	Am
1 Samuel	1 Sm	Obadiah	Ob
2 Samuel	2 Sm	Jonah	Jon
1 Kings	1 Kgs	Micah	Mi
2 Kings	2 Kgs	Nahum	Na
1 Chronicles	1 Chr	Habakkuk	Hb
2 Chronicles	2 Chr	Zephaniah	Zep
Ezra	Ezr	Haggai	Hg
Nehemiah	Neh	Zechariah	Zec
Tobit	Tb	Malachi	Mal
Judith	Jdt		
Esther	Est		
1 Maccabees	1 Mc		
2 Maccabees	2 Mc		
THE WISDOM BOOKS			
Job	Jb		
Psalms	Ps(s)		
Proverbs	Prv		
Ecclesiastes	Eccl		
Song of Songs	Sg		
Wisdom	Ws		
Sirach	Sir		

THE NEW TESTAMENT

THE GOSPELS		THE CATHOLIC LETTERS	
Matthew	Mt	James	Jas
Mark	Mk	1 Peter	1 Pt
Luke	Lk	2 Peter	2 Pt
John	Jn	1 John	1 Jn
		2 John	2 Jn
Acts of the Apostles	Acts	3 John	3 Jn
THE NEW TESTAMENT LETTERS		Jude	Jude
Romans	Rom		
1 Corinthians	1 Cor	Revelation	Rv
2 Corinthians	2 Cor		
Galatians	Gal		
Ephesians	Eph		
Philippians	Phil		
Colossians	Col		
1 Thessalonians	1 Thes		
2 Thessalonians	2 Thes		
1 Timothy	1 Tm		
2 Timothy	2 Tm		
Titus	Ti		
Philemon	Phlm		
Hebrews	Heb		

The Church

The Church is the Body of Christ—that is, the community of God's people who profess faith in the risen Lord Jesus and love and serve others under the guidance of the Holy Spirit. The Roman Catholic Church is guided by the pope and his bishops on the foundation of the Apostles.

Marks of the Church

1. *The Church is one.*

   The Church remains *one* because of her source: the unity—in the Trinity of the Father, Son, and Holy Spirit—in one God. The Church's unity can never be broken or lost because this foundation is itself unbreakable.

2. *The Church is holy.*

   The Church is *holy* because Jesus, who founded the Church, is holy, and he joined the Church to himself as his Body and gave the Church the gift of the Holy Spirit. Together, Christ and the Church make up the "whole Christ" (*Christus totus* in Latin).

3. *The Church is catholic.*

   The Church is *catholic* ("universal" or "for everyone") in two ways. First, she is catholic because Christ is present in the Church in the fullness of his Body, with the fullness of the means of salvation, the fullness of faith, sacraments, and the ordained ministry that comes from the Apostles. The Church is also catholic because she takes the message of salvation to all people.

4. *The Church is apostolic.*

   The Church's *apostolic* mission comes from Jesus: "Go, therefore, and make disciples of all nations" (Mt 28:19). The Church remains apostolic because she still teaches the same things the Apostles taught. Also, the Church is led by the pope and bishops, who are successors to the Apostles and who help to guide the Church until Jesus returns.

Moral Teaching

Morality refers to the goodness or evil of human actions. Listed below are several aids the Church offers for making good and moral decisions.

The Ten Commandments

The Ten Commandments are a main source for Christian morality. The Ten Commandments were spoken to the whole assembly of Israel. Jesus himself acknowledged them. He told the rich young man, "If you wish to enter into life, keep the commandments" (Mt 19:17). Since the time of St. Augustine (fourth century), the Ten Commandments have been used as a source for teaching baptismal candidates.

I. I am the LORD, your God: you shall not have strange gods before me.

II. You shall not take the name of the LORD, your God, in vain.

III. Remember to keep holy the LORD's day.

IV. Honor your father and your mother.

V. You shall not kill.

VI. You shall not commit adultery.

VII. You shall not steal.

VIII. You shall not bear false witness against your neighbor.

IX. You shall not covet your neighbor's wife.

X. You shall not covet your neighbor's goods.

The Beatitudes

The word *beatitude* means "happiness." Jesus preached the Beatitudes in his Sermon on the Mount (see Matthew 5:3–12).

Blessed are the poor in spirit, for theirs is the kingdom of heaven.

Blessed are they who mourn, for they will be comforted.

Blessed are the meek, for they will inherit the land.

Blessed are they who hunger and thirst for righteousness, for they will be satisfied.

Blessed are the merciful, for they will be shown mercy.

Blessed are the clean of heart, for they will see God.

Blessed are the peacemakers, for they will be called children of God.

Blessed are they who are persecuted for the sake of righteousness, for theirs is the kingdom of heaven.

Cardinal Virtues

Virtues—habits that help in leading a moral life—that are acquired by human effort are known as moral or human virtues. Four of these are known as the cardinal virtues, as they form the hinge (*cardinal* comes from the Latin word for "hinge") that connects all the others:

- Prudence
- Justice
- Fortitude
- Temperance

Theological Virtues

The theological virtues are the foundation for moral life. They are gifts infused into our souls by God.

- Faith
- Hope
- Charity

Works of Mercy

The works of mercy are charitable actions that remind you how to come to the aid of a neighbor and fulfill his or her bodily and spiritual needs.

Corporal Works of Mercy

1. Feed the hungry.
2. Give drink to the thirsty.
3. Clothe the naked.
4. Visit the imprisoned.
5. Shelter the homeless.
6. Visit the sick.
7. Bury the dead.

Spiritual Works of Mercy

1. Counsel the doubtful.
2. Instruct the ignorant.
3. Admonish sinners.
4. Comfort the afflicted.
5. Forgive offenses.
6. Bear wrongs patiently.
7. Pray for the living and the dead.

Precepts of the Church

The precepts of the Church are basic obligations for all Catholics dictated by laws of the Church. They are intended to guarantee for Catholics the minimum in prayer and moral effort to facilitate their love for God and neighbor.

1. You shall attend Mass on Sundays and on holy days of obligation and rest from servile labor.
2. You shall confess your sins at least once a year.
3. You shall receive the Sacrament of the Eucharist at least during the Easter season.
4. You shall observe the days of fasting and abstinence established by the Church.
5. You shall help to provide for the needs of the Church.

Understanding Sin

Being a moral person entails avoiding sin. Sin is an offense against God.

Mortal sin is the most serious kind of sin. Mortal sin destroys or kills a person's relationship with God. To commit a mortal sin, three conditions must exist:

1. The moral object must be of grave or serious matter. Grave matter is specified in the Ten Commandments (e.g., do not kill, do not commit adultery, do not steal, etc.).

2. The person must have full knowledge of the gravity of the sinful action.

3. The person must completely consent to the action. It must be a personal choice.

Venial sin is less serious sin. Examples of venial sins are petty jealousy, disobedience, or "borrowing" a small amount of money without the intention of repaying it. Venial sins, when not repented, can lead a person to commit mortal sins.

Vices are bad habits linked to sins. Vices come from particular sins, especially the seven capital sins: pride, avarice, envy, wrath, lust, gluttony, and sloth.

Steps for Celebrating the Sacrament of Penance

Before celebrating the sacrament, you should make time for an honest examination of conscience so that you can acknowledge any sins you have committed since your last confession and pray for God's mercy.

1. Sincerely tell God that you are sorry for your sins. Ask God for forgiveness and for the grace you will need to change what needs changing in your life. Promise God that you will try to live according to his will for you.

2. Approach the area for confession. Wait at an appropriate distance until it is your turn.

3. Make the Sign of the Cross with the priest. He may say, "May God, who has enlightened every heart, help you to know your sins and trust his mercy." You reply, "Amen."

4. Confess your sins to the priest. Simply and directly talk to him about the areas of sin in your life that need God's healing touch.

5. The priest will ask you to express your contrition or sorrow and to pray an Act of Contrition. Pray an Act of Contrition you have committed to memory. See page 328 for an example.

6. The priest may talk to you about your life, encourage you to be more faithful to God in the future, and will impose on you a penance for your sin. The penance corresponds as far as possible with the gravity and nature of the sins committed. It can consist of prayer, offerings, works of mercy, service of neighbor, voluntary self-denial, sacrifices, and patient acceptance of the crosses you must bear. Also, personally, you should continue in acts of penance, prayer, charity, and bearing sufferings of all kinds for the removal of the temporal punishment of sin that remains.

7. The priest will then extend his hands over your head and pray a prayer of absolution for your sins. You respond: "Amen."

8. The priest will wish you peace. Thank him and leave.

9. Go to a quiet place in church and pray your prayer of penance. Then, spend some time quietly thanking God for the gift of forgiveness.

Prayers

Some common Catholic prayers are listed below. The Latin translation for three of the prayers is included. Latin is the official language of the Church. There are several occasions when you may pray in Latin; for example, at a World Youth Day when you are with young people who speak many different languages.

Sign of the Cross

In the name of the Father,
and of the Son,
and of the Holy Spirit.
Amen.

In nómine Patris,
et Filii,
et Spíritus Sancti.
Amen.

Our Father

Our Father, who art in heaven,
hallowed be thy name.
Thy kingdom come;
thy will be done on earth as it is in heaven.
Give us this day our daily bread
and forgive us our trespasses
as we forgive those who trespass against us.
And lead us not into temptation,
but deliver us from evil.
Amen.

Pater Noster qui es in caelis:
sanctificétur Nomen Tuum;
advéniat Regnum Tuum;
fiat volúntas Tua, sicut in caelo, et in terra.
Panem nostrum quotidiánum da nobis hódie;
et dimítte nobis débita nostra,
sicut et nos dimíttimus debitóribus nostris;
Et ne nos inducas in tentatiónem,
sed libera nos a malo.
Amen.

Glory Be

Glory be to the Father,
and to the Son,

and to the Holy Spirit,
as it was in the beginning,
is now, and ever shall be,
world without end.
Amen.

Glória Patri
et Fílio
et Spirítui Sancto.
Sicut érat in princípio,
et nunc et semper,
et in saécula saeculórum.
Amen.

Hail Mary

Hail Mary, full of grace,
the Lord is with thee.
Blessed art thou among women
and blessed is the fruit of thy womb, Jesus.
Holy Mary, Mother of God,
pray for us sinners
now and at the hour of our death.
Amen.

Ave María, grátia plena,
Dóminus tecum.
Benedícta tu in muliéribus,
et benedíctus fructus ventris tui, Iesus.
Sancta María, Mater Dei,
ora pro nobis peccatóribus
nunc et in hora mortis nostræ.
Amen.

Memorare

Remember, O most gracious Virgin Mary,
that never was it known
that anyone who fled to thy protection,
implored thy help,
or sought thy intercession was left unaided.
Inspired by this confidence I fly unto thee,

O virgin of virgins, my Mother.
To thee do I come, before thee I stand,
sinful and sorrowful.
O Mother of the Word Incarnate,
despise not my petitions,
but in thy mercy hear and answer me.
Amen.

The Angelus

V. The Angel of the Lord declared unto Mary.
R. And she conceived of the Holy Spirit.
Hail Mary . . .
V. Behold the handmaid of the Lord.
R. Be it done unto me according to thy word.
Hail Mary . . .
V. And the Word was made flesh.
R. And dwelt among us.
Hail Mary . . .
V. Pray for us, O holy Mother of God,
R. That we may be made worthy of the promises of Christ.

Let us pray: Pour forth, we beseech thee, O Lord, thy grace into our hearts; that we, to whom the Incarnation of Christ thy Son was made known by the message of an angel, may by his Passion and Cross be brought to the glory of his Resurrection. Through the same Christ our Lord. Amen.

Grace at Meals

Before Meals
Bless us, O Lord,
and these thy gifts,
which we are about to receive from thy bounty,
through Christ our Lord. Amen.

After Meals
We give you thanks, almighty God,
for these and all the gifts
which we have received
from your goodness
through Christ our Lord. Amen.

Guardian Angel Prayer

Angel of God, my guardian dear,
to whom God's love commits me here,
ever this day be at my side,
to light and guard, to rule and guide. Amen.

Prayer for the Faithful Departed

Eternal rest grant unto them, O Lord,
and let perpetual light shine upon them.
May they rest in peace. Amen.

Morning Offering

O Jesus, through the Immaculate Heart of Mary, I offer you my prayers, works, joys, and sufferings of this day in union with the holy sacrifice of the Mass throughout the world. I offer them for all the intentions of your Sacred Heart: the salvation of souls, reparation for sin, and the reunion of all Christians. I offer them for the intentions of our bishops and all Apostles of Prayer and in particular for those recommended by our Holy Father this month. Amen.

Act of Faith

O my God, I firmly believe that you are one God in three divine Persons, Father, Son, and Holy Spirit. I believe that your divine Son became man and died for our sins and that he will come to judge the living and the dead. I believe these and all the truths which the Holy Catholic Church teaches because you have revealed them who are eternal truth and wisdom, who can neither deceive nor be deceived. In this faith I intend to live and die. Amen.

Act of Hope

O Lord God, I hope by your grace for the pardon of all my sins and after life here to gain eternal happiness because you have promised it who are infinitely powerful, faithful, kind, and merciful. In this hope I intend to live and die. Amen.

Act of Love

O Lord God, I love you above all things and I love my neighbor for your sake because you are the highest, infinite and perfect good, worthy of all my love. In this love I intend to live and die. Amen.

Act of Contrition

O my God, I am heartily sorry for having offended Thee, and I detest all my sins because of thy just punishment, but most of all because they offend Thee, my God, who art all good and deserving of all my love. I firmly resolve with the help of Thy grace to sin no more and to avoid the near occasion of sin. Amen.

Liturgy of the Hours

The Liturgy of the Hours is part of the official, public prayer of the Church. Along with the celebration of the sacraments, the recitation of the Liturgy of the Hours or Divine Office (office means "duty" or "obligation") allows for constant praise of and thanksgiving to God throughout the day and night.

The Liturgy of Hours consists of five major divisions:

1. Office of Readings
2. Morning Prayer (Lauds)
3. Daytime Prayers
4. Evening Prayers (Vespers)
5. Night Prayer (Compline)

Scriptural prayer, especially the psalms, is at the heart of the Liturgy of the Hours. Each day follows a separate pattern of prayer with themes closely tied in with the liturgical year and feasts of the saints.

Devotions

Devotions are external acts of holiness that are not part of the Church's official liturgy but simply popular spiritual practices of Catholics through history and today. Catholics have also expressed their piety around the Church's sacramental life through practices such as the veneration of relics, visits to churches, pilgrimages, processions, the Stations of the Cross, religious dances, the Rosary, wearing religious medals, and many more. Some popular Catholic devotions are included in this section.

The Mysteries of the Rosary
The Joyful Mysteries

1. The Annunciation
2. The Visitation
3. The Nativity
4. The Presentation
5. The Finding in the Temple

The Luminous Mysteries

1. The Baptism of Jesus
2. The Wedding Feast of Cana
3. The Proclamation of the Kingdom, with the call to Conversion
4. The Transfiguration

5. The Institution of the Eucharist

The Sorrowful Mysteries

1. The Agony in the Garden

2. The Scourging at the Pillar

3. The Crowning with Thorns

4. The Carrying of the Cross

5. The Crucifixion

The Glorious Mysteries

1. The Resurrection

2. The Ascension

3. The Descent of the Holy Spirit

4. The Assumption of Mary

5. The Coronation of Mary Queen of Heaven and Earth

How to Pray the Rosary

Opening

1. Begin on the crucifix and pray the Apostles' Creed.

2. On the first bead, pray the Our Father.

3. On the next three beads, pray the Hail Mary. (Some people meditate on the virtues of faith, hope, and charity on these beads.)

4. On the fifth bead, pray the Our Father and the Glory Be.

The Body

Each decade (set of ten beads) is organized as follows:

1. On the larger bead that comes before each set of ten, announce the mystery to be prayed (see above) and pray one Our Father.

2. On each of the ten smaller beads, pray one Hail Mary while meditating on the mystery.

3. Pray one Glory Be at the end of the decade. (There is no bead for the Glory Be.)

Conclusion

Pray the following prayer at the end of the Rosary:

Hail, Holy Queen
Hail, holy Queen, Mother of Mercy,
our life, our sweetness, and our hope.
To thee do we cry,
poor banished children of Eve.
To thee do we send up our sighs,
mourning and weeping in this valley of tears.
Turn then, most gracious advocate,
thine eyes of mercy toward us;
and after this our exile,
show unto us the blessed fruit of thy womb,
  Jesus.

O clement, O loving, O sweet Virgin Mary.

Pray for us, O holy Mother of God,
that we may be made worthy of the promises
of Christ.
Amen.

Stations of the Cross

The Stations of the Cross is a meditative prayer based on the Passion of Christ. This devotion grew out of the custom of Holy Land pilgrims who retraced the last steps of Jesus on his way to Calvary. Most Catholic churches have images or symbols of the Stations depicted on side walls to help Catholics imagine the sufferings of Jesus and focus on the meaning of the Paschal Mystery. Praying the Stations means meditating on each of the following scenes:

1. Jesus is condemned to death.
2. Jesus takes up his Cross.
3. Jesus falls the first time.
4. Jesus meets his Mother.
5. Simon of Cyrene helps Jesus carry his Cross.
6. Veronica wipes the face of Jesus.
7. Jesus falls the second time.
8. Jesus consoles the women of Jerusalem.
9. Jesus falls the third time.
10. Jesus is stripped of his garments.
11. Jesus is nailed to the Cross.
12. Jesus dies on the Cross.
13. Jesus is taken down from the Cross.
14. Jesus is laid in the tomb.

Some churches also include a fifteenth station, the Resurrection of the Lord.

Novenas

A novena consists of the recitation of certain prayers over a period of nine days. The symbolism of nine days refers to the time Mary and the Apostles spent in prayer between Jesus' Ascension into heaven and the descent of the Holy Spirit at Pentecost.

Many novenas are dedicated to Mary or to a saint with the faith and hope that she or he will intercede on behalf of the one making the novena. Novenas to St. Jude, St. Anthony, Our Lady of Perpetual Help, and Our Lady of Lourdes remain popular in the Church today.

The Divine Praises

These praises are traditionally recited after the Benediction of the Blessed Sacrament.

Blessed be God.
Blessed be his holy name.
Blessed be Jesus Christ, true God and true man.
Blessed be the name of Jesus.
Blessed be his most Sacred Heart.
Blessed be his most Precious Blood.
Blessed be Jesus in the most holy sacrament of the altar.
Blessed be the Holy Spirit, the Paraclete.
Blessed be the great Mother of God, Mary most holy.
Blessed be her holy and Immaculate Conception.
Blessed be her glorious Assumption.
Blessed be the name of Mary, Virgin and mother.
Blessed be St. Joseph, her most chaste spouse.
Blessed be God in his angels and in his saints.

Further Study: Your Life in Christ: Foundations of Catholic Morality

Imbued with Christ's presence from participation in the Seven Sacraments, Catholics are called to bring Christ to the world through the actions of their lives. As you continue to encounter Jesus in your studies, you will examine more clearly the good and moral behaviors that Christ expects of his followers. Listed below are some of the questions you will consider in a course on morality.

- How can the Catholic Church maintain that certain moral teaching applies to everyone and not only to Catholics?

- If God created humans with free will, can't I alone decide what is right or wrong?

- How can I tell if I made the right decision in the area of morality?

- Isn't it wrong to judge another person by telling them something they are doing is wrong?

- Why does God allow death?

- What is meant by "rising from the dead"?

- Where is heaven?

Final Words: Sacraments Draw You into God's Mystery

According to a Jewish legend a Caesar once went to Rabbi Joshua and said, "I want to see your God."

"You cannot," Rabbi Joshua told him.

"I am Caesar, and I insist that you show me your God."

"Very well," Rabbi Joshua said. "Meet me at noon on the day of the summer solstice."

The Caesar met the rabbi at the agreed-upon place on the day of the solstice. "Now show me your God," he said.

"First," Rabbi Joshua replied, "you must stand here and look directly at the sun."

"But I cannot!" Caesar exclaimed.

Rabbi Joshua responded, "If you cannot look directly at the sun, which is only one of the thousands of minions who serve the Holy One, how much less could you look on the Presence itself?"

You cannot "look upon God." You cannot touch him, and you cannot fathom him. God is infinitely beyond all human capacity of understanding. His thoughts and his ways are as high above yours as the heavens are above the earth. God is unsearchable mystery. And yet, God wants you to know him, love him, and serve him.

For this reason, God comes to you in ways that you can see, feel, and understand.

God comes to you in the sacraments.

GLOSSARY

abortifacient A drug that causes an abortion.

abortion The direct and deliberate ending of a pregnancy by killing the unborn child. Direct abortion, willed either as a means or an end, gravely contradicts moral law.

absolution The prayer by which a priest, through the power given to the Church by Jesus Christ, pardons a repentant sinner in the Sacrament of Penance.

Act of Contrition A prayer that expresses sorrow for sins.

adultery Infidelity in marriage wherein a married person has sexual intercourse with someone who is not the person's spouse.

Advocate A name for the Holy Spirit, who will live in you and guide you to truth.

age of reason Also called the "age of discretion," the age (typically the end of the seventh year) at which a person becomes capable of moral reasoning.

apocalyptic Relating to belief in the enactment of God's justice after death or in an end time when good people will be rewarded and evil people will be punished. In the Bible, the Books of Daniel and Revelation contain examples of apocalyptic writing.

apostolic succession An unbroken chain of power and authority connecting the pope and bishops to St. Peter and the other Apostles through the Sacrament of Holy Orders.

Baptism of blood The belief that martyrs—people who die for their faith in Jesus—who had not yet been baptized by water may receive forgiveness for their sins and experience God's saving mercy.

Baptism of desire The belief that catechumens who died before receiving the Sacrament of Baptism may receive forgiveness for their sins and experience God's saving mercy.

breviary A liturgical book from which priests and deacons pray the Liturgy of the Hours each day.

catechists Ordained ministers and laypeople who instruct others in Christian doctrine and for entry into the Church.

catechumenate From a Greek word that means "study or instruction." In the early Church, the catechumenate was a two- to three-year period of study about Jesus and the Christian faith. Celebration of the Sacraments of Christian Initiation did not occur until after the catechumenate.

catechumens Unbaptized persons who are preparing for full initiation into the Church through the Sacraments of Christian Initiation by engaging in formal study, prayer, and spiritual reflection.

celibacy The renunciation of marriage for more perfect observance of chastity made by those who receive the Sacrament of Holy Orders. Celibacy also extends to consecrated life and to those who forgo marriage for some honorable end.

chasuble The outer vestment worn by a bishop or priest at Eucharistic liturgy. Its color follows the liturgical seasons—purple for Advent or Lent; white for Christmas, Easter, and other feasts of Christ; red for Good Friday, Pentecost, and the feasts of martyrs; and green for Ordinary Time.

Chrism Mass An annual Mass, celebrated in a diocesan cathedral on or near Holy Thursday, in which the bishop consecrates the sacred chrism and other oils that will be used in the diocese throughout the year.

Chrismation The name in the Eastern rites for the Sacrament of Confirmation. It comes from the chrism used as part of the sacrament.

clergy From a Greek word for "lot," a term for ordained men.

collect The prayer appointed for the day or feast that concludes the Introductory Rites before the Liturgy of the Word begins.

common priesthood The priesthood of the faithful. Christ has made the Church a "kingdom of priests" who share in his priesthood through the Sacraments of Baptism and Confirmation.

Communion of Saints The unity in Christ of all those he has redeemed: the Church on earth, in heaven, and in Purgatory.

concupiscence The human inclination toward sin, caused by Original Sin.

confirmand A candidate for Confirmation.

Confiteor From the first word in Latin meaning "I confess," a prayer used during the Penitential Rite at the beginning of Mass and at other times to prepare to receive grace.

contraception Any artificial means (e.g., pills, condoms, diaphragms, surgeries) that deliberately and directly has an outcome of closing off one of the aims of sexual intercourse—the openness to life. Contraception also opposes the unitive aspect of the conjugal act by not allowing for the total self-giving of the couple to one another.

contrition Heartfelt sorrow for sins committed, along with the intention of sinning no more. This most important act of penitents is necessary for receiving absolution in the Sacrament of Penance.

dalmatic The outer liturgical vestment of a deacon. It may also be worn by bishops under the chasuble and at certain solemn liturgies.

declaration of nullity The Church's declaration that a particular marriage—whether presumed as a sacramental bond or simply a natural bond—was never valid.

Deposit of Faith The body of saving truth entrusted by Christ to the Apostles and handed on by them to be preserved and proclaimed by the Church's Magisterium.

diocese A geographic section of the Church, made up of parishes, that is headed by a bishop.

discern To perceive differences between more than one option. In the context of faith, to discern means to listen for the voice of the Holy Spirit when considering different options for action.

disposition The interior attitude of a person upon receiving the sacraments. "Celebrated worthily in faith, the sacraments confer the grace they signify" (*CCC*, 1127). Disposition includes the recipient's openness to the life of grace and willingness to avoid sin. Unrepented and unforgiven mortal sin affects a person's disposition to receive the sacraments.

divorce The dissolution of the marriage contract by the legal system.

domestic church A term for the family as the Church in miniature.

doxology A prayer of praise to the Blessed Trinity. The Eucharistic Prayer ends in a doxology.

Eastern Catholic Churches The twenty-one Churches of the East that are in union with the Roman Catholic Church and the bishop of Rome, the pope. They have developed their own liturgical and administrative traditions.

ecumenical council An assembly of all (or most) bishops from throughout the world in union with the pope. Such a council is the highest authority in the universal Church when it is conducted in unison with the pope.

epiclesis The prayer that petitions God to send the Holy Spirit to transform the bread and wine offered at the Eucharistic liturgy into the Body and Blood of Jesus Christ. This term also applies to the prayer said in every sacrament that asks for the sanctifying power of the Holy Spirit.

episcopal college The unity of all ordained bishops in the worldwide Church, in both the East and the West. The pope heads the episcopal college. The episcopal college is also called the "college of bishops."

eschatological Related to the "last things" (death, judgment, heaven, hell, Purgatory, the second coming of Christ, and the resurrection of the body).

Eucharistic Prayer The Church's great prayer of praise and thanksgiving to God that takes place during the Liturgy of the Eucharist. There are four main Eucharistic Prayers in the Roman Rite.

evangelization Bringing the Good News of Jesus Christ to others.

evangelize To bring the Good News of Jesus Christ to others.

examination of conscience An honest self-assessment of how well you have lived God's covenant of love, leading you to accept responsibility for your sins and to realize your need for God's merciful forgiveness.

excommunication A serious penalty that means a baptized person is no longer "in communion" with the Catholic Church.

exorcisms Prayerful rites in preparation for Baptism that invoke God's help in overcoming the power of Satan and the spirit of evil.

Extreme Unction A term from the Latin for "last anointing." It once referred to the reception of the Sacrament of the Anointing of the Sick just before death. It is accompanied by Viaticum.

fidelity From the Latin word *fides*, meaning faith. "Fidelity expresses constancy in keeping one's given word. God is faithful" (*CCC*, 2365).

Fraction Rite The time during the Communion Rite when the priest breaks the Body of Christ. He puts a piece of the consecrated bread into the chalice containing the Blood of Christ to signify the unity of the Body and Blood of Christ.

fruits of the Spirit Perfections that result from living in union with the Holy Spirit.

General Intercessions Also called the Prayer of the Faithful; prayers of petition for the sake of others.

Great Amen The affirmation by the faithful of the entire Eucharistic Prayer.

holy days of obligation The days in the Church Year when all Catholics are obliged to participate in Mass.

homily A reflection given by a bishop, priest, or deacon based on the Scripture read at Mass or a sacramental celebration. The homily helps you hear God's Word and apply it to your life today.

hypostatic union The doctrine of faith that recognizes two natures (one human and one divine) in the one Divine Person of Jesus Christ.

imprimatur A bishop's approval to print a religious text or pamphlet because its contents agree with Church teaching.

Incarnation The act by which the Father sent his Son into the world, and by the power of the Holy Spirit, the Son came to exist as a man within the womb of Mary. The Son of God assumed human nature and became man in order to accomplish salvation for humanity in that same nature. Jesus Christ, the Son of God, the Second Person of the Trinity, is both true God and true man, not part God and part man.

infallibility The charism or gift of the Church, offered by the Holy Spirit, in which the pope, and bishops in union with him, can definitively proclaim a doctrine of faith or morals for belief of all the faithful. It is a participation in the fullness of truth in Christ. The pope, as head of the episcopal college, enjoys this gift by virtue of his office. Infallibility is also present in the body of bishops, especially in an ecumenical council, when they teach on matters of faith and morals.

introit An antiphon, usually from a psalm, that is sung when the priest enters the church and approaches the altar.

invocation A call, request, or supplication for God's help.

laity All the unordained members of the Church who have been initiated into the Church through Baptism.

laying on of hands A gesture that is part of the essential rite and origin of the Sacrament of Confirmation. Acts 19:1–6 tells the story of a new group of disciples who, after being baptized, received the Holy Spirit when St. Paul laid hands on them.

lectio divina Literally, "divine reading"; a prayerful way to read, and meditate on, Sacred Scripture.

liturgical year Also known as the Church Year, it organizes the seasons of Advent, Christmas, Lent, the Easter Triduum, Easter, and Ordinary Time around the major events of Jesus' life.

liturgy The official public worship of the Church. The sacraments and the Divine Office constitute the Church's liturgy. Mass is the most important liturgical celebration.

Liturgy of the Hours The public prayer of the Church that makes holy the entire course of the day and night. It is also called the Divine Office.

Liturgy of the Word The part of the Mass that includes the "writings of the prophets" (the Old Testament reading and psalm), the "memoirs of the Apostles" (the New Testament epistles and the Gospel), the homily, the Profession of Faith, and the intercessions for the world.

mandate An official appointment from the pope that says a certain priest has been chosen to be a bishop.

marriage vows The promises made by the bride and groom to honor one another and to be faithful in good times and in bad, in sickness and in health, throughout their lives. By their consent to one another, the couple establishes a permanent covenant in love.

ministerial priesthood A unique sharing in the one priesthood of Christ received in the Sacrament of Holy Orders. By his ordination, a man is configured to Christ by a special gift of the Holy Spirit so that he can act as a representative of Christ, Head of the Church. As a representative of Christ, the ordained man is enabled to serve the common priesthood by building up and guiding the Church.

moral object A term for the material or content of a moral action, whether good, evil, or neutral. If the moral object of an act is evil, the act itself is evil.

mortal sin A serious, deadly violation of God's law of love that destroys sanctifying grace in the soul of the sinner. Mortal sins involve grave matter, full knowledge of the evil done, and full consent of the will.

motu proprio Literally "of his own accord," a papal document promulgated on the pope's own initiative.

mystagogia A Greek term that means "leading into the mystery"; the period following the Baptism of adults. During this time, the newly baptized are to open themselves more fully to the graces received in Baptism.

Natural Family Planning (NFP) A Church-approved method for regulating births within marriage; it is in accord with God's will because it is pursued by spouses without external pressure or motives of selfishness and is practiced through natural means of periodic continence and use of infertile periods.

neophytes Those newly received into the Church through the Sacraments of Christian Initiation at the Easter Vigil.

Nicene Creed The formal Profession of Faith recited at Mass. It came from the first two ecumenical councils, at Nicaea in AD 325 and Constantinople in AD 381.

nuncio An archbishop who acts as the official Vatican delegate for a nation. He is also called the apostolic delegate.

nuptial blessing A blessing intended for the bride and groom and the marriage covenant that takes place after the couple gives their consent to be married. The word *nuptial* comes from a Latin word that means "wedding."

oil of catechumens Olive oil that is blessed by a bishop at the Chrism Mass on or around Holy Thursday and used to anoint those preparing for Baptism.

oil of the sick Olive or another plant oil that is blessed by a bishop at a Chrism Mass or, in case of necessity, by any priest at the time of anointing. Anointing with the oil of the sick is an efficacious sign of healing and strength that is part of the Sacrament of the Anointing of the Sick.

ordinand A person receiving the Sacrament of Holy Orders at any level: episcopate, presbyterate, or diaconate.

ordinary bishop The name for the diocesan bishop. He is the pastoral and legal representative of his diocese.

original holiness and original justice The original state of human beings in their relationship with God before sin entered the world.

Original Sin The personal sin of Adam and Eve, which in an analogous way describes the fallen state of human nature into which all generations of people are born. Christ Jesus came to save the world from Original Sin and all personal sin.

Paraclete Another name for the Holy Spirit, it means "advocate," "defender," or "consoler."

particular judgment The individual judgment of every person right after death, when Christ will rule on his or her eternal destiny in heaven (after purification in Purgatory, if needed) or in hell.

penitent A person who admits his or her sins, is truly sorry for having sinned, and wishes to be restored to relationship with God and the Church.

Penitential Rite Part of the Introductory Rites at Mass when the priest invites people to repent of their sins and prepare themselves to encounter Christ in the Eucharist.

penitentiaries Books for confessors in the past that listed sins with corresponding penances.

Pentecost From a Greek word meaning "fiftieth day," the day on which the Church celebrates the descent of the Holy Spirit upon Mary and the Apostles.

polygamy Being married to two or more people at the same time. It is contrary to conjugal love, which is undivided and exclusive.

precepts of the Church Basic rules that bind Catholics who belong to Christ's Body. These are the minimal obligations for members to be in good standing in the Catholic Church. (See page 324 for a list of the precepts.)

presbyters The name for priests or members of the order of priesthood who are coworkers with the bishops and are servants to God's People, especially in celebrating the Eucharist.

Purgatory Purification after death for those who died in God's friendship but still need to be purified from past sins before entering heaven.

Real Presence The doctrine that Jesus Christ is truly present in his Body and Blood under the form of bread and wine in the Eucharist.

responsorial psalm A psalm sung or said at Mass in response to the first Scripture reading.

Rite of Christian Initiation of Adults (RCIA) The process by which an unbaptized adult or an adult baptized in another ecclesial community prepares for full initiation into the Catholic Church.

sacramental character An indelible spiritual mark that is the permanent effect of the Sacraments of Baptism, Confirmation, and Holy Orders. The mark is a permanent configuration to Jesus Christ and a specific standing in the Church. Because of their permanent effect, the reception of the Sacraments of Baptism, Confirmation, and Holy Orders is never repeated.

sacramental economy The communication or dispensation of the fruits of Christ's Paschal Mystery through the celebration of the sacramental liturgy.

sacramental seal The secrecy priests are bound to keep regarding any sins confessed to them.

Sacrament of Christian Initiation One of the three sacraments—Baptism, Confirmation, and Eucharist—through which a person enters into full membership in the Church.

sacraments Efficacious and visible signs of God's grace, instituted by Christ and entrusted to the Church, by which divine life is dispensed to us. The Seven Sacraments are Baptism, Confirmation, Eucharist, Penance, Anointing of the Sick, Holy Orders, and Matrimony.

sacred chrism Perfumed oil consecrated by the bishop and used for anointing in the Sacraments of Baptism, Confirmation, and Holy Orders.

Sacred Tradition The living transmission of the Church's Gospel message found in the Church's teaching, life, and worship. It is faithfully preserved, handed on, and interpreted by the Church's Magisterium.

sanctoral cycle The feasts of saints found throughout the year on the Church's liturgical calendar.

scrutinies Rites within the Rite of Christian Initiation of Adults that aid the elect in self-examination and repentance and support them through prayers of intercession and exorcism.

second coming of Christ Also known as the Parousia, the time when Jesus will return to earth, the Kingdom of God will be fully established, and victory over evil will be complete.

seminary The place where the training of candidates for the priesthood takes place. The Council of Trent instructed the bishops in each diocese to set up a seminary college to train men for the priesthood.

sterilization Any surgical procedure that prevents conception. Sterilization procedures in women include tying or cutting of fallopian tubes, removal of ovaries, and/or removal of the uterus. Sterilization procedures in men include vasectomy (cutting tubes carrying sperm from the testicles) or castration (removing the testicles). Deliberate sterilization is contrary to one of the characteristics of sacramental marriage, the openness to children.

stole A long, narrow band of fabric, like a scarf. A deacon's stole is worn diagonally from one shoulder. A priest's stole is worn straight from the shoulders.

synod of bishops A group of bishops, usually chosen from throughout the world, who come together to advise the pope on certain issues.

theological virtues Three important virtues, first infused at Baptism, that enable Catholics to know God and lead them to union with him; they are faith (belief in, and personal knowledge of, God), hope (trust in God's salvation and his bestowal of graces needed to attain it), and charity (love of God and love of neighbor). Catholics can also receive an increase in the theological virtues through reception of the other sacraments and through the application of the theological virtues in their lives.

transubstantiation What happens at the consecration of the bread and wine at Mass when their entire substance is turned into the entire substance of the Body and Blood of Christ, even though the appearances of bread and wine remain. The Eucharistic presence of Christ begins at the moment of consecration and endures as long as the Eucharistic species subsist.

venial sin A sin that weakens and wounds your relationship with God but does not destroy grace in your soul.

Viaticum The Eucharist received by a dying person. This is a Latin term that means "food for the journey."

vicar One who serves as a substitute, an agent, or a representative of another. Bishops are vicars of Christ; they take his place in the Church. The pope is the Supreme Vicar of Christ.

Words of Institution The words said by Jesus over the bread and wine at the Last Supper. The priest repeats these words over the bread and wine at Mass as they are changed into the Body and Blood of Christ.

SUBJECT INDEX

conversion from and Holy Orders, 263

transformation from, in Anointing of the Sick, 233–236

Seminary, 252–253

Sheen, Fulton J., Archbishop, 143

Sickness. *See* Anointing of the Sick; Suffering

Sign of Peace, 160

Sign of the Cross

Baptism and, 87

Penance and, 190–191

as sacramental, 70

Signs

Liturgy of the Word, 52, 154

of sacraments, 50

Sin(s)

absolution, 186, 194–195

concupiscence, 90, 183

confession of, 192–193

contrition, 191–192

death to, and Baptism, 90–91

Eucharist separating you from, 163–164

excommunication, 198–199

harm from, 196

Indulgence, 198

mortal, 164, 166, 187, 192

Original Sin, 86, 90–91

saying no to, and Baptism, 75–76

suffering and law of retribution, 216

venial, 163–164, 192

Sisters of the Blessed Sacrament, 173

Society, Christian families serving, 308–309

Society of Jesus, 234

Solemnities, 58

Solemnity of Christ the King, 58

Solemnity of Mary, Mother of God, 58

Sorin, Edward, Fr., 268

Stations of the Cross, 62

Stephen, St., 266, 267

Sterilization, 318

Stole, 230, 262–263

Suffering

Christ as Physician, 217–219

Church heals the sick, 221–222

as consequences of Original Sin, 216

healing miracles, 218, 219

Jesus taught about, 219

of Job, 216

as moral condition, 216, 217

Old Testament and, 216–217

Suffering Servant, 162

Suicide, risk of, 105

Synod of bishops, 273

Syriac Rite, 52

T

Tabernacle, 60, 175

Tantum Ergo, 43

Teacher, priests acting as Christ the Teacher, 267–270

Ten Commandments, Baptism and saying yes to culture of life, 76

Teresa of Calcutta, St.

Eucharist and, 165

life of, 242–243

Thanksgiving, 61

Theological virtues, 16

Thérèse of Lisieux, St., 233–234

Thomas Aquinas, St., 19, 118, 121

on Baptism, 92

on marriage, 294–295

on priesthood, 255

Thomas More, St., 310

Titular bishop, 271

Transfiguration of Jesus, 55

Transformation

from Penance, 200–202

from self-centeredness in the Anointing of the Sick, 233–236

Transitional deacons, 263

Transubstantiation, 150, 152

Tridentine Mass, 147–148

U

Understanding, as gift of Holy Spirit, 123

United States Conference of Catholic Bishops, 272–273

V

van Epp, John, 287

Venial sins

defined, 192

Eucharist and cleansing from, 163–164

Viaticum, 229–230

Visible sign

Church as, 9

in definition of sacrament, 3–4, 9

Visitation, 58

Vocal prayer, 62

W

Walterman, Mike, 35

Washing of regeneration and renewal by the Holy Spirit, 78

Water

blessing of, and Baptism, 88

immersion of, in Baptism, 88

Wedding at Cana, 304–305

Western (Roman) Catholic Churches

Anointing of the Sick, 227

baptismal rite, 87, 89

Confirmation, 112, 113–114, 118, 119

early liturgical traditions, 147

marriage, 295

reception of Communion, 160

Sacraments of Christian Initiation, 82

Whole Christ, 49

Wine

in Old Testament, 145

requirements for Eucharistic, 157

transubstantiation, 150, 152

Wisdom, as gift of Holy Spirit, 123

Wonder and awe, as gift of Holy Spirit, 124

Words of Institution, 157

World

communion with people throughout, 12

sacraments transforming, 14–18

World Meeting of Families, 294

Wurtz, Michael, Fr., 269

Z

Zacchaeus, 199

SCRIPTURE INDEX

OLD TESTAMENT

Pentateuch

Genesis

1:1–2, 79
1:1–2:2, 82
1:28, 303
2:4–25, 292
2:18–24, 53
2:24, 293
3:1–19, 216
6:5–8:22, 79
22:1–18, 82

Exodus

13:17–22, 131
14:10–31, 79, 96
14:15–15:1, 82
15:26, 219
16:2–4, 12–15, 53
17:3–7, 53
20:8–11, 151
20:12, 217
28–29, 32:25–29, 255
30:22–33, 112

Leviticus

8–9, 255
13–14, 219

Numbers

11:24–25, 255

Deuteronomy

1:9–14, 53
30:19–20, 79

Historical Books

Joshua

3:13–17, 79

1 Samuel

1–2, 293
16:13, 112

Ezra

36:16–28, 82
36:26, 111
37:1–13, 131

Wisdom Books

Job

42:7–9, 216

Psalms

42, 147
103:8, 305

Prophetic Books

Isaiah

1:10–18, 53
11:1–4a, 53
11:1–9, 131
11:2–3, 123
33:24, 217
54:5–14, 82
54:6, 7, 293
54:8, 10, 198
55:1–11, 82
61:1, 110
61:1–3a, 6a, 8b–9, 116

Jeremiah

31:33–34, 185

Baruch

3:9–15, 32–4:4, 82

Hosea

2:21–22, 293

NEW TESTAMENT

Gospels

Matthew

3:1–12, 53
3:13–17, 22, 79
4:19, 250
5:13–16, 6
5:17–20, 188
5:23–24, 200
6:9–13, 158
6:25–34, 240
6:33, 123
8:1–4, 53
8:14–15, 240
8:16, 218
9:1–7, 184
9:6, 199
9:15, 305
9:18–19, 23–26, 218

9:35–38, 22
10:1–42, 255
10:8, 221
12:1–8, 187
13:24–30, 6
13:31–33, 6
14:13–21, 49
14:35–36, 218
15:35–36, 145
16:18–19, 188, 256
16:19, 9
17:1–8, 58
17:1–9, 55
18:15–17, 201
18:18, 9
18:20, 42
18:21–22, 200
19:6, 293, 294
19:8, 293
19:16–30, 201
19:25, 201
19:26, 201
19:29, 283
22:37, 39, 58
25:35–46, 240
25:37–40, 233
26:28, 148
26:39, 42, 232
28:1–10, 82
28:16–20, 22, 39, 256
28:18–20, 87
28:19, 46, 80, 183
28:19–20, 86, 167, 270
28:20, 9, 41, 305

Mark

1:9–11, 79, 87
1:14–20, 53
1:15, 183, 185
1:17, 250
1:17, 3:13–19, 255
1:40–45, 22
2:1–12, 184
2:8–11, 217
2:17, 218
2:19, 305
3:1–6, 187
4:20, 125
5:21–24, 35–43, 218
6:13, 221

6:30–52, 172
6:34–44, 44
8:1–10, 172
8:22–26, 22
9:2–10, 55
9:7, 58
10:13–16, 87
10:14, 87, 166
10:37–38, 80
14:25, 145
16:1–8, 82
16:15, 256
16:16, 86

Luke

3:21–22, 79, 110
4:16–22a, 53, 110
4:18, 17
5:16, 45
5:17–26, 184
5:34, 305
6:19, 45
7:11–17, 218
7:22, 219
7:36–50, 22, 49, 184
7:50, 199
8:40–42, 49–56, 218
8:46, 45
9:11b–17, 53
9:28–36, 55
10:29–37, 49, 235
11:2–4, 158
11:33–36, 6
12:8–12, 22
12:11–12, 111
12:50, 80
13:10–17, 187
14:1–6, 187
14:15–24, 240
14:21, 219
15:11–32, 194, 197, 198
18:9–14, 194
19:1–10, 184, 199
19:10, 17–18
22:14–20, 22
22:15, 38
22:19, 146
22:19–20, 146
23:34, 184
24:1–12, 82

CATECHISM OF THE CATHOLIC CHURCH
INDEX

CHURCH DOCUMENTS INDEX

PHOTO CREDITS